The Humanities and Public Administration

The Humanities and Public Administration
An Introduction

Edited by

Edoardo Ongaro

Professor of Public Management, The Open University, UK

Giovanni Orsina

Professor of Contemporary History, LUISS School of Government, Italy

Lorenzo Castellani

Professor of History of Political Institutions and Lecturer, LUISS School of Government, Italy

Edward Elgar
PUBLISHING

Cheltenham, UK · Northampton, MA, USA

Published by
Edward Elgar Publishing Limited
The Lypiatts
15 Lansdown Road
Cheltenham
Glos GL50 2JA
UK

Edward Elgar Publishing, Inc.
William Pratt House
9 Dewey Court
Northampton
Massachusetts 01060
USA

Authorised representative in the EU for GPSR queries only: Easy Access System Europe – Mustamäe tee 50, 10621 Tallinn, Estonia, gpsr.requests@easproject.com.

A catalogue record for this book
is available from the British Library

Library of Congress Control Number: 2024952813

This book is available electronically in the **Elgar**online
Political Science and Public Policy subject collection
https://doi.org/10.4337/9781035333608

ISBN   978 1 0353 3359 2 (cased)
ISBN   978 1 0353 3360 8 (eBook)

Printed and bound by CPI Group (UK) Ltd, Croydon, CR0 4YY

Contents

List of contributors   vii

Acknowledgements   ix

1   The Contribution of the Humanities to the Advancement of
Public Governance and Public Administration   1
Edoardo Ongaro, Giovanni Orsina, and Lorenzo Castellani

2   Socratic Public Administration: The Relevance of Dwight
Waldo Today   23
Patrick Overeem

3   Public Philosophy and the Administrative State   36
Christopher Ansell

4   Philosophical Pragmatism and the Study of Public
Administration   50
Travis A. Whetsell

5   Benevolence, (Public) Ethics and Public Services: Revisiting
Public Value, Public Service Motivation, and Models of
Public Administration through the Ethics of Supererogation   68
Stefano Biancu and Edoardo Ongaro

6   Behaviour in Public Administration: In Search of
Foundational Insights   79
Jonathan Kamkhaji and Claudio Radaelli

7   Human Geography and the Study of Governance and Society:
Perspectives from the UK   94
Irene Hardill

8   The Concept of State in the Historical Studies   108
Leonida Tedoldi

9   Historiography and Public Administration: A Story of Disciplines   119
Fabio Rugge

10   History and Public Administration: Meanings, Problems,
     Usefulness in Policy-making   133
     Lorenzo Castellani

11   The Contribution of the Religious Studies and Theology
     Literatures to Public Administration: A Review and Outlook   152
     Michele Tantardini and Edoardo Ongaro

12   When Ideas Have Consequences: The Optical Illusion of
     Religion in Public Policy   176
     Pasquale Annicchino

13   Reconnecting government: On the existential layers of public
     administration   188
     Ronald van Steden

14   The Arts and Public Administration: How the Consideration
     of the Nature of Art can Provide Novel Ways to Understand
     Public Administration   207
     Edoardo Ongaro

15   The Arts and Public Administration: How Artworks Can
     Be a Source of Knowledge, Inspiration, Motivation, and
     Understanding in Public Administration   217
     Gjalt de Graaf and Hanneke van Asperen

16   Ambrogio Lorenzetti's Siena Frescoes and Public
     Administration Today   236
     Wolfgang Drechsler

17   Mind the Gap: A Strategy to connect Humanities (Arts) with
     Social Sciences (Public Administration)   253
     Geert Bouckaert

18   Humanism and Public Administration: Profiling the contours
     of Public Administration as Practical Humanism   275
     Stefano Biancu and Edoardo Ongaro

Index   283

Contributors

Pasquale Annicchino is at the University of Foggia, Italy, and a member of the OSCE/ODIHR panel of experts on freedom of religion or belief.

Christopher Ansell is Professor of Political Science at the University of California, Berkely, USA.

Stefano Biancu is Associate Professor of Moral Philosophy at LUMSA University, Rome, Italy, and Associate at the University of Notre Dame Rome, Italy.

Geert Bouckaert is Emeritus Professor of Public Governance at KU Leuven, Belgium, and Honorary Professor at University College London in the Institute for Innovation and Public Purpose, UK.

Lorenzo Castellani is Professor of History of Political Institutions and Lecturer at School of Government, LUISS, Italy.

Gjalt de Graaf is Professor of Public Administration at the Vrije Universiteit Amsterdam, the Netherlands.

Wolfgang Drechsler is Professor of Governance at TalTech, Estonia; Honorary Professor of University College London in the Institute for Innovation and Public Purpose, UK; and Adjunct Professor of Administrative Sciences at Universitas Indonesia.

Irene Hardill is Professor of Public Policy at Northumbria University, Newcastle, UK.

Jonathan C. Kamkhaji is a Postdoctoral Research Fellow at the Florence School of Transnational Governance, European University Institute, Italy.

Edoardo Ongaro is Professor of Public Management at The Open University, UK.

Giovanni Orsina is Professor of Contemporary History at LUISS, Italy.

Patrick Overeem is Associate Professor in Political Theory at the Vrije Universiteit in Amsterdam, the Netherlands.

Claudio M. Radaelli is Chair of Comparative Public Policy at the Florence School of Transnational Governance, European University Institute, and Professor of Political Science (on long-term leave) at University College London, UK.

Fabio Rugge is Professor Emeritus of History of Political Institutions at University of Pavia, Italy.

Michele Tantardini is Associate Professor of Public Administration at Penn State University, Harrisburg, PA, USA.

Leonida Tedoldi is Professor of History of International Relations at the University of Bergamo, Italy.

Hanneke van Asperen is Art Historian at Radboud University, Nijmegen, the Netherlands.

Ronald van Steden is Associate Professor in Public Administration at Vrije Universiteit Amsterdam, the Netherlands.

Travis A. Whetsell is Assistant Professor at Georgia Institute of Technology, Atlanta, GA, USA.

Acknowledgements

This book is the fruit of a quasi-casual encounter between three like-minded scholars. On occasion of the annual conference of the International Institute of Administrative Sciences (IIAS), jointly held at Rome Tor Vergata University and LUISS in June 2022, we three co-editors of this book had the opportunity to meet in person for the first time following on from the restrictions due to the COVID-19 pandemic – our previous meetings having been digital-only, most notably in 2021 on occasion of the presentation of the Italian translation of another Edward Elgar book authored by one of us, *Philosophy and Public Administration: An Introduction,* graciously organised by LUISS School of Government.

One face-to-face meeting and a few email exchanges later, and we were agreed that a book exploring the contribution of the humanities to the field of public administration was missing, that the gap should be filled, and that perhaps we could be the ones who might trigger the process that would lead other like-minded scholars to contribute to make this idea real.

And so it happened: we approached a number of prominent scholars and very dear colleagues – from both the field of public administration and the humanities – and to our so pleasant surprise we discovered it was as if everyone was just waiting to be summoned to engage with such an intellectual venture. If any new intellectual venture, like any daring human enterprise, requires a sprinkle of folly (as argued most famously by Desiderius Erasmus in his masterpiece In Praise of Folly), we definitely discovered we were not alone in partaking in this folly. We thus set up the enterprise of getting this book to become reality.

As key companion along the way, we found in Edward Elgar an incredibly supportive, always excellent, highly civilised publisher who welcomes intellectual challenges and supports truly interdisciplinary work. We are very grateful to Alex Pettifer and all the staff at Edward Elgar for their impeccable support for this intellectual project.

The conference promoted by LUISS School of Government, *The Contribution of the Humanities to the Advancement of Public Governance and Public Administration*, held in Rome on 10–11 May, 2024, was a pivotal event for the preparation of this book – and thence hopefully for the relaunch of more systematic scholarly attention for the contribution of the humanities to public administration. The team at LUISS School of Government managed the conference in an excellent way, and we wish to express our gratitude to Gaia Di Martino, Valentina Milano, Rosanna Sirianni, Lorenzo Valeri and all the staff of the School of Government.

In the most classical 'last but not least', we wish to thank all the contributors to the conference – Pasquale Annicchino, Chris Ansell, Stefano Biancu, Geert Bouckaert, Gjalt de Graaf, Irene Hardill, Jonathan Kamkhaji, Patrick Overeem, Claudio Radaelli, Fabio Rugge, Alessandro Sancino, Michele Tantardini, Leonida Tedoldi, Ronald van Steden, Travis Whetsell – and all those who were in attendance of the event. Wolfgang Drechsler and Hanneke van Asperen were not able to take part to the conference but kindly contributed to this book.

If 'the proof of the pudding is in the eating', as the English saying goes, we hope readers will find reading this book as enjoyable an experience as it was for its editors and authors writing it.

Edoardo Ongaro, Giovanni Orsina, Lorenzo Castellani

London, Rome, March 2025

1. The Contribution of the Humanities to the Advancement of Public Governance and Public Administration

Edoardo Ongaro, Giovanni Orsina, and Lorenzo Castellani

INTRODUCTION AND PURPOSE

This book stems from the consideration that the contribution the humanities can provide to the development of the field of public administration appears to have been overlooked in recent decades.[1] In fact, there appears to be a gap in the literature about the major contribution the humanities can and ought to make to the advancement of the study of public governance, government, public management, and public administration and policy – hereafter collectively referred to as PA, by which we mean both the field of academic studies of these areas and the 'reality out there' of governments in operation, as well as the public governance arrangements and administrative systems all over the world in their concrete functioning.[2] While social sciences such as political science, public policy, sociology, law, management, social psychology, and others are contributing to, and indeed part and parcel of, the 'administrative sciences', this has not been the case for the humanities – or at the very least, for most of the humanities, which have not been applied in a systematic and comprehensive way to the study of PA. It is the overarching goal of this book to fill such

---

[1] The call for the humanities to play a larger role is, of course, not new: it was in 1958 that Dimock claimed that 'Administration is, or at least ought to be, wedded to subjects such as philosophy, literature, history, and art, and not merely to engineering, finance and structure' (Dimock, 1958, p. 5) – yet it appears this and other calls have gone mostly unheard, for a host of reasons, to at least some of which we return and discuss throughout this book.

[2] For a detailed analysis of these notions, see Pollitt and Bouckaert, 2017; a critical discussion of the concepts from a historical perspective is provided by Franklin and Raadschelders, 2023.

a gap and provide an overview that is as comprenehsive as possible of how the humanities can contribute to PA.

A critical, systematic, and integrated exploration of the contribution of the humanities to the field of PA may be beneficial in a number of ways. First and foremost, because of the inherent contribution to the knowledge and understanding of PA that each of these perspectives may provide in its own right (as we argue throughout this book, in which most chapters focus on one selected perspective in the humanities and dissect the contribution it may provide to PA). Second, because providing a comprehensive and holistic view of the contribution of the humanities as a whole set of disciplines and perspectives (as opposed to fragmented and partial applications of the humanities to specific PA problems) may help better single out and highlight the specific contribution each individual discipline in the humanities can make. Third, because an examination and assessment of the potential contribution of the humanities to PA may also help revisit debates on the issue of humanism and its contemporary significance for PA.[3] This pursuit of a critical, systematic, and integrated exploration of the contribution of the humanities to the field of PA is the goal of this book.

RATIONALE

Bringing the humanities systematically and comprehensively into PA may provide a 'quantum leap' in our understanding of the field. We would indeed argue that 'reason' in the humanities (philosophy, theology and religious studies, historiography, literature and the fine arts, and so on) proceeds in ways,

---

[3] And support critically revisiting debates on post-humanism and trans-humanism in PA by enabling the revisitation of the nature and meaning of the human and rediscovering humanism in PA, and on these bases, also engaging with its alleged limitations (post-humanist perspectives), on one hand, and the transformative impact of new technologies on human life and the world (trans-humanist perspectives), on the other hand. In this regard, it is interesting to notice that the ancient Greek and Greco-Roman civilisation, which is at the roots of the humanities and of humanism in the West (through its rediscovery and reinvention over the historical period 1350–1550), was cosmos-centric rather than anthropo-centric (which is the reason why post-humanist claims about evolving ecosystems taking centre stage rather than human agency – thereby displacing the conscious and intentional human subject as the dominant source of agency – might in this sense find it useful to revisit ancient Greek thought in their elaboration of how change is enacted in the world). Yet, it is its rediscovery in 15th-century Italy which has brought about the flourishing of what has come to be defined as ('The') Humanism. A perspective on the meaning and application of humanism to contemporary PA is elaborated in chapter 18.

modes, levels, and forms that are different from reason in the natural and social sciences. Reason as employed and deployed in the humanities generates a kind of knowledge and understanding which is different and complementary to the knowledge generated by 'the scientific reason'.

We therefore also argue that the humanities and the social sciences, while operating at different levels – indeed exactly because of this – can and ought to complement one another: one set of disciplines 'invokes' the other when the capacity of reason to investigate reality at one level falls short, and it then requires another level of deploying human reason to tackle human and social problems. In this, we follow Floridi (2013, 2019) in assuming that 'levelism' – i.e., the approach of studying reality at different levels – can still, and should, be used in contemporary philosophising for understanding reality.

In this sense, this book also takes as one of its starting points the critique of the assumption, of (neo-)positivistic flavour, of the 'unity of science'; that is, that research methods and approaches patterned on the natural sciences are also the ultimate pattern for the studies of the social sciences and, as part of it, for the administrative sciences and the study of public administration. We argue that such a perspective, if brought to the extreme idea that 'knowledge ultimately can only be generated this way', precludes the further development of the field of PA, as it does not take into account the fundamental aspect that there are distinctive levels, forms, and modes of (human) knowledge and understanding: that human reason can also be deployed in different ways than those of the natural sciences, and that this does matter, including also for PA (Ongaro, 2020, chapter 1 in particular). The humanities and the natural sciences are predicated on different assumptions, and they are ultimately complementary, both being necessary; and the social sciences (of which the administrative sciences are a part as an applied area of the social sciences) may benefit from learning and incorporating into their objects and methods the contributions stemming from both the natural sciences, on one hand, and the humanities, on the other. Ultimately, this line of argumentation brings us to conclude that we need to bring forth forms of reasoning and understanding of reality that are drawn from the humanities if we are to succeed in bringing about a fuller appreciation of the realities of human life and society, and thence of public administration and public services as a (core) part of it.

The contribution of the humanities to PA enables to deepen the roots of PA as an interdisciplinary field of study by enlarging the gamut of academic disciplines that study PA. Importantly, our argument is that the humanities can and ought to *complement and supplement* (not displace) the social sciences (and other disciplines), thereby broadening and deepening our knowledge and understanding of PA. Our call is for an integrative approach, for *integrating the humanities with the social sciences into PA* (or, if the verb 'integrate' may appear too ambitious, at least 'combine' in a more systematic way the humanities and the social sciences): tackling crucial PA problems requires the joint contribution of the humanities and the social sciences. To reiterate: in and for the advancement of PA studies, the social sciences need the humanities, and the humanities need the social sciences, and by conjoining them, we may mobilise the intellectual resources needed for a broader and deeper understanding of PA problems. The humanities 'on their own' (so to speak) are no silver bullet/magic wand: indeed an acritical application of insights from the humanities, however valuable they may be on their own, without integrating such inputs with the insights drawn from the social sciences, might lead to misunderstandings about the functioning of administrative systems and ultimately might also lead to misconceived policy proposals for reforming the public sector and public services. It is only by systematically bringing the humanities into PA in a fruitful combination with the findings of the social sciences that we may attain a quantum leap improvement in the field of PA.

An even more precise formulation of our argument is that we argue for bringing *back* the humanities into PA, for *re*-integrating the humanities into PA, as the humanities have been part and parcel of the training of civil servants in many – possibly all? – administrative systems over history and across the world, from Confucian administrative systems to the British civil service. This book is therefore also a call for, and a map for, bringing back the humanities into the study of PA in the 21st century.

But what is the nature of PA? Alongside being an interdisciplinary field of studies (that is, the interdisciplinary study of government), PA has also been defined as: a profession, an art, and a form of practical humanism, in a four-fold definition of PA put forward in Ongaro (2020, chapter 1). So far, we have discussed the contribution of the humanities to PA as an interdisciplinary field, but we would argue that the humanities can provide a most valuable contribution to each of these constitutive features of PA.

As regards PA as a profession, the contribution of the humanities to PA as a profession begets important reflections about the ways in which the humanities may contribute to shaping the professional education and training of public personnel, and the various professions and professionalisms involved in public policy, public service, and public services management. It also brings about important debates about the contribution made by integrating the humanities into PA for purposes of skills development: what kind of 'professional skills' do the humanities contribute? This question also revolves around the somewhat elusive and at times controversial issue of how the humanities may contribute to 'employability' (in our case: preparation for public employment), and indeed whether they should contribute to employability at all, or whether the contribution the humanities can furnish belongs to a different realm.

As a contribution to the debate over the nature of PA as a profession, in defining specifically the nature of public management, Barzelay (2019) has wrought out an elaborate definition of public management as a 'professionally orientated design science'. It is interesting – for the purposes of this book – to dwell upon the term 'design', which is core to the above definition: in the celebrated Bauhaus School, which is credited with being a primary source of the very idea of design in the modern era, the notion of design encompasses architecture, industrial product design, graphic design, and fashion design. By the transitive property of deduction, the very notion of architecture gets associated with public management. The employment of the architecture metaphor in qualifying public management is especially pertinent: architecture is a form of both knowledge and human action that incorporates into its proceedings both the kind of knowledge that is generated by the 'hard sciences' – that is, the natural sciences and engineering on which it rests – and the kind of knowledge that is generated by the humanities. Architecture is predicated on the mastery of the laws of the natural world that come through the natural sciences and are then made to serve problem-solving purposes through engineering. At the same time, architecture is also predicated on the kind of knowledge that is proper to the humanities: the quest for meaning, beauty, symbolism, and for connecting the human to reality in its totality and the divine – all of which are proper to the humanities (we are here encompassing also the arts into the humanities: architecture being one of the seven main fine arts, see Ongaro, 2025, Chapter 14, this volume).

The consideration of public administration as a profession (via the notion of public management as a professionally orientated design science) helps us appreciate the obvious benefits of bringing the arts and artistic studies into the study of PA. This leads us to the third notion of PA, that of PA as an art. Relatedly, this leads us to delve into how the arts can enable our understanding and appreciation of PA. This is a central part of this volume: four chapters articulate the contribution of the arts to PA. For an in-depth elaboration of the ways in which the arts may be brought to bear on our understanding of PA and shed light on key profiles of it, see the chapters by Bouckaert (2025, Chapter 17, this volume); de Graaf and van Asperen (2016 and 2025, Chapter 15, this volume); and Drechsler (2001 and 2025, Chapter 16, this volume); and Ongaro (this volume) – to which we return later in this introduction.

Finally – in the most classical 'last but not least' fashion – bringing the humanities into PA is also crucial to progressing our understanding of PA as a form of practical humanism – our fourth definition of PA. To appreciate this point, a definition of humanism is in order. Humanism is a category that is, at the same time, historical, cultural, and axiological (Biancu and Ongaro, 2025, Chapter 18, this volume). It is historical in that humanism is an epoch of history, a specific time (ca. 1350–1550) and related to a specific place (Italy, then Europe). It is cultural in that humanism denotes an entire civilisation, and notably a civilisation that has an ethnic origin (the geographical-cultural borders of Europe) and at the same time a universalistic pretension: to have identified 'values' (rights and duties) that pertain to humankind in general, to each and every human being across time and space (one may see a link here to the United Nations' Universal Declaration of Human Rights). It is axiological in that humanism is a system of values and a horizon of sense, a conception of humankind as a mission and a goal. In other words, humankind as not just a matter of fact but a mission to accomplish, based on the assumption that humanity, that 'being human', is constitutive of each and every human being, and that promoting humanity in each and every human being is a (the) mission for each and every human being – in its axiological conception, humanism is a regulatory ideal.

In this sense, the appreciation of humanism as a historical and cultural phenomenon – and therefore bringing the humanities which investigate it into PA studies – may provide an underpinning for explicating the premises and implications of considering PA as a form of practical humanism, where humanism is intended as an axiological and mythical referent, furnishing a system of values and a horizon of sense, a conception of humanity as a mission to accomplish, in a way that is respectful of the natural world and attentive to the plurality of human cultures and the uniqueness of each human culture. Humanism in this perspective operates as a synthesising and generative category at the core of a constellation of notions – like 'human dignity' and 'human rights' – which are in need of being continuously renegotiated while remaining universally shared by humankind, as well as needing to be continually upheld, lest the vulnerable and the weakest get trampled by the very administrative systems and governance regimes that ought to support and protect them. In this conception, humanism is a regulatory ideal, providing an axiological basis for appreciating and evaluating the concrete functioning of administrative systems and public services.

The humanities enable us to better understand the fundamental humanity that all individual persons and all peoples of the world – living in and across the various political-administrative systems scattered across the globe – share in today's global society (Raadschelders, 2020). This is the same humanity whereby we (each and every human being) love and hate (Catullus); imagine and create; feel compassion for and deliver retribution to our fellow humans; exercise justice and effect injustice (Aristotle, Plato, Rawls); prove sympathy and antipathy for our fellow human beings (Hume); lead others and accept being led by others; care for ourselves and for others and the world (Heidegger), or exclusively for ourselves; imitate (what others have done) and innovate (fundamentally changing what our ancestors have done); admire and despise; search for the truth and conceal lies; feel pain and pleasure; let ourselves be driven by hope or despair, by instinct or reason, by fear or by courage, by anger or bonhomie; live in the past through memory, in the present through action, in the future through a project of life – while yearning for eternity; exercise volition and intent and be capable of renouncing any desires and even the willingness to will; be defined by individuality and relationality, by individualism and sociableness; think speculatively and practically; think of the particular and of the universal, of the necessary and of the contingent; embrace or reject destiny; be idle or active; be mind and body, soul and matter; aspire to the heavenly or covet the earthly, and often the hellish; organise socially in families, tribes, and communities, as well as internationally and globally; wage war and tenaciously pursue peace; belong to the local and to the global. All of this, and much more, is the humanity that humanism aims to put as a goal, as an end – not just as means, or matter of fact – of every expression of human life, thereby including our public life, and the public institutions and the public administration which compound it.

Crucially, (re-)bringing the humanities and humanism into PA both enables us to better answer the question famously posed by Immanuel Kant: 'what can we (human beings) know'? And also enables us to address the other question the German philosopher asked, and which the social sciences may not be geared to answer: 'what can we (human beings) hope for?' (see Bouckaert, 2020). It is only by enlarging the horizon from the world of 'scientific facts' to the world of the final goals, of the human aspirations, of the imagined and desired, that hope can be (re-)brought into our contemporary world.

To be sure, it is not only the humanities that enable a better and deeper knowledge of human nature (a somewhat elusive notion) by providing additional and (at least partly) different perspectives than the social sciences. Disciplines from the natural and life sciences, like (human) biology, also contribute, as do psychology and psychiatry, or primatology and palaeoanthropology. All these contributions should be tapped more systematically to complement the contribution of the social sciences to PA (an attempt to encompass at least some of these disciplines into the study of government and public administration is carried out by Raadschelders, 2020). Yet, the humanities do provide distinctive and unique perspectives about human nature, what it means to be human, how humans develop their lives in society, and why humans may aim to treat humanity not just as a means, but as a goal. The humanities can provide a treasure trove of knowledge and understanding, which has so far not been tapped as extensively and intensively as it would be worth doing, for the goal of the advancement of PA.

THE CONTRIBUTION OF THIS BOOK

What areas of the humanities are especially significant for the advancement of PA? This book aims to provide a multiplicity of entry points to analysing and critically discussing and appraising the contribution that the humanities may

– and ought to, in our view – provide to the field of PA, intended both as the academic field of study and the practice of it, the exercise of the profession of public administrator and public manager, the art and the practice of managing and administering public services.

The book is based on the contributions of a wide range of authors, selected on the basis of their mastery of both the field of the administrative sciences, public governance, and public administration on one hand, and at the same time one or more of the humanities, in which they are specifically versed, on their own or jointly as chapter co-authors. Importantly, while individual chapters tend to focus on one area of the humanities, and within it one specific perspective, to tackle one or more relatively specific PA problems, the *ensemble* of the chapters and the book as a whole traverses disciplinary boundaries. Indeed, the individual chapters and the book as a whole strive to provide the intellectual tools for enabling boundary-spanning intellectual inquiry, both across the various humanities and between the 'divide' of humanities and the social sciences as well as the other sciences more commonly associated with the study of PA. The thrust and spirit of this approach lie in refocusing on problems, rather than disciplines *per se*; evoking Popper, we (intellectuals) are students of problems, not of disciplines (Popper, 1962: 66–67).

The preparation of this book has itself been an exercise in boundary-spanning: with individual scholars teaming up around the core disciplinary area they are more versed in, to then networking and creating a broader 'community of teams' around and for the preparation of the chapters and clusters of chapters of this edited book.

The chapters in the remainder of this book illustrate and substantiate these thematic areas, topics, and problems in which bringing in the humanities – and the perspectives and forms of reasoning that are inherent to these areas of knowledge, understanding, and sapience – can contribute to the advancement of PA. In the remainder of this chapter, we briefly preview the contribution of each chapter before considering limitations and prospects and drawing some concluding remarks on this intellectual project as a whole.

OVERVIEW OF THE BOOK

Patrick Overeem (2025, this volume, Chapter 2) revisits Waldo's intellectual trajectory and contribution to the field of PA to argue that Waldo's perspective is inherently rooted in the humanities; it is a humanities-based interrogation of the nature of the field of PA. The chapter shows how the writings, style, and overall intellectual trajectory of Waldo point to a Socratic approach, in the literal sense of the unceasing interrogation of the very nature of reality which the ancient Greek philosopher Socrates championed – an approach that is much needed for a humanities-based rethinking of the nature and foundations of

PA. Such a claim about the contribution made by Waldo – one of the founding fathers of modern and contemporary PA studies – corroborates an assumption held by all the authors of this book: that the humanities need to be brought *back* to PA, as they were already there, having been part and parcel of the understanding of PA and the training of civil servants in many administrative systems over history and across the world.

In his chapter, Chris Ansell (2025, this volume, Chapter 3) works out an original and relevant approach to set to 'practical use' (much in the sense of the philosophy of Pragmatism, on which see also Whetsell, 2025, Chapter 4, this volume) the contribution the humanities can provide to PA. The author argues that we can appreciate the role of the humanities in PA through the lens of what he refers to as 'public philosophy,' intended as a system of principles and values that cohere (to some degree) and are invoked and utilised to guide public action and debate. Key features of a public philosophy include it being synoptic, non-arbitrary, public, and practical reasoning-orientated. Analytically, the chapter distinguishes two faces of public philosophy – one face refers to the principles and values embedded in our political cultures, while the other face refers to explicit philosophical traditions of political theorising. Both faces are important for justifying, understanding, critiquing, and defending the fraught role of a democratic administrative state. Recently, Ansell observes, this role has been challenged by the rise of populism, which regards the administrative state as usurping popular sovereignty in favour of technocratic elitism. The chapter briefly investigates three public philosophies of the administrative state – populism, liberalism, and civic republicanism – and points to some of their key principles and values. Two major flashpoints of debate about the administrative state are then discussed: the controversial question of the 'neutrality' of the state and the perennial debate over administrative discretion. The chapter therefore makes an important attempt to showcase the significance of the humanities for both the study and understanding of PA, on one hand, and for the practice of PA, including with a normative thrust, on the other, notably in the context of a democratic administrative state.

Travis A. Whetsell (2025, this volume, Chapter 4) revisits the history of a specific philosophical stream, Pragmatism, which has been intertwined with the field of PA, at least in the US, since its inception. The author argues that Pragmatism is endowed with some distinctive traits from other philosophies which may make it a 'natural' philosophical referent for the field of PA, thanks to its features of being: practical (hence in a sense sharing the same overarching thrust of PA), pluralist (in the ontological sense that reality is composed of more than one type of substance, and the epistemological sense that knowledge can be generated via more than one irreducible basic principle – thereby resembling the 'reality' of PA which is far from being a unified discipline oriented around a Kuhnian paradigm, and rather more an assemblage of theories applied eclectically to resolve public problems); participatory (which brings about the notion of 'community of inquiry', of the study and practice of PA as a fundamentally social and cooperative endeavour); and provisional (a status which most PA scholars might quickly recognise as quite constitutive of extant PA knowledge). Whetsell, referring most notably to the works of Patricia Shields, makes a strong and impassioned case for the significance of Pragmatism for PA – and within the process more broadly for the significance of a philosophy- and humanities-grounded understanding of PA. One lingering question may concern the extent to which Pragmatism as a philosophy of PA has travelled, or can travel, outside of a US intellectual PA context.

Stefano Biancu and Edoardo Ongaro (2025, this volume, Chapter 5) employ another branch of philosophy and the humanities, namely moral philosophy and philosophical anthropology (and theology). By adopting the theological notion of supererogation (which is concerned with those courses of action that a person undertakes beyond the call of duty), they revisit the anthropological foundations of key thematic areas in PA, which have been the subject of extensive social scientific inquiry over the past decades – namely integrity of governance, the theory of Public Value, Public Service Motivation theory, and models of public administration – from the standpoint of supererogation. To recall in this introduction chapter just one of the topics revisited by Biancu and Ongaro in their chapter, we may evoke the course of action undertaken by the town librarian so vividly depicted by Moore (1995) in his most famous, and most cited, book: the librarian who proactively reinvented the public service that the library used to provide in such way to cater to the needs of students pouring into the library in the afterschool time in search of a place to socialise (but not, to be noted, of a book to read). The librarian reimagined her library in such a way as to 'care for' the students, going well beyond her formal remit as a town librarian, to ultimately manage to create what Moore has described and theorised as 'Public Value' in his seminal work. The chapter interrogates the motives driving our town librarian from the perspective of the notion of supererogation, to then query whether the Public Value theory and practice posits – at least implicitly – a supererogatory view of the public servant, and noting these questions have not been asked in the public administration and management literature, and yet addressing them would provide a moral and anthropological foundation to the figure of the public manager creator of public value. They conclude by observing it may well be high time to ask such foundational questions: in the field of the Public Value theory as well as in other key areas of theoretical-empirical inquiry in PA. The chapter shows how the perspective of supererogation – and more amply the repertoire of notions and concepts that can be drawn from moral philosophy and philosophical anthropology – may be fruitfully brought into the field of PA.

Also centred on foundational issues about the individual person and human behaviour is the contribution by Jonathan C. Kamkhaji and Claudio M. Radaelli (2025, this volume, Chapter 6), who develop ontological hypotheses about the micro-foundations of PA, intended as the core individual-level properties of agents within PA. Of course, individuals interact in groups within PA and are constrained by institutional rules and organisational roles, and individuals that make up the public administration interact with other individuals with different micro-foundations, like elected politicians, citizens, pressure groups, and international organisations – but, as the authors argue: 'the story must start somewhere, and in this chapter our story starts with the ontology of the ideal-typical *homo* we find in public administration'. The chapter provides a fascinating theoretical journey towards the delineation of the civil servant/ bureaucrat/public manager as *homo faber*, who combines key traits of the *homo oeconomicus*, the *homo discentis* and, crucially, also the *homo emotionalis*. This chapter provides a theoretical journey which draws in an integrated way from psychology, the cognitive and the neurosciences, the social sciences, and from the humanities, at least to the extent its overall thrust is about working out an ontology of the human being and ontological hypotheses in the context of the administrative sciences.

With the thrust of bridging the individual and the 'context', Irene Hardill (2025, this volume, Chapter 7) revisits the contribution that human geography can provide to PA. She points out that, while human geography can be ascribed to the camp of the social sciences, historical geography lies in the field of the humanities: the two can and ought to be used in a combined way to shed light on aspects of the workings of administrative systems in context. Therefore, the contribution by Hardill shows that the border between social sciences and the humanities can be blurred, and it may be well worth traversing it in order to be better equipped intellectually to address PA problems (evoking again Waldo: ultimately, we should aim to study problems, not disciplines). It does so through the case of human geography in the UK context since WWII, also considering funding processes and how the institutional and infrastructural way of organising knowledge production affects interdisciplinary work.

The evocation of the perspective of history leads us to a cluster of chapters which examine the contribution of historiography to PA. In his contribution, Leonida Tedoldi (2025, this volume, Chapter 8) provides the first of three chapters centred on the contribution that the study of history, historiography, and the work of historians may provide to our understanding of PA. He focuses the level of the state and provides an account of the 'history of the historiography of the state', evidencing how it developed, between ups and downs, over the past decades, and its current state of the art in Europe.

Fabio Rugge (2025, this volume, Chapter 9) revisits, through the evocation of five distinct episodes, the status of administrative history as a specific and autonomous field of study. The narrative approach to writing employed by Rugge in his chapter is itself instructive: while the narrative style is quite common in historiography, it is less so in PA or the social sciences, so the writing style is itself part of the interdisciplinary dialogue this book attempts to make. In more broadly revisiting the contribution of history and historiography to PA, Rugge notices an inherent tension between historians working, through historiographical methods, on the uncovering and reconstruction of historical 'facts' and events in their 'uniqueness', so to speak, and who are cautious about drawing any generalisation beyond the extant historical episode being studied, on one hand; and, on the other hand, the usage of history and historiography for generalising purposes, that is, by uncovering historical evidence to provide social scientists with the 'raw material' for expanding the scope of the available evidence (beyond the present to also encompass the past) and thence for further testing or elaborating and refining theories and models by also utilising evidence from the past. At the roots of this tension is the inherent nature of a historical event being in a sense always 'foreign' to us living in another epoch, and yet through analogical reasoning, it can be possible to progressively approach it and make it meaningful also as a source of learning for our present. In a sense, the deeper the investigation of the causal texture of a past episode and the understanding of its genealogy, the stronger the learning can also be for contemporary purposes through analogical reasoning. Finally, historiography may enable the study not just of facts and events, but also of the thought of scholars of the past, thereby enlarging administrative thinking. For instance, see Rugge (2019), who revisits the thinking on public administration and the training of civil servants of Gian Domenico Romagnosi, an Italian intellectual of the 18th and early 19th centuries – something which is also done by Overeem with his interpretation of the thinking of Waldo in the already introduced chapter published in this volume.

In his contribution, Lorenzo Castellani (2025, this volume, Chapter 10) picks up on the key topic of the ways in which the past, history, and the study of it can be put to use for contemporary purposes. Administrative history, which is argued to be an autonomous field, can serve multiple purposes for both contemporary scholarly work and in assisting decision-makers. Regarding the former, i.e., scholarly work, he points to an intriguing feature of historiographic work: that of being profoundly ('intrinsically') interdisciplinary in nature (a historical event or process can be thoroughly analysed only by mobilising a wide range of disciplinary perspectives to delve into its complexity), and of possessing an interdisciplinarity which spans both the humanities and the social sciences: in a sense, historiography is itself a case in point of how the humanities and the social sciences can complement each other when studying phenomena of the past, thereby by its very existence furnishing an example of 'successful' interdisciplinarity. Even more notable is the latter aspect, that is amply elaborated by Castellani, who shows the multiple ways in which history and historiography can be brought to bear for public decision-makers. History can be a source of inspiration as it can provide 'real-life' material for analogical reasoning by decision-makers and is a tool with strong expressive power, hence likely to heavily influence decision-making – and Castellani rightly notices it is much better if professional historians provide such material for inspiration to decision-makers: otherwise, improvised analogies and misplaced interpretations of past events may warp decision-making. History can also provide a source for strategic planning in public management (Bryson, 2018; Ferlie and Ongaro, 2022), notably by means of the elaboration of imagined alternative futures, which historians can develop or at least enable through their work, and which can give us access to a wider range of human responses to the problems of society, ultimately enriching public administration thinking, and '[T]he skill of describing coherent, plausible alternatives can be applied in the development of scenarios, a central technique in strategy, not just in government but also in business and military contexts' (Castellani, Chapter 10).

Another cluster of chapters shifts the attention to religion and its manifold interconnections with public governance. The first of these chapters has been prepared by two authors (one being also a co-editor of this book and co-author of this introduction chapter) who have also devoted a book-length work (Ongaro and Tantardini, 2023a) to (re-)introducing religion into PA and have, for this purpose, elaborated a theoretical framework for the study of the influence of religion on PA. The chapter by Tantardini and Ongaro (2025, this volume, Chapter 11) provides the first (to our knowledge) systematic literature review of theology and religious studies' academic journals (in English) that investigates distinctive aspects of the relationship between religion and PA. The literature review, whose findings are reported in the chapter, has detected 58 journal articles which study aspects of PA by employing a theological or religious studies perspective. This contribution is in unison with the thrust of the present book to mobilise the humanities for generating valuable knowledge to address PA topics and themes, as religious studies and theology studies are generally classified within the field of the humanities (specifically, the relationship of the human to the divine, and its implications for individuals and society). Importantly, the authors combine the findings of the present literature review of theology and religious studies' journals with an analogous search with the same focus that they developed on academic journals in the social sciences, namely detecting articles addressing the topic of the influence of (aspects of) religion on (aspects of) PA. Conjoining the two searches has enabled the identification and initial examination of a combined 18 thematic areas into which it is possible to classify the influence of religion on PA (Tantardini and Ongaro, 2025, this volume, Chapter 11; see also Ongaro and Tantardini, 2024).

Pasquale Annicchino (2025, this volume, Chapter 12) shifts to the 'practical' implications of religion in its relationship to PA and provides a picture of the 'resurgence' of religion in contemporary societies across the world. He notices the misalignment of perceptions prevalent in the West due to the continual influence of the 'separation paradigms' that came to prevail in this region (and which include the separation 'of spiritual from secular, of religion from law') in the wake of the Enlightenment, with particular strength in the 20th century. Such separation paradigms worked on the assumption that Western liberal democracies had solved the problem of the relationship between state and religion, with constitutional secularism as a main plank of the solution – an assessment which nowadays seems somewhat naive and rushed, as Annicchino argues both by way of reasoning and with supporting evidence. While such an assessment about the limits of the 'inevitability of secularism' may be widely held and common wisdom for scholars of religious studies, outside of this circuit many, especially Western scholars, thereby including PA scholars, still work under the assumption of the separation paradigm. This may mean working under assumptions and presuppositions that may no longer hold in our contemporary world. As a minimum, differentiation must be developed among different clusters of countries, for which the interrelationship between religion and culture may entail that different sets of values tend to prevail. The comparative study of PA (and public policy) would benefit hugely from taking into account the important differences in the public dimension of religion across jurisdictions. Annicchino also argues that in policy-making, notably in relation to the role of PA, religion can acquire a problematic status, being seen either as a problem, a complication for policy-making, or as a contributor to effective policy-making (or both), with important implications for how policy-making processes unfold.

Ronald van Steden is definitely one of the PA scholars who is aware of and well understands how fallacious relegating religion to the margins may be for contemporary PA. Indeed, in his contribution (van Steden, 2025, this volume, Chapter 13), he tackles head-on one key issue for encompassing 'the religious factor' into PA studies; namely, how to bridge what seems to be incommensurable: the scientific investigation of social phenomena, on one hand, and the religious experience, which is located at another ontological-logical-existential level, on the other hand. The notion of resonance may provide a key to at least starting to build such a bridge, and hence provide the conceptual tools for encompassing religion into the explanatory factors of PA phenomena. He elaborates at length, and in depth, on how the notion of resonance might be employed in PA studies.

The next group of chapters then focuses specifically on the arts (notably the 'fine arts'), which we here group together into the broader category of the humanities – to which we should more precisely refer to as the 'arts and humanities'. Edoardo Ongaro provides an analysis of how the consideration of the key features – the essence, so to speak – of the arts and of artistic work may enlighten and provide novel ways of understanding a variety of aspects and profiles of PA, not just PA as an interdisciplinary object of study, but also of PA as a profession, and of PA as, indeed, an art (Ongaro, 2025, this volume, Chapter 14). The chapter notably dwells on and outlines what can be learnt for PA by considering the following inherent, constitutive aspects of art: (1) art as craftsmanship; (2) art as creation; (3) art as a means of expression; (4) art as a form of knowledge; (5) art as beauty. In his analysis, he encompasses all seven of the main 'fine arts', that is, alongside the three visual arts (painting, sculpture, architecture) also the performing arts (music, theatre, cinema) and writing/poetry.

Gjalt de Graaf and Hanneke van Asperen (2025, this volume, Chapter 15) revisit their own study of the famous frescoes by Ambrogio Lorenzetti's *Il Buon Governo* and track the academic impact of their article 'The Art of Good Governance: How Images from the Past Provide Inspiration for Modern Practice' (de Graaf and Van Asperen, 2016), which aimed at examining how Lorenzetti's frescoes can inspire modern-day conceptions of Good Governance, with the goal of probing whether the frescoes may inspire the development of fresh perspectives on what makes governance good governance. The key point is that the artistic work can be the core argument in a piece of PA research, not just a visual complement to it. In this vein, they then explore other artworks which can enhance our understanding of PA, and on that basis, and by revisiting the scattered works in PA that consider the significance of the contribution the arts can make to PA, they further develop conceptual bridges between the visual arts and PA, both in research and teaching.

Wolfgang Drechsler (2025, this volume, Chapter 16) also turns to the visual arts, and specifically to painting, and he too delves into the enduring significance of Ambrogio Lorenzetti's iconic frescoes of *Good and Bad Government and their Effects on City and Country* in the Town Hall of the Italian city of Siena. The chapter examines these masterpieces not only as a conduit to envisioning contemporary ideals of good public administration but also as a quintessential demonstration of art's ability to transcend temporal and spatial boundaries, following the thought of Hans-Georg Gadamer. By unraveling the philosophical underpinnings of communal existence depicted in these artworks, this chapter illuminates how visual art can directly articulate the foundational notion for PA of the Good Life in the Good State. Reference to the history of another famous, and probably much more successful over many consecutive centuries, Italian city-state, Venice, guides the reader to drawing the practical implications of the ideational bases of good government (and good governance) that can be inspired by artistic work.

The contribution by Geert Bouckaert (2025, this volume, Chapter 17) high-lights how the arts and the sciences need to combine to advance our knowledge and understanding, focusing especially on contemporary art, and reflecting on the meaning of 'contemporary' (as distinct from 'contemporaneous') as a pathway to futures, whereby 'contemporary' is not just about what is pro-duced today in art and science, but it is about what is produced today and what is relevant for tomorrow in terms of relevant futures. Bouckaert provides a comprehensive framework that starts from defining conceptual issues, to then consider both the intellectual strategy – from co-operation to constella-tion to co-production – and the practical 'how to' strategy, including institu-tional strategies and the development of infrastructural enablers, to facilitate such integrative thrust and to delineate what benefits can be reaped if such an undertaking is pursued (and conversely what we lose – as scholars, decision-makers, and society at large – when we do not operate to enable the conditions for such integration of arts and sciences, notably for application to PA). This chapter provides a major contribution to addressing one of the two overarching research questions of this intellectual endeavour and this book, namely, why and how the entirety of the arts and the humanities can be combined with the sciences – both the natural and, especially, the social sciences – for advancing PA. In addressing the question of whether the humanities and the social sci-ences are alternative or complementary, this contribution points out that they can be *made* to be complementary, for the ultimate purpose of a better PA.

Finally, in the most classical 'last but not least' fashion, the concluding chapter by Biancu and Ongaro (2025, this volume, Chapter 18) also tackles head-on another of the overarching research questions of this intellectual pro-ject and book, namely the question of whether we can speak of humanism of and for PA – and if so, with what meaning, and with what implications in terms of how humanism ought to infuse PA? Biancu and Ongaro notice that there are at least three senses in which the term 'humanism' is being used: the historical and historiographical sense (to denote certain points in European, and Western intellectual history); the cultural sense, to refer to humanism as a broad term in culture, a synthesising category that perhaps better than any other expresses the self-consciousness of European civilisation as a whole; and a third sense, one in which, other than being a historical and cultural term, humanism carries an axiological meaning and, as such, it has performed and can perform the role of a regulative ideal. Terms like 'humanism' and 'human-ity', in this third sense, are to all effects mythical categories that aim to estab-lish a symbolic space where recognition and a just order of relationships are made possible. Humanism in this perspective may operate as a synthesising and generative category at the core of a constellation of notions – like 'human dignity' and 'human rights' – which are in need of being continuously rene-gotiated and adapted to local cultures, while remaining universally shared by humankind and always needing to be continually upheld, lest the vulnerable and the weakest get trampled by the very administrative systems and governance regimes that ought to support and protect them. A humanism which is respectful towards nature and all other living beings, and is grounded by human dignity, can provide a regulatory ideal normatively driving the redesign of public governance for addressing the evolving challenges of humankind and nature in the 21st century. It is this humanism that substantiates the very notion of PA as practical humanism, which has first been introduced into the contemporary PA debate in Ongaro (2020, chapter 1).

LIMITATIONS AND PROSPECTS

In conclusion, we should point out that there are gaps we were not able to fill in the text contained between the two covers of this book. A glaring one concerns the contribution that anthropology and cultural anthropology may provide to PA – albeit a counterargument can be that the status of anthropology as being part of the humanities or rather the social sciences (and in some regards even of the natural sciences and the sciences of life; notably the studies of human evolution and the *hominis* carried out by palaeoanthropology) is contested, and indeed anthropology may be deemed to crosscut the humanities, the social sciences, and the natural and life sciences. Specifically, cultural anthropology can be considered the closest to (if not sitting squarely within) the humanities, and there is already significant work in the field of PA: Christopher Hood made a major contribution to public management by bringing a cultural anthropology theory (developed by prominent anthropologist Mary Douglas) into the field of public management (Hood, 1998). More recently, Raadschelders (2020) draws at least indirectly on this discipline in his interpretive history of government and public administration going back to the dawning of human civilisations.

Other areas of the humanities that could potentially benefit PA could not be covered here, due to limits of both resources and knowledge. However, the purpose of this book, as the title suggests, is to be an introduction to the topic of connecting the humanities and PA, a work capable of triggering a broader communal (to echo Whetsell's point in this volume) endeavour whose thrust is to bring back the humanities into PA. It is therefore our hope that this book will provide the stimulus for other authors to pursue the application to PA of those areas of the humanities that could not be addressed here. Furthermore, we should also stress that this book does not encompass areas such as the impact of technological evolution and revolutions on the humanities, and how these changes can reshape the very humanities and social sciences and the way research is being done in these areas, also for application to PA.

Importantly, this book does not directly cover the contribution of philosophy *tout court* to PA; that is, it does not encompass fields of philosophy like ontology and epistemology, rather the fields of philosophy that are more directly mobilised here are political philosophy and moral philosophy. This is not neglect, but simply division of labour, since the area of the connection between philosophy *tout court* and PA has been covered in a stream of recent works (see Ongaro, 2019, 2020, 2021, 2022 and forthcoming; Raadschelders, 2011; Lynch and Cruise, 2006). This book aims to engage in a dialogue with the perspective of philosophy and PA by bringing the humanities more widely into PA, while making the most of the division of intellectual labour between different publications and therefore not covering terrain already covered in other, recently published works. Those important contributions and – we hope – this book may together provide elements to build on for further developing the contribution of this important disciplinary area – crosscutting the humanities and social, and even natural, sciences – to PA.

As a final consideration, we notice that this book walks the path of connecting the humanities and PA in mainly one direction: from the humanities to PA. In more precise words: we identify the academic fields of the humanities as the *source domain* – that is, the field of knowledge which is used as a source (of theories, notions, and conceptual lenses) – for application to the field of PA as the *target domain*, that is, the field which may 'progress' (in the sense of advancing its state-of-art knowledge and/or expanding the theoretical-conceptual perspectives it employs) by employing knowledge drawn from the source domain. The individual chapters substantiate this one-way path by illustrating and expanding on how the humanities as the source domain can shed light on aspects of PA as the target domain.

It may well be argued that the path could be walked the other way around too: that is, it may be claimed (in a warranted manner, we deem) that the administrative sciences may also have something to offer and provide to studies in the field of the humanities, especially from the perspective of studying the state and power relationships, the interplay of administration as the process of running (complex) organisations, and the public dimension/publicness as constitutive components of any human society. PA studies may contribute to highlighting how these complex dynamics play out in philosophical thinking, or in literature and the arts at large, in historiography, and so on.[4] While addressing this question – what can PA studies contribute to the humanities? – is beyond the scope of this book, we hope this work may elicit interest in the multiple and two-way connections between the humanities and PA and that such interest may encourage scholars and practitioners alike to pursue this intellectual endeavour.

---

[4] We are indebted to an anonymous reviewer of the book proposal for pointing this out.

As to the present book, our focus is on how the treasure trove of knowledge, understanding, and wisdom that the humanities bestow upon us all can be harnessed to contribute to the advancement of the field of PA, or – if the term 'advancement' sounds too ambitious, and even too 'positivistic' – at least to the broadening of the intellectual perspectives and the cognitive maps that are employed and deployed in the 'art of the state' and in governing and administering any human society.

REFERENCES

Annicchino, Pasquale (2025, this volume, Chapter 12) 'When Ideas have Consequences: The Optical Illusion with Religion in Public Policy', in E. Ongaro, G. Orsina, and L. Castellani (eds.) *The Humanities and Public Administration: An Introduction.* Northampton, MA and Cheltenham, UK: Edward Elgar.

Ansell, Chris (2025, this volume, Chapter 3) 'Public Philosophy and the Administrative State', in E. Ongaro, G. Orsina, and L. Castellani (eds.) *The Humanities and Public Administration: An Introduction.* Northampton, MA and Cheltenham, UK: Edward Elgar.

Barzelay, Michael (2019) *Public Management as a Design-Oriented Professional Discipline.* Cheltenham, UK and Northampton, MA, USA: Edward Elgar.

Biancu, Stefano and Edoardo Ongaro (2025, this volume, Chapter 5) 'Benevolence, (Public) Ethics and Public Services: Revisiting Public Value, Public Service Motivation, and Models of Public Administration through the Ethics of Supererogation', in E. Ongaro, G. Orsina, and L. Castellani (eds.) *The Humanities and Public Administration: An Introduction.* Northampton, MA and Cheltenham, UK: Edward Elgar.

Biancu, Stefano and Edoardo Ongaro (2025, this volume, Chapter 18) 'Humanism and Public Administration: Profiling the Contours of Public Administration as Practical Humanism', in E. Ongaro, G. Orsina, and L. Castellani (eds.) *The Humanities and Public Administration: An Introduction.* Northampton, MA and Cheltenham, UK: Edward Elgar.

Bouckaert, Geert (2020) 'Foreword', in Edoardo Ongaro (ed.) *Philosophy and Public Administration: An Introduction* (pp. vii–ix). Cheltenham, UK and Northampton, MA: Elgar.

Bouckaert, Geert (2025, this volume, Chapter 17) 'Mind the Gap: A Strategy to Connect Humanities (Arts) with Social Sciences (Public Administration)', in E. Ongaro, G. Orsina, and L. Castellani (eds.) *The Humanities and Public Administration: An Introduction.* Northampton, MA and Cheltenham, UK: Edward Elgar.

Bryson, John M. (2018) *Strategic Planning for Public and NonProfit Organizations.* Hoboken, NJ: John Wiley & Sons.

Castellani, Lorenzo (2025, this volume, Chapter 10) 'History and Public Administration: Meanings, Problems, Usefulness in Policy-making', in E. Ongaro, G. Orsina, and L. Castellani (eds.) *The Humanities and Public Administration: An Introduction.* Northampton, MA and Cheltenham, UK: Edward Elgar.

de Graaf, Gjalt and Hanneke van Asperen (2025, this volume, Chapter 15) 'The Arts and Public Administration: How Artworks Can Be a Source of Knowledge, Inspiration, Motivation, and Understanding in Public Administration', in E. Ongaro,

G. Orsina, and L. Castellani (eds.) *The Humanities and Public Administration: An Introduction*. Northampton, MA and Cheltenham, UK: Edward Elgar.

de Graaf, Gjalt and van Asperen, H. (2018 – online first 2016) 'The Art of Good Governance: How Images from the Past Provide Inspiration for Modern Practice', International Review of Administrative Sciences, 84(2), 405–420.

Dimock, Marshall E. (1958). *A Philosophy of Administration: Toward Creative Growth*. New York: Harper and Row.

Drechsler, Wolfgang (2001) 'Good and Bad Government. Ambrogio Lorenzetti's Frescoes in the Sienna Town Hall as Mission Statement for Public Administration Today'. Local Government and Public Service Reform Initiative, Discussion Papers, No. 20, pp. 1–29.

Drechsler, Wolfgang (2025, this volume, Chapter 16) 'Ambrogio Lorenzetti's Siena Frescoes and Public Administration Today', in E. Ongaro, G. Orsina, and L. Castellani (eds.) *The Humanities and Public Administration: An Introduction*. Northampton, MA and Cheltenham, UK: Edward Elgar.

Ferlie, Ewan and Edoardo Ongaro (2022) *Strategic Management of Public Service Organisations: Concepts, Schools and Contemporary Issues*. London: Routledge.

Floridi, Luciano (2013) *The Philosophy of Information*. Oxford: Oxford University Press.

Floridi, Luciano (2019) *The Logic of Information: A Theory of Philosophy as Conceptual Design*. Oxford: Oxford University Press.

Franklin, Aimee L. and Jos C. N. Raadschelders (2023) *Introduction to Governance, Government and Public Administration*. Cham, Switzerland: Springer.

Hardill, Irene (2025, this volume, Chapter 7) 'Human Geography and the Study of Governance and Society: Perspectives from the UK', in E. Ongaro, G. Orsina, and L. Castellani (eds.) T*he Humanities and Public Administration: An Introduction*. Northampton, MA and Cheltenham, UK: Edward Elgar.

Hood, Christopher (1998) *The Art of the State*. Oxford: Oxford University Press.

Kamkhaji, Jonathan C. and Claudio M. Radaelli (2025, this volume, Chapter 6) 'Behaviour in Public Administration: In Search of Foundational Insights', in E. Ongaro, G. Orsina, and L. Castellani (eds.) *The Humanities and Public Administration: An Introduction*. Northampton, MA and Cheltenham, UK: Edward Elgar.

Lynch, Thomas D. and Peter L. Cruise (eds) *Handbook of Organization Theory and Management: The Philosophical Approach*. Boca Raton, FL: CRC Press.

Moore, Mark (1995) *Creating Public Value. Strategic Management in Government*. Cambridge, MA: Harvard University Press.

Ongaro, Edoardo (2019) 'The Teaching of Philosophy for Public Administration Programmes', *Teaching Public Administration*, 37(2), 135–146.

Ongaro, Edoardo (2020) *Philosophy and Public Administration: An Introduction*. Northampton, MA and Cheltenham, UK: Edward Elgar.

Ongaro, Edoardo (2021) 'Non-Western Philosophies and Public Administration', guest editorial, *Asia Pacific Journal of Public Administration*, 43:1, 6–10 - https://doi.org/10.1080/23276665.2020.1844027.

Ongaro, Edoardo (2022) 'Philosophy for and of Public Administration and Management', in K. Schedler (ed.) *Elgar Encyclopedia of Public Management*. Cheltenham, UK and Northampton, MA: Edward Elgar.

Ongaro, Edoardo (2025, this volume, Chapter 14) 'How the Consideration of the Nature of Art Can Provide Novel Ways to Understand Public Administration', in E. Ongaro,

G. Orsina, and L. Castellani (eds.) *The Humanities and Public Administration: An Introduction*. Northampton, MA and Cheltenham, UK: Edward Elgar.

Ongaro, Edoardo (forthcoming) *Connecting Philosophy and Public Administration: Directions of Inquiry*. London: Palgrave.

Ongaro, Edoardo and Michele Tantardini (2023a) *Religion and Public Administration: An Introduction*. Cheltenham, UK and Northampton, MA: Edward Elgar.

Ongaro, Edoardo and Michele Tantardini (2023b) 'Advancing Knowledge in Public Administration: Why Religion Matters', guest editorial, *Asia Pacific Journal of Public Administration*. 45(1), 1-6

Ongaro, Edoardo and Michele Tantardini (2024a) 'Contours of a Research Programme for the Study of the Relationship of Religion and Public Administration', *Public Policy and Administration*. 39(4), 521-530.

Ongaro, Edoardo and Michele Tantardini (2024b) 'Religion, Spirituality, Faith and Public Administration: A Literature Review and Outlook', *Public Policy and Administration*. 39(4), 531-555.

Overeem, Patrick (2025, Chapter 2, this volume) 'Socratic Public Administration: The Relevance of Dwight Waldo Today', in E. Ongaro, G. Orsina, and L. Castellani (eds.) *The Humanities and Public Administration: An Introduction*. Northampton, MA and Cheltenham, UK: Edward Elgar.

Popper, Karl R. (1962). *Conjectures and Refutations: The Growth of Scientific Knowledge*. New York: Basic Books.

Pollitt, Christopher and Geert Bouckaert (2017) *Public Management Reform – A Comparative Analysis: Into the Age of Austerity*. Oxford: Oxford University Press.

Raadschelders, J. (2011) *Public Administration: The Interdisciplinary Study of Government*. Oxford: Oxford University Press.

Raadschelders, Jos C. N. (2020) *The Three Ages of Government: From the Person, to the Group, to the World*. Ann Arbor: University of Michigan Press.

Rugge, Fabio (2019) 'Romagnosi, la formazione dei funzionari, le transizioni' [Romagnosi, the training of public officials, transitions], *Annali di Storia Moderna e Contemporanea*, 7, 15–26.

Rugge, Fabio (2022) 'Romagnosi, la formazione dei funzionari, le transizioni', *Annali di Storia Moderna*, 7, 15–26.

Rugge, Fabio (2025, this volume, Chapter 9) 'Historiography and Public Administration. A Story of Disciplines', in E. Ongaro, G. Orsina, and L. Castellani (eds.) *The Humanities and Public Administration: An Introduction*. Northampton, MA and Cheltenham, UK: Edward Elgar.

Tantardini, Michele and Edoardo Ongaro (2025, this volume, Chapter 11) 'The Contribution of the Religious Studies and Theology Literatures to Public Administration: A Review and Outlook', in E. Ongaro, G. Orsina, and L. Castellani (eds.) *The Humanities and Public Administration: An Introduction*. Northampton, MA and Cheltenham, UK: Edward Elgar.

Tedoldi, Leonida (2025, this volume, Chapter 8) 'The Concept of State in the Historical Studies', in E. Ongaro, G. Orsina and L. Castellani (eds.) *The Humanities and Public Administration: An Introduction*. Northampton, MA and Cheltenham, UK: Elgar.

van Steden, Ronald (2025, this volume, Chapter 13) 'Reconnecting Government: On the Existential Layers of Public Administration', in E. Ongaro, G. Orsina, and L.

Castellani (eds.) *The Humanities and Public Administration: An Introduction.* Northampton, MA and Cheltenham, UK: Edward Elgar.

Whetsell, Travis A. (2025, this volume, Chapter 4) 'Philosophical Pragmatism and the Study of Public Administration', in E. Ongaro, G. Orsina and L. Castellani (eds.) *The Humanities and Public Administration: An Introduction.* Northampton, MA and Cheltenham, UK: Edward Elgar.

2. Socratic Public Administration: The Relevance of Dwight Waldo Today

Patrick Overeem

INTRODUCTION

The question of what the humanities can contribute to Public Administration[1] can be approached from either the outside or the inside, so to speak. One can start with disciplines like history (including art history and the history of ideas), philosophy, linguistics, and theology and see how their insights, theories, and methods could be brought to bear on the study of public administration. Something like this has already been done for more adjacent disciplines like economics and law, as well as for more distanced ones such as biology and cybernetics, and it will surely be worthwhile to enrich Public Administration with 'input' from the *Geisteswissenschaften* as well. The alternative approach would be to look within the field of Public Administration itself to see whether attempts have already been made to do distinctively humanities-based work that could be continued further. Public administration hosts scholars with a wide variety of backgrounds, including the humanities, who often apply their disciplinary training in their new academic home; as well as generically trained students of public administration who have an interest in history, philosophy, and so on, and conduct their studies from those viewpoints. So, besides the more common 'outside' approach to our question, there is also a rarer and distinct 'inside' approach.

Here I want to adopt this latter approach and suggest a way to develop what I call 'Socratic Public Administration' by means of revisiting of the works of a giant in the field: the American scholar Dwight Waldo (1913–2000).

---

[1] Here I follow the custom, introduced by Waldo, to use 'Public Administration' (with capitals) to refer to the field of study and 'public administration' to its object. Thus, the phrase 'the study of public administration' refers to Public Administration, while 'the study of Public Administration' would refer to meta-reflections on that field.

Importantly, he was once an outsider to the field himself. Being educated first in English and then in political science, he continued his studies with a doctoral dissertation at Yale on pre-WW2 American administrative thought, which was explicitly meant as a study in political theory (Waldo 1984: I–II; Brown & Stillman 1986: 19–33). Soon after the publication of the now-famous book *The Administrative State* in 1948, the outsider became an insider. So much so, indeed, that he became seen as one of the most eminent administrative thinkers, while – ironically – being all but forgotten in political theory.

Picking up the thread of Waldo's work seems valuable for two reasons. One is that he offers an important corrective to the overly positivistic and technical ('managerial') approach to public administration that has become dominant in the field. As is generally known, Waldo had a brief but fierce *choc des esprits* with that other rising young star in the administrative sciences, Herbert A. Simon. The two men represented two fundamentally different approaches to the field: the former humanistic and *Geisteswissenschaftlich*, the other economistic and logico-positivistic. While, as I will note later, one can doubt whether Waldo won the 1952 battle, it is not at all doubtful who won the war: Simon's approach has become mainstream, while Waldo's has become marginal. By and large, Public Administration has developed into a positivistic social science like most other subject areas, including political science, its 'mother discipline' (Waldo 1987: 95). In this situation, which despite growing criticism is still fundamentally unchanged, the value of the humanities for Public Administration is easily neglected – something which may be redressed or corrected if we start taking Waldo seriously again.

There is also another, perhaps more controversial reason to pick up Waldo's work again. In the past few decades, the humanities themselves have changed character dramatically, to the point of becoming hardly recognizable. I am hinting at the rise of so-called 'critical studies' in virtually every humanities discipline: the wide array of approaches that include neo-Marxism, postmodernism, poststructuralism, 'standpoint theory', feminism, postcolonialism, and many related labels. Reading Waldo's work, one will be struck by the fact that he hardly engaged with any of these. Although working at the time of the Cold War for most of his career, neo-Marxism never took hold of him and he was utterly sceptical of postmodernism and its ilk (Bertelli & Lynn 2006: 178–179, note 7). And although far from naive about power, he never adopted the so-called 'critical' perspective so common today, that prefers to interpret social relations primarily, and often solely, from that viewpoint. Briefly put, his approach was Socratic, not sophistic; he aimed at reconstruction rather than deconstruction, and he was critical in the original instead of the current meaning of the term: prudently judging rather than prejudiced and judgemental. So, if one asks what the humanities can contribute to Public Administration, it matters immensely what kind of humanities one means. Waldo represents a classical approach within them that may not be very much *en vogue* today but is far more time-tested and open-minded than its hydra-like alternative.

THE SOCRATES OF PUBLIC ADMINISTRATION

Dwight Waldo can well be called the Socrates of Public Administration. Arguably, his mission was to turn Public Administration from a practical and somewhat primitive endeavour into a self-aware and self-critical academic field of study. Of course, there were students of public administration before Waldo, too, as there were pre-Socratics in philosophy. But Waldo was the first to awaken Public Administration from its 'dogmatic slumber' by raising *the* essential question: What is public administration? What is the subject matter, and what is the field of study devoted to it? This fundamental question had never been asked so incisively before. Earlier authors such as Woodrow Wilson and Leonard White in America, or Lorenz von Stein and Max Weber in Europe had given their working definitions and circumscriptions, to be sure, but they never seriously considered these among possible alternatives, let alone reflected on the enterprise of conceptualizing public administration and Public Administration itself. Waldo, however, like a real Socrates, raised the question explicitly and it has never been off the table since.

Waldo was also Socratic in his style: he raised the big questions and he did so incessantly. Never content with easy answers, certainly not with his own, he continued probing and wondering. This habit has also struck others, and they have appreciated Waldo for it: 'The truth is, the value of Waldo's work for me was not so much the answers that he gave but the questions that he raised together with his enthusiastic effort to help those of us willing to wrestle with these questions' (Werlin 2001: 294). Still, this probing style may also be a reason why reading Waldo has never been, and perhaps never will be, really *popular.* It takes a patient cast of mind to really appreciate him. Indeed, his writings can be so tentative and open-ended that many readers hoping for clear answers may easily get irritated – even up to the level of Thrasymachus's outburst against Socrates in Plato's *Republic*: 'You know very well it is easier to ask questions than to answer them. Give an answer yourself ...' (book I, 336c). Like Socrates, Waldo realized, however, that bringing your audience to a state of bewilderment (*aporia*) is necessary for bringing them to insight. And his writings, though sometimes deceptively simple and purposefully aporetic, do indeed also contain flashes of unrivaled deep insight.

Obviously, the analogy with Socrates only goes so far. Waldo was never forced to take hemlock; turning from a young radical into a gentleman-scholar, he even ceased to be controversial. The field that once received him with barely concealed antipathy bade him farewell with the highest honours. It named its most prestigious award after him and heaped much respectful praise upon him, both after his retirement (Gazell 1983; Laohavichien 1983; Marini 1993) and after his death (Carroll & Frederickson 2001; Frederickson 2000; Lowery 2001; Wamsley 2001; Werlin 2001). He is probably the only administrative scientist to whom a book-length interview has been devoted (Brown & Stillman 1986) and recently an important volume of selected writings has been published (Stillman 2021). Still, the careful observer will notice that those who praise him comprise only a relatively small set of 'Waldonians'. One might also notice that an even smaller set, consisting primarily of Waldo's own pupils, continues to address the issues that occupied him in his own manner. If Waldonians are relatively rare in the field of Public Administration, truly Waldonian work is even rarer. His name is respected, to be sure, and his writings (especially *The Administrative State*) are ritualistically cited, but few actually try to follow in his footsteps. He is appreciated mainly, I suspect, because of his major and indeed valuable 'negative' contribution, i.e., the demolition of the pre-Second World War Public Administration 'orthodoxy,' and not because of his later 'positive' contributions. In part, Waldo himself is to blame for this. Like Socrates and unlike, for instance, Aristotle, he did not leave behind a coherent system of thought. He will not be remembered for a theoretical model, an empirical finding, a breakthrough in resolving some long-standing puzzle, nor even a catchy slogan or concept. Instead, his legacy particularly consists of a hardly transferable *attitude*, a way of thinking and arguing about public administration and its study that is different from anybody else's.

RE-READING WALDO TODAY

Waldo, again unlike Socrates, left behind many writings. A handful of books (an important one of which is unfinished and so far unpublished; Waldo & Marini 1999; Overeem 2008) and dozens of articles, reports, and editorials are the most tangible fruits of a productive academic life spanning six decades. But the sheer quantity of writings alone does not warrant re-reading them. Instead, we want to know: what is their quality and remaining relevance? Why should we read Waldo today?

The qualifier 'today' is important here. It refers basically to our present, post-Cold War or even post-9/11 era. Why should one read Waldo in the age of artificial intelligence, climate change, terrorism, and the rise of Asia? Is paying attention to such issues not more compelling than reading some decades-old texts by a 'dead white male' who lived to see only glimpses of the 21st century? In a similar vein, 'today' can also mean 'by a new generation' of students that have not known Waldo directly. (To interject a personal note: I started my own studies of Waldo's writings in 2002 and, despite the privilege of getting in touch with several of Waldo's pupils, I came just too late to get to know him myself.) Present-day students are rarely required to read 'old' books and articles. Waldonians should realize not only that Waldo is barely known to younger generations, but also that his relevance is far from obvious.

Hence, again: why study Waldo today? One important reason is to understand the history of Public Administration as a discipline. Waldo can be regarded as one of the field's main historiographers. He never tired of writing overviews of its development. He clearly was not a historian, however; he rarely conducted archival work, never cared much about detail, and generally found interpretations more important than facts. Historiography, for him, was always secondary to and supportive of theoretical reflection. This is particularly clear in *The Administrative State*, his most famous book. Its rich argument can be summarized very simply as a set of three claims, namely: (1) 'orthodox' pre-war administrative thought in the US (e.g., scientific management) was determined by the material and ideological circumstances of the time; (2) contrary to its own claims, it was not a neutral and objective science, but rather a normative political theory in its own right; and (3) as such, it was highly undemocratic and thus antithetical to important American political values (Rosenbloom & McCurdy 2006: 2–4). The first claim was, surely, backed up by extensive historical studies of late 19th and early 20th century American Public Administration. Hence, *The Administrative State* and Waldo's later historiographic writings can assist present-day students of public administration to get a grasp of the intellectual development of their field. This can be a first immediate benefit of reading Waldo. But his key message had to do, of course, with the other two claims. They go beyond historiography and point us towards the most important part of Waldo's legacy: his unique theoretical approach. Let us consider the two claims in order.

PUBLIC ADMINISTRATION AS POLITICAL THEORY

The idea, firstly, that Public Administration can be understood as political theory in its own right was radically innovative when Waldo first presented it: 'In 1948, the idea that public administrative doctrine was also political theory came as a revelation. It opened up an entirely new way of looking at the study and practice of public administration' (Rosenbloom & McCurdy 2006, p. 2). It is also the idea to which Waldo stuck most steadfastly throughout his career, from his doctoral dissertation defended in 1942 until a book chapter published a decade after his retirement titled 'A theory of public administration means in our time a theory of politics also' (Waldo 1990). In between those two moments, he expressed the same belief as follows: 'I thought at the time [the 1940s] and firmly believe now that the literature of public administration contains elements that are political theory as this is conventionally understood' (Waldo 1984, p. x). As Waldo noted, this argument was in fact highly ironic, given the completely antithetical self-image of the field: '[I]ntriguing paradox, delicious irony – a movement that deprecated ivory-tower theorizing, that sought to bracket political theory if not to abolish it, proved on examination to be implicitly, and occasionally explicitly, engaged with political theory' (1984, pp. x–xi). The irony of the argument does not make it any less serious, however. Waldo wanted to be taken literally with his claim that Public Administration can be understood as political theory.

Although innovative when first presented, once grasped, this fundamental idea is actually not so strange at all. At their beginnings, all academic fields, from political science to economics and from history and philology to physics and biology, have been related to and even been part of philosophy. Philosophy is indeed the *principio* of all sciences. And this is not just a fact of the past; a 'philosophy gene' keeps running through them – or so at least it should be. For that characteristic, and that alone, is what makes scientific disciplines academic, since academic in the original (Platonic) and still most meaningful sense of the word means philosophical (Pieper 1952). So, Waldo was the Socrates of Public Administration because he was the first to make Public Administration philosophical and thus academic (Overeem 2018).

The third and final claim – that early American Public Administration had been highly undemocratic – is even more controversial than the second. It naturally raises the question of whether an alternative, more democratic theory of public administration could be possible. This is the key question that has continued to occupy Waldo ever since *The Administrative State*. It is the subject of his 1952 article to which Simon so fiercely responded (Waldo 1952) and of several later publications (Waldo 1977, pp. 81–98; 1980), as well as of his 'big unpublished book' (Waldo & Marini 1999). Indeed, I would argue that, from a Waldonian perspective at least, this is *the* core question of Public Administration as a field: How can efficiency and effectiveness be combined with responsiveness and accountability? How, to take a pair of terms that Waldo used mostly in his later writings, can bureaucracy and democracy go together? Does public administration not easily threaten democratic politics and vice versa? How far, then, should these two be distinguished in our thinking and separated in practice? Can we sensibly uphold a 'dichotomy' between them (Overeem 2008, 2012)? Such questions cut to the heart of Public Administration. They show that public administration can never be studied in isolation but should always be put in context. Since 'administration' is always the administration *of something* (a policy, a service), public administration is never a stand-alone phenomenon but inherently secondary: it implies a counterpoint that is primary to it, whether it be politics, democracy, or even civilization. By definition, Public Administration is public service. The question of how it relates to its 'master' was also not entirely new when Waldo raised it, but he urged the field to take it much more seriously and see it in a much wider context than had been done before.

WALDO AND PRACTICAL WISDOM

One helpful way to characterize Waldo's distinctive approach is to use Jos Raadschelders' (2008) analysis of Public Administration as an ongoing conversation between four intellectual traditions. These are the positivistic mainstream tradition of 'scientific knowledge' and three smaller sidestreams called 'practical wisdom' (roughly equating to interpretivism), 'practical experience' (relating to Pragmatism), and finally 'relativist perspectives' (consisting of critical theory and postmodernism) (see also Riccucci 2010).

How does Waldo fit in this landscape? The answer is not difficult. Waldo clearly belongs to the tradition of 'practical wisdom'. This tradition is reflective, aiming to be reasonable but not rationalistic, unashamedly normative, academic, humanistic, and generously interdisciplinary. According to Raadschelders, work in this tradition

> focuses on political (and, since the late 18th century, also administrative) theory and includes attention to, among other things, world view, public morality, the ruler's (since the late eighteenth century both political officeholders and civil servants) disposition towards and relation with citizens, and the development of grand theory (2008, p. 928).

Later on, he lists six characteristics of the 'practical wisdom' tradition: it is interdisciplinary, generalist, drawing on common sense, working with human background skills (tacit knowledge and intuition), acknowledging but not resigning itself to national traditions, and respectful of different viewpoints (Raadschelders 2008, p. 931). These characterizations all fit Waldo very well. His approach was indeed one of learning and erudition, concentrating on broader pictures and deep questions, aiming at understanding big real-world problems but never at providing small technical solutions. In essence, he remained a political philosopher who had ended up in Public Administration.

Waldo was not only critical of pre-Second World War 'orthodox' Public Administration (which had been strongly in the 'practical experience' tradition), but also of most of its post-war alternatives. His strongest antipathy was directed against 'scientific knowledge'. He seriously doubted that Public Administration could become an exact science, modelled after the natural sciences. His fierce debate, or rather collision, with Herbert Simon, of course testifies most directly to his resistance to this approach, but also in later years he expressed strong misgivings about the predominance of positivism and naturalism in Public Administration. It is safe to say, however, that Waldo has lost this war. Generally speaking, the field of Public Administration has followed in Simon's footsteps rather than his. He even, in my opinion, lost the exchange in 1952 because he did not articulate his own position clearly and because he misrepresented Simon's.[2] This is not to deny, however, that Waldo had the better part of the argument.

Waldo does not belong to the two other sidestreams either. Occasionally, Waldo has been called a Pragmatist, albeit a somewhat half-hearted one (Snider 1997), but clearly he never worked on the basis of the highbrow philosophical Pragmatism of Peirce, James, or Dewey – a philosophical strand that certainly has had considerable influence on American administrative thought (Shields 2003, 2008). Surely, however, Waldo was a pragmatist with a lower-case 'p': commonsensical, adverse to dogmatism, and ready to compromise with reality if ideals could not be realized. Indeed, he declared himself an adherent of this anti-philosophical kind of 'pragmatism':

> What it comes to is that I don't see pragmatism – and certainly not full-blown Deweyism – as an alternative to this or that philosophy or method, but as something of a 'bedrock' (...) to temper the other philosophies and to replace them as necessary. A lowercase pragmatism keeps us open to all new imputs – 'let's try it and see' – and at the same time keeps us from becoming fanatical about any of them. In a highly imperfect world, we could have a worse bedrock (Brown & Stillman 1986, p. 162; Waldo 1984, pp. xxxviii and xlviii).

Even further removed from Waldo's position, one finds postmodernism. Bertelli and Lynn have ascribed to him 'intimations of Derrida and deconstructionism' (2006, p. 48), but as they had to acknowledge themselves, he was in fact very critical of postmodernism (2006, pp. 178–179, note 7). Neither was he a 'critical theorist': it was never his goal to unmask ideologies, criticize established power structures, or emancipate the underprivileged. He even opposed the elevation of social equity to a kind of supervalue by the leftist New Public Administration movement that emerged from the Minnowbrook I conference he himself had launched. The reason was not that he was a right-wing capitalist without social values – if anything, he was the opposite – but because he had strong reservations about collective efforts to realize societal blueprints. Pithily, he declared himself 'basically sceptical of all faiths and philosophies' – including scepticism itself (1984, pp. lxii, note 39; cf. Marini 1993, p. 410).

Waldo's position of 'practical wisdom' is, as Raadschelders has pointed out, one position among others, but at the same time it offers a viewpoint from which to assess the landscape as a whole. None of the other perspectives gives

---

[2]   A decade later, Herbert J. Storing (1962) did a much better job of attacking Simon's position (cf. Chisholm 1989; Kirwan 1981; Morgan 2010).

such a rewarding birds'-eye view as this one. 'Scientific knowledge' and 'practical experience' both take the point of view of the 'insiders', namely from within Public Administration (as a discipline) and within public administration (as a profession), respectively. 'Relativist perspectives' do indeed take an outsider's perspective as well, but they look at Public Administration and public administration *from below*; that is to say, they focus on the lower motives and have the express aim to criticize, unmask, and ultimately deconstruct. Their ambition to change easily takes over from the aspiration to understand. They politicize Public Administration (and public administration no less) in a way that Waldo and other critics of the politics-administration dichotomy had never intended and would abhor. Indeed, in contrast to much recent theoretical work in Public Administration (particularly New Public Administration, critical theory, and even the Blacksburg movement), Waldo's understanding of Public Administration as political theory was remarkably *apolitical*. It is barely possible to figure out Waldo's political convictions and his stance in the American political landscape on the basis of his writings. One cannot even tell with certainty whether he endorsed the administrative state or not. In this sense, too, Waldo was first and foremost an academic scholar whose motto would be the exact reversal of Marx's famous dictum: 'Public Administration scholars have hitherto only aimed to change the world, in various ways. The point, however, is to understand it'. This is, indeed, what distinguishes Socratic Public Administration from its alternatives.

WALDO AND BEYOND

Again: why study Waldo today? As said, one can read him to become better acquainted with the development of (American) administrative thought. Another, and probably weightier, purpose is to become familiar with that wider Socratic tradition that Waldo established and represented. To be sure, this approach has never been much followed. Glimpses of it can be seen in the writings of Norton Long (1952, 1954, 1962), Herbert J. Storing (Besette 1995; Morgan et al. 2010), and a handful of others, as well as in the Blacksburg movement (Wamsley & Wolf 1996) and currently in the so-called Constitutional School – too big a name, probably, since it consists only of a very small number of people, but nevertheless is a promising initiative (Newbold 2010; Newbold & Rosenbloom 2017). Overall, however, the approach has always remained marginal.

This says much about mainstream, non-Waldonian Public Administration. For Waldo was everything the mainstream anxiously avoids being: qualitative, normative, generalist, philosophical, and inconclusive. The mainstream is under the spell of what Lawler has aptly called 'scientific populism': a combination of scientific (or rather scientistic) approaches towards the management of means and a deference to majoritarian democracy for the determination of ends (Lawler 1988). Against this combination of instrumental rationality and political irrationality, Waldo can help infuse Public Administration with what Weber famously called 'value rationality' and prudential reasonableness. By reading him with patience and open-mindedness, students of public administration can learn how to protect their field against itself, even save it from itself – from its scientific pretensions, from its isolationism, and from its narrow focus on 'organization and management'. Waldo urges us to face the big questions: What is public administration? How does it relate to politics? What is its place within the separation-of-powers framework? How can it be reconciled with democracy? What does it contribute to our civilization? Waldo's writings on these questions can still be easily read today because they (including his reflections on university turmoil in the 1960s and 1970s) are exceptionally timeless.

Studying Waldo seriously requires that we do not limit ourselves to *The Administrative State*. For sure, *The Administrative State* is a unique book, as Waldo himself realized: 'The thing that seems to me clearest about *The Administrative State* is that it is a "different" book. Put it this way: one would not say of it that it is better or poorer than book X (of a similar nature): there was not and is not anything much like it' (1965, p. 5). But however magisterial, it only covers American administrative thought in the first half of the 20th century. Hence, Waldo's later writings (up to the 1990s) are important as well. And they differ in important ways from his earlier writings: they are less polemic, more constructive, and more wide-ranging.

Still, *The Administrative State* sets the standard. Ultimately, one wonders whether a book comparable to it could be written for our times: not about the early 20th century, but about the late 20th and early 21st centuries, and not only about American administrative thought but about global administrative thought. What would a present-day 'study of the political theory of global Public Administration' look like? One can only speculate. The 'material and ideological background' (chapter 1 of *The Administrative State*), as well as the 'movements, the men [and women], the motifs' (chapter 2), have of course changed drastically, although old wine often does end up in new bottles. 'Scientific management', as Waldo himself noted in his later comments to chapter 3 (1984, pp. xxx–xxxiii), has turned into 'management science', particularly the science of public management. But this is all rather secondary. Most fundamental is part II, which addresses five classical questions of political philosophy: What is the meaning of the good life? What are the (moral) criteria for action? Who should rule? Should there be a separation of powers? Should there be centralization or decentralization? In answering, often indirectly and unwittingly, these and similar questions, contemporary Public Administration continues to add its own chapter to the long history of political theory. Laying bare how it does that is probably the main task of Public Administration scholars today. And when they do so, it is inevitable they will face the follow-up question as well: is this political theory of present-day Public Administration more democratic – indeed is it (as Socrates would want to know) more *just* – than the one that Waldo described in the 1940s? I hesitate to give a positive answer, but serious administrative theorists, whether they be Waldonians or not, must address this issue upfront.

TWO QUESTIONS

To conclude, when it comes to the theme of this volume, Public Administration as a field faces two consecutive questions. The first is whether it wants to shape itself after the model of (natural) science, technology, engineering, and mathematics (STEM), as the field, along with the other social sciences, has increasingly been doing, or whether it will allow itself to be inspired and informed by the humanities. And the second is: if it wants to do the latter, then what are the kinds of humanities it will draw upon? Are these the self-declared 'critical studies' that tend to see social reality exclusively through the lens of positionality and power, as, unfortunately, the humanities themselves are increasingly doing, or are they the more classical kinds of study that aim to understand social reality more comprehensively in its own terms? In other words, will Public Administration be Socratic or sophistic? Both questions have to be faced; neglecting them, or only addressing the former, will not do. It is clear, I hope, what Waldo's answer to each of them would be.

REFERENCES

Bertelli, A. M., & Lynn, L. E., Jr. (2006). *Madison's Managers: Public Administration and the Constitution*. Baltimore, ML: Johns Hopkins University Press.

Besette, J. M. (ed.) (1995). *Toward a More Perfect Union: Writings of Herbert J. Storing*. Washington, D.C.: The AEI Press.

Brown, B. E. S., & Stillman, R. J., II. (1986). *A Search for Public Administration: The Ideas and Career of Dwight Waldo*. College Station, TX: A&M University Press.

Carroll, J. D., & Frederickson, H. G. (2001). Dwight Waldo, 1913–2000. *Public Administration Review*, *61*(1), 2–8.

Chisholm, R. F. (1989). The Storing critique revisited: Simon as seen in *The Science of Politics*. *Public Administration Quarterly*, *12*(4), 411–436.

Frederickson, H. G. (2000, December). How I became a Waldonian. *PA-Times*, 11.

Gazell, J. A. (1983). Dwight Waldo, public administration, and the 'blooming, buzzing confusion'. *American Review of Public Administration*, *16*(2/3), 127–138.

Kirwan, K. A. (1981). Herbert J. Storing and the study of public administration. *Political Science Reviewer*, *11*(1), 193–220.

Laohavichien, U. (1983). Dwight Waldo: The leading light of public administration for three decades. *Philippine Journal of Public Administration*, *27*(1), 1–22.

Lawler, P. A. (1988). Public administration, constitutionalism, and political philosophy in America. *Teaching Political Science*, *15*(2), 50–56.

Long, N. E. (1952). Bureaucracy and constitutionalism. *American Political Science Review*, *46*(3), 808–818.

Long, N. E. (1954). Public policy and administration: The goals of rationality and responsibility. *Public Administration Review*, *14*(1), 22–31.

Long, N. E. (1962). Power and administration. In C. Press (ed.), *The Polity*. Chicago, IL: Rand McNally.

Lowery, G. (2001). Dwight Waldo: Putting the purpose in P.A. *Maxwell Perspective: The Magazine of the Maxwell School of Syracuse University*. Retrieved from: http://www.maxwell.syr.edu/perspective/Spr01_waldo_main.htm.

Marini, F. (1993). Leaders in the field: Dwight Waldo. *Public Administration Review*, *53*(5), 409–418.

Morgan, D. F., Kirwan, K. A., Rohr, J. A., Rosenbloom, D. H., & Schaefer, D. L. (2010). Recovering, restoring, and renewing the foundations of American public administration: The contributions of Herbert J. Storing. *Public Administration Review*, *70*(4), 621–633.

Newbold, S. P. (2010). Toward a constitutional school for American public administration. *Public Administration Review*, *70*(4), 538–546.

Newbold, S. P., & Rosenbloom, D. (2017). *The Constitutional School of American Public Administration*. London/New York: Routledge.

Overeem, P. (2008). Beyond heterodoxy: Dwight Waldo and the politics-administration dichotomy. *Public Administration Review*, *68*(1), 36–45.

Overeem, P. (2012). *The Politics-Administration Dichotomy: Toward a Constitutional Perspective* (2nd edition). Boca Raton, FL: CRC Press.

Overeem P. (2018). Making public administration academic [Book review essay]. *Public Admininstration*, *96*(2), 421–424.

Pieper, J. (1952). *Was Heißt Akademisch? Zwei Versuche über die Chance der Universität Heute*. München: I.M. Kösel.

Raadschelders, J. C. N. (2008). Understanding government: Four intellectual traditions in the study of public administration. *Public Administration*, *86*(4), 925–949.

Riccucci, N. M. (2010). *Public Administration: Traditions of Inquiry and Philosophies of Knowledge*. Washington, D.C.: Georgetown University Press.

Rosenbloom, D. H., & McCurdy, H. E. (2006). Introduction: Dwight Waldo's *The Administrative State*. In D. H. Rosenbloom & H. E. McCurdy (eds.), *Revisiting Waldo's Administrative State: Constancy and Change in Public Administration* (pp. 1–14). Washington, D.C.: Georgetown University Press.

Shields, P. M. (2003). The community of inquiry: Classical pragmatism and public administration. *Administration & Society*, *35*(5), 510–538.

Shields, P. M. (2008). Rediscovering the taproot: Is classical pragmatism the route to renew public administration? *Public Administration Review*, *68*(2), 205–221.

Snider, K. F. (1997). *Pragmatism and the Intellectual Development of American Public Administration* [PhD]. Virginia Polytechnic Institute and State University, Blacksburg, VA.

Stillman, R. J., II (2021). *Dwight Waldo: Administrative Theorist for Our Times*. New York/London: Routledge.

Storing, H. J. (1962). The science of administration: Herbert A. Simon. In H. J. Storing (ed.), *Essays on the Scientific Study of Oolitics* (pp. 63–150). New York: Holt, Rinehart and Winston.

Waldo, D. (1952). Development of theory of democratic administration. *American Political Science Review*, *46*(1), 81–103.

Waldo, D. (1965, March). The administrative state revisited. *Public Administration Review*, *25*, 5–30.

Waldo, D. (1977). *Democracy, Bureaucracy and Hypocrisy*. Berkeley, CA: Institute of Governmental Studies, University of California.

Waldo, D. (1980). *The Enterprise of Public Administration: A Summary View* (5th ed.). Novato, CA: Chandler & Scharp.

Waldo, D. (1984). *The Administrative State: A Study of the Political Theory of American Public Administration* (2nd ed.; first published in 1948). New York: Holmes & Meier.

Waldo, D. (1987). Politics and administration: On thinking about a complex relationship. In R. C. Chandler (ed.), *A Centennial History of the American Administrative State* (pp. 89–112). New York: Free Press.

Waldo, D. (1990). A theory of public administration means in our time a theory of politics also. In N. B. Lynn & A. Wildavsky (eds.), *Public Administration: The State of the Discipline* (pp. 73–83). Chatham, NJ: Chatham House.

Waldo, D., & Marini, F. (1999). *Bureaucracy and Democracy: A Strained Relationship*. Unpublished manuscript.

Wamsley, G. L. (2001). Reflections on the passing of Dwight Waldo. *Administration & Society*, *33*(3), 247–250.

Wamsley, G. L., & Wolf, J. F. (1996). *Refounding Public Administration: Modern Paradoxes, Postmodern Challenges*. Thousand Oaks, CA: Sage.

Werlin, H. H. (2001). Bureaucracy and democracy: An essay in memory of Dwight Waldo. *Public Administration Quarterly*, *25*(3), 290-315.

3. Public Philosophy and the Administrative State

Christopher Ansell

INTRODUCTION: THE SEARCH FOR PUBLIC PHILOSOPHY

This chapter argues that we can envision a rich role for the humanities in public administration through the lens of "public philosophy." A "public philosophy" neither implies professional philosophers coming down from their lofty heights to engage with common citizens, nor does it necessarily signal the importance of amateur or armchair philosophizing. Rather, a public philosophy is concerned with understanding and debating the principles and values that animate public life—whether they come from philosophers, activists, or citizens.

This chapter argues that it is important to understand the public philosophies that critique and defend the administrative state. Due to its coercive powers, the legitimacy of the state has always required justification. Why can the police put someone in jail? Why can public health authorities force you into quarantine? Why can environment ministries implement laws that prevent farmers from using their land as they like? As these questions suggest, the administrative state is often the instrument of the state's coercive power. As such, it may provide order, protection, and public goods, but it may also use its power as a source of personal wealth, political advantage, or arbitrary justice. Most challenging of all is the question of why the administrative state should have, or appear to have, relative autonomy from direct democratic control. Why, for example, do trade ministry experts get to determine competition regulations or why do central bankers have the autonomy to set interest rates?

While public philosophies can and do come to different conclusions about these questions, they are important precisely because they elevate them to a general level. Public philosophy can play a key role in helping the public understand and debate the basic principles and values that guide public life. Reflecting on the value of a public philosophy for addressing issues of women's inequality, for example, Martha Nussbaum (1998, p. 765) writes that public philosophy plays a role in: "… in articulating and debating norms of 'the quality of life.'" The field of public administration is, of course, well-positioned to lead this inquiry into the public philosophies of the administrative state (e.g., du Gay, 2005a; Bertelli and Lynn, 2006; Spicer, 2015a; Waldo, 2017). However, to do so, it must be prepared to draw on the wider humanities, especially history and philosophy.

The administrative state is particularly in need of public philosophy because it stands at a critical juncture. Populism presents a broad challenge to the administrative state as we know it, particularly but not exclusively in the US (Lee, 2018; Peters and Pierre, 2019; Campbell, 2022; Koliba, 2024). Muno and Pfeiffer (2022) argue that "state capture" is a key populist strategy, and Bauer and Becker (2020) argue that populists advance an "anti-pluralist reform agenda" that seeks to capture, dismantle, sabotage, or reform the administrative state. The populist attack on the administrative state is connected to the threat of "democratic backsliding" (Bauer, 2023) and challenges the presumptions of the "governance" paradigm to open the administrative state to partnering with civil society (Stoker, 2019).

There is nothing new about anti-statism (Stillman, 1995) or populism (Blokker, 2019; Urbinati, 2019) or indeed the public administration call for "public philosophy" (Dennard, 1995). Yet the somewhat surprising rise of populism raises fundamental questions about the role of public administration in an increasingly pluralistic world. To some degree, this attack on the administrative state is an opportunity to see and appreciate the administrative state in a new light, as a defender of pluralism (Arellano-Gault, 2020), a bulwark against democratic backsliding (Bauer, 2023), and a vehicle for civic engagement (Ansell, 2011). At the same time, populism raises fundamental and legitimate—and in a sense unanswered—questions about the relationship between public administration and democracy. It forces us to consider the causes and consequences of the "crisis of legitimacy" that the administrative state faces and how this may stem in part from its own "democratic deficit" (White and Neblo, 2021).

The remainder of this chapter has two primary goals. The first is to reflect on "public philosophy" and to consider how history, philosophy, and the interpretive social sciences can help public administration elucidate public philosophies of the administrative state. The second is to consider how three public philosophies—populism, liberalism, and civic republicanism—interpret, critique, and defend the administrative state. Since many books can be written about each of these public philosophies, the discussion is kept tractable by focusing on two key "flashpoints" in the debate about the administrative state—the issue of "state neutrality" and the issue of "administrative discretion."

WHAT IS PUBLIC PHILOSOPHY?

While the term "public philosophy" can have different meanings, it is used here to refer to a system of principles and values that cohere (to some degree) and that are invoked and utilized to guide public action and debate. These principles may be embedded in culture (the "theory implicit in our practice") or they may be formal and explicit philosophies (or both). In either case, the goal is to make this system of principles and values "public" so they can be collectively understood, evaluated, and debated. While some view "public philosophy" as a critique of or liberation from "academic philosophy" (Hanna, 2018; Brister, 2022), the approach adopted here interprets the adjective "public" to mean "collectively shared" rather than "popular" (which can imply a less erudite or sophisticated philosophy).

Why are public philosophies worth thinking about? The short answer is that public philosophies provide a synoptic and non-arbitrary basis for practical reasoning about the fundamental principles and values of public life. *Synoptic* means that they help us "see the big picture"; *non-arbitrary* means that they entail adopting a commitment to acting in a way that is consistent with these principles and values; *practical reasoning* means they help us make decisions about how to design public institutions and how to conduct ourselves in public life; and *public life* means that these principles and values are or could be collectively shared (i.e., we are not talking about your private philosophy) and they provide a basis for public debate and action. Note that the term "public philosophy" is not meant to imply that the public has a singular philosophy. Far from it. Most publics have plural and often rival systems of principles and values.

The Two Faces of Public Philosophy

Michael Sandel (2022, p. xiv) has given one of the most explicit treatments of the idea of public philosophy, which he refers to as the "theory implicit in our public life." In a review of Sandel's work, however, Ronald Beiner (1998, p. 10) distinguishes two different interpretations of public philosophy: "(1) an implicit but nonetheless cohering set of concepts associated with the reigning social, economic, and political practices of a society ... [or] (2) an explicit articulation of theoretical principles that has some significant causal role in the evolution of such practices." Beiner notes that while Sandel's definition of public philosophy is closer to the first meaning, Sandel often engages with public philosophy as if he understands it to be closer to the second meaning.

Rather than seeing these two different meanings as either contradictory or rival, it is more useful to see them as two different faces of public philosophy.

Doing so helps to illuminate the breadth of contributions that the humanities can make to public administration. The "first face" of public philosophy points to the principles and values embedded in our political cultures that shape our public life, regardless of whether they are explicitly recognized as "philosophy." Think of Martin Luther King's "I Have a Dream" speech. The "second face" of public philosophy points to explicitly and often abstractly codified systems of principles and values with application to public life. Think of John Rawls' *A Theory of Justice.*

Considering these two faces of public philosophy together—one culturally embedded, the other more explicit and abstract—brings the approach advanced here close to what sociologist Robert Bellah called the "Social Science of Public Philosophy" (SSPP) approach. In a review and clarification of this approach, Galen Watts (2022, p. 2) observes that Bellah and colleagues regard this approach as a "synoptic view, at once philosophical, historical, and sociological." This approach speaks to broad ethical issues but does not necessarily entail a commitment to any single philosophical perspective. It is, however, interested in fostering "constant invigoration of a public debate" (Watts, 2022, p. 6). Thus, it seeks to illuminate and elevate discussion of general values and principles about the "social and political conditions that enable human flourishing." It seeks to call out and clarify the evaluative criteria that can be used publicly and deliberatively for judging public institutions. Watts argues that SSPP is a form of immanent critical philosophy that is not detached from democratic practice.

Public philosophy's focus on principles and values calls upon the interpretive and hermeneutic techniques of the humanities. The precise skills required depend upon which face of public philosophy is being invoked: to uncover or recover the principles and values embedded in our public cultures, we must call upon the skills of the historian or interpretive social scientist; to discuss explicitly codified public philosophies, we must call on the skills of the philosopher and the political theorist. At least five distinct roles can be identified for the humanities with respect to public philosophies of the administrative state. The humanities can 1) reveal the principles and values already implicit in administrative life; 2) illuminate the meaning and implications of these principles and values for our public life; 3) create and articulate new principles and values to guide us; 4) demonstrate how general philosophical principles and values have been put into practice; and 5) clarify the ethical and moral choices that administrators must make. A short vignette is used to illustrate each of these roles.

Humanities as revealing

The humanities can help to reveal the public philosophies embedded in our history and culture. A good example is Camilla Stivers' (2000) research on "bureau men" and "settlement women," where she adopts a historical perspective on the US progressive movement and public administration. Buried in the standard accounts of progressive history, she discovers a less appreciated strain of thought associated with the settlement movement, which sought to facilitate the successful integration of immigrants. She argues that different gender roles led male and female progressive reformers to adopt different approaches to administrative reform. While "bureau men" focused administrative reform on fact-finding and administrative efficiency, "settlement women" sought to develop and provide social services. These different approaches to reform carried different values. While the stress on efficiency sought to make public administration more business-like, a key value of progressive women was benevolence and caring (Stivers, 2005). Through historical analysis, Stivers recovers a submerged public philosophy of administrative reform.

Humanities as illuminating
The humanities can also illuminate and clarify fundamental principles and values of public administration. A good example is Hannah Arendt's (2006) *Eichmann in Jerusalem,* where she covered the trial of the Nazi administrator of the Holocaust, Adolf Eichmann. Her basic argument, captured in the subtitle of her book—*A Report on the Banality of Evil*—was that Eichmann's crime was not his inherent evilness but rather his unthinking obedience to his superiors. Arendt's book is a fundamental critique of "bureaucratic anonymity," which she believed led to a vacuum of responsibility ("rule by Nobody") (Rodriguez, 2008; Stivers, 2015).

Humanities as creative
The humanities do not simply interpret an existing reality; they can also imagine new ways of living together. As Brister (2022, p. 44) writes in an essay on public philosophy, "One of the crucial roles of philosophy is to expand our moral imagination, to increase the range of what we perceive as our live options." A good example might be John Dewey's (1927) *The Public and Its Problems*, which sought to reimagine the meaning of the democratic state. Responding to Walter Lippmann's negative view of the role of citizens in democracy, Dewey argues that the scale and complexity of modern social life have undermined the ability of citizens to reason together about the consequences of living together. In this sense, he acknowledged Lippmann's critique. But he argued that the state could also help to give voice to more functional "publics" that could participate and collectively reason about their interdependence. In *The Public's Law: Origins and Architecture of Progressive Democracy*, Blake Emerson (2019, p. 85) writes that "Dewey reworked Hegel's ideas ... by developing a conception of the state as an institutional reflection of public discourse about shared social problems."

Humanities and values-in-action

While one role for the humanities is to reveal, illuminate, and create public principles and values, another is to track and analyze how a set of principles or values is concretely put into practice. The humanities can thus help us understand "values in action" in public administration. A good example is Gerald Berk's (2009) *Louis D. Brandeis and the Making of Regulated Competition, 1900–1932*. Berk shows how Brandeis forged populism and progressivism into a position that Berk calls "republican experimentalism" (with strong affinities to pragmatism), which ultimately led Brandeis to a strong but flexible antitrust doctrine. The book then explores how this republican experimentalism shaped Brandeis' role as an architect of the Federal Trade Commission (FTC) and how the early FTC took up Brandeis' agenda. Berk's historical analysis helps us to follow a "public philosophy in action."

Humanities and moral and ethical choice

The humanities can also help us understand the moral and ethical choices that public administrators must make. A recent book by Bernardo Zacka (2017)— *When the State Meets the Street: Public Service and Moral Agency*—exemplifies this possibility. Zacka investigates the moral and ethical dilemmas that street-level bureaucrats face in exercising their administrative discretion. To understand these dilemmas, he argues, it is important to understand the moral dispositions that bureaucrats bring to their work and to understand why bureaucrats are inclined to "reductive" dispositions (which Zacka categorizes as indifference, caregiving, or enforcement). The source of these dispositions, he argues, is the stress that bureaucrats must deal with in their job, which requires them to make difficult choices between competing values. These observations lead Zacka to reject both "personal autonomy" (Arendt) and "virtue ethics" as antidotes to reductive moral dispositions and to instead embrace a "practices of the self" approach. These practices require a continuous balancing of one's emotional responses against other commitments (via self-examination, calibration, and modulation).

Having argued that public philosophy is a useful lens through which to understand the contribution of the humanities to public administration, the chapter now briefly introduces three prominent public philosophies and their attitudes toward the administrative state.

POPULISM, LIBERALISM AND CIVIC REPUBLICANISM

Populism

While scholars observe that "populism" is a difficult concept to pin down (Webber, 2023), Urbinati (2019) points out that populism does have a political theory. She argues that populism in power is an "extreme majoritarianism" and its core concepts are "the nation" and "the people" (2019, p. 113). On the one hand, populism demands a restoration of democracy; on the other hand, it has an authoritarian bent that follows from its attempt to "take back" democracy for the people (Urbinati, 2019, p. 120). Urbinati writes that:

> Populist government is *pars pro parte*. It is essentially factional government: government by a part (defined as the best) that rules openly for its own good, satisfying its own needs and interests. This makes it a radical challenge to the party system, electoral representation, and constitutional democracy (2019, 123).

Webber (2023, p. 859) observes that a core feature of populism is a distrust of institutions, which are "typically seen as little more than obstacles to action." Arellano-Gault (2020) argues that the populist critique of the administrative state comes from its interpretation of the bureaucracy as a "technocracy serving elitist interests." As a result, populism seeks to either capture and tightly control the administrative state in the name of popular sovereignty, or, where this is not possible, to undermine it (Peters and Pierre, 2019; Bauer and Becker, 2020; Muno and Pfeiffer, 2022).

Liberalism

Liberalism is arguably the dominant philosophy of the administrative state, though it is itself a historical amalgam of different principles and values. Du Gay (2005b, p. 45) distinguishes between a more authoritarian liberalism associated with Hobbes and concerned with preventing social disorder; and a more "expressivist" liberalism that arose with demands for religious freedom and culminated in a "Kantian respect for the autonomy of free agents." As a result, "[t]he persona of the citizen as inhabitant of the sovereign state, and the persona of the practitioner of religious (or other forms of communal) self-governance, now represented two distinct and autonomous modes of comportment, housed in two distinct realms, of 'public' and 'private' conduct" (du Gay 2005b, p. 46). Classical liberalism preserves this clear separation between public and private via the idea of limited government (a "minimal state"), the "rule of law," and the "division of powers" (Heath, 2020). Despite this emphasis on limiting the powers of government, classical liberalism supports a "slim but strong and well-functioning state administration" that functions in a constitutional order (Armbrüster, 2005, p. 65).

Joseph Heath (2020, p. 149) distinguishes between classical and modern liberalism and points to "equality, efficiency, and liberty" as the core principles of the latter. These ideas underpin the development of the welfare state. He argues that efficiency is a particularly central value for this modern liberalism, especially as it applies to the administrative state. Armbrüster (2005, p. 68) refers to this modern liberalism of the welfare state as "liberal interventionism," and suggests that "neutral proceduralism is the central mechanism for achieving equal opportunities, equality before the law, and not favoring any particular conception of the good." While liberalism and democracy are generally seen as mutually reinforcing (i.e., liberal democracy), public administration scholars note that they can also be in tension, with the managerialism associated with some aspects of liberalism at odds with a more democratically or civically-oriented administration (Kravchuk, 1992).

Civic Republicanism

There are at least two branches of modern republicanism: an Aristotelian republicanism captured by Pocock's magisterial *The Machiavellian Moment*, which focuses on communal self-government and is associated with contemporary theorists like Hannah Arendt and Michael Sandel; and a Roman republicanism unearthed by Quentin Skinner in *The Foundations of Modern Political Thought*, which focuses on citizen participation as a strategy for preventing the arbitrary exercise of state power, and which is associated with contemporary theorists like Philip Petit. Aristotelian republicanism is more interested in cultivating civic virtue, while Roman republicanism is more interested in defending negative freedom (Barczewski, 2021).

Interestingly, this distinction between different versions of republicanism is reminiscent of one of the most important philosophical treatments of the American administrative state—Dwight Waldo's (2017) classic philosophical critique of the "orthodox" administrative perspective. Waldo argued that the executive-centered emphasis on efficiency advanced by the orthodox perspective is ultimately at odds with the democratic and constitutional principles of American politics. Rejecting the sharp distinction between "fact" and "value," Waldo famously argues that this "Greek" view of administration is incompatible with a "Roman" perspective that views administration as integrated into the governing process (see also Rosenbloom et al., 2006, for an enlightening discussion).

Administrative law scholar Mark Seidenfeld (1992) has articulated one of the most developed civic republican accounts of the administrative state. He argues that civic republicans view the Constitution as supporting the view that "… government decisions are a product of deliberation that respects and reflects the values of all members of society" (1992, p. 1514). Thus, the state's "primary responsibility is to enable the citizenry to deliberate about altering preferences and to reach consensus on the common good" (1992, p. 1514). He argues that civic republicanism "simultaneously seeks to foster individual freedom from government-imposed values and freedom collectively to define the values of the relevant political community" (1992, p. 1528). The common good arises from an inclusive and ongoing deliberative process, not mere processes of aggregation of preferences. He writes that civic republicanism seeks to counter factional competition, but he contrasts civic republicanism with pluralist perspectives that see policy arising through a competition of groups pursuing their private interests. He argues that the administrative state has a responsibility to uphold the civic republican emphasis on citizen deliberation.

Building on these brief descriptions of populism, liberalism, and civic republicanism, the next two sections call attention to their opposing positions on two key debates about the administrative state.

Neutrality of the State

One of the key flashpoints of debate about the administrative state is around the idea of the "neutrality of the state," which is a key principle of liberal theory that derives from Hobbesian thinking (du Gay, 2005b, p. 47). Neutrality is understood to be, at least in part, a procedural idea based on the rule of law. Barczewski (2021, p. 446) argues that "The liberal goal of state neutrality manifests itself in each regulatory decision." From this perspective, he writes, regulatory decisions are made by neutral technocrats whose decisions "do not interfere with an individual's ability to choose their own ends" (2021, p. 446).

Populism clearly opposes the neutrality of the state. Blokker (2019) argues that populists reject liberal constitutionalism and regard "legal rationality, the neutrality of the state, and formal–legal proceduralism" as weakening the state due to their lack of "symbolic, sentimental, and collective engagement" (Blokker, 2019, p. 536). Furthermore, populism "denounces the rule of law and the constitutional state as vehicles that promote the interests of minorities (elites) against the well-being of the people and claims to build a new constitutional order that will promote the common good against partial interests" (Blokker, 2019, p. 539).

Civic republicanism (which is sometimes lumped with communitarianism) also opposes the neutrality of the state, though for less factional reasons. Michael Sandel (2022) famously argues that the problems of the administrative state arise from liberalism's insistence on the neutrality of the state and the proceduralism that it cultivates. This neutrality ignores the importance of developing and supporting civic bonds and an overarching civic public philosophy (Armbrüster, 2005). Bureaucracy is suspect because it is particularly committed to neutral proceduralism rather than to the cultivation of civic virtues. From a civic republican perspective, state policies should advance civic life and citizenship rather than remain neutral towards it (Kalu, 2003). From the civic republican perspective of Hannah Arendt, Camilla Stivers (2015) criticizes American progressivism's emphasis on state neutrality. Stivers points out that Arendt was committed to public dialogue as an antidote to the "sameness" embraced by bureaucracies (Stivers, 2015, pp. 246–247).

Both populism and civic republicanism also regard "expert" or "technocratic" decision-making (an embodiment of state neutrality) as undemocratic and biased in favor of interest groups and elites. Barczewski (2021, p. 463) argues that only a "robust form of republicanism that supports widespread and direct participation in administrative decisions" can offset this bias. This is because "only politics can accommodate the divergent interests of citizens, provide a forum for the expression of those interests, encourage the development of qualities needed to express interests to fellow citizens, promote the formation of common interests above private ones, and show the way toward a consensual understanding of the common good."

Can Administrative Discretion be Defended in a Democracy?

Administrative discretion is another flashpoint of debate between populism, liberalism, and civic republicanism. There is little debate about whether the administrative state actually has *de facto* discretion; the debate is whether this is desirable. As Zacka (2017, p. 35) writes, "It is one thing to explain why street-level bureaucrats do have discretion and how they should deal with it; it is another to explain whether they should have discretion in the first place."

The issue is somewhat different from the debate about neutrality because discretion can be seen as problematic from both the populist perspective of popular sovereignty and from the liberal perspective on the rule of law. A populist, for instance, may argue from a "social compact" perspective that the people are sovereign and may not "transfer their power and responsibility to govern themselves to any other body" (Postell, 2016, p. 1012). From a liberal "rule-of-law" perspective, administrative discretion can be seen as "illicit" and "arbitrary" and as producing legal uncertainty (Heath, 2020, pp. 260–261). Both the populist view and this version of liberalism lead to what Seidenfeld (1992, p. 1516) calls a "transmission belt" perspective in which "agencies merely carry out Congress's statutory plan and do not themselves exercise political judgment" (Zacka [2017] refers to this same idea as the "compliance" model).

While liberals may reject administrative discretion from a rule-of-law perspective, they may support it based on the principle of neutrality. Experts are delegated discretion in part because of their ability to make effective and efficient decisions, but also because they are neutral—they can make "non-partisan" decisions. Mark Seidenfeld (1992) notes that civic republicans also support administrative discretion, but on different grounds than liberals. He argues that this "transmission belt" perspective is "seriously flawed" because the idea that "an agency can exercise judgment in implementing statutes without influencing and reshaping the political balance struck by Congress is, in most instances, a fiction" (1992, p. 1517).

While civic republicans are less interested in granting administrative discretion based on technocratic (neutral) grounds, they are interested in acknowledging the importance of "judgment" as a basis of discretion. Stivers (2015) discusses how Arendt's discussion of publicness contrasts "judgment" with "rule." She notes that for Arendt, judgment is "the essential political human capacity, because it both relies on and makes possible the sorting out of what is the same in what is different" (2015, p. 248). Arendt argued that judgment is based on experience and the ability to see things from other people's points of view.

There is one other basis for liberals to argue in favor of administrative discretion—in regards to the role that civil servants play in upholding constitutions. Dennard (1995) discusses Rohr's work on public administration and argues that the discretion of public servants is linked to constitutionalism. Paraphrasing Rohr, she argues that "Administrators practice discretion. Would you rather have this discretion exercised by constitutional officers or by those who feel no particular allegiance to the Constitution and what it stands for?" (1995, p. 51). It is worth noting that administrative law scholars have also stressed that agencies are central to the actualization of the constitution, referring to this role as "administrative constitutionalism" (Metzger, 2012; Lee, 2018).

CONCLUSION

How can the humanities contribute to public administration? The argument of this chapter is that they can contribute to revealing, illuminating, and creating our public philosophies of the administrative state. They can also show how the principles and values of public philosophies are put into concrete administrative action, and they can help us understand the ethical and moral dilemmas that arise in public administration. These contributions are particularly relevant in the present moment because the administrative state as we know it is facing a fundamental populist attack on its dominant—primarily liberal—principles and values. However, we should not be merely defensive. Populism raises legitimate concerns about the relationship between democracy and administration that our prevailing administrative principles and values do not fully answer.

The chapter stresses the importance of "public philosophy" to public administration. Public philosophy is understood here as a synoptic and non-arbitrary system of principles and values that cohere (to some degree) and that are invoked and utilized to guide public action and debate. While power and interests may shape our institutions as much or more than public philosophy, clarifying the philosophical basis of public life helps to create a framework for better understanding and discussing our administrative institutions. Too often, the values and principles that guide their design are not clear, and hence the trade-offs entailed by different designs are obscure (and more subject to determination by power and interests).

Public philosophy has at least two faces. On one fact, public philosophy is embedded in our political cultures, though often hidden in plain sight. Historians and interpretive social scientists can play a critical role in discovering and illuminating these embedded values and principles. On the other face, public philosophy draws on philosophy as a distinctive field of study. Long and distinguished traditions of philosophy debate and refine philosophical concepts, revealing their consequences and implications. Both faces of public philosophy are important for public administration.

The chapter provided short descriptions of three public philosophies of the administrative state—populism, liberalism, and civic republicanism. Each of them expresses different attitudes toward the administrative state. Populism is deeply suspicious and sees the administrative state as a threat to popular sovereignty. Liberalism has a more positive conception, stressing state neutrality, the rule of law, and constitutionalism. Republicanism is less suspicious of the administrative state than populism but interprets the administrative state from the point of view of its commitment to public deliberation and civil society.

The chapter concludes with a discussion of two flashpoints of debate about the administrative state. The first is the liberal defense of state neutrality. Based on a long history of civil strife, liberals have come to defend the view that the state should not take sides or impose a particular philosophy or set of values on society. This position is familiar to public administration from the work of Weber and Wilson and their defense of the neutrality of civil servants. However, philosophical objections to this position may be less familiar. Populists see neutrality as disguising bias, and civic republicans perceive proceduralism as preventing the cultivation of civic values. The other flashpoint is around the issue of administrative discretion—another common public administration topic. Again, populists see discretion as a loss of popular sovereignty, while liberals defend expert discretion on the basis of neutrality, and civic republicans defend it on the grounds of judgment. Neither of these two flashpoints was resolved by the discussion, but the discussion demonstrates that public philosophies can reveal and illuminate the principles and values that shape public life.

REFERENCES

Ansell, C. (2011). *Pragmatist Democracy: Evolutionary Learning as Public Philosophy.* New York: Oxford University Press.

Arellano-Gault, D. (2020). Responding to the populist attack on public administration. *Asia Pacific Journal of Public Administration*, 42(1), 6–8.

Arendt, H. (2006). *Eichmann in Jerusalem: A Report on the Banality of Evil*. Penguin.

Armbrüster, T. (2005). Bureaucracy and the controversy between liberal interventionism and non-interventionism. In du Gay, P. (ed.), *The Values of Bureaucracy*. Oxford: Oxford University Press, pp. 63–88.

Barczewski, B. M. (2021). Politicizing regulation: Administrative law, technocratic government, and republican political theory. *Nebraska Law Review*, 100, 424.

Bauer, M. W. (2023). Public administration under populist rule: Standing up against democratic backsliding. *International Journal of Public Administration*, 1–13.

Bauer, M. W., & Becker, S. (2020). Democratic backsliding, populism, and public administration. *Perspectives on Public Management and Governance*, 3(1), 19–31.

Beiner, R.S. (1998). Introduction: The quest for a post-liberal public philosophy. In Allen, A. L., & Regan, M. C. (eds.), *Debating Democracy's Discontent: Essays on American Politics, Law, and Public Philosophy*. Oxford: Oxford University Press, pp. 1–17.

Berk, G. (2009). *Louis D. Brandeis and the Making of Regulated Competition, 1900–1932*. Cambridge: Cambridge University Press.

Bertelli, A. M., & Lynn, L. E. (2006). *Madison's Managers: Public Administration and the Constitution*. Baltimore: Johns Hopkins University Press.

Blokker, P. (2019). Populism as a constitutional project. *International Journal of Constitutional Law*, 17(2), 536–553.

Brister, E. (2022). The value of public philosophy. In: McIntyre, L. C., McHugh, N., & Olasov, I. (eds.), *A Companion to Public Philosophy*. Hoboken, NJ: John Wiley & Sons, pp. 41–52.

Campbell, J. L. (2022). *Institutions under Siege*. Cambridge: Cambridge University Press.

Dennard, L. (1995). Asking different questions in the search for public philosophy. *Administrative Theory & Praxis*, 17(1), 46–54.

Dewey, J. (1927). *The Public and Its Problems*. New York: Holt Publishers.

Emerson, B. (2019). *The Public's Law: Origins and Architecture of Progressive Democracy*. Oxford: Oxford University Press.

du Gay, P. (ed.). (2005a). *The Values of Bureaucracy*. Oxford: Oxford University Press.

du Gay, P. (2005b). Bureaucracy and liberty: State, authority, and freedom. In du Gay, P. (ed.), *The Values of Bureaucracy*. Oxford: Oxford University Press, pp. 41–62.

Hanna, R. (2018). How to escape irrelevance: Performance philosophy, public philosophy and borderless philosophy. *Journal of Philosophical Investigations*, 12(24), 55–82.

Heath, J. (2020). *The Machinery of Government: Public Administration and the Liberal State*. New York: Oxford University Press.

Kalu, K. N. (2003). Of citizenship, virtue, and the administrative imperative: Deconstructing Aristotelian civic republicanism. *Public Administration Review*, 63(4), 418–427.

Koliba, C. (2024). Liberal democratic accountability standards and public administration. *Public Administration Review*, 85(1), 21–31.

Kravchuk, R. S. (1992). Liberalism and the American administrative state. *Public Administration Review*, 374–379.

Lee, S. Z. (2018). Our administered constitution: Administrative constitutionalism from the founding to the present. *University of Pennsylvania Law Review*, 167, 1699-1747.

Metzger, G. E. (2012). Administrative constitutionalism. *Texas Law Review*, 91, 1897.

Muno, W., & Pfeiffer, C. (2022). Populism in power—A comparative analysis of populist governance. *International Area Studies Review*, 25(4), 261–279.

Nussbaum, M. C. (1998). Public philosophy and international feminism. *Ethics*, 108(4), 762–796.

Peters, B. G., & Pierre, J. (2019). Populism and public administration: Confronting the administrative state. *Administration & Society*, 51(10), 1521–1545.

Postell, J. (2016). The people surrender nothing: Social compact theory, republicanism, and the modern administrative state. *Missouri Law Review*, 81, 1003.

Rodriguez, M. (2008). The challenges of keeping a world: Hannah Arendt on administration. *Polity*, 40(4), 488–508.

Rosenbloom, D. H., McCurdy, H. E., Durant, R. F., Romzek, B. S., Cadigan, J. J., Terry, L. D., ... & Kettl, D. F. (2006). *Revisiting Waldo's Administrative State: Constancy and Change in Public Administration*. Washington, D.C.: Georgetown University Press.

Sandel, M. J. (2022). *Democracy's Discontent: A New Edition for our Perilous Times*. Cambridge, MA: Harvard University Press.

Seidenfeld, M. (1992). A civic republican justification for the bureaucratic state. *Harvard Law Review*, 1511–1576.

Spicer, M. W. (2015a). Neutrality, adversary argument, and constitutionalism in public administration. *Administrative Theory & Praxis*, 37(3), 188–202.

Stillman, R. J. (1995). The refounding movement in American public administration: From "rabid" anti-statism to "Mere" anti-statism in the 1990s. *Administrative Theory & Praxis*, 17(1), 29–45.

Stivers, C. (2000). *Bureau Men, Settlement Women: Constructing Public Administration in the Progressive Era*. Baltimore: Johns Hopkins University Press.

Stivers, C. (2005). A place like home: Care and action in public administration. *The American Review of Public Administration*, 35(1), 26–41.

Stivers, C. (2015). Rule by nobody: Bureaucratic neutrality as secular theodicy. *Administrative Theory & Praxis*, 37(4), 242–251.

Stoker, G. (2019). Can the governance paradigm survive the rise of populism?. *Policy & Politics*, 47(1), 3–18.

Urbinati, N. (2019). Political theory of populism. *Annual Review of Political Science*, 22, 111–127.

Waldo, D. (2017). *The Administrative State: A Study of the Political Theory of American Public Administration*. Abingdon: Routledge.

Watts, G. W. (2022). Social science as public philosophy revived. *Civic Sociology*, 3(1). https://doi.org/10.1525/cs.2022.35299.

Webber, J. (2023). Understanding populism. *Social & Legal Studies*, 32(6), 849–876.

White, A., & Neblo, M. (2021). Capturing the public: Beyond technocracy & populism in the US administrative state. *Daedalus*, 150(3), 172–187.

Zacka, B. (2017). *When the State Meets the Street: Public Service and Moral Agency*. Cambridge, MA: Harvard University Press.

4. Philosophical Pragmatism and the Study of Public Administration

Travis A. Whetsell

INTRODUCTION

Public administration scholars have maintained broad interest in philosophical pragmatism throughout the course of the development of the discipline. While this interest has not always been explicit, it is not hard to find evidence of pragmatism in the major landmarks of public administration scholarship. There are many varieties of philosophical pragmatism. In this chapter, I will primarily focus on the ideas of John Dewey for the reasons described below.

As philosophical scholarship in public administration is relatively sparse, I have been pleasantly surprised to find that again and again philosophers are not too difficult to locate in the halls of public affairs, administration, and policy schools and departments. The same can also be said of scholarship in the discipline, particularly in those articles that touch on broad meta-topics about the discipline itself. Thinking through the nature, identity, and purposes of the discipline often quickly leads to the observation that public administration is a pluralistic discipline involving many others from social science, humanities, law, and even natural science. Furthermore, public administration contains both scholars and a substantial presence in practice, often featuring former and active members of government and non-profit sectors. Wrestling with these facts of the discipline inevitably incites philosophical questions about ontology (what is the nature of the studied objects?), epistemology (what counts as knowledge with regard to these objects?), axiology (what ethical positions and dilemmas relate to the decision-making process?), and teleology (what are the ultimate purposes of policy and administration?).

Philosophical pragmatism provides insights into many of these questions. Scholars of public administration have recognized and applied many of these to numerous topics key to the discipline. While much of the early and middle 20th century public administration scholarship is implicitly driven by a pragmatic ethos, it isn't until the 1990s that substantive advocacy on the topic emerges. In this chapter, I tell the story of pragmatism in public administration from the early 20th century to the present day.

The following chapter is organized as follows. First, I present a simplified conceptual framework for the comprehension of pragmatist philosophy. Next, I present a brief intellectual history of pragmatism in public administration, moving through the early to late 20th century, also exploring the eclipse of pragmatism by logical positivism and identifying some of the recent developments in public administration.

A CONCEPTUAL FRAMEWORK FOR PRAGMATIC PUBLIC ADMINISTRATION

In this section, I will provide a brief description of pragmatism. I attempt to extract from a turbulent stream of ideas a potable set of concepts, both as a means of adequately sampling the conceptual space and to provide a useful mnemonic for understanding pragmatism and its relation to public administration. In the following sub-sections, I describe four general principles of pragmatism.

Four Principles of Pragmatism

I first learned about the Four Ps of pragmatism in a discussion as an MPA student with my then-professor and future co-author Patricia M. Shields at Texas State University in 2010. By that time, I had read many of the classics in philosophy but knew virtually nothing about *pragmatism*. Over the previous two decades, Shields (1996, 2003, 2008; Shields & Tajalli, 2006) had written several articles arguing the relevance of this philosophy to the discipline and practice of public administration. In "Rediscovering the taproot", Shields (2008) advanced the handy mnemonic device: practical, pluralistic, participatory, and provisional. She had borrowed the device from Brendel (2006), who was interested in leveraging pragmatism to *heal* the theory-practice gap in psychiatry. Public administration as a discipline featured a similar gap between academic theory on the one hand and the knowledge of practitioners in and around government on the other. Shields (2008) found the device useful for conceptualizing pragmatism, and indeed, it had staying power in my mind as well. I have continued to use these categories as a conceptual framework to organize my own observations of pragmatism along the way.

Pragmatism is practical
The adjective *practical* is probably the first concept that comes to mind in conjunction with pragmatism. As the Oxford English Dictionary (OED) defines it, practical means "Of, relating to practice or action ..." particularly "... as

opposed to speculation or ...", and de-emphasized in this chapter, "... theory". This definition is appropriate as a pithy description of pragmatism's theory of the truth. The theory goes something like this: the truth value of an idea depends upon its consequences in the world.

While many ideas may be technically true, often these ideas have no practical use and thus lack truth in the pragmatic sense. This may seem somewhat harsh, especially for those scholars who prioritize pure reason. However, this practical truth criterion is often necessary, especially when weighing the value of public policies or programs. The father of pragmatist philosophy, C.S. Peirce, generated what is now known as *the pragmatic maxim*, which embodies this pragmatic theory of truth. As the maxim goes, "Consider what effects, which might conceivably have practical bearings, we conceive the object of our conception to have. Then, our conception of these effects is the whole of our conception of the object" (Peirce, 1868). While the language is certainly from an older era, the idea itself is timeless: the consequences of an idea in action constitute the whole of its intellectual content. Of course, we may play with ideas, imagining possible worlds, but until they are put to the test, we cannot assess their truth. Thus, an idea's consequences in the world are deeply intertwined with its truth or falsity. As the pragmatist William James (1907) referred to it, an idea's "cash value" is identified as it is put to work. In the realm of public administration, we can only identify the cash value of a program or policy after observing its consequences for the public. This concept appeals to many scholars and practitioners in the public administration community because it suggests something about proposed public policies and programs. The old cliché that the policy idea is "good on paper, but bad in practice" reveals the theory at work. Pragmatism cares not for the paper value of an idea, only the cash value derived from practice.

But there are all sorts of calculations derivable from the pragmatic maxim. We might employ a positive version that suggests comparison by the best possible outcomes of a policy. We could let the markets run their course, and eventually the price mechanism produces the incentive to find a cure for the disease. Or we might use state action to stimulate inter-organizational cooperation and get there quicker. Conversely, we might employ a pessimistic version that suggests comparison of policies based on their worst possible outcomes. If we leave the markets to their own devices, they will fail under the weight of pure public goods, in which case millions will continue to suffer every year. But if we intervene with targeted government support, fewer might die needlessly. Perhaps we combine the two and take a range of positive to negative consequences of a policy or program.

We can imbue policy and administrative decisions with any number of practical criteria. My point here is that the pragmatic theory of truth dictates that policymakers and public administrators *should* consider the consequences of implementing this or that policy or program before implementation. Our deontological motivations are not good enough to justify implementation. In practice, policy analysis might begin with a thought exercise but often involves programmatic experimentation.

Further, the practical element of pragmatism suggests a deeper theory of the ontology of the public. Dewey (1927) argued that the public emerges when the practical consequences of private interaction have unregulated effects on third parties. The classic example here is negative externalities such as pollution. Ostrom et al. (1961) argued that Dewey's original theory formed the foundation for the public choice theory of externalities. In contrast to a variety of existing theories on the public, pragmatism suggests that the public is to be identified as an emergent property of a complex system of actors, interactions, and consequences (Whetsell, 2024). The practical element therefore emphasizes the relational rather than individualistic nature of public problems.

Pragmatism is pluralistic

The adjective *pluralistic* is packed with a variety of useful meanings, all converging on the basic notion of one versus many. As the *Oxford English Dictionary* proposes, in philosophy, pluralism refers to the idea that reality is composed of more than one type of substance; in epistemology, it means "more than one irreducible basic principle" (*OED*, 2). Pluralism is opposed to dualism and monism. As William James (1907) argued in *A pluralistic universe*, reality is more like a diverse collection of experiences than a unified monistic entity. This is particularly true of social reality and has become a standard assumption in many disciplines of social science. Pluralism is both a particular view of epistemology and the more familiar case in democratic politics. In other words, in a pluralistic democracy such as the United States, there are a variety of cultures, ethnicities, religions, and political factions. While the political system is pluralistic, the counterpart epistemology is one of intellectual pluralism.

As I argued (Whetsell, 2013), public administration is less a unified discipline oriented around a Kuhnian paradigm and more an assemblage of theories applied eclectically to resolve public problems. The principle of pluralism in public administration epistemology requires the application of numerous sometimes overlapping theoretical lenses to adequately describe the content of problems. Borrowing heavily from the problem-solving approach of contemporary pragmatist philosopher of science, Larry Laudan (1977), I employed the term *theory-pluralism* to describe this epistemic viewpoint. But the basic idea grew from rumination over a metaphor developed by William James (1907) and echoed by Shields (1996) almost 100 years later. The metaphor is worth directly quoting.

[Pragmatism] lies in the midst of our theories, like a corridor in a hotel. Innumerable chambers open out of it. In one you may find a man writing an atheistic volume; in the next someone on his knees Praying for faith and strength; in a third a chemist investigating a body's properties. In a fourth a system of idealistic metaphysics is being excogitated; in a fifth the impossibility of metaphysics is being shown. But they all own the corridor, and all must pass through it if they want a practicable way of getting into or out of their respective rooms. (James, 1907, p. 22)

The basic idea here, at least the one that I took from it, is that public administration as a discipline must be less like a single occupant of a hotel room and more like a competent navigator of the corridor itself. Each hotel room is occupied by a particular Kuhnian paradigm, where a single theory is ascendant, e.g., utility maximization in neoclassical economics. Navigating the corridor requires a meta-cognitive perspective that resists capture by any single paradigm. The scholar of public administration avoids becoming overly entangled by any single theory and efficiently grapples with multiple theories simultaneously. Concurrently, the practitioner of public administration must serve multiple distinct communities without being captured by the interest of any single stakeholder group.

Raadschelders (2011) used a similar metaphor in describing the interdisciplinarity of public administration. The picture he paints is one of a harbor where ships come to dock for a time, then head back out into the open sea. The ships represent different academic theories or disciplines. They come to dock in the harbor of public administration, which serves as a protective intermediary between them and facilitates the exchange of intellectual and material resources. The metaphor is again quite useful for illustrating the type of epistemic position we have at hand. Sil and Katzenstein (2010) used a similar logic to wrangle and leverage multiple theories in international relations, coining the term *analytic eclecticism.*

Pragmatism is participatory

The adjective *participatory* by now is a familiar one for scholars of public administration in democracies, where, for example citizen participation and participatory decision-making have become important topics. The OED defines participation as , "sharing in an action, sentiment, etc.; active involvement in a matter or event, esp. one in which the outcome directly affects those taking part". In pragmatism, the term has a couple of unique meanings and concomitant sets of implications. One such idea is embodied in the term, the *community of inquiry,* introduced to public administration by Shields (2003). The term is built on the ideas of C. S. Peirce (1868), and John Dewey (1938) elaborates on the notion extensively in the epistemological opus *Logic: The theory of inquiry.*

In a nutshell, the *community of inquiry* indicates that the pursuit of knowledge is very often, if not always a social, cooperative, and participatory endeavor. Yes, new knowledge may be generated by individuals working in isolation, but lone epistemic pursuits are only possible by "standing on the shoulders of giants." The entire context of scientific inquiry is based on the existence of social reality, perhaps most obviously illustrated by the necessity of a common language in which such truths may become articulated and formalized (Dewey, 1938). Knowledge is further validated by the attention of those interested minds to these new propositions. Looking back to the previous section, while the truth or falsity of an idea may be found in its practical consequences, a community of inquiry ultimately determines which consequences matter.

As Peirce (1868) stated it, "the very origin of the conception of reality shows that this conception essentially involves the notion of a COMMUNITY, without definite limits, and capable of a definite increase of knowledge." Following on in a later work, Peirce (1868) states, "The opinion which is fated to be ultimately agreed to by all who investigate, is what we mean by the truth, and the object represented in this opinion is the real." In other words, knowledge is discovered and adjudicated within communities of inquiry, and its promulgation depends upon their acceptance. Dewey (1938) elaborates on the idea, pointing out that logic itself depends on communities. In a certain sense, the pragmatic maxim is applied here to the process of inquiry, where the truth value of new knowledge depends on its cognitive effects upon members of the relevant epistemic community. These insights, of course were dampened by the ascendence of logical positivism in the mid-20th century. They began to gain traction again with the development of post-positivist history of science after Thomas Kuhn's *The Structure of Scientific Revolutions*.

An important metaphor illustrating the difficulty of generating knowledge within communities of inquiry was described by Shields (2003); that of the blind men and the elephant. Each individual inquiry is like a blind man with a limited physical interaction with an elephant. One believes himself to be dealing with a rope, another a large fan, another a tree trunk, and another a wall. They cannot possibly hope to identify the elephant from their limited viewpoints. However, by combining their insights, it might be possible to uncover the truth of the mystery.

These aspects of pragmatism, dealing with participation as a fundamental element of scientific inquiry, are useful to the scholar of public administration, but there is another aspect also relevant to practice. Especially in a democracy, participation by citizens in the decision-making processes of government through elections and deliberative forums is critical to its functioning and legitimacy. Not only this, but the very notion of a *public* depends on the participatory quality of democracy. As Dewey (1927) argued, a collection of individuals that are affected by uncontrolled externalities is not realized as a public until they become cognizant of these effects and begin to adapt. Dewey (1927) provided a specific role for the public administrator of assisting in the organization of such communities as publics. This point was later developed by public administration scholars examining aspects of deliberative democracy; for example, the development of minipublics (Moore, 2014; Fung, 2015).

Pragmatism is provisional

As the OED it, *provisional* means "provided or adopted for the time being". In particular, the pragmatic philosophy of science detailed by Peirce and Dewey maintains a provisional attitude regarding the truth status of scientific theories. The implication for public administration is that it has no Kuhnian paradigm, no period of normal science, and no major revolutions signaling sea change events. In contrast, the science of administration seeks to construct useful theories. Scholars treat theories as instruments to explore, describe, and explain structures and processes relevant to public issues. Maintaining relevance to the issues entails that instrumental theory building is context-dependent, and hence *provisional*. Even our best theories of structure and process are subject to future revision.

One important implication of the provisional element of pragmatism is that continuous experimentation is necessary to assess whether our best theories still obtain in new social, economic, and political environments (Dewey, 1927). One of the biggest shifts in public management over the past few decades has been the decentralization of service delivery through networks of public, private, and non-profit actors. This general trend has led to a decline in significance of traditional constructs of hierarchy and authority and elevated others such as accountability.

Similarly, overturning traditional theories is generated not only through historical evolution but also through the development of theory in adjacent disciplines. For example, many of the assumptions of public choice economics were overturned by developments in judgment and decision-making research in psychology (Pallesen & Pedersen, 2023). The important point is not to treat assumptions of scientific theory as fixed, unchanging, and unchallenged. In short, our best theories are provisionally true and subject to future revision.

A VERY BRIEF HISTORICAL OVERVIEW OF PRAGMATISM AND PUBLIC ADMINISTRATION

In this section, I provide a chronological ordering of concepts as they manifest in tandem by philosophers and public administration theorists. This second approach is conducted by tracing explicit mentions of pragmatic philosophy and citations of the works and concepts of pragmatic philosophers by prominent scholars in public administration. This section begins with early 20th-century scholarship but also examines a contemporary debate on the applicability of pragmatism to public administration academics and practice.

As a formal system of philosophy, American pragmatism maintains an important influence upon public administration. Part of the reason for this influence is the co-evolution of American public administration and classical philosophical pragmatism during the post-Civil-War Reconstruction era in the United States. Menand (2002) argued that the origin of pragmatism can be traced to an intellectual salon called "The Metaphysical Club" that formed in the 1870s and included Charles Sanders Peirce, William James, and John Dewey. These three are often considered the primary founding figures of philosophical pragmatism. Another notable pragmatist of the time was Jane Addams. The role of Jane Addams was not fully appreciated until recently (Shields, 2017), but she played a crucial part in the development of pragmatism in early public administration through her work in the settlement house movement (see Addams, 1911) as well as through her intellectual and personal influence on John Dewey (Menand, 2002).

Since I have chosen to focus on a philosophy that was developed during the late 1880s and early 1900s, a note on the prevailing ideologies of the time is in order. According to Menand (2002), the thought of both William James and John Dewey escaped the contagion of bigotries prevalent at the time. Dewey appears to be the most progressive of the group and was a well-known advocate for equal rights. Dewey was a founding member of the NAACP and the ACLU and was also active in promoting women's inclusion in higher education and, of course, the suffrage movement. Dewey was also the most prolific of the pragmatist philosophers, which is evidenced by the size of his collected works. His thought is most associated with philosophical pragmatism and was arguably the most influential in public administration. As Menand (2002) illustrates, the ideological commitments of C.S. Peirce may be more problematic. In this chapter, I focus on Dewey's works as the most well-developed of the pragmatist philosophers and the most relevant to public administration.

While it is difficult to demonstrate any direct effect of philosophy on the conduct of government, there were many developments in government at the time that aligned well with the pragmatic ethos. Public administration was becoming more developed, professionalized, and efficient. The Pendleton Civil Service Reform Act of 1883 eliminated the political patronage system and implemented a merit-based system for public servants. The emergence of the city manager form of government during the Progressive Era further reflected the separation of partisan influence from administration and the elevation of a more practical approach to government (Shafritz and Hyde, 2016). The practical criterion of efficiency was elevated as a core value in administration during this period, popularized by figures such as Luther Gulick.

John Dewey had become a prominent intellectual, popular in progressive circles for reforms in education, advocacy for racial and gender equality, and as a champion of democracy. Jane Addams made significant contributions through the settlement movement to women's suffrage, and won a Nobel Peace Prize for her work in promoting peace during the First World War. Many PA scholars now consider the settlement movement to represent an important vision of administration at the founding (Stivers, 1995; Shields, 2017). Theodore Roosevelt, a former student of William James who was also associated with Jane Addams, is widely considered a pragmatist president who made significant contributions to the administration of wildlife and land conservation in addition to other progressive causes. The Brownlow Committee advising Franklin Roosevelt, himself considered a pragmatist, was known to be influenced by principles of pragmatism (Fry & Raadschelders, 2013).

Examples of pragmatism influencing great events in government abound as the Progressive Era itself was broadly suffused with an ethos of pragmatism that originally grew out of the healing of America after the Civil War. It flourished at the turn of the 20th century, ripe with optimism about government action, economic growth, expansion of political rights, the development of new technologies, and progress on a variety of fronts. A core element of the zeitgeist was the prevailing notion that social and economic problems could be addressed through government action. The culmination of this view is evident in the numerous programs developed under the New Deal.

Pragmatism also appears to have influenced many of the early authors in public administration. However, it is much more difficult to identify influences through bibliometric methods during the early 20th century as referencing in books and papers was far less frequent than today. Furthermore, I should note that Snider (2000) has argued against the position that pragmatism influenced early administration. Nevertheless, it is possible to identify pragmatism in the works of many early authors in public administration. For example, Dimock (1936, p. 8) argued that pragmatism was an essential mode of understanding public administration, supplying both the concept of "administration as experience" and providing an instrumentalist approach to theory that situated administration as a tool for the resolution of problems. Gaus (1936) references Dewey's *The public and its problems* directly, arguing that a philosophy of public administration may be derived therein. Incidentally, this is what I have attempted in a recent publication (Whetsell, 2024). In a retrospective on trends in public administration since the founding of the American Society of Public Administration, Gaus (1950) argued again for the importance of Dewey's philosophy in connecting a theory of social change with the administrator and administration.

As Fries (1943), Waldo (1952), and Long (1954) all noted with varying tones of approval, Dewey's view of scientific inquiry as an experimental endeavor proved to be quite influential in public administration. Waldo (1948) appears to be skeptical of Dewey's view of science and administration or at least Fries' (1943) endorsement of it. On the matter, Waldo (1965) later refers to himself as a "confused, revolving eclectic." Setting aside Waldo's eclecticism, he nevertheless provides an important statement about pragmatism's intellectual trajectory during the middle of the 20th century while simultaneously reaffirming its place as a philosophy of public administration. As Waldo (1965) states it:

> Of Pragmatism one would have to say that it has sharply declined as a "fashionable" philosophy ... its decline has been precipitous, a remarkable event in intellectual history. Of course, pragmatism can exist without Pragmatism, and of the lower-case variety there is plainly a great deal; we impart a great deal of it in teaching Public Administration and it is the unarticulated working philosophy of much public administration. (Waldo, 1965, p. 11)

The Eclipse of Pragmatism by Logical Positivism

The World War II and post-war periods elevated administrative sophistication but dampened the progressive pragmatic philosophical ethos. On the one hand, many new administrative structures were created out of necessity in prosecuting the war. On the other hand, the philosophical mode shifted toward a more excessive emphasis on the hard and practical elements of pragmatism while simultaneously downplaying the softer participatory, pluralistic, and provisional elements of the philosophy. The philosophy of logical positivism came to embody this new ethos in science and in government.

Logical positivism was a philosophical movement that sought to systematically eliminate all non-empirical elements from scientific investigation (Ayer, 1959). Thus, it eliminated all metaphysical concerns about the nature of the studied object, what we now typically refer to as ontological questions, and focused only on developing an epistemology of facts. The term of art at the time was verification by reference to *the given* (Hempel, 1959). In other words, scientific theories could never be proven true or false but only sensible or nonsense considering empirical observations. Nonsense in this case is a technical term which literally means lacking any sense data (Whetsell & Shields, 2015). Data derived from observations would be the final arbiter of the truth value of scientific claims. Of course, this approach invalidated wide swaths of scholarship that would have been considered scientific.

Curiously, early logical positivists could not even admit "unobservables" such as atoms. It was only in the last decade or so that scientists first directly observed an atom with microscope technology. Imagine the scoffing and eye-rolling at the mention of something like public service motivation. Whetsell and Shields (2015) discussed positivism in public administration, arguing that its use in the field is often a misnomer. Scholars tend to lump all quantitative empirical research into the positivist mode, remaining in the dark about the distinctions between positivism, realism, and pragmatism. The contemporary pragmatist philosopher Larry Laudan (2012) does a wonderful job illustrating the differences through the rhetorical method of a Socratic dialogue.

In short, logical positivism would not allow theory based on unobservable entities and is thus considered anti-realist. This is in sharp contrast to the popular notion that positivism is objectivist; in fact, it is better understood as instrumentalist about studied objects. In this sense, it actually has some commonalities with pragmatism. In contrast, realism posits the potential validity of developing theory on unobservable entities which may be regarded as potentially "real" (Psillos, 2005). Bringing this back to PA, it is difficult to think of any objects of study in public administration which are directly observable. In fact, a strict logical positivist might discard the whole field. Many of the constructs of interest, particularly in intra-organization public administration, such as dealing with psychological concepts, would be discarded as nonsense by logical positivism. This is the philosophical point of contention behind the administrative behavior movement, which sought to build theory only on observable behavior. However, it isn't clear to me how even behavior would survive perspective. Thus, my contention is that there really can be no strict logical positivists in public administration. Individuals inclined to such views would be more comfortable in the natural sciences, where direct observations are far less problematic.

Pearl (2018) noted that this distinction manifests in enduring quarrels between statisticians interested in correlation on one side and scientists interested in causal inference on the other. As Pearl lays it out, the originators of modern statistics, Francis Galton, and especially Karl Pearson, espoused that there is nothing more in science than correlation and that speaking of causal relations is nothing more than metaphysics. Statistical correlation requires no assumptions about mechanisms in the world, and so a purely statistical approach to science might rest comfortably on a philosophy of logical positivism. In contrast, scientists interested in investigating cause and effect relationships cannot comfortably rest here since such relationships often depend on unseen forces, e.g., gravity, magnetism, etc. Pragmatists have taken on a variety of positions regarding this point, with some, such as Richard Rorty, taking a pragmatic anti-realist position and others, such as Hilary Putnam, taking a pragmatic realist position.

Logical positivism became widely popular first in the philosophy of science in the 1920s–1930s and began to spread into adjacent disciplines through the influence of many prominent intellectuals during the World War II period. This was the result of the appeal of the intuitive ambition that we could and should base all our scientific theories only on observable facts, but also the result of political turmoil, which forced many prominent scholars from their home institutions in Austria to the United States. These included, for example Rudolf Carnap, Carl Hempel, and Hans Reichenbach, among others from the Vienna Circle.

Herbert Simon (1997) cited several of Carnap's works in *Administrative Behavior* while articulating the now infamous fact-value distinction in public administration, stating "the conclusions reached by a particular school of modern philosophy – logical positivism – will be accepted as a starting point" (p. 55). Simon later revised the statement, saying that he intended logical "empiricism". As Whetsell and Shields (2015) explained, the distinction here is something like the following: logical positivists abandoned the strict verification criterion of meaning based solely on observable facts since, among other reasons, the criterion itself could not be verified. They subsequently moved to a criterion of coherence, where the meaning of scientific theories could be derived from their coherence with other theories. This shift from foundationalism to coherentism was represented in logical empiricism.

However, it would be a vast oversimplification to call Simon a logical empiricist and move on. Simon (1997) also cites the pragmatists John Dewey and William James in several areas in the same book, noting their influence on his behavioral insights. In fact, I can think of no more pragmatic principle than the one Simon is perhaps most well-known for, that of "satisficing". We humans, from time to time, are of course known to engage in rational optimizing. Personally, any time I make a major purchase, such as a new car, I engage in an extensive and exhausting process of optimizing, weighing all the relevant variables and alternatives until finally making a choice. This is true of a great deal of the decision-making humans do, and it is reflected in the *homo economicus* approach of neo-classical economics. However, such processes are often not possible, particularly under time constraints. Thus, satisficing is pragmatic decision-making.

In summary, even though pragmatism appeared to be eclipsed by logical positivism during the middle of the 20th century, public administration remains a practitioner-oriented discipline and so maintained a lower-case pragmatic mode throughout. By the late 1980s and early 1990s, pragmatism was beginning to enter the third contact from behind its eclipse.

Pragmatism in Contemporary Public Administration

Despite the prevalence of logical positivism and other modes of philosophy, such as existentialism and post-modernism, that arose during the middle of the 20th century, pragmatism, and John Dewey in particular, continued to be sprinkled throughout the public administration literature, often accompanied by references to *The public and its problems* (e.g., Backoff, 1974; Murray, 1975;

Sherwood, 1976; Cooper, 1980; Long, 1981; Gates & Herbert, 1984; Mathews, 1984).[1] As pragmatism was eclipsed, only the corona of its light escaped around the edges. This changed in the 1990s when pragmatism entered its "Third Contact", and new scholarship on the topic gradually emerged, which delved into Dewey's philosophy more deeply.

One of the first articles to substantially investigate pragmatism in public administration was by Stever (1993), who compellingly argued for the relevance of Dewey's philosophy as a contribution to organization theory as well as philosophy of technology. As Stever suggests, Dewey's relevance was overlooked because his style was distinct from that of the administrative scholars. Stever argues that Dewey's philosophy entails that "organizations are inevitably the central focus of a liberal society," and further that technological progress had begun to interfere with the bedrock element of organization, that of social interaction. Dewey's insights could not have been more prescient to the contemporary scene. In less than ten years, starting somewhere in the late 2000s, mobile devices and social media apps upended the basic structure of culture itself. Face-to-face interaction is now heavily substituted, complemented, or mediated by technology. We are now more interconnected than ever but simultaneously more isolated and estranged from basic forms of community.

A few years later, Shields (1996) applied and developed Dewey's theory, suggesting that pragmatism is more than an attitude shared broadly among practitioners in public administration. Instead, as she argued, pragmatism is an *organizing principle* that explains the pragmatic *imprint* of administration. By imprint, Shields indicates that pragmatism is to administration as efficiency is to the economist, power is to the politician, or profits are to business. However, the imprint is merely its practical impression, while its substance resides in the deeper philosophy, e.g., articulated in the 4Ps above. As Shields noted, pragmatism's instrumental, problem-oriented use of theory; its emphasis on experience and consequences; and its evolutionary view of truth in context are all well suited to the chaotic world of public administration.

A few years after Stever (1993) and Shields (1996) advanced pragmatism for public administration, Evans (2000) made a similar call to reorient the discipline around Dewey's philosophy. She sought to *reclaim* Dewey and provided recitations of several of his works, placing them in the context of public administration. Evans emphasized the logic of community, the place of the individual in the community context, and the role of the public manager in fostering participatory and deliberative democracy. Curiously, Evans' (2000) reclamation project failed to appreciate that Shields (1996) made an effective

---

[1]   These were identified by a full-text keyword search of Dewey in the archives of *Public Administration Review* and *Administration & Society*.

attempt four years earlier. At the same time, a tranche of articles supporting and critiquing Evans (2000) emerged simultaneously.

Shortly after Evans' call to reclaim John Dewey for public administration, Shields (2003) advanced a new concept for public administration called "the community of inquiry". As I briefly touched on in a previous section, the participatory approach to science found in pragmatism emanated from the belief that truth happens to an idea within the context of the relevant epistemic community. Shields (2003) argued that practitioners in public administration routinely find themselves enmeshed in an array of problematic situations, from setting meeting agendas to organizing a large-scale crisis response. To comprehend the nature of public problems, practitioners develop working hypotheses, propositions, and middle-range theories that are used as instruments in their resolution. The entire process unfolds through the participation of numerous stakeholders to the problem. These groups form *communities of inquiry.*

From the perspective of individual psychology, the problematic situation presents a type of doubtful indeterminacy where the actions and outcomes are often unknown. Practitioners often assemble communities – for example, town hall meetings – to conduct inquiry into a problem situation in a way that is open, participatory, and democratic. That is not to say that expertise is not valued in this approach, but that experts are simply included in the process along with all the other stakeholders to the problem. This process of investigation leverages a plurality of participants, allowing the public manager to transform an indeterminate situation into a unified whole, and in so doing, generate pragmatic truth. Shields is fond of using Jane Addams' example of managing a lively and chaotic settlement house, which exemplifies all these principles, as well as the enduring causes of public health, sanitation, housing, social reform, and community building.

Shields (2003) kicked off a period of debate between classical pragmatists and neo-pragmatists in the pages of *Administration & Society*. While this debate should be of interest to philosophically minded public administration scholars, it will not be reviewed at length here. In a nutshell, the debate centered on the question of whether experience or language takes precedence in the establishment of pragmatic truth claims, with classical pragmatists emphasizing experience and the neo-pragmatists emphasizing language.

In 2008, Shields again advanced philosophical pragmatism for public administration, arguing that pragmatism serves as a kind of taproot that might be recognized to renew public administration. Here, Shields is interested in exploring the potential reasons that pragmatism was never strongly integrated into public administration, suggesting that pragmatism was internalized from the inception of public administration during the late 19th and early 20th centuries. This is the sense in which pragmatism may serve as a taproot for renewal.

Since then, a number of works have been published focusing on the application of pragmatism to public administration. Ansell (2011) provided a compelling argument for integrating pragmatism in democratic governance more broadly. Whetsell (2013) argued that pragmatism provides an epistemological basis for methodological pluralism in public administration. Shields and Whetsell (2017) detailed how pragmatism can be applied to provide a flexible framework for research methods in public administration. Ansell and Geyer (2017) connect pragmatism to new concepts in complexity science emerging in public administration. Ansell and Boin (2019) suggested pragmatism is an effective way to conceptualize crisis management. Pedersen (2020) explored Dewey's conception of the state as the manifestation of the organized public. Finally, Whetsell (2024) applied Dewey's *The public and its problems* to articulate a unique ontology of the concept of the public based on the consequences of social interaction.

CONCLUSION

In this chapter, I have sought to describe philosophical pragmatism in the context of public administration. I have also sought, through rehearsing my own understanding, to reinforce the idea that pragmatism is indeed suitable as a philosophy for public administration. Pragmatism has been quite durable across time, it is adaptable to developments in contemporary theory, and it may continue to serve as a useful organizing principle for public administration. Pragmatism will continue to face challenges on the one hand from the hard science side for being too perspectival and from the humanities side for being too instrumental. That is the plight of the moderate position. To paraphrase William James, the goal of the pragmatist is not to specialize in any particular domain but to be able to competently navigate the corridors between all domains.

REFERENCES

Addams, J. (1911). *Twenty years at Hull House*. Macmillan.
Ansell, C. (2011). *Pragmatist democracy: Evolutionary learning as public philosophy*. Oxford University Press.
Ansell, C., & Boin, A. (2019). Taming deep uncertainty: The potential of pragmatist principles for understanding and improving strategic crisis management. *Administration & Society*, 51(7), 1079–1112.
Ansell, C., & Geyer, R. (2017). "Pragmatic complexity" a new foundation for moving beyond "evidence-based policy making"?. *Policy Studies*, 38(2), 149–167.
Ayer, A. J. (ed.) (1959). *Logical positivism*. Simon and Schuster.
Backoff, R. (1974). Operationalizing administrative reform for improved governmental performance. *Administration & Society*, 6(1), 73–106.

Brandom, R. B. (2004). The pragmatist enlightenment (and its problematic semantics). *European Journal of Philosophy*, 12(1), 1–16.

Brendel, D. H. (2006). *Healing psychiatry: Bridging the science/humanism divide.* MIT Press.

Cooper, T. L. (1980). Bureaucracy and community organization: The metamorphosis of a relationship. *Administration & Society*, 11(4), 411–444.

Dimock, M.E. (1936). "The Meaning and Scope of Public Administration". In *The Frontiers of Public Administration* (J.M. Gaus, White, L.D., and Dimock, M.E, Eds) New York, Russell & Russell.

Dewey, J. (1927/2008). *The Later Work of John Dewey, 1925–1953: Volume 2: 1925–1927, Essays, Reviews, Miscellany, and "The Public and its Problems"* (J. A. Boydston, Ed.). Southern Illinois University Press.

Dewey, J. (1938/2008). *The Later Works of John Dewey, 1925-1953*: Volume 12: *Logic: The Theory of Inquiry* (J. A. Boydston, Ed.). Southern Illinois University Press.

Evans, K. G. (2000). Reclaiming John Dewey: Democracy, inquiry, pragmatism, and public management. *Administration & Society*, *32*(3), 308-328.

Fries, H.S. (1943) Liberty and Science [Review of *The Machiavellians, defenders of freedom*, by J. Burnham]. Public Administration Review, 3(3), 268–273.

Fry, B. R., & Raadschelders, J. C. (2013). *Mastering public administration: From Max Weber to Dwight Waldo.* CQ Press.

Fung, A. (2015). Putting the public back into governance: The challenges of citizen participation and its future. *Public Administration Review*, 75(4), 513–522.

Gates, B., & Herbert, A. W. (1984). Knowledge, networks, and neighborhoods: Will microcomputers make us better citizens?. *Public Administration Review*, 44, 164–171.

Gaus, J. M. (1936). "American Society and Public Administration". In *The Frontiers of Public Administration* (J.M. Gaus, White, L.D., and Dimock, M.E, Eds) New York, Russell & Russell.

Gaus, J. M. (1950). Trends in the theory of public administration. *Public Administration Review*, 10(3), 161–168.

Hempel, C. G. (1959). The empiricist criterion of meaning. In A. J. Ayer (ed.), *Logical positivism* (pp. 108–129). Free Press. (Original work published 1950).

James, W. (1907). Pragmatism: *A new name for some old ways of thinking.* Longmans, Green and Co.

Laudan, L. (1977). *Progress and its problems: Towards a theory of scientific growth* (Vol. 282). University of California Press.

Laudan, L. (2012). *Science and relativism: Some key controversies in the philosophy of science.* University of Chicago Press.

Long, N. E. (1954). Public policy and administration: The goals of rationality and responsibility. *Public Administration Review, 14*(1), 22–31.

Long, N. E. (1981). The SES and the public interest. *Public Administration Review*, 41(3), 305–312.

Mathews, D. (1984). The public in practice and theory. *Public Administration Review*, 44, 120–125.

Menand, L. (2002). *The metaphysical club: A story of ideas in America.* Macmillan.

Moore, M. H. (2014). Public value accounting: Establishing the philosophical basis. *Public Administration Review*, 74(4), 465–477.

Murray, M. A. (1975). Comparing public and private management: An exploratory essay. *Public Administration Review*, 364–371.

Ostrom, V., Tiebout, C. M., & Warren, R. (1961). The organization of government in metropolitan areas: a theoretical inquiry. *American Political Science Review*, 55(4), 831–842.

Pallesen, T., & Pedersen, K. Z. (2023). Model of human fallibility: Traveling behavioral assumptions in public governance. *Perspectives on Public Management and Governance*, 6(2–3), 119–130.

Pearl, J. (2018). *The book of why: The new science of cause and effect*. Basic Books.

Pedersen, K. Z. (2020). John Dewey on public office and representative democracy. *European Journal of Cultural and Political Sociology*, 7(1), 75–95.

Peirce, C. S. (1868). Some consequences of four incapacities. *The Journal of Speculative Philosophy*, 2(3), 140–157.

Psillos, S. (2005). *Scientific realism: How science tracks truth*. Routledge.

Raadschelders, J. C. (2011). *Public administration: The interdisciplinary study of government*. Oxford University Press.

Rorty, R. (2009). *Philosophy and the mirror of nature*. Princeton University Press.

Shafritz, J. M., & Hyde, A. C. (2016). *Classics of public administration*. Cengage Learning.

Sherwood, F. P. (1976). Action research: Some perspectives for learning organizations. *Administration & Society*, 8(2), 175–192.

Shields, P. (ed.) (2017). *Jane Addams: Progressive pioneer of peace, philosophy, sociology, social work and public administration* (Vol. 10). Springer.

Shields, P. M. (1996). Pragmatism: Exploring public administration's policy imprint. *Administration & Society*, 28(3), 390–411.

Shields, P. M. (2003). The community of inquiry: Classical pragmatism and public administration. *Administration & Society*, 35(5), 510–538.

Shields, P. M. (2008). Rediscovering the taproot: Is classical pragmatism the route to renew public administration?. *Public Administration Review*, 68(2), 205–221.

Shields, P. M., & Tajalli, H. (2006). Intermediate theory: The missing link in successful student scholarship. *Journal of Public Affairs Education*, 12(3), 313–334.

Shields, P., & Whetsell, T. (2017). Public administration methodology: A pragmatic perspective. *Foundations of Public Administration*, 75–92.

Sil, R., & Katzenstein, P. J. (2010). Analytic eclecticism in the study of world politics: Reconfiguring problems and mechanisms across research traditions. *Perspectives on Politics*, 8(2), 411–431.

Simon, H. A. (1997). *Administrative behavior: A study of decision-making processes in administrative organizations* (4th ed.). Free Press.

Snider, K. F. (2000). Response to Stever and Garrison. *Administration & Society*, 32(4), 487–489.

Stever, J. A. (1993). Technology organization, freedom: The organizational theory of John Dewey. *Administration & Society*, 24(4), 419–443.

Stivers, C. (1995). Settlement women and bureau men: Constructing a usable past for public administration. *Public Administration Review*, 522–529.

Waldo, D. (1948). *The administrative state*. Ronald Press Company.

Waldo, D. (1952). Development of theory of democratic administration. *The American Political Science Review*, 46(1), 81–103.

Waldo, D. (1965). The administrative state revisited. *Public Administration Review*, 25(1), 5–30.

Whetsell, T. A. (2013). Theory-pluralism in public administration: Epistemology, legitimacy, and method. *The American Review of Public Administration*, 43(5), 602–618.

Whetsell, T. A. (2024). What is the public? A pragmatic analysis of a core concept in public administration. *Perspectives on Public Management and Governance*, 7(1–2), 27–36.

Whetsell, T. A., & Shields, P. M. (2015). The dynamics of positivism in the study of public administration: A brief intellectual history and reappraisal. *Administration & Society*, 47(4), 416–446.

5. Benevolence, (Public) Ethics and Public Services: Revisiting Public Value, Public Service Motivation, and Models of Public Administration through the Ethics of Supererogation

Stefano Biancu and Edoardo Ongaro

INTRODUCTION[1]

This chapter attempts to connect a key notion and topical area in moral philosophy and philosophical anthropology with key themes in public administration and public management (PA). We interrogate whether and how the notion of supererogation may enable us to critically revisit key themes in PA. Supererogatory actions and attitudes are usually considered morally positive and yet beyond the call of duty – they are not required nor demandable: while they may be perceived as mandatory from a first-person perspective (i.e., by the agent at the moment of deliberation), they are not so from a third-person perspective (i.e., from the point of view of an external observer). The reason for this is that they are in some way necessary. The agent feels they have to do what is not required nor demandable to the extent that it is a condition of the possibility of liberty and humanity. We consider how the perspective of supererogation may enable us to critically revisit key theories and notions in PA, such as the theory of Public Service Motivation (PSM), Public Value management and governance (PV), and models of PA reform.

The chapter unfolds as follows: first, the notion of supererogation is introduced and discussed. Then, questions for PA scholars (and practitioners) are

---

[1]   The chapter is the joint work of the authors; however, in the final writing Stefano Biancu has written the sections "Introduction", "The notion of supererogation" and "Beyond the Call of Duty", while Edoardo Ongaro has written the other sections of the chapter.

raised. The chapter then presents how the notion of supererogation may help problematise and critically revisit key theories and notions in PA, such as PSM, PV, and models of PA reform. We conclude by discussing the helpfulness of further bridging moral philosophy and philosophical anthropology and the field of PA.

THE NOTION OF SUPEREROGATION

Supererogatory actions and attitudes are morally positive and yet beyond what is required and demandable – they are optional. The concept of supererogation (Heyd, 1982; Janiaud, 2007) has its origins precisely in the Vulgate, the Latin translation of the Christian Bible dating back to the 4th century CE and, in particular, in the parable of the Good Samaritan, in Chapter 10 of the Gospel according to Luke. Current English translations of the parable read:

> 25 There was a scholar of the law who stood up to test him [Jesus] and said, 'Teacher, what must I do to inherit eternal life?' 26 Jesus said to him, 'What is written in the law? How do you read it?' 27 He said in reply, 'You shall love the Lord, your God, with all your heart, with all your being, with all your strength, and with all your mind, and your neighbor as yourself.' 28 He replied to him, 'You have answered correctly; do this and you will live.' 29 But because he wished to justify himself, he said to Jesus, 'And who is my neighbor?' 30 Jesus replied, 'A man fell victim to robbers as he went down from Jerusalem to Jericho. They stripped and beat him and went off leaving him half-dead. 31 A priest happened to be going down that road, but when he saw him, he passed by on the opposite side. 32 Likewise a Levite came to the place, and when he saw him, he passed by on the opposite side. 33 But a Samaritan traveler who came upon him was moved with compassion at the sight. 34 He approached the victim, poured oil and wine over his wounds and bandaged them. Then he lifted him up on his own animal, took him to an inn and cared for him. 35 The next day he took out two silver coins and gave them to the innkeeper with the instruction, "Take care of him. If you spend more than what I have given you, I shall repay you on my way back." 36 Which of these three, in your opinion, was neighbor to the robbers' victim?' 37 He answered, 'The one who treated him with mercy.' Jesus said to him, 'Go and do likewise.' (Lk 10, 25–37)

In the instructions the Samaritan gives the innkeeper, so that he takes care, in his absence, of the unfortunate pilgrim, the Vulgate reads: '*Curam illius habe, et, quodcumque supererogaveris, ego, cum rediero, reddam tibi*' (Lk 10:35). As we have just seen, the Latin verb '*supererogaveris*' is translated, in the current versions of the biblical text, by the periphrasis, 'If you spend more'. Supererogation has therefore to do with a 'surplus' and, in particular, with an additional cost, an extra expense. This is why the attitude of the Samaritan has traditionally become the emblem of supererogation – he did good and he did more than was required of him.

Starting from the Gospel, the fathers of the Church introduced the term into the technical language of theology, using it to refer to actions recommended by the spiritual tradition, but contrary to natural inclinations, such as fasting and chastity (Dentsoras, 2014, pp. 351–372). But it is only with Thomas Aquinas that the term became relevant (Witschen, 2004, pp. 27–40). According to Aquinas, a good moral action can be either commanded or advised. That is, it can be the object of either an obligation (the sphere of *'praecepta'*) or a recommendation (the sphere of *'consilia'*, such as chastity, poverty, obedience). This second category includes supererogatory actions, i.e., actions which, while being morally positive, are beyond the call of duty. According to Aquinas, counsels are morally superior to commandments. If the latter concern what is good, the former concern a better good.

Aquinas' perspective on supererogation became canonical, remaining substantially unchanged for a few centuries, at least until Luther and the other Reformers (Konrad, 2005, pp. 119–140). In their eyes, supererogatory actions took the shape of human claims to obtain salvation thanks to one's own merits. The Anglican Declaration of Faith (the famous '39 articles') is a good example of the Protestants' attitudes vis-à-vis supererogation. Article 14, which was first composed in 1552/1553 and has been unchanged since, reads: 'XIV – OF WORKS OF SUPEREROGATION Voluntary Works besides, over, and above, God's Commandments, which they call Works of Supererogation, cannot be taught without arrogancy and impiety.'

In the following centuries, the notion of supererogation lost its relevance and centrality, at least until 1958, when the British philosopher James Urmson published his short essay 'Saints and Heroes' (Urmson, 1969). According to Urmson, moral philosophy had traditionally disregarded two types of actions, the saintly and the heroic. Such actions would not fall into the commonly accepted classification, according to which moral actions would be divided into: (1) morally right obligatory actions, (2) morally wrong prohibited actions and (3) morally neutral permitted actions. When they are performed beyond the call of duty, saintly and heroic actions do not fit in this classification as long as they are morally good actions that are not obligatory, not required, nor demandable. More precisely, although they may be perceived as mandatory from a first-person perspective (i.e., by the subject at the moment of deliberation), they are not so from a third-person perspective (i.e., from the point of view of an external observer). According to Urmson, compared to the 'basic moral duties', those actions would represent 'the higher flights of morality'. Following Urmson's seminal article, a huge debate has opened up in Anglo-Saxon moral philosophy about the concept of supererogation: about its definition, about the taxonomy of supererogatory actions and attitudes, and about some paradoxes inherent in the notion (Archer, 2018; Cowley, 2015; Heyd, 2016).

BEYOND THE CALL OF DUTY: WHAT DOES IT MEAN FOR PA?

Taking the notion of supererogation seriously urges a rethinking of the notion of duty (Biancu, 2020a, pp. 25–39, Biancu 2020b). In particular, it is necessary to distinguish at least three different levels of duty. A first experience of duty is situated at a legal level: my duty corresponds to what is established by a law or even by the right of another person. By setting boundaries and limitations, legal duties aim to protect everybody's original freedom and rights, which are supposed to be an original human feature, as the 1948 Universal Declaration of Human Rights puts it, 'All human beings are born free and equal in dignity and rights' (Article 1).

A second experience of duty is situated at an ethical level. A form of responsibility comes up at each encounter between humans. Not only am I responsible for my own actions (which I might be asked to justify), but I am in some way responsible for the other's life and destiny (Levinas, 1961; Waldenfelds, 1997; Waldenfelds, 2002). An implicit call for love is present in each human encounter and I have to respond as suitably as possible to this call of the other – 'I hope you will love me', which means I hope my life and fate are not irrelevant to you. The subject feels they have to respond as adequately as possible to this call for love.

A third experience of duty is situated at an anthropological level. At this level, the idea that all human beings are born free is an abstraction (Ferry, 2004, p. 201). Humans are actually born able to *become* free. Freedom has its own conditions, and love is one of these conditions. Not only do I need to be free in order to love, but I also need to receive and give love to become free. Only if I act out of love – love for myself and for others – can I can truly be free.

It is clear that supererogation is beyond duty at a legal level, i.e., beyond what the moral agent might be required to do by either a law or respect for a third person's rights. At this level, no one has the right to bother me by asking me to love them (i.e., to forgive, to be generous, to give my life for someone, etc.). But supererogation is not beyond the call of duty at an ethical level: I have to respond as suitably as I can to the call for love of my neighbour, since both their and my destiny depends on my response. This is what Jaspers called a 'metaphysical' responsibility, based on an original solidarity among humans (Jaspers, 1946, p. 11).

Supererogation is not beyond the call of duty on an anthropological level either. At this level, duty is what I actually need in order to become free, to fulfil myself. In other words, in order to really become a subject who is perfectly equal to themselves (Biancu, 2014). Something is due to the extent that it is a condition of my flourishing as a person. I truly become a subject by freely and suitably responding to someone who in some way bothers me by asking me for love. Not by chance, one of the most important meanings of the term *'humanus'* is benevolent (Giustiniani, 1985).

Given this distinction between at least three different levels of obligation, duty is not only what is established by a law or required by someone else's rights. Duty can also be also understood as a necessary condition of the possibility of freedom, of subjectivity, of humanity – if I need to, then I have to. Being one of these conditions of possibility, supererogation exceeds the mere legal understanding of duty, but not duty itself. In other words: supererogation can be considered as a 'maximum' if compared to the 'minimum' which cannot and must not be missed – i.e., the area of what is required either by a law or by respect for a third person's rights. Since it is one of the conditions of freedom and subjectivity, this 'maximum' is nevertheless in some way 'necessary'.

Let's think of the three pillars of modern politics – liberty, equality, fraternity (Biancu, 2021a; Biancu, 2021b). Liberty and equality are usually considered as required. Protests around the world are always demands for either more liberty or more equality. The state, and therefore PA, must guarantee and protect these pillars. Compared to them, fraternity is usually considered supererogatory – it is good to have a more fraternal society, but it is not demandable and required.

Rather, by contributing to creating truly human and free subjects, the supererogatory attitude of fraternity needs to be understood as a condition of the possibility for both liberty and equality. When fraternity is missing, freedom and equality are purely formal. Fraternity makes them substantial. Since the liberal state needs citizens who are truly free human subjects, fraternity fulfils those premises on which – according to Böckenförde – the liberal state lives without being able to guarantee them by itself: *'Der freiheitliche, säkularisierte Staat lebt von Voraussetzungen, die er selbst nicht garantieren kann'* (Böckenförde, 2006, p. 112).

Good examples of supererogatory actions and attitudes are saintly and heroic acts, beneficence, volunteering, acts of forbearance; forgiveness, mercy and pardon, and even acts of kindness. All these kinds of actions are beyond both what a public institution is expected to do vis-à-vis the citizens and what it can ask the citizens to do. All these actions cannot be imposed – like the gift (Mauss, 1925), they only make sense if they are free. And yet they are necessary, even to the liberal state and its PA, to the extent they are a substantial condition for fully free and equal citizens (and institutions). In many ways, PA can positively encourage these actions and attitudes within itself and in society, without limiting the spaces of negative freedom of its workers and the citizens: for instance, in terms of kindness while addressing citizens, in terms of favouring pro-social actions like beneficence and volunteering, in terms of favouring pro-social attitudes like forgiveness, and in terms of giving good examples of saintly and heroic actions, i.e., actions which are respectively performed by the agent against their self-interest and even involve putting their life at risk.

The perspective of supererogation can therefore be seen as a viewpoint from which to interrogate, from a moral philosophy and philosophical anthropology perspective, the key issue of what is 'duty' in the public service, for both public servants and citizens. We try to delineate some of the implications for the scholarly research of PA, notably by highlighting how the notion of supererogation may be brought to bear on some key, 'mainstream' thematic areas of inquiry in the field.

REVISITING INTEGRITY OF GOVERNANCE, THE THEORY OF PUBLIC VALUE, PUBLIC SERVICE MOTIVATION THEORY, AND MODELS OF PUBLIC ADMINISTRATION FROM THE STANDPOINT OF SUPEREROGATION

Adopting an ethical and anthropological perspective, and specifically the consideration of the notion of supererogation, may offer a philosophical perspective from which to revisit some key theoretical streams and debates in the field of PA. First is, it goes without saying, the area of public ethics and the integrity of governance, which is one of the relatively few areas in the field of PA to directly connect philosophical preoccupations, in the form of ethical questions and issues, and the field of PA as currently practised across academia. Such a stream of research – developed by authors such as Gjalt de Graaf, Wolfgang Drechsler, George Frederickson, Leo Huberts, Michael Macaulay, Mark Rutgers, amongst others – has not, to our knowledge, directly employed and deployed the notion of supererogation. A first line of scholarly inquiry that may therefore be inspired by the introduction of the notion of supererogation into the academic field of PA is public ethics.

The consideration of public ethics also leads us to the two areas of inquiry about public values (in the plural) and the distinct, yet related, strand of Public Value (in the singular) governance and management (PV). Notably, we may revisit the motives of the 'public manager creator of public value' so vividly theorised by Mark Moore (1995) and query: does the entire PV theory (and practice) implicitly posit a supererogatory view of the public servant?

In his most famous, and most cited, book, Moore (1995) vividly depicts the action of a town librarian who proactively reinvented the public service that the library used to provide on an afternoon between 3:00 and 5:00 pm, in such a way to cater to the needs of students pouring into the library during afterschool hours in search of a place to socialise (but not, it should be noted, of a book to read). To make a long – and very famous, at least within the community of PA scholars and practitioners – story short, the librarian reimagined her library in such a way as to 'care for' the students, going well beyond her formal remit to ultimately manage to create what Moore has described and theorised as 'public value'. The motives driving our town librarian are not fully discussed in Moore's initial work (disclosure: the librarian is a partly real, partly imagined figure). From the perspective we have taken in this chapter regarding the notion of supererogation, we may therefore well ask: is our librarian driven by a supererogatory attitude? A question which brings us to our initial research question: does the entire PV theory and practice posits – at least implicitly – a supererogatory view of the public servant? To our knowledge, these questions have never been asked in the public administration and management scientific literature, and yet addressing them would provide a moral and anthropological foundation to the figure of the public manager as a creator of public value. It may well be high time to ask such a question.

A stream of research in PA, which is perhaps less evidently connected to the perspective of benevolence and supererogation that we take in this chapter, is the theory of Public Service Motivation (PSM – Perry, 1996; Perry and Wise, 1990). It is now a now well-established and highly researched theoretical perspective that delves into the motives driving people to join the public service and spend their professional lives in it. It has long been queried – and to our knowledge is still the subject of intense debate – what the nature of PSM is: is it about intrinsic motivation, extrinsic motivation or pro-social motivation (within self-determination theory), or a combination of all of these? Is PSM linked to a combination of extrinsic autonomous motivation (through the internalisation of socially transmitted values, which then become personally endorsed values) and pro-social 'long-term' motivation (a pro-social motivation matched with the rational consideration that working in and for public institutions may produce positive outcomes for society in the longer term, longer than through other forms of social engagement)? If so, what are the ethical roots of such motivational drivers?

To our knowledge, in the burgeoning literature on PSM, the perspective of supererogation has never been employed. If it were employed, it might provide, from an ethical and philosophical anthropology perspective, a foundation for the motives that seem to drive people into public service. We promptly recognise that the theory and social construct of PSM, on one hand, and the philosophical (and theological) perspective of benevolence, on the other hand, are notions pegged at different logical-ontological levels, namely the empirics of individual agency vs. the anthropology of it. Yet – perhaps exactly because of their being located at different logical-ontological and epistemological levels – they may shed mutual light and complement each other in any discourse about what drives public servants to choose this walk of life and pursue it. In a sense, one invokes the other: when one queries 'what happens empirically?', the philosophical perspective of supererogation calls on the social sciences, and PSM theory specifically, for the theme to be meaningfully investigated. When, complementarily, PSM theory queries, or at least elicits the question of 'what underpins what PSM purports about human action and behaviour?', it is this social science (and social psychology) theory within the field of PA, and therefore the very field of PA, that invokes the contribution of philosophy and theology for bringing the ethical-moral discourse into the picture.

Finally, we may shift from the level of individual human beings and their moral agency (the level to which this process of bridging between PA and the theological-philosophical notion of supererogation is most directly developable, given that in this chapter we take the move from a perspective of ethics and morality) to the level of the reform of public governance and the public sector at the system level. Here too, we query whether the philosophical perspective of benevolence and supererogation may shed new light on well-rehearsed debates. We argue that it may. In fact, if we consider (in an extremely stylised way) the storyline of public sector reform doctrines[2] having shifted in emphasis and centrality from an 'old' public administration (OPA) to, at first, the New Public Management (NPM), and then to a blend of doctrines which include, as the 'next big thing', the perspective of collaborative governance (CG) (Ansell and Gash, 2008), then we may tentatively query: has this shift also meant a shift from perspectives predicated on public servants performing only their duty – a 'duty only' assumption of human behaviour – to perspectives predicated on public servants 'going the extra mile', that is, in more philosophically rigorous terms, premised on supererogatory action of the public servants?

The thesis that we put forward here (to provoke discussion) is that:

- OPA and NPM = the doctrines of reform of the public sector are designed assuming duty only by both public servants and citizens/users of public services.
- CG = premised on supererogatory actions by both public servants and citizens/users and, indeed, whoever engages in processes for co-creating public value.

This proposition is put forward in a tentative and, in a sense, provocative way, to hopefully spark and stimulate a reflection in the field of PA about the (almost

---

[2] We use the term 'doctrine' to identify a form of knowledge that is inherently normative-prescriptive in nature; that is, which is about 'how things ought to be'. In our case, reform doctrines concern forms of knowledge about how to reorganise the public sector with the ultimate purpose of making it function 'better', in some sense (i.e., with reference to certain criteria of performance and accountability – see Pollitt and Bouckaert, 2017).

always implicit) philosophical assumptions on which we rely in our scholarly inquiry, even when studying topics and issues, like administrative reform doctrines, which are ultimately normative in their stance.

CONCLUDING REMARKS AND PERSPECTIVES OF INQUIRY

This chapter tackles the questions of whether and how the moral philosophy notion of supererogatory action may enable us to critically rethink key issues in PA. We argue that it does, and demonstrate how the adoption of the perspective of supererogation can enable us to revisit foundational issues in areas of PA inquiry, like the theory of PV, the theory of PSM and the doctrines of reform of the public sector that have successively appeared, grown in significance – at least in the reform talk if not in actuality – and quite often later on eclipsed (possibly to resurface in partially new guises) over the decades and internationally.

This contribution is part of an intellectual effort to connect philosophy and the field of PA (Ongaro, 2020 and forthcoming). Philosophical anthropology and PA theories are pitched at different logical-ontological (and moral-ethical) levels, and yet, in a sense precisely for this reason, they may complement each other: theories and propositions at one level invoke the others in order to be complemented and completed. PA theories can make assumptions about individual agency and human behaviour in relation to moral issues, but they can only rely on philosophical anthropology to explain and ground their assumptions. In turn, moral philosophy and philosophical anthropology become 'concrete', addressing and engaging with 'real life' contemporary problems, when they are applied to societal issues – and PA is a key part of any society. Findings of PA theories may then, in turn, interrogate the moral philosopher (and, indeed, also the moral theologian) by furnishing 'real life' instances and situational issues which elicit circumstantiated questions for the moral philosopher to consider (quite in the spirit of casuistry, an approach to addressing issues in moral philosophy which has been so aptly developed over the centuries by the Jesuit fathers).

Bridging and then traversing these two levels – the level of morality addressed by moral philosophy, and the level of society and the social scientific study of it addressed by PA theory and practice – is indeed a valuable, perhaps even (morally) necessary activity. We are here assuming that 'levelism' – i.e., the approach of studying reality at different levels – can still be used in contemporary philosophising, as Floridi argues (Floridi, 2013, chapter 3). This chapter attempts to illustrate how this can happen in the specific, yet majorly significant, case of the field of PA and the moral implications of administering and managing public policies and public services in the contemporary world.

Doing so means undertaking a worthwhile intellectual enterprise. This consists of shifting the analytical focus from a segmented understanding of reality – the moral dimension of life as studied by moral philosophy, the social dimension of life as studied by the social sciences and specifically PA studies as part of the social sciences, and the two segments of reality remaining insulated from each other – and towards a more holistic view of the human being: yes, even when s/he is a bureaucrat!

REFERENCES

Ansell, C. and A. Gash (2008) 'Collaborative Governance in Theory and Practice', *Journal of Public Administration Research and Theory*, 18(4), 543–571.

Archer, A. (2018) 'Supererogation', *Philosophy Compass*, 13(3).

Biancu, S. (2014) 'Capograssi: l'autorité et sa crise. In: G. Capograssi (ed.), *Essai sur l'État*, pp. 5–62. Paris: Éditions de la revue Conférence.

Biancu, S. (2020a) *Il massimo necessario. L'etica alla prova dell'amore*. Milano: Mimesis.

Biancu, S. (2020b) 'Héros et saints: un autre (trans)humanisme', *Transversalités*, 153, 25–39.

Biancu, S. (2021a) *La genealogia dell'umano. Una filosofia dell'autorità*. Milano: Vita e Pensiero.

Biancu, S. (2021b) 'Fraternity And Supererogation. Some Philosophical Ideas On The Encyclical 'Fratelli Tutti'. *Educa*, 7, 58–62.

Böckenförde, E. W. (2006) 'Die Entstehung des Staates als Vorgang der Säkularisation' In: *Recht, Staat, Freiheit. Studien zur Rechtsphilosophie, Staatstheorie und Verfassungsgeschichte*, pp. 92–114. Frankfurt A.M.: Suhrkamp.

Cowley, C. (2015), 'Introduction: The Agents, Acts and Attitudes of Supererogation'. In: *Supererogation* (Royal Institute of Philosophy Supplement, Volume 77, October), pp. 1–23. Cambridge: Cambridge University Press.

Dentsoras D. (2014) 'The Birth of Supererogation'. *Epoché. A Journal for the History of Philosophy* 18(2), 351–372

Ferry, J.-M. (2004) *Les Grammaires de l'intelligence*. Paris: Éd. du Cerf.

Floridi, L. (2013) *The Philosophy of Information*. Oxford: Oxford University Press.

Giustiniani, V. R. (1985) 'Homo, Humanus, and the Meanings of "Humanism'''. *Journal of the History of Ideas*, 46(2), 167–195.

Heyd, D. (1982) *Supererogation: Its Status in Ethical Theory*. Cambridge: Cambridge University Press.

Heyd, D. (2016) *Supererogation*. In: E.N. Zalta (ed.), *The Stanford Encyclopedia of Philosophy* (https://plato.stanford.edu/archives/spr2016/entries/).

Janiaud, J. (2007) *Au-delà du devoir. L'acte surérogatoire*. Rennes: Presses Universitaires de Rennes.

Jaspers, K. (1946) *Die Schuldfrage. Ein Beitrag zur deutschen Frage*. Zürich: Artemis.

Konrad, M. (2005) *Precetti e consigli: Studi sull'etica di san Tommaso d'Aquino a confronto con Lutero e Kant*. Roma: Lateran University Press.

Levinas, E. (1961) *Totalité et Infini*. La Haye: Nijhoff.

Mauss, M. (1925) 'Essai sur le don. Forme et raison de l'échange dans les sociétés archaïques'. *L'Année Sociologique,* 30–180.

Moore, M. (1995) *Creating Public Value*. Cambridge, MA: Harvard University Press.

Ongaro, E. (2020) *Philosophy and Public Administration: An Introduction*, 2nd edition. Cheltenham, UK and Northampton, MA: Edward Elgar.

Ongaro, E. (forthcoming) *Connecting Philosophy and Public Administration: Directions of Inquiry*. London: Palgrave.

Perry, J. L. (1996) 'Measuring Public Service Motivation: An Assessment of Construct Reliability and Validity', *Journal of Public Administration Research and Theory*, 6(1), 5–22.

Perry, J. L. and L. R. Wise (1990) 'The Motivational Bases of Public Service', *Public Administration Review*, 50, 367–373.

Pollitt, C. and Bouckaert, G. (2017) *Public Management Reform. A Comparative Analysis: Into the Age of Austerity*. 4th edition. Oxford: Oxford University Press.

Urmson, J. (1969) 'Saints and Heroes'. In: Feinberg J. (ed.), *Moral Concepts*, pp. 60–73. Oxford: Oxford University Press.

Waldenfels, B. (1997) *Topographie des Fremden. Studien zur Phänomenologie des Fremden 1*. Frankfurt A.M.: Suhrkamp

Waldenfels, B. (2002) *Bruchlinien der Erfahrung*. Frankfurt A.M.: Suhrkamp

Witschen, D. (2004) 'Zur Bestimmung supererogatorischer Handlungen: der Beitrag des Thomas von Aquin'. *Freiburger Zeitschrift für Philosophie und Theologie*, 1–3(51), 27–40.

6. Behaviour in Public Administration: In Search of Foundational Insights

Jonathan C. Kamkhaji and Claudio M. Radaelli

INTRODUCTION

What are the motivations, preferences, and values that inform the behaviour of a public manager? What is essential and unique about a civil servant? This question is wide – practically, it takes us to the foundational ideas about what public administration is. Even the terminology we use has its own implications. If we say "civil servant" instead of "public manager" or "bureaucrat", for example, we borrow some presuppositions about why public administration exists – to serve the state and the citizen, to manage processes efficiently, or to follow routines.

One way to deal with such a huge question is to make hypotheses about the ideal-typical foundations of individual behaviour. To reason ideal-typically means that we identify a few properties of the individual we are interested in. We do so by abstracting from the infinite variety of individuals in different real-world types of public administration, and we search for what is foundational, in terms of properties, about the phenomenon – even if in reality we may not find an individual with exactly these *properties*. In other words, we develop ontological hypotheses about the micro-foundations of public administration (PA). This is in a sense one of the key missions of this volume; that is, to get to the core of administrative phenomena and public governance by mobilizing a vast range of complementary traditions and disciplines, including the humanities. For sure, an interrogation on the nature of the individual triggers a vast array of propositions from the philosophy of public administration (Ongaro, 2020) to psychology, experimental economics, public policy, and the administrative sciences.

Micro-foundations are the core individual-level properties of agents. Of course, individuals then interact in groups within PA. They are constrained by organizational roles. Institutions and rules determine which groups and organizations can do what, when, and how in the policy process, and more generally in governance processes. In turn, individuals that make up the public administration interact with other individuals with different micro-foundations, like elected politicians, citizens, pressure groups, and international organizations. But the story must start somewhere, and in this chapter our story starts with the ontology of the ideal-typical *homo* we find in public administration.

In the remainder of the chapter, we will provide different versions of the story. To begin with, there is a story about economic motivations, costs and benefits, utility, efficiency, and so on. Max Weber provided the ideal-type of a public manager that is motivated by efficiency – impassionate and precise, mindful of standard operating procedures and the rules of the game in the bureaucracy. This ontology can be developed in various ways: as perfectly rational *homo oeconomicus*, or the boundedly rational *satisficer* of Herbert Simon, or the puzzling and learning individual of Hugh Heclo. Indeed, there is an important story about cognition and learning: the story of the learning individual, the *homo discentis,* goes beyond costs, benefits, and efficiency calculations. Yet this is still a *homo* that proceeds inferentially, with some important and quite fundamental traits of rationality, logic, and calculation in the observable behaviour.

To make things more complicated, but at the same time more realistic, we also have to tell a story about emotions – in this story, Weber is turned upside down because emotions tell the mind what to do, not vice versa. With emotions we no longer see an inferential brain driving behaviour, like for example in the *homo discentis.* Some emotions are pre-cognitive, impulsive, fast responses to stimuli. This emotional component adds warmth and passion to the ontology of the individual we are exploring. One important point we shall make is that the different ontologies are present together in administrative behaviour. Hence, we need to bring all the stories together to find a proper conclusion of our journey.

Indeed, in the conclusions we shall gather these multiple ontologies into the label of *homo faber.* The *homo faber* is not the *homo politicus* – we will reason – because the main motivation in public administration is not to win elections. This does not imply that, in the civil service, individuals do not think politically about their mission, departments, and the policies they manage. But, as we shall see, the micro-foundations of public managers are different.

An important caveat is that we do not want to take a normative stance: we are not motivated by the desire to prove that one *homo* is better than others, or that there *should be* some necessary properties of the public manager. Our aim is rather to capture the essential character of individual behaviour. The result intends to be a multifaceted yet unitary account of the multiple ontologies that characterize the public manager.

Once we have done that and we have talked about the complexity of the *homo faber*, we shall move to the implications for public administration and administrative reforms in the conclusions.

SETTING THE STAGE: FIELD AND RESEARCH QUESTIONS

Although this may sound trivial, we start by noting that the public administration (PA) is populated by public managers. Hence, it makes sense to raise general questions about the foundational assumptions we make about the ideal-typical public manager. To motivate this focus on the ontological nature of the public manager, we also espouse a branch of sociological institutionalism that sees institutions as inhabited organizations: "Institutions such as bureaucracy are inhabited by people and their interactions [...] [they] are not inert categories of meaning; rather they are populated with people whose social interactions suffuse institutions with local force and significance" (Hallett and Ventresca, 2006, p. 213).

We start our inquiry, hence, by asking in general terms:

Who is the (ideal-typical) public manager?

As mentioned in the Introduction, we focus on three types, or three brains, or three ways of thinking about how public managers behave – the *homo oeconomicus*, the *homo discentis*, and the *homo emotionalis*. We will draw on general theories of decision-making, not specific public administration theories (although all of these theories have been heavily applied to PA). This choice allows to fish in the big pond of *models of man* (to paraphrase Simon; today we would say *models of the individual*) developed in the social sciences and the humanities.

It follows that ours is a *study of being*, if we want to dig into the philosophical, or a *study of agency in the PA*, if we want to be more pragmatic. But, what *being*? Which *agent*? If, as we said above, we accept there is something like a public administration where the jobs, ethos and values of bureaucrats are generated and cultivated, we have to have some ideas in mind about the public manager. Historically, these ideas have come by answering two overarching, yet simple questions about the PA as an inhabited institution:[1]

---

[1] Before starting, we acknowledge that theoretical models are useful tools to make sense of complex empirical realities (by simplifying and somewhat dumbing them down), hence our own syncretic unitary model of *homo faber* may be over-specified and prove of little help for supporting empirical analysis. Yet, we find it hard to imagine an individual, let alone a public manager, who acts only upon her full or bounded rationality, learning needs, or other emotional drivers. The empirical reality drives us to reckon that all of these ontologies co-habit in the public

1. What are the major *models of individual* that have historically emerged in the administrative sciences when it comes to the characterization of a key inhabitant of the real-world PA, that is, the public manager?
2. What are the ontological traits of these models? Or, in other words, what are the micro-foundations of the different models of individual agents that underpin behaviour?

MICRO-FOUNDATIONS

To answer the above questions, we make at least one important assumption based on methodological individualism; that is, we ask the reader to reason with us in terms of micro-foundations. Micro-foundations – their characterization, qualification, and eventual aggregation – are, we believe, necessary conceptual and analytical steps for the study of social and collective action.

In the Introduction we said that individuals work in groups, organizations, and political institutions. True. But to understand collective action and aggregate levels of analysis, we must first start from empirically robust models of individual motivation and behaviour, and only after this step, one can engage in the problem of aggregating these models and evaluating group/social dynamics, decision-making, and outcomes. To be clear, our position draws on methodological individualism, but it is far from assuming that collective action and outcomes are the mere sum of individual behaviours. We do not discount the so-called problem of aggregation (see Kamkhaji and Radaelli, 2022). Yet, here we focus on comparing and discussing different micro-foundational models with the aim of finding common grounds – and possibly integrating different models in a unitary view.

Micro-foundations are hence key assumptions about the cognition and behaviour of individuals. Let us begin our journey by exploring the micro-foundations of the first of our *homines*.

THE *HOMO OECONOMICUS*

When it comes to micro-foundations, economics is the social science which more heavily employs this concept and methodically infuses macro-level research with micro-models of behaviour. Macro outcomes are often considered the sum of the choices and behaviour of so-called representative agents (read as: the typical agent, e.g., the typical household, the typical firm, the typical consumer, or investor. For our purposes, we will focus on the typical

---

manager – for difficult it may make empirical analysis. And for difficult it makes theorizing, as we shall see in a while.

decision-maker within the PA). The representative agent, according to economics, is, a bit tautologically, the *homo oeconomicus (HE)*.

In the hardcore/pure Adam Smith version, the *HE* possesses full/perfect rationality. "Full" in the sense of being able to calculate the pay-offs of a vast range of alternative courses of action, and order them in terms of the utility they bring to the agent. Decisions, in the end, are solved computationally, by calculating which course of action brings the highest expected return (utility) to the agent. The *HE* is eminently and entirely self-interested, engages in (constrained) utility maximization, and has such things as perfect foresight (Bray, 1990). Alongside multiple applications in fields such as economics, finance, and management, the *HE* has latitude also in the study of the PA. Historically, the transposition of the *HE* as underpinning public decision-makers came in three fashions.

First, there is the rather faithful impression of the perfectly rational *HE* featuring in rational choice models (Becker 1976). In fact, the self-interested utility maximizer also lies at the heart of rational choice theorizations of the PA. Among them, perhaps the purest form of *HE* can be found in public choice theory (Buchanan and Tullock 1965). Noticeably, the fully rational and fully self-interested bureaucrat of public choice is not moved by drivers different than those of the Smithian butchers, brewers, and bakers. She also has also a fully individualistic view of the collective, whereby public interest is an artifact composed of the aggregation of individual/group (partisan) interests. The equilibrium is typically found on Pareto-efficiency grounds.

A somewhat milder version features in public finance theories (Musgrave and Peacock, 1958). In fact, when this *HE* faces collective action problems within the PA, drawing on a perfect rationality framework, she still does engage in utility maximization, but not in *individual maximization*. She rather maximizes *social utility*. Whereas public choice collective action is a grand bargain among self-interested actors who struggle to fulfil their individual preferences (possibly supporting social welfare through invisible hand effects), in public finance, collective action overtly aims at social utility. Since the assumptions of full rationality and perfect foresight are retained, the ideal-typical public manager of public finance is a benevolent or sociotropic *HE* who, by using taxes to stabilize, allocate, and redistribute, maximizes on a collective utility curve, given a collective budget constraint.

Perfect foresight and information are the core assumptions that allow this benevolent, collectivist *planner* to optimize the allocation of scarce resources to reach full employment. When carefully guided by this version of the HE, the economy reaches the state of general equilibrium. The same assumptions made with micro-foundations allow us to follow equilibrium-seeking decisions that are first individual, then in markets, and finally across the whole economy. Interestingly, this *HE* may be naturally sociotropic or benevolent, or she may be so because she acts behind a Rawlsian veil of ignorance. Yet, introducing a veil of ignorance is a crack to the perfect rationality vase (and an informational tragedy to the central planner). If information is not full, rationality may also not be. The two models (self-interested vs. benevolent or sociotropic) are antithetic in terms of their profound motivations of behaviour (Buchanan and Musgrave, 1999) but agree on perfect rationality, which, as we said and shall see, proves to be problematic.

The first reactions against the *HE* perfect rationality are internal to economics. The Austrian school embraces a philosophical approach where information and rationality need not be perfect to reach an equilibrium in a decentralized order like that of perfectly competitive markets. Behavioural economics instead has an inductive take, where choices *are* revealed preferences and full rationality gets empirically disproved again and again in the most disparate experimental settings (Gerrard, 1993).

But those disciplines that reacted more forcefully and meaningfully to the perfect rationality totem are administrative science (to which we now turn) and public policy analysis (we will talk about the latter in the next section). Pioneered by Herbert Simon (1955), the framework of bounded rationality is nowadays foundational for the study of decisions in the PA. The boundedly rational public manager is, first of all, *Socratic* in that she is aware that her cognition is fallible and biased. She also knows that her knowledge (information) is far from being complete or perfect – but even if it were, her rationality may not be able to process it efficiently.

For Simon, it is impossible to ask the human brain to calculate the alternative pay-offs of a sufficiently wide range of alternative courses of action. Uncertainty and limited computational ability make this simply not feasible. This pragmatic way of thinking about decisions takes us to the core question whether we are still talking about the *HE* or not. The answer is yes: a boundedly-rational individual is still *oeconomicus* in the sense that she prefers more than less. Her preferences are monotonic. The motivation is still to get as much as possible. Yet maximization is impossible. Therefore, this individual is content with *satisficing* (rather than maximizing) behaviour. The search for alternative courses of action is stopped when there is a satisfying level of utility, given the uncertainty of the context and computational limitations to comprehend, describe, and analyse. Instead of comparing all options, the agent takes the first decision that passes a sort of acceptability test, a viable second best. Importantly, instead of tackling rationality, Simon points to informational deficiency. Ontologically, however, we have not shifted to another ground.

And yet: by pointing to the cognitive skills of agents, Simon opens an important pathway to learning. If agents do not have full information about the world and make decisions on the basis of satisficing criteria, they will learn from past mistakes. The public manager observes the outcomes of decisions made with bounded rationality – the world provides new information continuously. Reflecting on the changing state of the world, the public manager adapts expectations. The comparison between past expectations and actual realizations opens the door to learning as a micro-foundation. It is now to the *homo discentis* that we turn. Here we will find the contribution of policy analysis.

THE *HOMO DISCENTIS*

Learning as micro-foundation of behaviour is particularly important in public policy analysis, as shown by the family tree of policy learning (Dunlop et al., 2018). This is also because the opening to the psychological/cognitive dimension marked by the bounded rationality revolution is nowadays a standard feature of much public policy and policy process research. Scholars like Karl Deutsch and Hugh Heclo start from the observation that when optimization is not possible, decisions in public administration and, more generally, public governance are taken in a context of radical uncertainty. As a result of this (Knightian) uncertainty, no single actor can calculate which decision will increase her power. Instead of powering, actors in public administration react to the complexity and uncertainty of the environment by puzzling (Heclo, 1974): public administration is an order of things where individuals constantly wonder about *how to solve problems*, so to speak. And, consequently, making decisions in public administration becomes a problem of learning.

Learning is central in policy theories also because it accommodates ambiguity, as well as uncertainty. Ambiguity means that participants change across time, the search for alternative courses of action takes place in different fora, problems are constantly redefined, and solutions are combined with the changing nature of problems (Zahariadis, 2016).

Importantly, if uncertainty and the computational limitations of humans can be addressed by smart and big data or re-organizations, ambiguity is there to stay in the world of public decisions. It is not a variable that can be reduced to zero. Politics and administration "breathe" ambiguity. Here is an example. A problem may start being addressed in a government department; then questions are asked in Parliament and the issue becomes politicized; a scandal revealed by the press may give the problem a different connotation; economic pressure groups may appear with their own solutions to the problem, whilst experts carry out the search for solutions in technical institutions like independent regulatory agencies; incoming elections may modify the expectations of lead departments and the core executive; international organizations may chip in with their "best practice" and "reviews", suggesting options that had not been considered before. All this is ambiguity: problems, participants, solutions are randomly combined and re-arranged in what is called a garbage can-like process (Cohen et al., 1972).

The dyadic nature of this new (administrative) "man", a boundedly rational agent in an environment of ambiguous collective problems, does not only fit bounded rationality but it also envisages that information and foresight are far from complete or perfect. As a result, a public decision-maker is one that continuously processes new and old information (Jones, 2017) and, crucially, learns out of them and changes behaviour thereof – also in contingent and non-fully inferential ways (Kamkhaji and Radaelli, 2017 – see also the following section).

In terms of stability and equilibrium, learning takes us far away from homeostatic equilibria. It does not imply going back to the previous points of equilibrium in the system. Learning in public policy is the capacity to pursue changing goals. This is an important property of the public manager, especially in a fast-changing environment and under conditions of crisis. Indeed, the kind of learning that Deutsch has in mind is similar to the zigzagging of a rabbit in a field, contingent but self-aware. The rabbit moves from one place to another and re-assesses where to go on the basis of the new point of observation and the things that can be seen and evaluated from the newly-acquired position. What was good-enough, or satisfying, before may no longer be good now.

This learning environment chimes with Heclo's maze in which the walls are re-patterned all the time; individuals are bound in groups acting together; the group disagrees on how to get out of the maze and more fundamentally on whether getting out is the best solution to the problem; there are many groups, not just one, inside the maze, and each group keeps getting in each other's way (Heclo, 1974, p. 308). Clearly, learning belongs to a complex world, more complex than the world of *HE*. But we can still theorize about decisions in this world of complexity and ambiguity. This is the message of learning theories.

Specifically, learning brings us to a new model of the individual, that is, the *homo discentis (HD)*, who is empowered by knowing. To quote Dunlop and Radaelli's approach to the micro-foundations of learning (2018, p. 53), "within learning as framework, *Homo discentis* – the learning, studying and practicing person – is at the heart of all policy-making. No matter what policy environment we operate in, what our role or standpoint, whether we work alone or in a collective, learning is the governing dynamic of our activities. Learning is how people make sense of the world".

But one can go further and take learning as full-blown ontology of policy making – an ontology that complements the classic power-based understanding of politics and political science as a study of power in society (Lasswell, 1936). In this ontological view, learning becomes a systemic and ubiquitous trait of policy-making, implicit and inherent to any form of social interaction, and even more so to any set of policy interactions. This reminds us that policy-making is commonly intended as "a knowledge-intensive process, long associated with concepts of learning" (Hall, 1993, p. 277).

According to this ontological perspective, in every domain of policy-making and in every policy process, new knowledge is always created by and diffused among actors, because of interaction or new evidence becoming available. The creation and exchange of knowledge spawned by policy interactions, crucially, is not an extrinsic feature of the policy process but an immanent one. One can argue that learning takes place systematically, *regardless* of its causal effect on the policy process – *regardless* also because this is what each *homo sapien* does when facing ambiguous decisions. Accepting the banal truism of learning being a legitimate overarching and immanent aspect of knowledge-based social interaction in general, and of a markedly knowledge-intensive process like policy-making in particular, renders us a vivid picture of the *HD* and the differences with respect to the various qualifications of the *HE* discussed above.

Learning further implies bounded rationality and accommodates both self and collective interest perspectives (learning can be political, sociotropic, or individualistic). But still, even the *HD* it is not a radical departure from rational models of cognition and behaviour. Decisions are still taken by individuals who reason on what they observe. These individuals are information processors. Or, in a milder form, they are Bayesian explorers: they keep on making inferences and adjust their prior probabilities about the state of the world when they see new evidence. Crucially, they make decisions with their thinking, reasoning mind, not with pre-cognitive impulses, instinctive reactions to events, and, in one word, emotions. Now, is this always true? Or do emotions play a role in public decisions, choices made in public administration, and ultimately the behaviour of public managers? Indeed, the story can carry on with emotions, as we shall see in the next section.

THE *HOMO EMOTIONALIS*

So far, we have reviewed two broad models of the individual that can help us figure out the micro-foundations of the bureaucracy. We told different stories. A foundational story comes from economics with the *HE*. By means of evolution and permutations, different variations of *HE* took us to the story of cognition and learning: *HD* entered the scene and is here to stay, in administrative sciences as well as in theories of the policy process.

The *HE* does not necessarily have to be a selfish individual / utility maximizer – we have seen sociotropic variations in public economics, for example. Bounded rationality kicked in with a story of a more self-aware *HE* but also paved the way for a more complex (yet realistic) model of individual action: the *HD*.

That being said, the *HD* micro-foundation also comes with its own problems. Although the *HD* is aware of bounded rationality, her puzzling / information processing / learning sequence is not as neat as the story says and, most importantly, it is not what we see in empirical settings, especially in crisis conditions (see our previous work: Kamkhaji and Radaelli 2017; Radaelli, 2022). As we want our models to be empirically robust at the micro level and applicable to crisis situations (after all, today we say we live in a world of poli-crisis and crisis as the new normal),[2] we have, hence, to accept that policy learning, as theorized so far, is an abstract post-hoc observational modelling of one of the most ubiquitous individual cognitive processes. In reality, the true empirical story of learning is one of fast, pre-cognitive reactions to stimuli. Beliefs do not change under conditions of crisis (Kamkhaji and Radaelli, 2017) – yet behaviour does. Decisions are taken, but not on the basis of inferential reasoning about evidence, that is, not on the basis of the adjustment of priors determined by what is observed and learned. So, what could be triggering these behavioural changes?

Enter emotions, or the story of the *homo emotionalis (HEM)*. Yet again, we start from the basics. Individual behaviour is for sure explained by emotions, as shown by a vast literature in psychology. Yet emotions are completely absent from the models that assume rationality as a general framework of action. The *HE* foundations, dominant in economics and part of political science and public administration, can become blinkers. They do not allow us to "see" the role of emotions. And once we widen our peripheral view to acknowledge emotions, the question appears whether emotions are so "irrational" after all. Actually, emotions can build rational, efficient decisions (Haidt, 2012).

One way to explore the story of emotions is to add them to the *HD*. To go back one more time to crisis conditions, some authors have spoken of associative learning, Precisely, "associative learning is thought to be fast acting, automatic, and would require little cognitive resources to act" (Morís et al., 2014: pp. 77–78). This insight, strongly supported by empirical evidence, leads us to acknowledge the presence of emotions like fear (for example, of financial markets), contempt (of corrupt politicians), empathy (for refugees), and anger (for wrong decisions). Emotions are empirically verifiable and often efficient triggers or mechanisms of decision-making (see the literature cited in Haidt, 2012).

---

[2]   The pre-eminence of the puzzling dimension for the public manager can also be anchored to the observation that historically, and increasingly so, bureaucratic action is also called upon to stop crises and solve all sorts of failures.

This is then our final micro-foundation: the *homo emotionalis*. This model is innovative because it integrates rather than excludes the multiple ontologies that underpin the bureaucracy. Importantly, emotions are also part of cognition. They can be considered evolutionary mechanisms developed to perfect behavioural responses under specific circumstances. Think of the importance of emotion regulation for everyday individual and organizational life. In terms of micro-foundational thinking, it has been recently found that conscious awareness, the foundation of rationality and inferential learning, may well be a post-hoc cognitive product rather than the standard way we process information and behave upon it: "Well before conscious awareness becomes available, the human brain can and does considerable preconscious processing of sensory and interoceptive inputs" (Sawada et al., 2022, cited in Marcus, 2023). The investigation of emotions can lead us further, into the realms of literature for example, where so many novels have puzzled and explored the many ways in which emotions "decide" behaviour and the whole trajectory of life. Similarly, emotional responses to arts go beyond the simple stimuli-response patterns and indeed hinge, and are possibly part of, the preconscious ontology that underpins the *HEM*.

The findings on emotions have dramatic implications for the models we have reviewed so far, as they all see rationality as a basic framework for behaviour: instead, what we call rationality may well be a normative ex-post reconstruction of a decision taken on emotional basis (Haidt 2012). If conscious awareness is not instantaneous, this may imply that pre-rational cognitive mechanisms, such as emotions and associative processes, may be influencing rationality, or what we think it is, in ways that are far detached from our current understanding of it. As Marcus (2023, p. 4) puts it:

> Research in the neurosciences challenges the long-held normative view that consciousness is the preferred platform for judgment. It does so because conscious awareness is not capable of executing the normative imperatives long thought to be reasoning's responsibility (Bechara et al., 1997; Pinker, 2021). Consciousness is a platform that is very limited in its ability to construe the world. That diminishes the importance of subjective feeling states in as much as many of the actions humans undertake are deftly executed well before the conscious availability of feeling states (Zajonc, 1980; Hoffman, 2019).

CONCLUSIONS: *HOMO FABER*

We can wrap up our different stories now. Our position is not that there is a single dominant micro-foundation. Rather, a realistic model of the individual takes into account all the varieties we have reviewed – and possibly more. In public administration, there is room for rational calculations of costs and benefits, but also for evidence-informed policy and emotional reactions to events or triggers.

And so, forget Max Weber – at least, forget his argument about a single ideal-type of bureaucrat. After all, Weber was interested in what the civil servant should be, not in describing different types of individuals inside a bureaucracy. Moving beyond Weber then, we argue that robust explanations of administrative behaviour need a unitary micro-foundational consideration or perspective of the "administrative man" if not a unitary "model" – if by model we mean a technical /mathematical formulation of hypotheses and conjectures.

In empirical research, this unitary view must take into account the transition from micro-foundations to group and macro aggregates. We, as society, can use science against a pandemic to avoid political contestations of decisions (*HE*) and learn incrementally (*HD*) even if individually we are scared (*HEM*). Policy-makers in office can change the public narrative about vaccines that reach individuals (*HEM*) to increase the take up of vaccinations in a community and, arguably, generate popularity gains for the incumbent (*HE*). We can leverage the individual fear of inflation "eating up the purchasing power of my salary" (*HEM*) to promote collective austerity policies that create inequalities (*HE*). The models take us on a journey, not to a single station.

Two important questions arise. First, are the micro-foundations in hierarchical order? This is difficult for us to answer, although we acknowledge that in psychology the debate is alive, arguably with a tendency to put emotions on top. The elephant guides the rider, as in the famous book by Haidt (2012). Yet the rider may learn something about emotions regulation, and use some degrees of *HD* and *HE* to tame the elephant, as shown by the public policy interventions inspired by behavioural insights (Thaler and Sunstein, 2021).

Second, what is a distinctive characteristic of the *homo* in the bureaucracy? Is the public manager a variation of the *homo politicus*? In an important contribution, Boda (2013) talks about the anthropology of the *homo politicus*. The politician can be selfish or sociotropic, Boda argues. If motivated by public / social concerns, the *homo politicus* leverages calculations, learning, and emotional triggers to obtain gains for the audience she cares about the most. This audience can be the political party, the government, or the country of the *homo politicus*.

This core motivation cannot be applied to the public manager mechanically. Bureaucrats do not necessarily work with the aim of serving the interests of a party or an electoral district. They are not re-elected, hence they do not have a predefined audience or manifesto to implement. For this reason, our ideal-typical bureaucrat is not, quintessentially, a *homo politicus*. We would rather like to think of a *homo faber*. A public manager with a "can-do" attitude, who is in control of rationality, cognition, and emotions. Rather than colliding, the three elements can be leveraged to improve on public decisions and public policy. Rather than succumbing to emotions, the *homo faber* has the skills and the power to exercise emotional regulation in the design and implementation of public policy. With this observation, we realize we have gone far from our empirical intent, and moved into a normative dimension of what the bureaucracy should do and for whom. This is a very interesting line of research that can be usefully pursued in the future.

Flying back down to earth from the normative sky, we can point to practical implications for administrative behaviour and reforms. One is that all the major applications of artificial intelligence that are on the table for the foreseeable future should be designed by acknowledging that both bureaucrats and citizens are also *HEM*. Emotions should matter far more in the design of chat-bots, for example. Imagine the difference between an empathic chat-bot and a purely *HE* chat-bot. Diagnosing fear and apprehension can be crucial in delivering a service online to a citizen.

Another implication is about how to reduce red tape in public administration. All too often we forget that what makes an administrative obligation a burden is not the time it takes to comply with it, but the irritation it causes, its lack of consideration of the citizen, its stupidity. The *homo emotionalis* feels and judges when a form is sensible and when it becomes a burden, even keeping time-related and cognitive complexity-related variables constant.

Finally, in their public communication about policies, public administrations should be in control of the emotional content of their narratives. It is one thing is to tell a story about migrants or innovation. It is another to tell an emotional story that involves and transports the audience. The emotional dimension can make a difference in terms of delivery and implementation, but it is forgotten by the impersonal bureaucratic language that still dominates how public administration communicates with companies and citizens.

ACKNOWLEDGEMENTS

We gratefully acknowledge the support of the Horizon MORES project, Moral Emotions in Politics, Grant no. 101132601. We are also very grateful to Edoardo Ongaro and the participants at the Luiss Conference on the *Contribution of the Humanities to the Advancement of Public Governance and Public Administration: Perspective and Issues*, Luiss, Rome, 10–11 May 2024.

REFERENCES

Bechara, A., Damasio, H., Tranel, D., and Damasio, A. R. (1997). Deciding advantageously before knowing the advantageous strategy. *Science* 175, 1293–1295. doi: 10.1126/science.275.5304.1293.

Becker, G. (1976) *The economic approach to human behavior.* University of Chicago Press.

Boda, Z. (2013) Homo politicus: Towards a theory of political action and motivation. *Wordl Political Science Review*, 9(1): 71–96.

Buchanan, J.M., and Musgrave, R.A. (1999) *Public finance and public choice: Two contrasting visions of the State.* MIT Press.

Buchanan, J.M. and Tullock, G. (1965) *The calculus of consent: Logical foundations of constitutional democracy.* University of Michigan Press.

Bray, M. (1990) Perfect foresight. In Eatwell, J., Milgate, M., and Newman, P. (eds.) *Utility and probability.* Palgrave Macmillan.

Cohen, M.D., March, J.G., and Olsen, J.P. (1972) A garbage can model of organizational choice. *Administrative Science Quarterly*, 1–25.

Dunlop, C.A. and Radaelli, C.M. (2018) Does policy learning meet the standards of an analytical framework of the policy process?. *Policy Studies Journal*, 46: S48–S68.

Dunlop, C. A., Radaelli, C. M., and Trein, P. (2018) "Introduction: The family tree of policy learning" in Dunlop C.A., Radaelli, C.M. & Trein P. (Eds.) *Learning in public policy: Analysis, modes and outcomes*, Springer Nature, pp. 1–25.

Gerrard, B.J. (ed.) (1993) *The economics of rationality.* Routledge.

Haidt, J. (2012) *The righteous mind: Why good people are divided by politics and religion.* Vintage.

Hall, P. A. (1993) Policy paradigms, social learning, and the state: The case of economic policymaking in Britain. *Comparative Politics*, 275–296.

Hallett, T. and Ventresca, M.J. (2006) Inhabited institutions: Social interactions and organizational forms in Gouldner's Patterns of Industrial Bureaucracy. *Theory and Society*, 35: 213–236.

Heclo, H. (1974) *Modern social politics in Britain and Sweden.* Yale University Press.

Hoffman, D. D. (2019). *The Case Against Reality.* Bristol, United Kingdom: Allen Lane.

Jones, B.D. (2017) Behavioral rationality as a foundation for public policy studies. *Cognitive Systems Research*, 43: 63–75.

Kamkhaji, J.C. and Radaelli, C.M. (2017) Crisis, learning and policy change in the European Union, *Journal of European Public Policy*, 24(5): 714–734.

Kamkhaji, J.C. and Radaelli, C.M. (2022) Don't think it's a good idea! Four building sites of the "ideas school". *West European Politics*, 45(4): 841–862.

Lasswell, H. (1936) *Politics: Who gets what, when, how.* Whittlesey House.

Marcus, G.E. (2023) Evaluating the status of theories of emotion in political science and psychology. *Frontiers in Political Science*, 4: 1080884.

Morís, J., Cobos, P.L., Luque, D., and Lopez, F.J. (2014) Associative repetition priming as a measure of human contingency learning: Evidence of forward and backward blocking. *Journal of Experimental Psychology: General*, 143(1): 77–93.

Musgrave, R.A., and Peacock, A.T. (eds.) (1958) *Classics in the theory of public finance.* Springer.

Ongaro, E. (ed.) (2020) *Philosophy and public administration: An introduction*, 2nd edition. Cheltenham, UK and Northampton, MA: Edward Elgar.

Pinker, S. (2021). *Rationality: What It Is, Why it Seems Scarce, Why it Matters* (1st ed.). New York, NY: Viking Press.

Radaelli, C.M. (2022, September) Policy learning and European integration. *JCMS: Journal of Common Market Studies,* 60(S1), 12–25.

Sawada, M., Adolphs, R., Dlouhy, B. J., Jenison, R. L., Rhone, A. E., Kovach, C. K., et al. (2022). Mapping effective connectivity of human amygdala subdivisions with intracranial stimulation. *Nat. Commun.* 13, 1–20. doi: 10.1038/s41467-022-32644-y.

Simon, H.A. (1955) A behavioral model of rational choice. *Quarterly Journal of Economics*, 69(1): 99–115.

Thaler, R. H., and Sunstein, C. R. (2021). *Nudge: The final edition.* Yale University Press.

Zahariadis, N. (2016) Powering over puzzling? Downsizing the public sector during the Greek sovereign debt crisis. *Journal of Comparative Policy Analysis: Research and Practice*, 18(5): 464–478.

Zajonc, R. B. (1980). Feeling and thinking: preferences need no inferences. *Am. Psychol.* 35, 151–175. doi: 10.1037/0003-066X.35.2.151.

7. Human Geography and the Study of Governance and Society: Perspectives from the UK

Irene Hardill

INTRODUCTION

In this chapter I critically reflect on the linkages and synergies between human geography and the study of governance and society by employing a biographical approach focusing on the United Kingdom (UK). Today, human geography is taught at over 70 UK universities in departments where human geography is often alongside physical geography and environmental science (https://www.thecompleteuniversityguide.co.uk/league-tables/rankings/geography-and-environmental-science). Human geography focuses on the way in which social processes express themselves over space and in turn are enabled and limited by those spatial arrangements (Cox, 2023, 1), including governance structures and public policies. There are different approaches to the study of human geography, first *systematic*: the study of a particular element of geography such as agriculture or settlement, seeking to understand the processes that influence it and the spatial patterns that cause it (Hardill et al, 2001, 243); and second, *regional*: the study of geography through areal differentiation (ibid, 242). Regional geographers can make connections with physical geography. These two geographical traditions offer competing ways of understanding geographical space, with tensions between Euclidean and relational space (Cox, 2023; Massey, 1984).

After this brief introduction the chapter is divided into three sections, first I provide a brief policy context as in the UK the higher education sector because the research we undertake is highly regulated, there is a strong 'audit culture' (ESRC, 2012, 7). I then focus on the human geography governance and society nexus, followed by a conclusion.

UK HIGHER EDUCATION: POLICY CONTEXT

There is a long history of engagement between the world of policy, social science, the humanities and indeed the wider academy. UK social science, which includes human geography, has received direct government funding for postgraduate training and research since 1965 following the Heyworth Report.[11] Government funding for arts and humanities research and postgraduate training started in 1998 following the Dearing Report (AHRC, 2024; Herbert, 2008). Human geography research and postgraduate training is largely funded by the ESRC, but some historical geography projects are funded by the AHRC. Applications for research funding are peer reviewed by academics and 'research users' (from policy and professional practice), and then approved by the relevant research council. The research councils will fund salaries and research expenses (ESRC, 2024).

In addition to providing financial support for the social sciences and the humanities through the UK research councils, the UK Government also gives some financial support to the arts, humanities and social sciences through a grant to the British Academy (BA).[22] The BA now promotes the humanities and the social sciences, 'mobilising the social sciences and humanities for the benefit of everyone', and funds some research (BA, 2023, 5).[33]

Second, another nexus between the worlds of social science, the humanities, and the study of governance and society is the long tradition of academics, professionals and policy makers studying social problems *together*, thereby mobilizing multiple knowledges, not merely epistemic knowledge, but also techne and phronesis (the knowledge of practitioners and citizens) (Flyvbjerg, 2001; Ongaro, 2017). In 2006, for example, members of a multi-disciplinary learned society, the Regional Studies Association (including geographers and policy makers https://www.regionalstudies.org/) collaborated to produce a book on the English regions (Hardill et al, 2006). The book was inspired by the need to make sense of a policy dilemma, namely the struggles with English regional devolution. The response was to try to make sense of the failure of

---

[1] The Social Science Research Council (SSRC) was founded following the establishment of a Committee by the UK Labour Government of Harold Wilson, chaired by Geoffrey Heyworth, who had been Chairman of Unilever in the 1940s and 1950s (Nichol, 2001). In 1983, the SSRC was renamed as the Economic and Social Research Council (ESRC) arguably for political reasons.

[2] The BA received its royal charter in 1902 for the 'promotion of historical philosophical and philological studies' (https://www.thebritishacademy.ac.uk/about/charter-british-academy/).

[3] The BA funds larger projects, including Academy Research Projects Scheme (ARP, https://www.thebritishacademy.ac.uk/funding/academy-research-projects/).

that political experiment and the return of the English devolution question. There are countless examples of such publications in the UK and elsewhere. One example, this time from France, where there has been a strong policy emphasis on regional policy since the 1980s, was led by Marcel Baleste (2001). A team of geographers wrote *La France: les 22 regions* to help understand the key socio-economic challenges of the French regions. Their work has been updated several times.

Third, the careers of individuals can embrace the worlds of public policy, professional practice and the academy (Davies, 2018). Economist William Beveridge, for example, was an expert in unemployment, and former Director of the London School of Economics (LSE) who had spells as a civil servant during the First and Second World Wars. He was a civil servant when he wrote The Beveridge Report (1942, https://www.parliament.uk/about/living-heritage /transformingsociety/livinglearning/coll-9-health1/coll-9-health/). This report outlined five social policy problems, which he termed 'giant evils': idleness, ignorance, disease, squalor and want, and solving these problems framed public policy making in post war Britain. The underpinning evidence Beveridge assembled included various reports and surveys, including locality studies undertaken by social scientists in the 1930s (Beveridge, 1942, 165).

I will end this section by referring to the UK 'audit culture' (ESRC, 2012, 7), including the discipline-based Research Excellence Framework (REF, https:// waw/w.ref.ac.uk/). Human geography forms part of Unit of Assessment (UoA) 14 (Geography and Environmental Studies) and 56 submissions were made from UK universities in the last census of 2021.[44] University-based submissions include nominated research publications of academics,[55] the amount of research income generated etc. over a census period (https://results2021.ref.ac .uk/profiles/units-of-assessment/14). For a number of years the wider impact of research on economy, environment and society undertaken by academics has been assessed through impact case studies. In 2021, 185 U0A 14 impact case studies were assessed (https://results2021.ref.ac.uk/impact). The British Academy and the Academy of Social Sciences[66] commissioned researchers at the Leverhulme Centre for Democratic Science, Oxford University (Wagner et

---

[4] Human geographers at some universities were returned under other UoAs, including social policy.

[5] Articles and books are assessed for their: originality, significance and rigour and graded on a four point scale: world leading, internationally excellent, recognised internationally, recognised nationally. The underpinning research must be new, generating new knowledge, such as theories, data, insights, policies.

[6] The Academy of Social Sciences is a registered charity that promotes the social sciences, it includes 48 member learned societies from across the social sciences and over 1500 Fellows from academia, public, private and third sectors.

al., 2024) to undertake an analysis of the 2021 REF impact case studies from the social sciences, arts and humanities. A recurring theme in these case studies is of scientific 'relevance' to economy and society (cf Staeheli and Mitchell, 2005), a theme I develop further in the next section.

Universities make strategic decisions as to which UoA research active staff are submitted, indeed these decisions often influence staff hiring decisions. While publication strategies are shaped by the REF and the discipline clusters academics are members of, to secure research funding, especially from the UK research councils (social sciences (ESRC) or humanities (AHRC)), an interdisciplinary approach to understand our complex social and economic problems is increasingly encouraged. This tendency is growing in intensity – particularly post-COVID[77] (Hardill et al, 2022a), and the discourse is dominated by talk of mission-oriented research, moonshots etc. (cf Mazzucato 2018). REF results have implications for UK university budgets, which was alluded to back 2012 in the *ESRC benchmarking review: human geography*,[88] 'by the 1990s, with significant prestige and financial awards at stake, competition in the research environment intensified both between and within departments, and administrative and research horizons were focussed around generating outputs for the periodic performance assessments. There was some concern at the time that longer-term intellectual projects are threatened' (ibid, 7). Nonetheless, the Report concluded that accountability aided an improvement in overall research standards and has supporters especially among university departments who have benefited substantially with high performance scores.

UK HUMAN GEOGRAPHY AND THE STUDY OF GOVERNANCE AND SOCIETY

In the remaining part of the chapter, I look in more detail at UK human geography. From the nineteenth century, interest in 'regional studies' in a variety of forms, grew in the UK and elsewhere (Hardill et al, 2006, 5). The French school, and, in particular, Paul Vidal de la Blache, had a strong interest in understanding the causes of regional geographical particularities and these ideas influenced UK geography. The concept of *terroire* was articulated to explain the complex relationship between physical environment, patterns

---

[7] In 2022 I was commissioned along with O Moss (Teesside University), D Wheatley (Birmingham University) and E Speed (Essex University) to undertake an Evaluation of the impact of COVID-19 on methodological innovation. This involved an analysis of almost 200 ESRC/UKRI social science research projects funded as part of the COVID-19 call.

[8] In the 2010s the ESRC commissioned panels of international experts to undertake a series of benchmarking reviews of UK social science disciplines.

of land use, agricultural practices and social formations. Vidal de la Blache (1922) incorporated nature as a dynamic element in human geography, his approach was concerned with the *milieu*, the basic differentiation of the earth's surface; *genres de vie*, lifestyles of a particular region, reflecting the economic, social, ideological and physiological identities imprinted on landscapes; and *circulation*, the disruptive process by which human contact and progress took place between regions (Unwin, 1992).

When looking at the geography of the UK some geographers have adopted a regional approach, others systematic, or indeed combined the two approaches. A regional approach attempts to give a portrait of a region. Until the mid-1970s regional geography was seen as a central component of mainstream geographical scholarship, combining aspects of physical and human geography. This is reflected in the literature, in Mackinder's (1902) classic study *Britain and the British Seas*, for example, or in Demangeon's (1927) *Les Isles Britanniques*. Some authors such as Stamp and Beaver (1933) adopted a systematic approach to understand the UK, focusing on studying the natural resources of the British Isles[99] and the uses made of them. In my much later co-authored undergraduate textbook on the UK (Hardill et al, 2001) we deliberately blurred the regional and systematic approaches to understand the socio-economic landscape.

Following the election of the New Labour Government headed by Tony Blair in 1997 placed emphasis on evidence-based policy making, foregrounding the human geography and the governance and society public policy nexus, including the contribution geographers could make through their focus on 'place' effects (James et al, 2004, 1902–3). Moreover, there is a distinction between policy driven (more instrumental, targeted work on specific government policies) and policy relevant research (engagement with policy through a critique of public policy and support of alternative social organisations, such as trade unions, environmental groups etc.) (ibid, 1904).

The human geography and the governance and society public policy nexus is a recurring theme when trying to understand uneven geographies, at various spatial scales, the region, locality, the city. This nexus was explored in a paper in the *Annals of the Association of American Geographers* when Staeheli and Mitchell (2005) examined what makes research 'relevant'. They noted that relevance had concerned geographers since the nineteenth century, but since the 1960s it had taken a particular significance in 'English-language geography', posing questions of why research should be relevant, how the research becomes relevant and for whom it is (or is meant to be) relevant, and the issues of how relevance cannot be separated from the person making the evaluation (ibid, 358). Each question is challenging, but they concluded that geographers in the

---

[9] The UK and Ireland.

English-speaking world have a broad commitment to addressing problems facing the world. Kevin Ward (2006) picked up the theme of relevance in a review article on the geography public policy nexus by building on Burawoys' writings on public sociologies. He reflected on English language human geography on both sides of the Atlantic, and ended his essay by asking us to reflect on how the public engagement of today might become the policy reform of tomorrow (ibid, 501).

I end this section with a comment on human geography and research methods. Archives have emerged as a subject of methodological interest across the social sciences and humanities, in a range of disciplines beyond history, including human geography (Brewis et al, 2023; Hyacinth, 2019, Mills, 2013a). This 'archival turn' is partly indebted to a Foucauldian analysis of the archive as an artefact of knowledge production (Foucault, 1972). Archives whether containing public records or the archives of private organisations, including charities, are used by geographers and rather than being seen simply as a system of files, the archive is defined as the practice that determines what is filed (Basu and De Jong, 2016, 5–6). This involves a move from considering 'archive as source' to 'archive as subject' that examines 'the practices of collecting, classifying, ordering, display and reuse' (Ashmore et al, 2012, 82; Stoler, 2002). Crucially archives can contain the records of 'hidden voices', offering different perspectives. While archival work is often perceived to be a solitary process, Ashmore et al (2012, 81) reflected on their experiences of working with the owners of archival collections as a 'collaborative practice, communal knowledge formation' (ibid, 82).

In the remaining part of this chapter I use three UK government-funded projects I have been involved with as indicative case studies to illustrate the connections between human geography and the study of governance and society (Stake, 1994). Turning firstly to my PhD. In 1980, I began my postgraduate studies thanks to UK government funding from the then SSRC (now ESRC). My SSRC 'quota' Human Geography award did not stipulate a particular topic, so I was able to scope the precise focus of my thesis with my supervisor, economic geographer Professor John Goddard who had an interest in uneven development (Goddard, 1975).

The economic geographers who inspired my work worked in the UK and North America, and included Doreen Massey (1984), Linda McDowell (1991), Jan Monk (2004) and Susan Hanson (Monk and Hanson, 1982). These feminist geographers highlighted the linkages between paid and unpaid work, and the clustering of women's jobs spatially and sectorally. Doreen Massey's 1984 work, for example, embodies a strong relational approach to thinking about space and place. My PhD focused on the UK wool textile industry, an industry with a strongly feminised labour force.

I received my postgraduate training and subsequently worked in an interdisciplinary social science research centre attached to the Geography Department of Newcastle University, UK, the Centre for Urban and Regional Development Studies (CURDS). The Centre – still operating today – has a tradition of interdisciplinary and collaborative research with research 'users'. The title of my thesis was '*The Regional Implications of Restructuring in the Wool Textile Industry*' and in 1987 I slightly modified my thesis and published it as a book (Hardill, 1987). Although the thesis was deeply spatial, human geography and public policy were intertwined.

I used previously unavailable secondary source data from the private archive of the Wool Jute and Flax Industry Training Board to evaluate the spatial implications of restructuring (1972–1981). The industrial training boards were established following the Industrial Training Act of 1962 to make better provision for the training of workers in specific industries. I gained access to the Board's records on individual employers and I gathered information on wool textile companies, recording the number of employees etc, computerised the data and analysed it. The geographical heart of the industry, West Yorkshire, at the time of my studies was classified as an 'assisted area' (in terms of regional policy) and benefited from spatially-targeted regional policies to boost the economy. Chapter Four of my thesis was devoted to an examination of another government policy initiative *The Wool Textile Scheme* which was launched in 1972 and offered employers all over the UK grants for scrapping old machinery. This scheme focused on improving equipment and productivity.

Immediately after my PhD I continued to research the changing world of work through the many meanings of work, paid and unpaid in the home and in the community with funding from the Leverhulme Trust[10] and ESRC. My analysis of paid work included the study of gender and careers, work (paid and unpaid) and the life course, mobility and work, as well as how people juggle paid and unpaid work, they were all human geography (e.g Hardill, 2002; Hardill et al, 1997).

For the past twenty years my research has focused on unpaid work outside the home, helping non-kin, specifically unpaid voluntary action through social welfare voluntary organisations (charities) helping the young and old. These studies have been interdisciplinary, still place-based and with a strong policy focus, undertaken by teams of social scientists and supported by a series of grants from the ESRC, reflecting in part increasing emphasis on interdisciplinarity by the research councils. But our publication strategy was shaped by

---

[10]   The Leverhulme Trust is a registered charity established in 1925 following a bequest of the philanthropist Lord Leverhulme via scholarships and research.

the REF, including a range of journals for specific UoAs (geography, social policy etc).

One of these grants was for the *Discourses of Voluntary Action at two 'Transformational Moments' of the Welfare State, the 1940s and 2010s* project. From 2017–2021 I led a multi-disciplinary team of social scientists (geography, sociology, social and public policy) and a social historian, with charities as project partners who granted us access to their archives.[11] The 1940s and 2010s can be considered 'transformational moments' in which the boundaries between the state, voluntary action and others were rethought (Brewis et al, 2021). The 1940s when the welfare state was created, and 2010s when economic austerity radically changed – for the worse – the welfare state. While the austerity regime has not abolished the welfare state altogether rather Koch and James (2022) argue that the 'state of the welfare state' is marked not by a straightforward withdrawal or loss of welfare services but rather by an ever more complex reconfiguration of market, state and civic-society or third sector relations, one which draws a range of actors into the job of governing welfare. We argued that it was extremely timely given the considerable transformation to the ways in which welfare services across one policy area, England, with specific implications for the voluntary sector.

The overarching aim of the project was to explore the ways in which different narratives of the role, position and contribution of the voluntary and community sector (VCS) in social welfare provision in England, from voluntary sector representatives, government officials, and the general public, were articulated in the 1940s (1942–51) and the 2010s (2010–18). It focused on four fields of voluntary action: children, youth, older people and the voluntary movement/sector as a whole.

We worked with the Mass Observation Archive[12] to explore public narratives, while government policy documents, speeches and parliamentary debates from the National Archive were used for exploring state narratives, and the private archives of our partner English charities for voluntary sector perspectives. Voluntary sector archives may preserve records of marginalised individuals and communities, whose lives are not recorded elsewhere. But

---

[11] One of our project partners, Children England closed in 2023, and one of our original partners the National Council for Voluntary Youth Services (NCVYS) established in 1936 closed in 2016 just as our research was beginning. We were able to save their archive as it was donated to UCL Special Collections in association with this project.

[12] Mass Observation (MO) was a research project set up in 1937 to study everyday life, which was active until the mid 1950s. It was re-launched in the early 1980s, as the Mass Observation Project (MOP) and is located at the University of Sussex.

these records are often in-house, not necessarily catalogued, and semi-private (Mills, 2013a).

Our project was affected first by Brexit, and then the COVID-19 pandemic. In 2019, one big dissemination event at the House of Lords had to be postponed when Parliament was prorogued (suspended) by Prime Minister Johnson because of the challenges of negotiating a Brexit settlement, and then the rescheduled event had to be delivered online because of emergency legislation that restricted daily life during the COVID-19 pandemic. This legislation prevented us holding our rescheduled event in-person. We have subsequently produced a book on our findings (Brewis et al, 2021) and published a human geography methods paper on the use of private archives, dissemination with the REF in mind (Brewis *et al,* 2023).

The final project is one I led during the COVID-19 pandemic, again with funding from UK government, as part of the ESRC element of the UKRI COVID-19 programme. The project *Mobilising Voluntary Action in the four UK jurisdictions: Learning from today, prepared for tomorrow* involved a multidisciplinary team of academics (geographers, sociologists, and social policy) and co-researchers from key charities active in the four jurisdictions of the UK (England, Scotland, Wales and Northern Ireland) working remotely to undertake a comparative study of social welfare voluntary action responses to the pandemic. The involvement of the charity sector was essential as through their networks evidence was gathered on the impact of the pandemic on the work of volunteers and voluntary organisations.

The devolved nature of the UK policy landscape shaped the design of the project as policies to support voluntary action are 'non-reserved', i.e., public policy is the responsibility of the devolved administrations, so across the four UK jurisdictions public policy towards the voluntary sector is different. Devolution in policy making was very evident during the pandemic emergency including in legislation restricting daily life, such as shopping, social distancing, health policy, opening and closing schools, also varied across the four jurisdictions, and affected the delivery of services by charities. One of the aims of our project was to investigate the ways the voluntary action policy frameworks adopted by the four nations in response to COVID-19 differed, and how effective they were. We focused on the policy and organisational response to co-ordinating and managing volunteers during the pandemic and a publisher quickly published (open access) our findings (Hardill et al, 2022b).

CONCLUSION

In this concluding section I focus on three themes: first the human geography and public policy nexus; second, human geography, the social sciences and the humanities nexus, and third the production of knowledge. A recurring theme in this chapter has been the importance of the human geography and public policy nexus, as illustrated through indicative case studies. For example, in my PhD my data were derived from unpublished data from a UK Government Scheme, and three national and regional policies shaped the restructuring processes I was studying namely: the training of employees; second grants to enterprises to replace old machinery, and third, financial assistance to companies located in certain economically 'distressed' regions. My more recent work on charities and social welfare has also been underpinned by the UK public policy context. The devolved nature of the UK policy landscape, for example, shaped the design of my COVID-19 pandemic project as policies to support voluntary action are 'non-reserved', i.e., public policy is the responsibility of the devolved administrations, so across the four UK jurisdictions policy towards the voluntary sector is different. The 2012 international analysis of UK human geography in the *ESRC benchmarking review of UK human geography* noted that the 'versatility of [human] geography in an interdisciplinary milieu is regarded as a bankable asset' (ESRC, 2012, 35). Human geography is a discipline that is open to interdisciplinary approaches, but dissemination strategies are often geared to REF discipline-specific targets set by an academic's employer university.

Second, human geography, the social sciences and the humanities. Is human geography a social science or part of the humanities, or indeed does it bridge the two? As I mentioned earlier there are different approaches to the study of human geography: *systematic and regional.* These two traditions offer competing ways of understanding geographical space, with tensions between Euclidean and relational space (Cox, 2023; Massey, 1984). When a temporal focus is adopted to the study of social processes and spatial arrangements as in historical geography, then human geography falls within the Humanities whereas when studying economic restructuring, as I undertook in my PhD, my economic geography thesis was social science and funded by the SSRC.

Human geography today is a complex discipline as the 2012 ESRC benchmarking study noted. It is at the convergence of the social sciences, the natural sciences and the humanities, interdisciplinarity and openness to innovation are core characteristics. The international reviewers noted that historical geographers work with those in museum and media studies, political geographers engage with those in international relations etc, and this is conducive to creative experimentation (ibid). I should also mention that an important part of geography is physical geography, and with our current climate challenges there is a renewed interest in this nexus. But this is beyond the scope of our discussion.

Another way human geographers draw on the Humanities is through the methods we employ. I have seen this at first hand through undertaking archival research since the beginning of my academic career, and more recently when trying to understand the evolution of the British Welfare State. As I noted earlier there is a growing trend across the social sciences to engage with pub-lic and private archives, accessing 'hidden voices'. Within human geography this engagement has stimulated a debate about the nature of archives, includ-ing moving from considering 'archive as source' to 'archive as subject' (Mills 2013 a; b). Mills also teases out other important issues for example, she refers to the gaps and silences in archives. If we are serious about understanding the politics of knowledge production, do we – in all our work – need to think more systematically about how we engage with, and re-present our findings? Does the engagement with archives by human geographers act as a bridge between the social sciences and the humanities? Or is archival work just another social science method and data source, representing a shift in perspective?

In my recent work with social historians we have built on and extended this thinking and suggest that an even more active appreciation of the dynamic nature of relationships between researchers, owners of records, and archival material is needed. In using private archives we have highlighted how the dif-ferent iterative processes involved in collaborative archival research lead to the production of co-curated collections. Co-curation involves the negotiated iden-tification, selection, preparation, and interpretation of archival materials. This has implications for both research processes and the new substantive insights they produce (Brewis et al, 2021). Should we think about our research infra-structure, including public and private archives, and how it is supported and protected, the vital enablers of research?

I want to end by reflecting on the production of knowledge, and how we may mobilise multiple knowledges in our research. The social sciences and humanities matter, as do the disciplines we are specifically focusing on in this book because they can help us understand the current complex challenges confronting society wherever we live and undertake research. And this under-standing can be enriched through the mobilisation of multiple knowledges, not merely epistemic knowledge, but also techne and phronesis (the knowledge of practitioners and citizens) (Flyvbjerg, 2001).

In his book on *Philosophy and Public Administration* Ongaro (2017 – 2nd edition 2020) develops this theme with specific reference to public adminis-tration when he highlights public administration as practical experience, the roots of this approach he notes are found in the writings of Plato and Aristotle (ibid, 263). Finally Ongaro's (2017, 266) work on the intellectual tradition of public administration, and the importance of learning from history to under-stand contemporary problems as Machiavelli articulated in *The Prince* and *Discourses on Livy*. There is much to be learned from insights and reflections from the past as Machiavelli articulated, and many of us want our knowledge to bring about change, and looking back can help us contextualise the pre-sent, we are hoping to change the world not merely interpret it (to misquote

Marx) (Johnson et al, 2023). To this end I am a member of the *UK Common Sense Policy Group* https://hosting2.northumbria.ac.uk/commonsensepolicygroup/).[13][13] In anticipation of the UK election in 2024 we worked to produce *Act Now: A vision for a better future and new social contract* an example of policy-relevant social science that looks back to the foundations of the welfare state in the 1942 Beveridge Report, and looks forward presenting actionable plans with the potential to become the policy reform of tomorrow (cf Ward, 2006, 501).

ACKNOWLEDGEMENTS

I am particularly grateful to Edoardo Ongaro, Sarah Mills, Darren Smith and Oliver Moss for their most helpful comments on earlier drafts.

REFERENCES

AHRC (2024) https://www.ukri.org/who-we-are/ahrc/who-we-are/ accessed March 14 2024

Ashmore, P., Craggs, R. and Neate, H. (2012). Working-with: talking and sorting in personal archives. *Journal of Historical Geography* 38, 81–89.

Baleste, M., Boyer J-C., Montagne-Villette, S., Gras, J. and Vareille, C. (2001) *La France: les 22 regions* Paris: Armand Colin

Basu, P. and De Jong, F. (2016) Utopian archives, decolonial affordances: introduction to special issue, *Social Anthropology* 24:1, 5–19

Beveridge, W. (1942) *Social Insurance and Allied Services.* Cmd. 6404, London: HMSO. (see also https://www.parliament.uk/about/living-heritage/transformingsociety/livinglearning/coll-9-health1/coll-9-health/) accessed March 14 2024

Brewis, G., Ellis Paine, A., Hardill, I., Lindsey, R. and Macmillan, R. (2021) *Voluntary action and social welfare: England in the 1940s and 2010s* Policy Press, Bristol, UK

Brewis, G., Ellis Paine, A. Hardill, I. Lindsey, R. and Macmillan R. (2023) Co-curation: Archival interventions and voluntary sector archives. *Area* 55:3, 332–39 (https://rgs-ibg.onlinelibrary.wiley.com/doi/pdf/10.1111/area.12768).

British Academy (2023) *Strategic Plan: 2023–7, Understanding our world, shaping a brighter future* British Academy, London

British Academy (2024) Royal Charter (https://www.thebritishacademy.ac.uk/about/charter-british-academy/). accessed March 13 2024

British Academy (2024) Small Grants Scheme (https://www.thebritishacademy.ac.uk/funding/ba-leverhulme-small-research-grants/) accessed March 13 2024

---

[13] The Common Sense Policy Group comprises academics, policymakers, third sector leaders, community representatives, media figures and people with lived experience. We present consensus on feasible, affordable and overwhelmingly popular evidence-based policies that can form the basis for a programme for progressive Government.

British Academy (2024) Academy Research Projects Scheme (ARP, https://www.thebritishacademy.ac.uk/funding/academy-research-projects/) accessed March 13 2024

Common Sense Group (2024) *Act Now: A vision for a better future and new social contract* MUP: Manchester

Cox, K. R. (2023) *Geography Indivisible: How and why configuration matters*, Routledge, London and New York

Davies, J. (2018) Clement Attlee and the social service idea: modern messages for social work in England *British Journal of Social Work* 48, 5–20

Demangeon, A. (1927) *Les isles britanniques* Paris: Libraire Armand Colin

ESRC (2012) *International benchmarking review for United Kingdom Human Geography* ESRC, Swindon

ESRC (2024) Research Grant Scheme (https://www.ukri.org/opportunity/esrc-research-grant/) accessed March 13 2024

Flyvbjerg, B. (2001) *Making social science matter: why social inquiry fails and how it can succeed again* Cambridge, CUP

Foucault, M. (1969, 1972) *The archaeology of knowledge*, A M Sheridan Smith (trans.) Routledge, London

Goddard, J. B. (1975) *Office location in urban and regional development* Oxford: OUP

Hardill, I. (1987) *The regional implications of restructuring in the wool textile industry* Aldershot: Gower.

Hardill, I., Green, A. E., and Dudleston, A. C. (1997) The 'Blurring of Boundaries' between 'Work' and 'Home': Perspectives from Case Studies in the East Midlands. *Area* 29:3, 335–43

Hardill. I, Graham, D. T. and Kofman, E. (2001) *Human geography of the UK: An introduction* London: Routledge.

Hardill, I. (2002) '*Gender, Migration and the Dual Career Household*' International Studies of Women and Place series London: Routledge

Hardill, I., Benneworth, P., Baker, M. W. and Budd, L. C. (eds) (2006). *The rise of the English regions?* Regions, Cities and Policy book series Routledge: London. This book was published to mark the 40th anniversary of the learned society, the Regional Studies Association

Hardill, I., Moss, O., Wheatley, D. and Speed, E. (2022a) *The impact of COVID-19 on methodological innovation: an analysis of ESRC/UKRI social science research projects (July 2020- July 2021)* ESRC, Swindon

Hardill, I., Grotz, J. and Crawford, L. (2022b) *Mobilising Voluntary Action in the UK: Learning from the pandemic* Policy Press, Bristol, UK

Herbert (2008) *Creating the AHRC: An arts and humanities research council for the United Kingdom in the twenty-first century* London: British Academy

Hyacinth, N. (2019) Black Archives in the UK Report: Opportunities, Challenges and Moving Forward A Race, Culture and Equality Working Group Report, Royal Geographical Society (https://raceingeography.org/ accessed August 2nd 2019).

James, A., Gray, M., and Martin, R. (2004) (Expanding) the role of geography in public policy *Environment and Planning A*, 36:11, 1901–5

Johnson, E. A., Hardill, I., Johnson, M. T. and Nettle, D. (2023) Breaking the Overton Window: on the need for adversarial co-production, *Evidence and Policy*, 1–13 https://www.researchgate.net/publication/374113635_Breaking_the_Overton_Window_on_the_need_for_adversarial_co-production

Koch, I. and James, D. (2022) The state of the welfare state: advice, governance and care in settings of austerity. *Ethnos* 87:1, 1–21

McDowell, L. (1991) Life without father and Ford: the new gender order of post-Fordism *Transactions of the Institute of British Geographers* 16:4, 400–19

Mackinder, H. J. (1902) *Britain and the British Seas* London: Heinemann

Massey, D. (1984) *Spatial divisions of labour: social structures and the geography of production* London: Macmillan

Mazzucato, M. (2018) Mission-oriented research and innovation in the European Union, European Commission, Brussels

Mills, S. (2013a). Cultural-Historical geographies of the archive: fragments, objects and ghosts. *Geography Compass*, 7, 701–713. https://doi.org/10.1111/gec3.12071

Mills, S. (2013b) Surprise! Public historical geographies, user engagement and voluntarism. *Area*, 45, 16–22. https://doi.org/10.1111/area.12001

Monk, J. J. (2004) Women, gender and histories of American geography. *Annals of the Association of American Geographers* 94:1, 1–22

Monk, J. J. and Hanson, S. (1982) On not excluding the other half in human geography *Professional Geographer* 34:1, 11–23

Nichol, A. (2001) *The Social Sciences Arrive* Swindon: ESRC (https://www.ukri.org/publications/ssrc-and-esrc-the-first-forty-years/) accessed March 13 2024

Ongaro, E. (2017, 2nd edition 2020) *Philosophy and public administration* Cheltenham, UK and Northampton, MA: Edward Elgar

Research Excellence Framework (2024) https://www.ref.ac.uk/ accessed February 24 2024

Staeheli, L. A. and Mitchell, D. (2005) the complex politics of relevance in geography *Annals of the Association of American Geographers* 95:2, 357–72

Stake, R. (1994) Case studies, in Denzin, N., and Lincon, Y (eds) *Handbook in qualitative research*, pp 236–48, London: Sage

Stamp, D. and Beaver, S. H. (1933) *The British Isles: a geographic and economic survey* London: Longman

Stoler, A. L. (2002) Colonial archives and the arts of governance. *Archival Science* 2, 87–109

Unwin, T. (1992) *The place of geography* Harlow: Longman

Vidal de la Blache, P. (1922) *Principes de geographie humain* Paris: Libraire Armand Colin

Wagner S., Rahal, C., Spiers A., Leasure, D.R., Verhagen, M., Zhao, B., Li, L., Lu, Y. REF 2021 LCDS Project team and Mills, M. C. (2024) The shape of research impact, London: Academy of Social Science and British Academy (https://acss.org.uk/publications/the-shape-of-research-impact/, accessed April 3 2024)

Ward, K. (2006) Geography and public policy: towards public geographies *Progress in Human Geography* 30:4, 495–503

8. The Concept of State in the Historical Studies

Leonida Tedoldi

The study of the State as an object of historiographical inquiry grew during the latter decades of the twentieth century, between the 1970s and '90s, concurrently and congruently with the advancements in historical investigation concerning 'political authority' (Bezes, 2017, p.251). For this reason, from the 1980s onward, historiography emerged as a vital support for augmenting the scholarly investigation of the State, a domain hitherto predominantly within the purview of legal, political science, and occasionally economic disciplines, mirroring trends observed in the Anglo-Saxon academic sphere. Thus, it was only in the final decades of the twentieth century that historical scholarship began to engage with the State in a more comprehensive manner.

Despite the efforts of the historian Otto Hintze (1861–1940), urging scholars to consider the State not only as a legal construction or an autonomous sovereign entity but also to deem it necessary to place it within its historical process, the relationship between historiography and other scientific disciplines concerning State institutions was conditioned by what an Italian historian, Guido Melis, termed 'the cultural bias against the State': a mindset widely prevalent within the Marxist cultural sphere (Bolaffi, 2002), but not limited to it.

This concept is tied to a culture according to which state institutions would either be a superstructure shaped by the economic structure or a 'mere form' and therefore irrelevant. Such bias was based on a view of the state and its administrative apparatus as instruments of bourgeois oppression that would eventually collapse under their own contradictions.

For these ideological reasons, the bias was also intertwined with the image of the crisis of the 'statehood', highly cherished by liberal jurists, and which has a remote origin (Fioravanti, 1995). So much so that, as some historians of political doctrines affirm, at the beginning of the twentieth century, the crisis of the State was already 'commonplace.' This concept has also deeply influenced European historiography.

In fact, at the beginning of the twentieth century, historiographic notions based on nineteenth-century theoretical and cultural frameworks, particularly of German origin, were being questioned. The crisis of European legal-publicistic thought—and of a certain liberal ideology—also stemmed from the increasing difficulty in interpreting the complexity of the relationship between state institutions and civil society in the first decade of the twentieth century. Not least, anarchist-socialist and Catholic intellectuals had led to pessimistic diagnoses regarding the crisis of the modern idea of the State.

In Italy, jurists such as Vittorio Emanuele Orlando, Alfredo Rocco, and especially Santi Romano were prominent figures who proclaimed the decline of the State, the form of the State based on liberal law, and as it was termed, the 'modern State.' In his essay 'L'ordinamento giuridico' published in 1918, Romano argued that the crisis stemmed from the breakdown of the modern State and its unity into social bodies, consolidated by the economic and professional interests of society. This transformation was occurring during the Giolittian age, spurred by the institutionalization of workers' movement organizations. Rocco, on the other hand, articulated the theory of the crisis of authority of the liberal State in the face of problems arising from social conflicts within fascism. According to Rocco, the danger lay in the increasingly evident emergence of individualistic and anti-State spirit—a core aspect of liberalism—which led to actions of disintegration among individuals and groups, directly affecting the State (D'Alfonso, 2004; Lanchester, 2004; Ferrajoli, 1997).

In the debate on the demise of the State, which was well underway in the first decade of the twentieth century, Hans Kelsen also intervened. Around 1920, the Bohemian jurist asserted the need to dispose of the very concept of sovereignty upon which the entire construction of the State rested—a notion already theorized by other prominent jurists such as Hermann Heller. This included challenging the State itself as the centerpiece of nineteenth-century legal doctrine. The underlying attempt was to dismantle the 'formalistic' conception of the 'State-person', a product of legal positivism, and instead advocate in political discourse a theory centered on the 'positive State' (Portinaro, 2005, p.4).

The 'resurgence of Leviathan', fueled by Carl Schmitt's influential essay 'Political Theology' in 1922 and the fragmentation of the Weimar constitutional experience, revived the myth of sovereignty through the theoretical assertion of the 'total State,' based on the monopoly of the 'ultimate decision'.

Therefore, to summarise, the history of the crisis of Stateness has deep roots, dating back at least to the late nineteenth century. It is worth noting that Hans Kelsen revisited these themes in his 1944 essay 'Peace through Law,' proposing a theory of sovereignty limitation aimed at introducing judicial guarantees against violations of peace outside states and human rights within them. Subsequently, the aftermath of totalitarian regimes prompted scholars to reflect on the boundaries and political significance of sovereignty.

The complementarity between the 'rule of law' and the 'power-State' became an antinomy, to borrow Pier Paolo Portinaro's words (Portinaro, 2002, pp.387–404).

As Pietro Costa writes, the new phase of post-war European political-institutional reconstruction 'stimulated the widespread establishment of constitutional rule of law that ensured judicial oversight of legislative actions and appeared to provide secure protection of fundamental rights' (Costa, 2002). So, in the post-World War II era, 'liberal statism' began a phase trajectory, and a 'new cycle of political primacy' emerged, re-centering the debate on the sovereignty of Constituent Power and the primacy of the Constitution as a 'fundamental choice for a particular system of values'. At this juncture, European institutionalist historical research, which had been culturally aligned with democratic theory, contributed significantly to the debate on the legitimization processes of state institutions and administration.

At this time, institutionalist historical research distanced itself from the 'Hegelian tradition of the State', thereby offering a perspective on the dynamics of governance and legitimacy. In Germany, this is quite evident, for example, in the 1960s, when the culture of philosophy of history deteriorated, and a close collaboration began among German historiography and that of the Anglo-Saxon and European traditions in historical research on State institutions and public administration. In many respects, this also marked the overcoming of exclusive political interpretations.

In Italy, unlike Germany, between the 1950s and 1960s, historical research on public administration took on a programmatic and organizational character coinciding with the centenary of unification. Moreover, during these years, the reconstruction of the history of administrative sciences, and particularly of the science of administrative law, was not part of the debate or 'research agendas.' Administrative law was understood not only as a set of norms but also as a science. Until the 1970s, in most contemporary theories of politics, political institutions (legislative assemblies, the judicial system, etc.) saw their importance reduced compared to the role they played previously in theories, for example, of political scientists, economists, and even sociologists. In the meantime, in the second half of the 1960s, political science strengthened its scientific production on the theme of the (Western) State.

In the author's view, the works of Stanley Hoffmann provided a significant impetus to reflection on what appeared to be the irreducibility of the crisis of the Nation-State. At the same time, he demonstrated the potential 'capabilities' of the State as a subject capable of consolidating itself within the international system (Hoffmann, 1966, pp.862–915). Hoffmann transcends the view, which, however, was destined to last until the end of the 1970s, of political institutions as mere arenas within which political behavior was enacted.

However, in the 1970s, the most significant cultural influence for studies on the State came from historical and sociological analyses rather than political science ones. During this era, thanks to contamination with Anglo-Saxon and American sociologist culture and historiography, or perhaps one should say an interdisciplinary approach, scholars began to adopt certain definitions and concepts, such as 'limited State', 'State of the apparatus', and 'post-modern State'. In a way, scholars acknowledged that the 'State paradigm' (and therefore also the administrative State) was a crucial conceptual reference point, thus beginning to provide significant support for research on the State (and public administration).

The 'institutionalist' historical research, increasingly viewed as a social science, engaged deeply with the intellectual legacy of Max Weber, often mediated through the works of scholars like Hintze, and definitively forged links with sociology. In Italy, notable contributions emerged in the form of three volumes on the State and the history of administration in major European states of the modern era, overseen by historian Ettore Rotelli and historian of doctrines Pierangelo Schiera (Rotelli and Schiera, 1971–1974). These volumes not only advanced the study of administrative history in Italy, but also lent support to the broader field of administrative sciences.

It should also be added that these scientific publications accounted for the results of research by French historiography, which was the first to develop a methodological transformation even in studies on public administration (let us say so even if it is not correct to use the term 'administration' in the ancien régime), addressing the persistence of institutional practices, specialized languages, and administrative cultures (Legendre, 1968; Thomas, 1995).

Simultaneously in Italy, another influential figure in the study of institutions, Roberto Ruffilli, integrated his scholarship with insights derived from the intersection of institutionalist historiography and social theory (Ruffilli, 1979). This perspective, which viewed the State as the 'social group of its officials', placed the administrative State at the core of analysis. Consequently, even in German historiography, the focus shifted away from the State as an exclusive object of investigation, instead achieving greater recognition in the field of administrative history.

So, in the second half of the 1970s, the enrichment of historiography in the study of public administration is most notably evidenced by the historical analysis of the social groups within the State bureaucracy, social mobility, and consequently, the role of the State apparatus and public administration as avenues for social ascent. This exceeds the notion of high bureaucracy solely as a ruling and dominant class, a perspective commonly found in political science and sociology research. These interpretive trends within European historiography lent cultural support to the reevaluation of the State.

For instance, during this period in Germany, historical scholarship delved into the role of representative assemblies of provincial states in the modern era and examined the autonomous administration of municipalities, such as Ruhr, as fundamental political and democratic structures, representing a form of municipal socialism that laid the groundwork for the welfare State. Subsequently, a second phase of research focused on the high bureaucracy and the issue of mobility within the elite ranks of public administration officials.

European historical scholarship also intersected with the reception of sociological research paradigms, leading to the incorporation of theories concerning the structural and functional systems of State apparatuses and their interplay with historical studies on the exercise of power, notably derived from Weberian principles ('administration is power in everyday life'). Furthermore, notable contributions, such as Hans-Ulrich Wehler's *Das Deutsche Kaiserreich , 1871–1918* (Wehler, 1985), underscored the enduring role of the State as a 'power State', central to the decision-making process and the implementation of policies. According to Wehler, the action of the State (and public administration) succeeds when it represents the majority of existing interests; it fails when it no longer represents the interests of those who hold power. Clear allusions to Weber are apparent, as he posited that the modern bureaucratic state, or bureaucracy, constituted the most efficient organizational structure for achieving any objective, albeit without ascribing it autonomy.

A push towards strengthening 'interdisciplinarity' on these research topics was propelled by the volume *Bringing the State Back In* (Evans, Rueschemeyer, and Skocpol, 1985) in the midst of the neoliberal conservative revolution and the attack on welfare. The volume took shape at a crucial moment for global politics and the social sciences. In the preceding decades, new nations had emerged during the process of decolonization.

The revolutions had shaken some regimes in the 'Third World,' echoing themes of previous social revolutions in Europe and China. Throughout the world, national governments had become more active in promoting economic development. Yet, the post-war social theories, especially in the academic circles in the US, had treated this as a reflection or 'by-product' of social, economic, and cultural dynamics. Therefore, according to this research group, there was a need for improvement in conceptualizing the structures and capacities of States to more adequately explain how they are formed, organized, and how they influence society.

For these scientific reasons, the research group, comprising sociologists led by Evans, Rueschemeyer, and Skocpol, considered it essential to pay greater attention to States as potential autonomous actors and to the ways in which their actions and institutional structures indirectly shaped politics. The research group demonstrated the effectiveness of the relationship between sociological and historical research in examining the State in its structures and the role of its structures and policies in capitalist industrial democracies.

There were three research tracks: the State in the decolonization process, the 'conceptualization of structures' and 'capacity' of States, and the latter as autonomous actors shaping politics through State institutions. The research group once again followed the investigations of Hintze and Weber on the subject of the 'State', in terms of assemblies, apparatuses, and public administrations claiming control over territories and people; apparatuses seen as resources of money, personnel, violence, and expertise.

Thus, *Bringing the State Back In* surpassed the preference for studying informal structures (gender, class, particular interests) that had previously dominated American sociology. In doing so, it simultaneously challenged the cultural dominance of 'behaviorist' analysis, which was highly influential in political science and had prioritized the 'microphysics of informal powers' over the formal dynamics of power. The 'State paradigm' became the 'central explanatory variable' for understanding the formation of social and political interests (Barkey and Parikh, 1991).

As Carlo Galli wrote in 1983, the identification of this 'variable' marked, for the liberal tradition, the newly acquired awareness of the autonomy of the State (Galli, 1983, pp.111–131). Let us not forget that structural-functional studies of neo-Marxist derivation interpreted the State as a structural phenomenon; that is, as a variable dependent on the economic process.

During the same period, the research conducted by sociologist Michael Mann illustrated to historiography the resurgence of sociological inquiry (Mann, 1986) into the autonomy of political systems through an institutional and functional problematization of the levels of analysis concerning the logics and organization of social power, characterized by ideological, economic, military, and political elements (comprising the so-called IEMP model). These interpretative trends were further advanced by scholars such as Brian Downing (1992), Theda Skocpol, and Anthony Giddens. Very much in tune with Weberian theory, Mann significantly influenced English and French historiography and, perhaps more than commonly believed, Italian historiography as well. He also undoubtedly influenced German historiography, as evidenced by the considerable importance given to his work in Wolfgang Reinhard's 'Geschichte der Staaatsgewalt'.

From the mid-1980s, while the state paradigm became a predominant area of Anglo-Saxon research, from another perspective Luhmann's theoretical-sociological approach appeared to diminish. According to this approach, the State could not be aligned with the logic of a complex society; instead, it would increasingly demonstrate its growing impotence in the face of lobbies and the impossibility of hierarchically governing a society from the center. In fact, for instance in Italy, the fifteen years (1980–1995) that separate Ruffilli's book, mentioned earlier, from Romanelli's book (Romanelli, 1995) and the important research of the 1990s, were years of profound epistemological reflection on the conception and role of the State and State sovereignty. During these years, a segment of Italian historiography argued that linking the notion of the State to the development of power dynamics in the nineteenth and twentieth centuries was weak and sustained only by 'legal ideology.'

Evidence of this is found in Pietro Costa's work, *Stato immaginario* (Costa, 1986), which favored the history of disciplinary discourses that constructed and imagined the State over the pursuit of strengthening the historiography of the State itself. Meanwhile, another segment of historiography, in a nearly opposite manner, believed that the notion of the State retained a precise meaning that was 'inextricably material and ideal' (Rugge, 1997, p.124).

This debate led to an expansion of differing viewpoints within historiography, contrasting an early modern State, which was less Weberian,[1] with a 'modern', 'Weberian', constitutional, and national State. More importantly, it reinforced the conviction that the viability of the State paradigm could be considered without starting from its presumed crisis, but by identifying its strengths. So, it was necessary to conceive of States and their structures not as arenas of contending social forces, but as sets of organizations (Pedersen, 1991, pp.125–148; Almond, 1988, pp.853–874). Sociological research on this topic has disassembled and reassembled the forms of Statehood, aiming to highlight primarily ideological evasions.

Simultaneously, this period initiated a wave of studies on power, which had been relegated to the sidelines in administrative sciences. In response to this momentum, historiography also questioned the meaning, idea, and logic of the State. In this regard, I would like to borrow a phrase from historian Alberto Tenenti. In 1987, he wrote, 'The State is what connects the various forms of power and the awareness of their nature' (Tenenti, 1987) – particularly concerning the maintenance of its legitimacy and organizational articulation.

These are the years when German historiography of the modern age focused on the 'State for Estates' and drew attention to the corporate-estate society that acted in the centuries of the gestation of the 'modern State' in Europe, mobilizing a variety of power organization models. In this way, the 'pluralistic' structure of power in 'ancien régime' societies emerged. And this approach

---

[1] The historiography concerning the State in the early modern period defines what could be termed the State as a form of integration process towards a 'common horizon' or a 'coherent system', or even towards a 'political imaginary', where 'political' denotes a blend of hierarchy, necessity, effectiveness, justice, and dynamic respect for the interests of the institutional subjects involved. This 'paradigm' does not exclude the recognition of a trajectory of power concentration, which began to take shape during the 14th century.

led to an interpretive turning point not only in historiography (contemporary historiography as well) but also in the very idea of the State.

Historical and sociological inquiries illuminated that State institutions were not merely 'receptacles' for individual and collective behaviors subjected to political maneuvering. Instead, they emerged as pivotal determinants in political dynamics, in the manner of social classes, economic paradigms, and technological changes.[2] Therefore, from the late 1970s through the early 1980s, the State became 'genuine' historiographical subjects.

The administrative State emerged as a focal point of scholarly investigation for institutionalist historians and political science researchers alike. In the latter field, the study of the influence of public institutions on society began to dismantle the dominance of rational choice theory, which was less inclined to consider the role of institutions in societal dynamics (March and Olsen, 1989). It was recognized that the State is constituted by concrete institutions, relationships, processes, and the production of preferences and meanings for citizens.

Additionally, the 'autonomy' of political institutions was acknowledged, as well as the fact that institutions not only serve as arenas where diverse social and political forces interact, but also possess the capacity to define values, norms, and identities, alongside establishing a political order and influencing societal change.[3]

European historians absorbed much of this theoretical discourse on institutions from Anglo-Saxon scholars. Consequently, in the 1980s, historians embraced 'deconstruction' as a methodological tool for historical investigation, almost as if they had internalized Derrida's theoretical framework.[4]

Through the study of the interactive factors that determined the vertical and horizontal ties between institutions and society, the 'adaptive capacity' of the State and public administration, as well as political power over time, was highlighted. Moreover, as argued by Clegg, Courpasson, and Philipps, political power is 'defined as a generalized capacity to influence the allocation of resources for attaining collective goals' (Clegg, Courpasson, and Phillips, 2006, p.193). These research directions subsequently bolstered the analysis

---

[2] It should not be forgotten that, from this point of view, the historical-economic research of Douglas North has further enriched such interpretations.

[3] On these topics, I believe it is interesting to examine the works of the Italian jurist and historian Sabino Cassese, whose studies have gained widespread recognition across Europe.

[4] Moreover, historical research also embraced the methodological shift in the sociological field that proposed applying models developed by 'systems theory' to the study of the State, intersecting with administrative science, which envisaged the 'autonomization' of the State as a political-administrative subsystem, alongside other subsystems of society.

of other research topics, such as the 'politicization of administrative activity,' which is what Wolfgang Reinhard laid out in his work *Geschichte der Staatsgewalt* (Reinhard, 1999).

For all these reasons, historical studies enriched the debate on two research topics: first, the analysis of the monoply on the legitimate exercise of bureaucratic power and decision-making processes, and second the examination of the legitimacy underlying the implementation of political decisions. The State, more generally, has become the focal point for the resolution of social conflicts originating from the struggle for the conquest of available resources of power, wealth, and public reputation. Over time, this issue has taken on a certain prominence alongside the analysis of decision-making processes.

Moreover, the analysis of the relationship between normative frameworks and real-world implementation, as well as the scrutiny of 'administrative practices' as mediators between State action and its recipients (the society), has become imperative (Bourdieu, 2012).

Additionally, a whole strand of studies has consolidated in these years, finding its references in the works of Alan S. Milward on the Nation-State, particularly around the end of the 1980s when the wave of globalization began to reach Europe. From this perspective, Milward's works are milestones and remain pivotal references for historical studies, especially concerning the trajectory from the reassertion of the Nation-State as a political actor after World War II to its decline in the 1990s with the end of the Cold War (Hall, 2003), and its intertwining with European integration. The British historian demonstrated the strength of the state in society within the context of the bipolar conflict until its project-based expiration.

This transitional phase not only progressively affirmed a redistribution of capital in favor of richer countries but also shifted the redistribution of political power from democratic institutions to financial interests, leading to democratic deficits and the growth of inequalities (Milward, 1992; Milward, 1993). Milward was an economic historian and his works were, in a sense, the culmination of a long reflection on the concept of the State in historiography, which intertwined with economic history and the history of European institutions.

In some ways, Milward further developed the reflections presented in the volume *Bringing the State Back In*, particularly on the concept of the 'autonomy' of the political actor 'State' as an object of investigation. In this regard, his work became a point of reference for historiography in the following decades, which essentially are our contemporary times. This is also because he transcended the concept of crisis as the 'perennial condition' of the State, rearticulating a historical analysis that provided ground for dialogue among historians, political scientists, jurists, and economists on the concept of the State in the face of changes imposed by globalization (Bickerton, 2013; 2017).

These discussions continue today; for example, when we debate the role of the Maastricht Treaty and the European Union.

To conclude, I would like to echo the words of Italian historian Marco Meriggi from 2005: the State, the 'real' one, can be defined as an institutional enterprise capable of manifesting in various forms (patrimonial, bureaucratic, etc.) that adapts over time, not depleting itself entirely, but rather transforming into a 'terrain of contention' and certainly not an 'inert body' (Tedoldi, 2005, pp.9–11).

This is precisely what is happening in our current era.

REFERENCES

Almond, G.A. (1998). The Return to the State, *American Political Science Review*, 82(3).

Barkey, K., Parikh, S. (1991). Comparative Perspectives on the State, *Annual Review Sociology*, 17, 525–525.

Bezes, P. (2017). The Neo-Managerial Turn of Bureaucratic States, More Steering, More Devolution, in King, D., Le Galès, P. (eds.) *Reconfiguring European States in Crisis*. Oxford, Oxford University Press.

Bickerton, C.J. (2013). *European Integration: From Nation-States to Member States.* Oxford, Oxford University Press.

Bickerton, C.J. (2017). Nation-State to Member State: Trajectories of State Reconfiguration and Recomposition in Europe, in King, D., Le Galès, P. (eds.) *Reconfiguring European States in Crisis*. Oxford, Oxford University Press.

Bolaffi, A. (2002). *Il crepuscolo della sovranità. Filosofia e politica nella Germania del Novecento.* Roma, Donzelli.

Bourdieu, P. (2012). *Sur l'État. Cours au Collège de France 1989–1992.* Paris, Seuil.

Clegg, S., Courpasson, D., Phillips, N. (2006). *Power and Organizations.* London, Sage.

Costa, P. (2002). Lo Stato di diritto. Un'introduzione storica, in Costa, P., Zolo D. (eds). *Lo Stato di diritto. Storia, Teoria, Critica.* Milano, Feltrinelli.

Costa, P. (1986). *Lo Stato immaginario. Metafore e paradigmi nella cultura giuridica italiana fra Otto e Novecento.* Milano, Giuffrè.

D'Alfonso, R. (2004). *Costruire lo Stato forte.* Milano, FrancoAngeli.

Downing B.M. (1992). *The Military Revolutions and Political Change: Origins of Democracies and Authocracy in Early Modern Europe.* Princeton, Princeton University Press.

Evans, P., Rueschemeyer, D., Skocpol, T. (eds.) (1985). *Bringing the State Back In.* Cambridge, Cambridge University Press.

Ferrajoli, L. (1997). *La sovranità nel mondo moderno. Nascita e crisi dello Stato nazionale.* Milano, Feltrinelli.

Fioravanti, M. (1995). Lo stato di diritto come forma di Stato. Notazioni preliminari sulla tradizione europeo-continentale, in Gherardi R., Gozi, R. (eds.) *Saperi della borghesia e storia dei concetti fra Otto e Novecento.* Bologna, il Mulino.

Galli, C. (1983). Lo Stato come problema storico-politico. Osservazioni su alcuni recenti contributi, *Il Mulino*, 285.

Hall, A. (2003). Nation-States in History, in, Paul, T.V., Ikenberry, G.J., Hall, J.A. (eds) *The Nation State in Question.* Princeton, Princeton University Press.

Hoffmann, S. (1966). Ostinate or Obsolate? The Fate of the Nation-State and the Case of Western Europe, *Deadalus*, 95(3).

Lanchester, F. (2004). *Pensare lo Stato. Giuspubblicisti nell'Italia unitaria*. Roma-Bari, Laterza.

Legendre, P. (1968). *Histoire de l'administration française de 1750 à mos jour*. Paris, P.U.F.

Mann, M. (1986). *Sources of Social Power, Volume I: History from the Beginning to 1740 AD*. Cambridge, Cambridge University Press.

March, J.G., Olsen, J.P. (1989). *Rediscovering Institutions, Organizational Basis of Politics*. New York, The Free Press.

Milward, A.S. (with the assistance of G. Brennan and F. Romero) (1992). *The European Rescue* to *the Nation-State*. London, Routledge.

Milward, A.S. (with F.M.B. Lynch, R. Ranieri, F. Romero, V. Soresen) (1993). *The Frontier of National Sovereignty: History and Theory, 1945–1992*. London, Routledge.

Pedersen, O.K. (1991), Nine Questions to a Neo-institutional Theory in Political Science, *Scandinavian Political Studies*, 14(2).

Portinaro P.P. (2002). Oltre lo stato di diritto. Tirannia dei giudici o anarchia degli avvocati?, in Costa, P., Zolo, D. (eds.). *Lo Stato di diritto. Storia, teoria, critica*. Milano, Feltrinelli.

Portinaro, P.P. (2005). Una disciplina al tramonto? La Staatslehere da Georg Jellinek all'unificazione tedesca, *Teoria politica*, XXI(1).

Reinhard, W. (1999). *Geschichte der Staatsgewalt Eine vergleichende verfassungsgeschichte Europas von den Anfängen bis zur Gegenwart*. Berlin, Beck.

Romanelli, R. (ed.) (1995). *Storia dello Stato italiano dall'Unità ad oggi*. Roma, Donzelli.

Rotelli, E., Schiera, P. (eds.) (1971–1974). *Lo stato moderno*, I–III. Bologna, il Mulino.

Ruffilli, R. (ed.) (1979). *Crisi dello Stato e storiografia contemporanea*. Bologna, il Mulino.

Rugge, F. (1997). Storia dello Stato: Istituzioni e dottrine giuspubblicistiche, *Storica*, 7.

Tedoldi, L. (2005). Introduzione. Quel che resta dello Stato, in Tedoldi, L. (ed.) *Lo stato dello Stato. Riflessioni sul potere politico nell'era globale*. Verona, Ombre Corte.

Tenenti, A. (1987). *Lo Stato: Un'idea, una logica. Dal comune italiano all'assolutismo francese*. Bologna, il Mulino.

Thomas, Y. (1995). *Histoire de l'administration*. Paris, La Découverte.

Wehler H.-U. (1985). *The German Empire from 1871 to 1918*. Oxford, Berg.

9. Historiography and Public Administration: A Story of Disciplines

Fabio Rugge

INTRODUCTION

My approach to the subject of this chapter will be neither theoretical nor normative. I am not going to theorize on how the relationships between historiography and public administration *have been* practiced; nor will I formulate any sort of instruction on how they *ought to be* practiced. In the typical historians' fashion (and occasionally mimicking it), I will rather recall five episodes capable of shedding light on those relationships. The episodes will be followed by an epilogue. This rhetorical ploy will allow me to introduce the reader to a question – the one summarized in the title – which is as complex as it is instructive, and whose systematic treatment would require much more space than I have at my disposal. The sequence of episodes will also help me in proposing some final, very general considerations.

Before starting this 'story of disciplines', two clarifications are in order. In the following, I will happen to consider public administration equivalent to administrative science or administrative sciences. This equivalence is certainly arguable, but for the purpose of this text, it is – I believe – acceptable. My second clarification concerns a character who will hover over this 'story of disciplines' but will not feature in it: law. The triangulation between history, administrative studies, and law is of extreme interest and should not be neglected. I will do it here, partially at the expense – I admit – of the truthfulness of the story. However, the reader will find traces of the 'hidden character's' action here and there.

FIVE EPISODES

Somewhere in Alabama

The scene of my first episode takes place in a classroom of the University of Alabama in 1956. There, Dwight Waldo, a professor at Berkeley, holds the third lecture of a series titled *Perspectives on Administration* (Waldo, 1956). This particular lecture is dedicated to the 'Perspectives of History'. Waldo has already published his *The Administrative State* (Waldo, 1948), a significant contribution to the field of Public Administration. Also, in 1952, he has crossed swords with the Nobel Prize-winner-to-be, Herbert Simon, on the pages of the *American Political Science Review*, in one of the most 'memorable and acrimonious' debates in the intellectual history of American Public Administration (Harmon, 1989: 437; Raadschelders, 2023).

Waldo is not yet *the* leading figure of that field, but he will soon become one, as vice president of the American Political Science Association and president of the National Association of Schools of Public Affairs and Administration, as well as a member of the editorial board of *The American Political Science Review* (1959–1963) and of *Public Administration Review* (1958–1966). Of this last journal, he will be the editor-in-chief for about eleven years, from 1966 to 1977 (Brown and Stillman II, 1986).

All this is yet to come; but in his Alabama lecture, Waldo already speaks for the discipline. He believes that public administration scholars have a lot to learn from history. In *The Administrative State*, especially in its opening chapter, he has already shown his sensitivity to history; that is, to the influence that the historical context has on the development of administrative ideas and the administrative enterprise. And, later on, in 1967, when, during a reception, the New York governor Nelson Rockefeller asked him what his field of research was, he simply answered, 'History' (Stillman II, 2021: 129).

In this lecture, Waldo spells out explicit and precise opinions on the usefulness of historiography for the Public Administration scholar. He maintains that the observation of the past can provide general teachings (he calls them 'philosophical') as well as problem-solving techniques. On this point, he takes up and cites *verbatim* a 1951 article by Harvey C. Mansfield on the 'Uses of History' (Mansfield, 1951), which he has already drawn from in his book, *The Study of Public Administration* (Waldo, 1955).

Beside this, Waldo shows appreciation for Max Weber's typological approach, and also displays a fair knowledge of a more genuinely historiographical literature. For instance, he mentions Charles A. Beard, one of the most influential American historians of the first half of the 20th century, and makes reference to a couple of excellent history books. Among others, he names Tout's *Chapters in the Administrative History of Mediaeval England* (Tout, 1920–1933) and Dorwart's *The Administrative Reforms of Frederick William I of Prussia* (Dorwart, 1953) (the latter a work he reviewed a couple of years earlier in the *American Political Science Review* [Waldo, 1954]).

Many of Waldo's research interests therefore come together in his Alabama lecture. Nonetheless (or possibly because of this), his treatment of the relationships between historiography and Public Administration is far from systematic. He himself states that he proceeds 'by "free association" without too much regard for logical progression and consistency' (Waldo 1956: 54).

Indeed, the conceptual structure of the lecture is not impeccable. For instance, in his discussion, Waldo does not seem to distinguish between *history* and the *past* (Lanzalaco, 1997: 46–47; Jenkins, 1995: ch. 1, sect. 1); whereas this difference is not only relevant in theory but can prove crucial when dealing with practical problems of governance, administration, and management (Brändström et al., 2004: 194; Rugge, 2008: 705). In any case, Waldo does not envisage the establishment of administrative history as a specific field in which studies on administration and history can converge and integrate. His crucial concern stays with Public Administration, whose autonomy from political science he will soon start asserting.

Cambridge, UK

My second scene opens in Cambridge, UK, in another continent and a different disciplinary province. There operates Geoffrey Rudolph Elton, a Jewish scholar, born as Gottfried Ehrenberg in Tübingen before fleeing to the UK. As Waldo is lecturing at Alabama University, some students possibly have on their desks the book Elton has recently published: *The Tudor Revolution in Government: Administrative Changes in the Reign of Henry VIII* (Elton, 1953). It is the first of several works that will make Elton the most authoritative interpreter of Tudor absolutism. His thesis is that the essence and the tool of that absolutism was the creation of a modern bureaucratic system by Thomas Cromwell.

Administration and its transformations were crucial in Elton's research. To him, the 'real' history, the 'hard' history 'must consist of the actions of governments and the governed in the public life' (Elton, 1967: 172). In an article concerning the early Tudor Council, Elton specifies what a historian needs to reconstruct when dealing with an administrative institution: its 'structure, membership, functions, procedure, manifold manifestation, and changing nature' (Elton, 1964: 296). This sounds like an appropriate program for an administrative historian. But the author does not hesitate to tackle topics that could certainly be of interest to scholars of Public Administration and Public Management. For example, in the article I just cited (my next episode will clarify why I insist on this one text), Elton discusses the following statement: 'A large Council cannot be a working Council' (Elton, 1964: 274).

The assertion evokes a classical discussion on the size of political bodies (e.g., Heller, 1996: 1182; Sartori, 1975) and would probably be worthy of a painstaking discussion in a retreat of meeting scientists ('meeting science' is – I learned – a 'relatively new', 'flourishing' field, focusing on meetings and never to be confused with 'team science' [Olien et al., 2015]). Yet, nothing would be more distant from Elton's attitude than such a 'scientific' approach. The Cambridge historian analyzes the Tudor Council with the precise and sole objective of ascertaining whether Henry VII's decision to increase the number of members of his Council to forty led to a greater or lesser participation of those councilors in the life of the body. No overall conclusion or generalization on the subject shines through.

Much in the vein of Leopold Ranke's source-based historiography, Elton believed that it is the historian's craft to gather evidence of the facts as they have really happened and then to narrate them as objectively as possible. Edward Carr, who opposed Elton in a famous debate, would have characterized his opponent's position in these terms: 'First get your facts straight, then plunge at your peril into the shifting sands of interpretation' (Carr, 1987: 16).

To Elton, the historian's craft requires not only 'the analytical eye of the investigator', but also the 'comprehensive eye of the story-teller' (Elton, 1967: 84). In fact, Elton is a master in the art of narrating, which he deems inextricably linked to historiographical work. He did not want to know of typologies and much less of any nomothetic historiography.

His fascinating *Star Chamber Stories* (Elton, 1958) proves how much the life of a governmental device (such were the courts in the Ancien Régime) is intertwined with the life of society. Nevertheless, in his manifesto book *The Practice of History*, Elton attacks the 'sociologizing historian' (Elton, 1967: 35), and would resolutely reject any cross-disciplinary hybridizing of historiography with social sciences, let alone the administrative ones. In fact – as Quentin Skinner pointed out – he never seriously attempted to 'convey some sense of why the study of administrative and constitutional history might still be thought to matter even in a post-imperial culture dominated by the social sciences' (Skinner, 1997: 313).

Milan, Italy

Our third episode takes us to Milan in Italy. There, a professor of political science, Gianfranco Miglio, strives to give a twist to our story (Miglio, 1981; Miglio, 2011). Miglio was trained as a jurist and was reportedly qualified by Carl Schmitt as 'one of the most cultured men in Europe' (Ulmen, 1994: 129). So far, the two protagonists of our story, historiography and Public Administration, have been flirting without coming to an engagement. In Milan, in 1964, that engagement is celebrated. The promotion of administrative history becomes the mission of an *ad hoc* institution: the FISA: Fondazione Italiana per la storia amministrativa (Italian Foundation for the Administrative History).

In his contribution to the first issue of the Foundation's Annals (*Annali*), Miglio claims the disciplinary autonomy of the history of administration and blames the administrative historians for having failed to establish that autonomy for too long. As to methodology, Miglio takes inspiration from Weber, of course, and insists on the relevance of both genealogy and analogy in the study of history. Miglio extols 'the richness of the territories to be discovered by an up-to-date administrative historiography' and, in fact, he begins to map those territories with remarkable comprehensiveness and accuracy (Miglio, 1964: 14). Growth and international breadth of the research work attributable to administrative history are also demonstrated by the extensive bibliography that Giuliana Nobili edited for each issue of the Annals.

To carry out his task, the Annals' editor gathered around himself a formidable army. Johannes Winckelmann, the editor of Weber's works, features in the first issue of the Annals with a paper on Weber's administrative studies (Winckelmann, 1964). Tche-hao and Josiane Tsien, outstanding experts on Chinese institutions, contribute to the second issue with an account of the traditional Chinese administrative systems (Tsien and Tsien 1965). The iconoclast sociologist and theologian Jacques Ellul opens the third issue with a discussion on the usefulness of 'concepts' in history (Ellul, 1966). A profound interpreter of the modern state, Gerhard Oestreich, contributes to the same issue with an article on Otto Hintze and the comparative history of administration (Oestreich, 1966). Even the staunch historian Geoffrey Elton contributed with the article I repeatedly quoted in the previous episode of this story (Elton, 1964).

There is no use making any further references. Each issue of the Annals is a treasure trove of reflections and research work, with contributions of the highest quality. However, I do not want to put these old volumes aside before mentioning Pierre Legendre, the jurist and heterodox psychoanalyst.

Two years after contributing to the Annals with an account of the history of the French debate about public administration (Legendre, 1966), Legendre published one of the most beautiful and stimulating histories of French administration. 'History' – writes Legendre in the introduction to his volume – 'is Geology of the Administrative Science', it is its 'main support'. 'Without the analysis of the lower layers one cannot be certain of the solidity of the ground … nor can one lay the foundations of an effective perspective /on the present/' (Legendre, 1968: 20) – a clear and suggestive metaphor for the relationships between historiography and Public Administration.

With interlocutors of this caliber and of such beliefs, FISA represented a unique intellectual experience. Unfortunately, that experience ended too soon. After four issues, the Annals ceased publication and the Foundation itself was discontinued. But Miglio's action was not limited to FISA. In 1959, together with Feliciano Benvenuti, a prominent administrative jurist, he created the Institute for the Science of Public Administration (ISAP). Of the five departments into which this research center was divided, one was entitled 'Typology and History' (Rotelli, 2010: 47–48). In the following years, ISAP warranted if not the integration, then at least the proximity between historiography and administrative sciences. Later on, especially starting from the 1980s, it produced a wide range of studies on administrative history. We will talk about it again in the epilogue.

Brussels, Belgium

The fourth chapter of our story is set in Brussels, home to so many cosmopolitan enterprises. This time, the main character is André Molitor, a Belgian senior civil servant, King Baudouin's private secretary, and also a professor at the University of Leuven. It is 2 December 1982, and we can imagine ourselves in a meeting room of the International Institute of Administrative Sciences (IIAS), then located at 25 Rue de la Charité. There, a working group on the history of the administration is established (WG), that Molitor, also the vice-president of IIAS, will chair for about ten years.

Molitor explains the reasons for the creation of the working group in an article in the Institute's journal. I would like to highlight only two passages of this text, those most relevant to our story of disciplines. In the first one, Molitor underlines that every historical experience is unique and therefore 'ransacking history for codes and models of behavior applicable to new situations' is a very risky exercise. It seems like a caveat explicitly addressed to the 'administrative scientist,' possibly too prone to generalizations that do not recognize the primacy of the context (Pollitt, 2013).

The second passage concerns a 'trap' in which 'historical studies' often fall: that of dealing 'only with long-established industrialized nations'. The WG was called to circumvent this pitfall thanks to the study of 'post-independence administrative structures in Latin American States' as well as 'the historic analysis of administrative aspects of colonization and decolonisation in Africa and Asia' (Molitor, 1983: 1). The topicality of both warnings is evident – just think of how often superficial and hasty generalizations ally with Western-centrism to produce deceptive 'administrative gospels', disregarding the context in which they are preached and ignoring the 'weight' of history (Rugge, 2006). But, let us go back to our story.

It was not obvious that the Brussels Institute should be named after 'administrative sciences' in the plural. In fact, over time, that title generated some controversy (Drewry, 2005: 64–65). Furthermore, the contrast between that plural and the singular of 'Public Administration', with its alleged lack of disciplinary 'boundaries' (Raadschelders, 2010), could trigger a huge epistemological and semantic debate. I will not climb this mountain in these pages. The fact is that in Brussels it had been decided that the administrative sciences would be professed in the plural and, from December 1982 onwards, historiography (and therefore administrative history) was officially and institutionally one of those sciences.

Over the years, the WG established by Molitor put out a series of *Cahiers*. Apart from the first experimental issue (1983), each subsequent *Cahier* had a monographic topic. For example, the second volume was dedicated to the diffusion of the merit system in the recruitment of administrative personnel (Cassese and Pellew, 1987). Usually, the contributions to the *Cahiers* came from around ten or a dozen countries, offering very interesting material for comparative historical research (more on that later in this chapter). As for the disciplinary issue we are concerned with, I think it is appropriate to give the floor to Vincent Wright, one of the successors to Molitor.

Wright was a political scientist equally versed in the study of the past and of the present of public administration. One could say – as it has been written – that he was 'pulled in conflicting directions by the contrasting concerns and methodological demands of history and politics' (Hayward and Hazareesingh, 2002: 440). In fact, Wright jokingly admitted to his 'intellectual schizophrenia', but declared he lived happily with it, profiting 'from the networks of colleagues and friends created and consolidated by both politics and history' (Wright, 1997: 176).

Such a scholar certainly could not fail to observe the internal dynamics of a group that was quite composite from a disciplinary point of view (not to mention its heterogeneity in terms of national academic traditions). Wright wrote in 1995: 'inevitably tensions were bound to emerge in the group between the generalizing and modeling attitude of political scientists and the historians' deep skepticism and unconquerable idiosyncrasy toward both generalizations and models' (Wright, 1995).

Before closing this fourth episode, let me just point out, in an ideal picture of the members of the IIAS team, a particularly active participant, Jos Raadschelders. It was he who animated the discussion on the use of models in history, to which Wright probably refers when speaking of tensions within the WG. In one of the *Cahiers*, a note by Raadschelders was published, intended as a 'reply' to Guy Thuillier, also a participant in the WG, who had denied the existence of a 'Napoleonic model' of administration (Wunder, 1995: 263–268). We shall meet Raadschelders again later.

Baden-Baden, Germany

Administrative history is at center stage of our fifth and last episode, set in the romantic city of Baden-Baden, Germany. In 1989, in a fortuitous but fortunate coincidence with the fall of the Berlin Wall, the German publisher Nomos brought out a *Yearbook of European Administrative History* (*JEV*). Nomos specialized in legal publications, but – as anticipated – this is no clue that we are going to follow now.

The elegantly bound *Jahrbuch* will regularly appear for no less than twenty years. Its editor is a jurist, Erk Volkmar Heyen, a scholar with strong interests in philosophy and sociology (later on, in 2013, he will publish a book titled *Verwaltete Welte – Administered Worlds* – illustrating how European painting has been reflecting the vicissitudes of political-administrative structures over centuries [Heyen 2013]). Alongside Heyen, we find, as co-editors or members of the scientific committee, personalities we have already met such as Vincent Wright and André Molitor.

In his preface to the inaugural issue of the Jahrbuch 1, Heyen speaks of administrative history as a field that 'in spite of remarkable advancements' is still 'struggling to establish itself in a properly unitary sense'. The statement could be called into question if we consider the progress made, at that date, by the studies that defined themselves as administrative history. Just two years earlier – and precisely in Heyen's homeland – a mighty scholarly undertaking had been completed: a history of the German administration in six volumes (Jeserich et al., 1983–1988). And, in 1989, the authoritative legal historian François Burdeau introduced his own history of French administration with the following claim: 'The history of administration is a field that has long been explored' (Burdeau, 1989: 11).

Yet, Heyen's statement refers to a 'unitary' disciplinary statute; and this actually did not exist at that date – nor can it be said that it was achieved through the JEV experience. As of 1998, the JEV community, surveyed on the basis of the institutional affiliation of the Annals' contributors, was made up of a good portion of Germans. French and Italians were in second place with an almost equal share of contributions. But the British component was also large, and other nations were significantly represented: the Netherlands, Belgium, the United States, and Denmark (Rugge, 2000a). The backgrounds, interests, and methods of the JEV community were equally varied.

This variety perfectly reflects the editor's personal opinion about administrative history, an opinion that was far from being dogmatic. The title of an article published by Heyen in 2000 can well attest to that. It reads: 'There are many paths leading to administrative history, and some lead through Europe' (Heyen, 2000). The second part of this title alludes to an issue that – in my opinion – is still of burning relevance today: the very limited knowledge that

American Public Administration has of the tradition of administrative studies in continental Europe. But we need not discuss this today. What we want to underline instead is Heyen's vision of administrative history as a world more suitable for disciplinary encounters than fearful of encroachments.

As a matter of fact, Heyen's Yearbook pays much attention to the relationships between the history of public administration and other histories, such as the history of legal doctrines and even art history. For example, one of JEV's (always thematic) issues is devoted to the 'images of the administration in memories, caricatures, novels, architecture' (JEV, 1994). And – as the editor does not hesitate to claim – some of the articles included in the Yearbook 'might have been published in political science periodicals as well' (Heyen, 2000: 728).

In this regard, it is worth mentioning that the 1993 issue of JEV hosts a contribution urging deeper cooperation between historiography and the science of administration. Yet, the data presented in the article are far from encouraging. According to a detailed survey of four of the most important Public Administration journals (two European and two American), those journals pay only scant attention to the past (Rugge, 1993). The disciplinary divide between historiography (even in its version of administrative history) and Public Administration remains deep and daunting.

Epilogue

Yet, in the 1990s, administrative history in itself seemed to enjoy a favorable situation. As an epilogue to my five episodes, I shall briefly recall some circumstances connected with the characters and institutions we have already met. They can give an idea of the fruitful intellectual season I am talking about. In a three-year span (1993–1995), two periodic publications dedicated almost exclusively to administrative history made their debut in Italy: *Storia Amministrazione Costituzione* (*SAC*) and *Le Carte e la Storia*. The latter, directed by Guido Melis, was, and is still today, the organ of the Society for the Studies on History of Institutions. The former, *SAC*, directed by Ettore Rotelli, was edited by ISAP, the already cited Milanese institute, which in the meantime had carried out an impressive quantity of studies on Italian administrative history (ISAP, 1985, 1990).

In the editorial that inaugurates *SAC*'s more than twenty-year existence, the names of great Public Administration scholars like Lorenz von Stein and Dwight Waldo appear, alongside the names of authors of both constitutional history (such as Frederic Maitland and Otto Brunner) and social history (such as George M. Trevelyan and Lucien Febvre). Moreover, it is *SAC*'s declared project to make administrative history a meeting point not only of other historiographies, but also of disciplines such as economics, law, and political science (p.a., e.r., f.r., 1993: 14).

Over two decades, between 1991 and 2010, the Working Group of the IIAS published no fewer than nine books, dedicated to topics as diverse as, e.g., the administration of cultural heritage (Fisch, 2008), corruption in the civil service (Tiihonen, 2002) wartime administrations (Rugge, 2000b), the governance of migrations (Arnold, 2010), and the management of water resources (Raadschelders, 2005). The selection of themes was based on the idea that the reconstruction of historical events could contribute to Public Administration studies and serve to practically address highly topical issues.

In 1998, Jos Raadschelders, whom we already met as a member of the IISA WG, published the first *Handbook of Administrative History* (Raadschelders, 1998, 1994). Five years later the *Handbook of Public Administration*, edited by Peters and Pierre, hosted a robust section on 'Administrative history', introduced by the same Raadschelders (Raadschelders, 2003). There, the author provided his own authoritative recipe regarding the relationships between historiography and Public Administration – the typical set of recommendations and warnings that makes what we call a discipline (Stichweh, 2001).

CONCLUDING CONSIDERATIONS

Faithful to my purpose of not entering into a normative discussion, I will not dwell on Raadschelders' prescriptions. I shall rather submit to the reader some considerations drawn from my five episodes (and their epilogue). If I had to give them a title, I could suggest 'Administrative History: The Rise of a Discipline'. But my take on the story is actually different. The turbulent dialectic between historiography and public administration, from which the quasi-discipline of administrative history emerged, teaches me a different lesson.

Those vicissitudes give evidence of how much disciplines and their quest for so-called autonomy are double-edged. On one side, the existence of a disciplinary statute compels researchers to continually question the consistency of their methods and subjects with the discipline's statute. This sharpens and specializes the scholars' analytical gaze. On the other side, that scholar easily loses sight of what lies outside the disciplinary perspective, while the methodological orthodoxy reduces the variety and perceptiveness of his or her research methods.

To overcome the resulting paralyzing alternative and advance beyond any disciplinary dogmatism, we need scholars who dare to cross the borders of their discipline like Waldo or Miglio did. We need people who are intellectually robust and daring enough to seek contact with other academic tribes. We need what management scholars would call boundary spanners (Tushman, 1977).

The figure of Weber, whose name, not by coincidence, has frequently turned up in my story, can provide us with a model. I am not talking of Weber's unattainable genius. As Winckelmann underlines with admiration in the above quoted article, Weber was 'a lawyer by training', but 'his historical researches set trends'; he was also a prominent economist, but possessed the qualities of a 'great sociologist and political scientist' (Winckelmann, 1964: 27). It should be noted, however, that this genius could flourish in a cultural climate – the 19th-century academia – in which specialism had not yet led to an exasperated fragmentation of knowledge. At that time, top universities and top scholars were working not at parting the different threads of knowledge but at weaving them (by the way, the German word *Weber* translates precisely to weaver!).

This weaving work could find a welcoming environment in the German faculties of *Staatswissenschaften*, the 'sciences of the state', embracing philosophy and economics, law and history (Ellwein and Hesse, 1991); or it could be the goal of adventurous and visionary initiatives like those generated by the 'powerful ideal' of the 'unity of science', pursued by a movement active in the interwar period (Kamminga and Somsen, 2016).

The fact is that the 20th century witnessed a pressing push in the opposite direction, towards the 'disunity' of the sciences, with a growing number of disciplines proclaiming their 'autonomy' and shaping education accordingly. Thus, in 1927, the philosopher John Dewey was already complaining about the 'social science' being divided into 'independent and insulated branches' (history, sociology, economics, political science), lacking the 'cross-fertilization' typical of the 'physical Knowledge' (Dewey, 1927: 171).

Luckily, our time is marked by a growing awareness of the flaws of specialism and by a mounting drive for interdisciplinarity. We all believe this to be good. After all, as Karl Popper once put it: 'we are students of problems not of disciplines' (Popper, 1962: 66–67). Debating the relations between different fields – as this book does – can be the *via regia* to discover new, more comprehensive paradigms of research. Such a commitment will always find the sympathy of those who believe that research work, as an unbiased and rigorous intellectual enterprise, is *one and the same* irrespective of the field in which we undertake it.

REFERENCES

Arnold, Peri E. (ed.) (2010). *National Approaches to the Administration of International Migration*. Amsterdam: IOS Press.

Brändström, Annika, Bynander, Fredrick, and 't Hart, Paul (2004). Governing by Looking Back: Historical Analogies and Crisis Management. *Public Administration*, vol. 82, no. 1, pp. 191–210.

Brown, Brack, and Stillman II, Richard J. (1986). *A Search for Public Administration: The Ideas and Career of Dwight Waldo*. College Station, TX: Texas A&M University Press.

Burdeau, François (1989). *Histoire de l'administration francaise du 18e au 20e siecle*. Paris: Montchrestien.

Carr, Edward H. (1987). *What is History?* London: Penguin.

Cassese, Sabino, and Pellew, Jill (eds.) (1987). *Le système du mérite / The Merit System*. Bruxelles: Institut International des Sciences Administratives.

Dewey, John (1927). *The Public and Its Problems. An Essay in Political Inquiry*. New York: Henry Holt.

Dorwart, Reinhold August (1953). *The Administrative Reforms of Frederick William I of Prussia*. Cambridge, MA: Harvard University Press.

Drewry, Gavin (2005). The Administrative Sciences – The Intellectual Context of an Institutional History. In Fabio Rugge and Michael Duggett (eds.), *IIAS/IISA: Administration and Service 1930–2005*. Amsterdam: IOS Press, pp. 61–79.

Ellul, Jacques (1966). Est-il légitime d'utiliser des Concepts en l'Histoire. *Annali della Fondazione Italiana per la Storia Amministrativa*, vol. 3, pp. 3–23.

Ellwein, Thomas, and Hesse, Joachim Jens (eds.) (1991). *Staatswissenschaften: Vergessene Disziplin oder neue Herausforderung?* Baden-Baden: Nomos.

Elton, Geoffrey R. (1953). *The Tudor Revolution in Government: Administrative Changes in the Reign of Henry VIII*. Cambridge, UK: Cambridge University Press.

Elton, Geoffrey R. (1958). *Star Chamber Stories*. London: Meuthen.

Elton, Geoffrey R. (1964). Why the history of the early-Tudor Council remains unwritten. *Annali della Fondazione Italiana per la Storia Amministrativa*, vol. 1, pp. 268–296.

Elton, Geoffrey R. (1967). *The Practice of History*. New York: Thomas T. Crowell Company.

Fisch, Stefan (ed.) (2008). *National Approaches to the Governance of Historical Heritage over Time: A Comparative Report*. Amsterdam: IOS Press.

Harmon, Michael M. (1989). The Simon/Waldo Debate: a Review and Update. *Public Administration Quarterly*, vol. 12, no. 4, pp. 437–451.

Hayward, Jack, and Hazareesingh, Sudir (2002). Vincent Wright (1937–1999). *Proceedings of the British Academy*, vol. 115, pp. 439–463.

Heller, Hermann (1996). The nature and structure of the state. *Cardoso Law Review*, vol. 18, pp.1129–1137.

Heyen, Erk Volkmar (2000). There are many paths leading to administrative history, and some lead through Europe. Administrative *Theory & Praxis*, vol. 22, no. 4, pp. 719–731.

Heyen, Erk Volkmar (2013). *Verwaltete Welten. Mensch, Gemeinwesen und Amt in der europäischen Malerei*. Berlin: Akademie-Verlag.

ISAP (1985). *L'amministrazione nella storia moderna*, 2 vols. Milano: Giuffrè.

ISAP (1990). *Le riforme crispine*, 4 vols. Milano: Giuffrè.

Jenkins, Keith (1995). *On 'What Is History?': From Carr and Elton to Rorty and White*. London: Routledge

Jeserich Kurt G. A., Pohl, Hans, and Unruh, Georg-Christoph (eds.) (1983–1988). *Deutsche Verwaltungsgeschichte*, vol. 6. Stuttgart: Dt. Verl.-Anst.

Jev (Jahrbuch für europäische Verwaltungsgeschichte) (1994). *Bilder der Verwaltung. Memoiren, Karikaturen, Romane, Architektur*. Baden-Baden: Nomos.

Kamminga, Harmke, and Somsen, Geert (2016). *Pursuing the Unity of Science: Ideology and Scientific Practice from the Great War to the Cold War.* London: Routledge.

Lanzalaco, Luca (1997). Storia, amministrazione e teoria politica in Dwight Waldo. *Storia Amministrazione Costituzione*, vol. 5, pp. 27–50.

Legendre, Pierre (1966). Évolution des systèmes d'administration et histoire des idées: l'exemple de la pensée française. *Annali della Fondazione Italiana per la Storia Amministrativa*, vol. 3, pp. 254–274.

Legendre, Pierre (1968). *Histoire de l'administration de 1750 à nos jours.* Paris: Presses Universitaires de France.

Mansfield, Harvey C. (1951). The uses of history. *Public Administration Review*, vol. 11, no. 1, pp. 51–57.

Miglio, Gianfranco (1964). Premesse ad una metodologia della storia amministrativa. *Annali della Fondazione Italiana per la Storia Amministrativa*, vol. 1, pp.11–19.

Miglio, Gianfranco (1981). *Le regolarità della politica. Scritti scelti.* Milano: Giuffrè.

Miglio, Gianfranco (2011). *Lezioni di politica. 1. Scienza della politica; 2. Storia delle dottrine politiche.* Bologna: il Mulino.

Molitor, André (1983). The history of administration. *International Review of Administrative Sciences*, vol. 49, no. 1, pp. 1–3.

Olien, Jessie, Rogelberg, Steven G., Lehman-Willenbrock, Nale, and Allen, Joseph. A. (2015). *Exploring Meeting Science: Cambridge Handbook of Meeting Science.* Cambridge: Cambridge University Press.

Oestreich, Gerhard (1966). Otto Hintze und die vergleichende Verwaltungsgeschichte. *Annali della Fondazione Italiana per la Storia Amministrativa*, vol. 3, pp. 59–80.

p.a., e.r., f.r. (1993). Editoriale. *Storia Amministrazione Costituzione*, vol. 1, pp. 9–14.

Pollitt, Christopher (ed.) (2013). *Context in Public Policy and Management: The Missing Link?* Cheltenham, UK: Edward Elgar.

Popper, Karl R. (1962). *Conjectures and Refutations. The Growth of Scientific Knowledge.* New York: Basic Books.

Raadschelders, Jos C. N. (1994). Administrative history: Contents, meaning and usefulness. *International Review of Administrative Sciences*, vol. 60, no. 1, pp. 117–129.

Raadschelders, Jos C. N. (1998). *Handbook of Administrative History.* New Brunswick: Transaction.

Raadschelders, Jos C. N. (2003). Administrative history: Introduction. In: B. Guy Peters and Jon Pierre (eds.), *Handbook of Public Administration.* London: Sage, pp. 161–168.

Raadschelders, Jos C. N. (ed.) (2005). *The Institutional Arrangements for Water Management in the 19th and 20th Centuries.* Amsterdam: IOS Press.

Raadschelders, Jos C. N. (2010) Identity without boundaries: Public administration's canon(s) of integration. *Administration and Society*, vol. 42, no. 2, pp. 131–159.

Raadschelders, Jos C. N. (2023). Review of the book by Stillman, Dwight Waldo: Administrative theorist. *Public Administration Review*, pp. 1859–1861.

Rotelli, Ettore (2010). Per una storiografia della scienza di Feliciano Benvenuti. Introduction to F. Benvenuti (ed.), *Amministrazione pubblica. Autonomie locali.* Milano: Giuffré, pp. 13–140.

Rugge, Fabio (1993). Eine Wissenschaft ohne Vergangenheit? Eine Geschichte ohne Zukunft? Ein kleiner Streifzug durch verwaltungswissenschaftliche Zeitschriften. *Jahrbuch für europäische Verwaltungsgeschichte*, vol. 5, pp. 369–380.

Rugge, Fabio (2000a). Dieci anni di JEV: 'Annuario per la storia amministrativa europea'. *Storia Amministrazione Costituzione*, vol. 8, pp. 287–299.

Rugge, Fabio (ed.) (2000b). *Administration and Crisis Management: The Case of Wartime*, Bruxelles: International Institute of Administrative Sciences.

Rugge, Fabio (2006). Social and cultural dimensions in institution building: The weight of history. *Il Politico. Rivista italiana di Scienze politiche*, vol. 71, no. 211, pp. 141–147.

Rugge, Fabio (2008). Critical review of the book by Christopher Pollitt, *Time, Policy, Management: Governing with the Past. International Review of Administrative Sciences*, vol. 74, no. 4, pp. 703–706.

Sartori, Giovanni (1975). Will democracy kill democracy? Decision-making by majorities and by committees. *Government and Opposition*, vol. 10, no. 2, pp. 131–158.

Skinner, Quentin (1997). Sir Geoffrey Elton and the practice of history. *Transactions of the Royal Historical Society*, vol. 7, pp. 301–316.

Stichweh, Rudolph (2001). History of the scientific disciplines. In *The International Encyclopedia of the Social and Behavioral Sciences*, vol. 20, pp. 13727–13731.

Stillman II, Richard J. (2021). *Dwight Waldo: Administrative Theorist for our Times*. New York: Routledge.

Tiihonen, Seppo (ed.) (2002). *The History of Corruption in Central Government*. Amsterdam: IOS Press.

Tout, Thomas Frederick (1920–1933). *Chapters in the Administrative History of Mediaeval England: The Wardrobe, the Chamber, and the Small Seals*, 5 vols. Manchester: Manchester University Press.

Tsien, Josiane, and Tsien, Tchen-Hao (1965). Histoire de la fonction publique en Chine traditionnelle. *Annali della Fondazione Italiana per la Storia Amministrativa*, vol. 2, pp. 409–433.

Tushman, Michael (1977). Special boundary roles in the innovation process. *Administrative Science Quarterly*, vol. 22, no. 4, pp. 587–605.

Ulmen, Gary (1994). Beyond Schmitt? Reply to Miglio. *Telos. Critical Theory of the Contemporary*, vol. 100, pp. 129–133.

Waldo, Dwight (1948). *The Administrative State: A Study of the Political Theory of American Public Administration*. New York: Ronald Press.

Waldo, Dwight (1954). Review of Dorwart, the administrative reforms of Frederick William I of Prussia. *American Political Science Review*, vol. 48, no. 2, pp. 576–577.

Waldo, Dwight (1955). *The Study of Public Administration*. Garden City, NY: Doubleday

Waldo, Dwight (1956). *Perspectives on Administration*. Alabama: University of Alabama Press.

Winckelmann, Johannes (1964). Max Webers historische und soziologische Verwaltungsforschung. *Annali della Fondazione Italiana per la Storia Amministrativa*, vol. 1, pp. 27–67.

Wright, Vincent (1995). Il gruppo di lavoro sulla 'storia dell'amministrazione' dell'IISA. *Storia Amministrazione Costituzione*, vol. 3, pp. 311–314.

Wright, Vincent (1997). The path to hesitant comparison. In: Hans Daalder (ed.), *Comparative European Politics: The Story of a Profession*. London: Pinter, pp. 162–176

Wunder, Bernd (ed.) (1995). *The Influences of the Napoleonic 'Model' of Administration on the Administrative Organization of Other Countries*. Bruxelles: International Institute of Administrative Sciences.

10. History and Public Administration: Meanings, Problems, Usefulness in Policy-making

Lorenzo Castellani

INTRODUCTION

In 1946 the English historian A.L. Rowse (1946: 5) argued: "History is one of the recognized roads into its [i.e., the Civil Service's] higher ranks; it is an important subject in the entrance examination. And it might quite rightly have greater influence attached to it; for history gives you the right background for most of the affairs with which you will have to deal in the administrative Civil Service." In the United States, the study of history was considered important to aspiring public servants until the end of the 19th and beginning of the 20th century. Woodrow Wilson's 1889 study is illustrative and he, like many of his contemporaries, was convinced that a student of public administration should have grounding in history. Indeed, in the past, history was the topic to study for those preparing for a career in the public service.

Today the study of administrative history, and history in general, is not as popular or central to the education of the ruling class as it was in the past.

However, in terms of research and academic understanding the link between history and public administration remains strong and important for a wide number of reasons; by way of example, one may think of the detection of administrative traditions or the comparison between administrative reforms in a certain era or the analysis of the cultural environment within which public administrations developed. Moreover, history is useful not only for reconstructing the past and opening perspectives on the present but also for evaluating possible future developments through its tools (Van Creveld, 2020), especially in the field of policy and administrative reforms.

The aim of this chapter is to outline the interplay between history and public administration, considering definitions of administrative history, the usefulness of history for public administration from an applied history perspective, the toolkit that historian can deploy in public administration, the meaning of history for policy-making and administrative reforms, and the relationship between history and social sciences in public administration.

FROM ADMINISTRATIVE HISTORY TO ADMINISTRATIVE HISTORIES

The great historian of the modern state Joseph Strayer once wrote that most attention is given to the glamorous institutions (such as sovereignty, kingship, nation-state, judiciary, high councils of state) while too little attention is paid to the details of the recruitment, training, career patterns, and financial rewards of the people who make the institutions work (1975: 504).

The major postwar administrative theorist Dwight Waldo would agree with that observation as he remarked that a genuine administrative history has yet to be written and that the history of government as such – its functions, institutions, and operations – is still a non-subject (Waldo, 1987: 90).

For these reasons, the definition of the very concept of administrative history is still being discussed today. Caldwell (1955: 455) defines administrative history as "the study of the origins and evolution of administrative ideas, institutions and practices".

More elaborate is Raadschelders, who defines administrative history proper as "the study of structures and processes in and ideas about government as they have existed or have been wanted in the past and the actual and ideal place of public functionaries therein" (1998a: 7). But this definition *strictu sensu* is considered too narrow by other scholars, who point out that administrative history should also have an eye for the legitimacy of government, the societal context in which it is embedded, as well as the balance between public and private institutions rather than being focused merely on structures, processes, and ideas regarding public functionaries.

Indeed "if administrative history is to mean anything at all, it must always be related to the society from which it springs" (Cromwell 1966: 254–255). This is administrative history in a broader sense: the interplay between government and society at large.

It is best not to get too lost in definitional or classification questions. It is clear that history embraces a complex array of issues, even if one limits oneself to analyzing the public administration object, which cannot be confined within limits that are too precise. On the other hand, the very definition of "public administration" is uncertain and variable, depending on the countries and their history and the context, so it would perhaps be better to talk about *administrative histories*, which can take on a variable level of detail of observation.

On the other hand, if history is the realm of the accidental, the involuntary, the contingent, the new and the different, the irrational and the emotional, how can history be restricted to single fixed variables of public administration?

History stands out from other disciplines precisely for its generality, for the ability to outline contexts, including different aspects and levels of analysis.

The process is similar to the analysis of an object under a microscope: you can choose the level of detail, which in this case can range from the history of the government-as-a-whole in its relationship with society-as-a-whole up to the history of a single public administration. This "variable geometry" approach makes any historical research useful for better understanding the history of public administration in a given context. In a matter that is by nature complex, interconnected, and vast, it makes little sense to narrow the field of investigation.

DIFFERENT INTERPRETATIONS OF ADMINISTRATIVE HISTORY

Once we have assumed that a broad definition of administrative history is more useful than a narrow one, and that administrative histories in the plural is better than administrative history in the singular, we have to analyze the position of administrative history within the different academic systems because national traditions influence the way in which history and public administration interact and in which scholars studied them.

Caldwell and Raadschelders define administrative history as an independent field of study within the field of public administration and of history proper. According to their view, the core business of public administration can only be grasped as a historical phenomenon. A historical perspective is thus far from a mere annex to the study. It might well be the major approach in public administration. Indeed, a study of public administration that aims at grasping reality is intrinsically historical (Raadschelders et al., 2000).

This approach is realistic because in every nation the role of history is central to the development of public administration as an institution and as a field of study.

However, even if we confine our overview only within the Western world, we would see that history occupies a different position depending on how public administration studies are conceived of and organized within the academia.

The first macro division is the one between the Anglo-American tradition and the continental European one. In the former, over the last century a field of study has developed which is interdisciplinary but unified in nature and which is called simply "public administration", while in the latter the study of public administration is, for the most part, split among various disciplines, such as administrative law, history of political institutions and administration, public management, and public policies (Painter and Peters, 2010).

A further sub-division could be made, dividing the countries in which administrative history falls within the field of history and those in which it is encompassed within public administration. In countries like France, Italy, Spain, Germany, and the UK administrative history is generally found within the broad field of history, or constitutional history and legal history, depending on the academic tradition; while in countries like the United States, Australia, New Zealand, and the Netherlands, history tends to be encompassed within the field of public administration (Raadschelders et al., 2000).

For American and Dutch scholars in particular, history has to be incorporated in public administration (Raadschelders et al., 2000). Public administration exists as an autonomous subject in these countries and the dimension of this academic field is wide enough to include administrative history in it. But for the rest of the Western world the tradition is different: public administration does not exist as an autonomous subject of academic inquiry, and administrative history deals with the fields of law, public management, or politics, while it remains within the broader academic field of historical studies.

There is a risk in the first model: that of an administrative history entirely included within the field of public administration. As Raadschelders et al. (2000) suggest, the risk lies in reducing the scope of the study of history too much and having a dialogue only with the administrative sciences, when, instead, the interaction should be with modern history, with all its political, social, and cultural nuances, in order to enrich the understanding of public administration in the past.

For these reasons, an interdisciplinary dialogue is essential when we consider administrative history. A common approach in administrative history is possible only when considering these differences and building up a dialogue among historians and other scholars, and through the development of a comparative approach.

THE PRISM OF ADMINISTRATIVE HISTORY AND ITS METHODOLOGY

Administrative history is a multifaceted subject: an effective historical investigation of institutions requires political, social, legal, and economic knowledge. This intrinsic interdisciplinarity is the added value of this discipline, a feature that should be emphasized by scholars as much in teaching as in research. The timeframes of public administrations are often diachronic with respect to those of political and economic history, and this characteristic demands a continuous search for continuities and changes that lead to questioning the periodizations of politics/economy. The relationships betwthat can stimeen administrations and the actions of political-institutional actors unfold in a subterranean and asymmetrical manner with respect to pure politics: this is why the study of biographies, networks, practices, and of the osmosis between different sectors (e.g., public-private) takes on a particular value for this discipline.

For these characteristics, historical methodology is particularly relevant to analyze the development of public administration. History enables the consideration of elements often neglected by public administration scholars which can better outline that the context within continuity and change are unfolding. To accomplish this task, the historian is relying on primary sources – archives, legislation and regulation, correspondences, newspapers – and secondary sources, like public administration literature of the period/place analyzed, memories of civil servants, public debates on government, academic and professional reviews and journals. Moreover, when possible, oral history can also be helpful, in order to consider the views of the protagonists of a certain historical phase. When a single public administration or a civil servants' group are investigated, prosopography (Stone, 1971), which is the description of a person's social and family connections, career, etc., or a collection of such descriptions and network analysis, which is the interplay of connections among individuals or groups, among institutions and within institutions are useful (Wetherell, 1998). Biographies, personal and group background, and connections which informed networks could show the dynamics of the machinery of government and public administration in a very clear manner. Moreover, biographical investigation of relevant protagonists in public administration, as top public managers and civil servants, are important for studying institutional change, culture, and mentality of an age (Castellani, 2023). Just to mention a few examples, think of characters, in different historical ages and countries, such as Bernard Baruch (1910s, USA), Derek Rayner (1980s, UK), Alberto Beneduce (1930s, Italy), or Michel Debré (1940s, France).

Finally, the understanding of the present through administrative history is enhanced when approached by means of comparative analysis. Administrative history in this sense is comparison over time, enabling us to see through the political and administrative fads and fashions of the day and getting a perspective on more fundamental differences and similarities between present and obsolete structures, operations, and policies. To cite Alexis de Tocqueville: "There are far more ways of structuring society than man, living in a specific country, is able to envisage" (in Jacoby 1973: 222). Reality is bound by both time and place, and comparative administrative history holds the promise that it can break through these boundaries.

Indeed, knowledge of the past enlarges and sharpens our insights in regards to the how and why of contemporary administrative structures and processes and their origins. Administrative history may contribute to the notion that all innovations in administration are relative and that administrative revolutions are rare (Elton, 1955).

It would be equally interesting, for example, to see if, how, and when certain administrative ideas and practices penetrated Western countries. Creel (1964) for instance suggested that medical and civil service exams originated in China and – via Baghdad – were introduced and implemented at the court of King Roger Il of Sicily (1095–1154). Furthermore, he suggests that several Chinese administrative techniques found their way to the West, especially in the area of financial management, and he points out the influence of the Indian civil service on the 19th-century British one. As we can see, the procedures and methods of history are useful for establishing comparisons, analogies, and contextualizations that help us understand the dynamics of development of administrative institutions even with references that are very distant in time and space. But at the same time, history can also have more practical implications, offering policymakers useful knowledge for making decisions about the present and the future.

Last but not least, administrative history is useful not only for investigating the past and for a deeper understanding of the present, but also for thinking about future scenarios and directions for public administration reform.

THE PRACTICAL USE AND USEFULNESS OF HISTORY IN PUBLIC ADMINISTRATION

Applied History for Public Administration

Historians are often reluctant to share their ideas and introduce their works in parliamentary halls and government offices, mindful of the "uses and abuses" committed by politics against history during the 20th century (Green, 2016: 13). But this mistrust cannot cancel out the fact that a direct relationship between citizens, institutions, and history takes place every day "without the mediation of academic discipline" (Green, 2016: 14). At the heart of applied history there is the desire to reaffirm that the relationship between history and politics is not and must not be instrumental but rather utilitarian: knowledge of the past can help to form an aware citizenship and to develop far-sighted policies. However, for this knowledge to be useful and – as such – scientifically founded, historians must not shy away from confrontation with political and administrative authorities. Historians can address the link between historical discourse and the public scene and reaffirm the pragmatic character of historical knowledge. Within the framework of general thought on applied history developed by historians such as John Tosh, Niall Ferguson and Graham Allison, the discipline stands out for the promotion of a historical approach to policymaking and for having re-proposed the relationship between historiography and politico-administrative issues in an original way.

According to applied history, history is not only an interpretative framework of the past but is also an orientation for present and future political strategies. The relationship between history and politics is complicated and protean but nevertheless inextinguishable, since all political and administrative choices mature within a historical framework in which the present is connected to the past as it originates from it. Applied history, however, does not limit itself to appealing to a mere didactic conception of history for policy-makers. It instead undertakes to identify trends and to develop analytical lenses that can stimulate and enrich decision-making processes at governmental level. Applied history proposes a vision of history at the same time as a critical assessment of the facts and as a tool for investigating new, possible forms of acting. The approach is useful for administrative history: analyzing the past, comparing administrative systems, but also offering a compass for future reforms. The refusal to establish a division between the theoretical moment and the practical moment of the investigation constitutes, indeed, the specific instance of applied history. Peter Stearns suggested looking at the latter as a hybrid discipline, capable of combining the method of historical research with the objectives of social sciences, economics, and political sciences *in primis*:

> In a sense, applied historians are taking into the policy realm the larger interest in a new union between history and social sciences. Many applied historians, like their social science history counterparts, see their mission mainly in terms of fuller historical data to accomplish the basic purposes of social science: better theory, more precise methodology, and [...] a closer alignment to policy needs. (Stearns, 1994: 224)

The applied historian would also be distinguished from the contemporary historian both by the selection of the research themes (dictated by the politico-administrative contingencies and by the needs of the institutions with which the applied historian collaborates, or by circumstances external to the researcher) and by the way of sharing the results of the investigation, to the extent that the applied historian would renounce a discursive analysis. One of the principal differences between applied history and contemporary history, *de facto*, is the former's avoidance of a narrative mode in favour of an analytical style. The applied historian is looking for elements in the past that will explicate, possibly orient to solution, a current problem. The applied historian is not satisfied to provide a mere introductory background statement, which will locate and inform serious policy research but not be a part of the policymaking process (Stearns, 1994: 222). Applied history's theory tries to fulfill two specific objectives: to highlight the affinities between the historiographical investigation and its political counterpart; to examine the analytical toolkit of the historian and evaluate how and to what extent it can be of help to politicians and their advisors.

Regarding the first objective, the applied historians affirm a substantial homology between history and politics, since "both originate from a problem that needs to be explained" (Green, 2016: 80). History is a synthetizing discipline; it proceeds through the study of heterogeneous sources and arranges the collected data in a chronological and interpretative framework. History, like politics, policy and public administration, works on the analysis and integration of information. However, the mere management of data and facts does not exhaust the task of historical research because, if this were the case, it would limit itself to describing a scenario without explaining or interpreting it. Historians have to explain and interpret the evidence, the context, and the process for helping policymakers and decision-makers. Indeed, busy policymakers, immersed in the advice offered by economists, statisticians, jurists, and other professionals, will not have time – even if they did have the inclination – to become regular readers of academic history. In this sense, the challenge for historians is twofold. First, it is in communicating the value of history to a policy and public administrators' audience, then, if this value is accepted, to persuade policymakers to listen to and act on these historical insights.

Usefulness of Applied Administrative History

Applied history offers different questions and points of observation compared to those of other disciplines and compared to the parameters generally used by decision-makers. For example, how can we point out the importance of the irrational and the emotional and make room for the unforeseen and for fate or luck in our institutions, if not by using history? How do we assess the contribution of an individual or an elite in a certain time? How do we make the past usable for policymakers? Could history make policymakers see reality as a whole by teaching them to look at all of historical reality instead of focusing on only those aspects that are considered relevant in a particular disciplinary context (e.g., sociology, political sciences, law, economics; Graham, 1983: 16–18.) Possibly this argument can gain new momentum at a time when knowledge and expertise are becoming ever more fragmented.

Caldwell states that: "Its [administrative history's] relevance to the theory and practice of administration depends upon its instructive value. Its ultimate justification depends upon its success in utilizing historical experience to contribute to the solution of administrative problems" (1955: 458) and "granting the limitations upon the practical applicability or accuracy of administrative history" (Caldwell, 1955: 460), he believes "practical lessons" can be provided (p. 459) and that "the larger relevance of administrative history to the lives of men lies in its ability to contribute first to understanding, and second to rational control of the course of man's development of his latent capacities as a morally creative individual and member of society" (p. 465).

Other authors, such as Luton, suggest, with an Enlightenment thrust, that history can "provide insight into the potential meanings of our lives" (1999: 214). Raadschelders expects a "civilizing and liberating influence" from administrative history (1994: 123), and Plumb points to the fact that in the past, perhaps somewhat more realistically, "its purpose was educative, and hopefully moral" (1971: 301). Assuming that administrative history helps us understand the relationship between society and government, it may also enhance our sensitivity and responsiveness to social change in our time. In this case, history acquires a civilizational value, as it is considered capable to help the improvement of the future. In regards to other authors, Miewald observes that "history promised some sort of foundation for the field" and helped in the "search for a disciplinary identity" (1994: 320). From this perspective, history is the solid ground on which social sciences can develop and define themselves. History is the springboard of the social disciplines. Raadschelders aims to bring these approaches together in a single definition, stating that the "usefulness of administrative history" can be summarized in three steps: 1. Acquiring knowledge for itself to serve (better) understanding of the present; 2. Listing practical lessons from this knowledge about developments; and 3. Contributing to the solution of current problems and the shaping of society in the future with realistic expectations (Raadschelders, 1998a: 13).

Neustadt and May provide an interesting argument for the practical value of history. In their *Thinking in time: The uses of history for decision makers* (1986), they argue that history is going to be used by decision-makers, whether it is taught to them or not and most likely by drawing upon misconceived analogies.

History is useful for public administration scholars too. They could learn a lot from the way historians conduct discourse analysis or collect and interpret source material. "Why don't social scientists use the past as an alternative?" they would ask. It, after all, provides an endless collection of real-life experiments (Monkkonen, 1994). And there is more hidden history in use. In much public administration research, historical material is studied in abundance; for instance, historical archive research is undertaken constantly when a study involves the (re)construction of the history of a policy or organization. Neither the cases nor the research are often recognized by their authors as being historical studies, and therefore lack the safety margins a historian would provide, especially the awareness that the choice and availability of sources influences reconstructions and turns historical conjectures into subjective narratives. Indeed, history is the science of context and historians are conscious that they are providing one of the possible interpretations of this context that could be revised in the future. They bring into the public administration discipline the concept that every scientific activity, including ones subjected to Weberian typification, is always subject to exceptions and revisions.

To sum up: public administration scholars do generate histories, i.e., undertake research with strong historical dimensions. Therefore, they should account for the problems and the tools of historical interpretation as well.

Once the usefulness of history for policymakers and decision-makers working on public policies and public administration reform has been established, it is time to consider the tools that historians can deploy for their applied analyses.

THE TOOLKIT OF THE HISTORIAN

Theorists of applied history have isolated four instruments of historiographic investigation which, in their opinion, would be of the utmost importance, namely: periodization, contextualization, analogy, and integration of evidences (Castellani, 2022).

Periodization and Contextualization

Periodization and contextualization are interrelated procedures. When a certain problem is examined by the historian, the construction of a chronological framework is an essential operation in order to place that given problem in a correct historical perspective. Historians may approach an administrative topic by disassembling the apparent configuration of historical building blocks, but they must then suggest fresh ways of rebuilding them. Periodization is, therefore, an important idea. By examining and questioning the inherent or received periodization of public administration in the past, the historian can hope to refresh current thinking on an issue. Here, historians must deal critically with their own, as well as policymakers', world of ideas. Periods are part of our mentality and notions about power, significance, progress, justice, identity, and so on are enmeshed in how we conceive and describe them (Jordanova, 2017). Critical scrutiny may not, therefore, be easy for the historian but it can be productive, and not only in policy and administrative terms. The formulation of fresh chronological frameworks for understanding political and administrative development through the applied work of history holds an intellectual promise that will surely extend beyond political and administrative history (Zelizer, 2005).

By reassembling the historical building blocks of an administrative topic, the historian also exposes the contingencies of past decision situations. Once it is recognised that a course taken was not inevitable – other routes were considered, imagined, or even intended – then the future may be similarly open. The historian enlarges the options for policy action in the present by showing the array of alternatives that were plausible and feasible in the past. Those imagined futures – sometimes lost, sometimes suppressed – are themselves a rich resource for historians. These "scenarios" can give us access to a wider range of human responses to the problems of society that enhance historical understanding and historical methods but can also enrich public administration thinking.

The skill of describing coherent, plausible alternatives can be applied in the development of scenarios, a central technique in strategy, not just in government but also in business and military contexts. This can be accomplished through the chronological organization – the patterning of time – that the historian offers to policy development. Historians have insights to offer on the scale, nature, and pace of different kinds of change. The tracing of *trends* – and the associated tasks of identifying turning-, starting-, and end-points – are obvious contributions' given we have trends and associated tasks. Knowing where you are in the uptake of a particular technology (say the 5G network) or in social attitudes (for example, in regards pervasive use of social networks) may help determine the timing of a policy intervention and thus maximize cost effectiveness or minimize the risk to political capital. Historians are, further, able to categorize change and "give it coherence", to assess "differential speeds" of change, to distinguish "fundamental from superficial change" and to recognize the continuities "even in an apparently evolving environment" (Stearns, 1982: 19–20).

In turn, the contextualization is necessary both to ascertain a coherent evolutionary path of the issue, and to trace alternative scenarios: by reassembling the historical building blocks of an administrative issue, the historian enlarges the options for policy action in the present by showing the array of alternatives that were plausible and feasible in the past (Bédarida, 1987). In policy and administrative science, context is "a conceptual device to compensate for the lack of behavioral rules and methods to compare behavior across time, space, organizations, and functions" (Ashford, 1992: 13). For historians, the weaving of context is essential to the historical account. If our accounts are to be more than chronicles, we must rely on contextual analysis to interpret sources, assess their significance, identify continuity and change, make valid distinctions or comparisons, and so on. Contextual analysis also serves to authenticate our accounts and provide a guide to our intellectual labour in the scholarly apparatus. Context is therefore much more than its usual synonyms, such as setting, environment, milieu, and background, suggest. In terms of history in government, however, context tends to be understood in these more limited senses: preface rather than policy. Articulating the power of contextual thinking for policymaking and administrative reformers is therefore an important task. The weaving of context involves asking questions that create connections between present knowledge and the circumstances of the past. The process is a swinging pendulum between past and present, which incrementally builds up a map or image representing the historian's understanding of the past in the present. Questioning allows the historian to crystallize what is not known; once gaps are identified, a new focus for the enquiry is gained. The value of such skilled questioning to the collective puzzling of policy and administrative learning is clear. The historian on the inside can, of course, acquire "knowledge of historical specifics" relevant to a task pursued in the mixed unit but such content cannot be a substitute for contextual thinking (Green, 2016: 77).

The preliminary phase of contextualization allows individuals to articulate the historical facts that led to the emergence of a specific situation within a unitary sequence and therefore to consider them not as isolated moments, but linked events of the same pattern. This organic perspective on the past implies, according to the applied historians, certain interpretative advantages that the ruling classes could exploit to plan long-term strategies (Neustadt and May, 1986, 235; Stearns and Tarr, 1981: 522).

Analogy

Formulating an action in the light of the practice and knowledge of historiographic investigation would also prevent the perpetration of the fallacious use of a conceptual device typical of the historian but nevertheless highly appreciated by policymakers and reformers: analogy.

The appropriate use of analogy is what distinguishes a conscious and effective use of the past from its empty actualization. Analogy is a tool with a strong expressive power and represents the form in which, mainly, history relives in the political debate. Analogy condenses phenomena of the past, watershed moments in history, and transforms them into symbolic syntheses: the Marshall Plan, appeasement, the New Deal, to name some of the most recurrent analogies, become macro-categories capable of creating immediate references between the past and present, on the basis of which political initiatives are explained and legitimized. The use of analogy by those who are not used to working professionally with historical facts has obvious limits and it is precisely by virtue of this misuse of comparison with the past that applied historians claim the need to introduce historians into ministries and into government offices. Removing the analogies from the imprecise applications they have often been the subject of represents, for applied history, the first step towards redeveloping the role of history in the political debate. The comparison between different political phenomena and historical circumstances can be misleading, if not harmful, from a strategic point of view. An example of the distortions caused by a careless use of analogy is provided by May in his *Lessons of the past*, which underlines the error of assessment committed by the Truman administration in believing that the European situation after World War II would match that of 1919 and, specifically, in having identified a correspondence between Soviet expansionism in the Balkans with that of Nazi Germany in continental Europe (Achenbaum, 1987).

Integration of Evidences

All disciplines create meaning from information, using approaches from within the parameters of their discourses. The information may not be specific to a discipline but what scholars *do* with their materials is an important aspect of disciplinary distinctiveness. History is an eclectic field; historians actively seek out a plurality of data from which to derive evidence and develop interpretations. There is no form of information that could not, potentially, fall within the historian's purview – from the more conventional letters, diaries, and official papers to sketchbooks and statistics, films and field notes – nor is any form of human knowledge without a historical dimension. History is inevitably "history of …" and so its practitioners have always drawn on and engaged with evidence from other scholarly domains as an integral part of their pursuit of historical meaning. The absence of a canon equivalent to those found in the social sciences perhaps aids these creative appropriations (Guldi and Armitage, 2014: 10; Jordanova, 2017). Trained through exposure to competing approaches to a topic, historians are generally accustomed to crossing, challenging, and revising paradigms and work with a relatively open interplay between theories, concepts, and evidence (Fulbrook, 2002: 68 and 109).

Given the complexity of administrative issues and the multiple perspectives involved, historians' ability to make sense of a wide variety of often incompatible and conflicting data should be a strength. The need to integrate evidence, to bring coherence to the mess of information, is an important affinity between history and policy. So, "[i]t is precisely the ability to embrace complexities while making sense of them, and to think flexibly about diverse phenomena at distinct analytical levels, that characterises the historian's purchase on the past" (Jordanova, 2017: 71).

The policymaker must assess different forms of external evidence and integrate the conclusions with a multiplicity of other factors, such as feasibility and public opinion, as well as the mechanisms available within the political system. There is an inherent pragmatism to both historians' and policymakers' endeavours, which seeks to reconcile disparate data into a coherent account in the absence (and impossibility) of perfect knowledge. Both begin with issues that require explanation. Historians do not start from a blank sheet but turn to the sources with "questions about problematic aspects of the past within pre-existing collective frameworks of assumed knowledge, theories, and moot points or dark spots for further investigation" (Fulbrook, 2002: 67). Similarly, policy commitments and administrative initiatives proceed from problems that are enmeshed in prior understandings: of the functions of the state, for example, the nature of a good society, or the priorities for government action.

A number of scholars have suggested that their fellow historians are more able than those from other fields to convene efforts to address policy and administrative problems, due to the ability to weigh and draw together incompatible data, perspectives and ideas. History can blend in a meaningful way "economic, political, intellectual, cultural, climatic, geographic, demographic, scientific, technological, organizational, and psychological factors and concepts in order to 'see matters'" (Graham, 1983: 11; Gaddis: 2004 69). This practice of synthesis and integration is particularly valuable for administrative decision-making, as the problems with which governments are concerned inevitably cross the boundaries that have been constructed around academic disciplines.

RELATIONSHIP WITH OTHER DISCIPLINES

In the past decades, general arguments advocating for the study of administrative history included: the formulation of ever-higher levels of generalization (Caldwell, 1955: 454), the development of grand theory (Nash, 1969: 63), and the preference for macro-causal analysis (Skocpol and Somers, 1980: 175–180).

At present, a historical perspective is pursued within the neo-institutional school, and more specifically by the historical institutionalists (to be distinguished from the rational choice group) (cf. Thelen and Steinmo, 1992), departing from such embracing concepts as path dependency and critical junctures. Moreover, history is fundamental to detect, to conceptualize, and to test administrative traditions in comparative perspective (Painter and Peters, 2010; Ongaro, 2010; Peters, 2021).

According to Adams, administrative history can shed more light on and improve the epistemological basis of the field: "Critical, historically-based studies are sorely needed to address in a meaningful way both the political and epistemological dimensions of modernity as they bear on public administration" (1992: 373). History of political and administrative thought, for example, is very helpful in assessing the evolution of debate and ideas on public administration reforms (Castellani, 2021).

Historians thus seem to understand that in the social sciences an evolutionary hypothesis does not constitute a universal law but is merely a historical statement (Nisbet, 1969; Popper, 1974). Evolution is a unique historical process that may proceed according to some kind of causal law such as natural selection, but unlike the natural sciences, the social sciences do not claim to have identified such universalities (i.e., natural laws), but only suggest stages, patterns, and mechanisms. This fits well with the use of ideal-typical constructs in the social sciences, which are used as means to interpret reality. They by no means are real themselves. They are abstractions that exist primarily in the mind, "out of time and out of place" (Boudon, 1986). History is useful to contest ideal-types established by scholarship in public administration and not only to build them.

Furthermore, the historical perspective study of public administration should blur the boundaries both between generalists and specialists and between the humanities and social sciences (Raadschelders, 2011). The aim of public administration as discipline could not be bordered only within a scientific approach, in a sheer explanatory manner. Indeed, the aim of public administration would be rather optimizing public administration in the widest sense, that is, making the state work as legitimately, fairly, effectively, and efficiently as possible. Historically, a number of civil services (like the British one) used to train civil and public servants mainly in the humanities. Public servants were seen as "amateurs" whose main skills lay in general culture and in learning by practising, or learning "on the job". A philosophical, historical and literary culture was seen as pivotal in the public service. The underlying conception was one in which "understanding" comes before technical and managerial "knowledge" (Castellani, 2018). This is a conception of public administration in which the emphasis is on understanding rather than disciplinary knowledge, in which to be centre stage is the bridging of knowledge and action through understanding and linking the explanatory (why? what? questions) to the normative (the "should" questions, e.g., what should administration do?). Public administration is in this respect an art (Hood 2000): it is about the capacity to bridge understanding and knowledge, the normative and explanatory, in order to create, maintain, or renew an administrative system. If we take this composite definition of public administration, it is evident how history can be an essential element of this field of research due to its "natural ability" to act as a bridge, and often as a basis, between different disciplines and between different times and spaces.

But public administration may also be seen – alongside being a science, an art and a profession – as a form of "humanism" (Waldo 1987; Biancu and Ongaro, Chapter 5, this volume). Public administration is in this sense part of the humanities too, administering being concerned also and intrinsically with the making of value-laden decisions, which demand the decision-makers exercise judgement and wisdom (Hodgkinson, 1978). Public administration is human-made, it is made by humans for humans, and hence it must be informed by knowledge and understanding about human nature: its traits, needs, motivations, and aspirations to well-being – and the rights and obligations associated with our human condition (Ongaro, 2020). To reinforce the case for bringing public administration back to the humanities, it is also worth recalling the admonitions that Hannah Arendt (1958) issued to the contemporary rulers when she referred to the death of Socrates as the death of wisdom in both public governance and society at large: from this consideration stems her call to rediscover philosophical wisdom alongside, and in a sense over, technical expertise as the only way forward for a better and more humane society and public governance. In sum, the nature of public administration as both science and also, in an integrated way, an art, a profession, and a form of humanism, drawing from the humanities, is part and parcel of its nature (Ongaro, 2020, chapter 1). To the extent public administration is science, it is perhaps better intended as episteme, as rigour in generating knowledge; and as *Wissenschaft*, a field of intellectual inquiry conducted through an approach that encompasses a systematic consideration for values and meanings in the study of social phenomena (Gadamer, 1960/1975; Weber, 1922). Within the framework of this broad conception of science, we intend "explanation" as both the process of identifying the causes of something and the process of attributing meaning to something (Demeulenaere, 2011). Public administration draws from the social sciences and shares with them the common problems and quandaries of social scientific knowledge; at the same time, due to its composite nature, it partly transcends those boundaries to enter the terrain of the canons and practices of a profession, like medicine or engineering; of a human activity, which is also inherently an art – the art of governing and administering; and of the humanities, the making of value-laden decisions and the attributing of meaning to the public space (Ongaro, 2020).

CONCLUSIONS

In conclusion, administrative history has multiple sources of relevance for public administration. If administrative history is not defined with too stringent criteria, but by including different levels of analysis and perspectives, it turns out to be very valuable for the study of public administration for a variety of reasons. It is relevant for society-at-large as it can be found in historical sensitivity toward how government is influenced by its environment and how it might enhance the ability to both appreciate more as well as adequately criticize the government of one's own era. It can be important for policy-making and its practical implications because knowledge and insight in administrative development might be important for the day-to-day actions and behavior of politicians, civil servants, and citizens. Finally, the study of history is central for the epistemic community for its prismatic and multifaceted characteristics. Administrative history is interdisciplinary in itself; the historical mindset and the historian's toolkit can help decision-makers craft reforms and policies. History offers strong connections with other disciplines which are involved in the study of public administration.

REFERENCES

Achenbaum, W.A. (1989). Politics, power, and problems: Perspectives on writing public history. *Journal of Policy History* 1: 206–231.

Achenbaum, W.A. (1987). Public history's past, present and prospects. *American Historical Review* 5: 1162–1174.

Adams, G. B. (1992). Enthralled with modernity: The historical context of knowledge and theory development in public administration. *Public Administration Review*, 363–373.

Arendt, H. (1958). The modern concept of history. *The Review of Politics*, 20(4), 570–590.

Ashford, D.E. (ed) (1992). History and Context in Comparative Public Policy, Pittsburgh, University of Pittsburgh Press.

Bédarida, F. (1987). The modern historian's dilemma: conflicting pressures from science and society. Economic History Review, 335–348.

Boudon, R. (1986). The problems of the philosophy of history. *Social Science Information*, 25(4), 861–880.

Caldwell, L.K. (1955). The relevance of administrative history. *International Review of Administrative Sciences* 21: 453–466.

Castellani, L. (2023). Alberto Beneduce. A technocrat in the fascist era. *Contemporary European History*. Published online by Cambridge University Press: 30 March 2023.

Castellani, L (2022). Thinking with history in policy, in C. Domper, G. Priorelli (eds.) *Combining political history and political science: Towards a new understanding of the political*. Routledge.

Castellani, L. (2021). *The history of the US civil service: From postwar years to the twenty-first century*. Routledge.

Castellani, L. (2018). *The rise of managerial bureaucracy: Reforming the British Civil Service*. Palgrave Macmillan.

Creel, H.G. (1964), The beginnings of bureaucracy In China. *The Journal of Asian Studies* 23(2): 155–184.

Cromwell, V. (1966). Interpretations of nineteenth-century administration: An analysis. *Victorian Studies* 9(3): 245–255.

Demeulenaere, P. (Ed.). (2011). *Analytical sociology and social mechanisms.* Cambridge University Press.

Elton, G. (1955). *The Tudor revolution in government.* Cambridge University Press.

Ernest, R. (1973). *May, Lessons of the Past: The Use and Misuse of History in American Foreign Policy.* Oxford, Oxford University Press.

Fulbrook, M. (2002). *Historical theory: Ways of imaging the past.* Routledge.

Gadamer, H. G. (1960). Aesthetics and hermeneutics. *The continental aesthetics reader*, 181–186.

Gaddis, J.L. (2004). *The landscape of history: How historians map the past.* Oxford University Press.

Gawthrop, L.C. (1993). The ethical foundations of American public administration. *International Journal of Public Administration* 16(2): 139–163.

Graham, O.L. Jnr. (1983). The uses and misuses of history: Roles in policymaking. *The Public Historian* 2: 5–19.

Green, A. (2016). *History, policy and public purpose: Historians and historical thinking in government.* Palgrave Macmillan.

Guldi, J. and Armitage, D. (2014). *The history manifesto.* Cambridge University Press.

Hodgkinson, C. (1978). The failure of organizational and administrative theory. *McGill Journal of Education/Revue des sciences de l'éducation de McGill*, 13(003).

Hood, C. (2000). *The art of the state: Culture, rhetoric, and public management.* Oxford University Press.

Jacoby, H. (1973). *The bureaucratization of the world.* University of California Press.

Jordanova, L. (2017). *History in practice.* Hodder Arnold.

Luton, L.S. (1999). History and American public administration. *Administration & Society,* 31, 205–221.

May, E.R. (1973). *"Lessons" of the past: The use and misuse of history in American foreign policy.* Oxford University Press.

Miewald, R.D. (1994). European administrative history and American public administration, in E.V. Heyen (ed.), *Yearbook for European administrative history,* Vol. 6. Bilder der Verwaltung: Memoiren, Karikaturen, Romane, *Architektur = Images de Vadministration: Memoires, caricatures, romans, architecture* (pp. 319–328). Nomos Verlagsgesellschaft.

Monkkonen, Eric H. (1994). "Lessons of Social Sience History." Historical Social Research/Historische Sozialforschung (1994): 140–146.

Nash, G.D. (1969). *Perspectives on administration: The vistas of history.* Institute of Governmental Studies, University of California.

Neustadt, R.E. and May, E.R. (1986). *Thinking in time: The uses of history for decision makers.* The Free Press and Collier Macmillan Publishers.

Nisbet, R.A. (1969). *Social change and history: Aspects of the Western theory of development.* Oxford University Press.

Ongaro, E. (2010). The Napoleonic administrative tradition and public management reform in France, Greece, Italy, Portugal and Spain. In M. Painter and B.G. Peters (eds.), *Tradition and public administration* (pp. 174–190). London, UK: Palgrave Macmillan.

Ongaro, E. (2020). *Philosophy and public administration.* Cheltenham, UK and Northampton, MA: Edward Elgar.

Painter, M. and Guy Peters, B. (2010). *Tradition and Public Administration,* Palgrave Macmillan.

Peters, G.B. (2021). *Administrative traditions: Understanding the roots of contemporary administrative behavior.* Oxford University Press.

Plumb, J. H. (1971). Reason and unreason in the eighteenth century: the English experience, in In the Light of History, New York: Delta Books.

Popper, K. R. (1974). *Scientific reduction and the essential incompleteness of all science.* Studies in the philosophy of biology: Reduction and related problems, 259–284.

Raadschelders, J. C. (2011). *Public administration: The interdisciplinary study of government.* Oxford University Press.

Raadschelders, J. C. N. (1999). A coherent framework for the study of public administration. *Journal of Public Administration Research and Theory* 9: 281–303.

Raadschelders, J.C.N. (1998a). *Handbook of administrative history.* Transaction Publishers.

Raadschelders, J.C.N. (1998b). Evolution, institutional analysis, and path dependency: An administrative-historical perspective on fashionable approaches and concepts. *International Review of Administrative Sciences,* 64, 565–582.

Raadschelders, J.C.N. (1997). Size and organizational differentiation in historical perspective. *Journal of Public Administration Research and Theory,* 7, 419–441.

Raadschelders, J.C.N. (1994). Administrative history: Contents, meaning, and usefulness. *International Review of the Administrative Sciences* 60: 117–129.

Raadschelders, J.C., Wagenaar, P., Rutgers, M.R., and Overeem, P. (2000). Against a study of the history of public administration: A manifesto. *Administrative Theory & Praxis* 22(4): 772–791.

Rowse, A.L. (1946). *The use of history.* Hodder & Stoughton.

Skocpol, T. and Somers, M. (1980). The uses of comparative history in macrosocial inquiry. *Comparative Studies in Society and History* 22: 174–197.

Stearns, P. (1994). Applied history and social sciences. *Social Science History* 2: 219–226.

Stearns, P. (1982). History and policy analysis: Toward maturity. *The Public Historian* 4(3), 5–29.

Stearns, P. and Tarr, J. (1981). Applied history: A new-old departure. *The History Teacher* 4: 517–531.

Stone, L. (1971). Prosopography. *Daedalus*, 46–79.

Joseph Strayer, On The Medieval Origins of the modern State, Princeton University Press, Princeton, 1975.

Thelen, K. and Steinmo, S. (1992). Historical institutionalism in comparative politics. In Steinmo, S. Thelen, K., and Longstreth, F. (eds.), *Structuring politics: Historical institutionalism in comparative analysis* (pp. 1–32). Cambridge University Press.

Van Creveld, M. (2020). *Seeing into the future. A short history of prediction.* Reaction Books.

Waldo, D. (1987). Politics and administration: On thinking about a complex relationship. *A centennial history of the American administrative state*, 89–112.

Weber, M. (1922). Gesammelte aufsätze zur wissenschaftslehre. JCB Mohr.

Wetherell, C. (1998). Historical social network analysis. *International Review of Social History* 43(S6): 125–144.

Wilson, W. (1889/1898/1918). *The state: Elements of historical and practical politics.* (The 1889 edition had an extra subtitle: *A sketch of institutional history and administration*). Heath.

Zelizer, J. E. (2005). New Directions in Policy History. *Journal Of Policy History*, vol. 17, no.1, 1–12.

11. The Contribution of the Religious Studies and Theology Literatures to Public Administration: A Review and Outlook

Michele Tantardini and Edoardo Ongaro

INTRODUCTION

In a review of the English language scientific journals in three disciplines of the social sciences – namely public administration, political science, and business/management – Ongaro and Tantardini (2024d) found that the influence of religion, faith, and spirituality on public administration (hereafter: PA) had been mostly overlooked. The findings were even more limited if religion alone was considered. In order to have a more comprehensive understanding of the manifold relations between religion and PA and a more complete picture of what has been written on this topic, a good starting point is, therefore, to take stock of the literature outside the social sciences and explore the literature pertaining to the disciplines of religious studies and theology.

Religious studies and theology are generally grouped within the field of the humanities, a branch of knowledge concerned with studying human beings and their values, culture, literature, history, art, religions, and philosophy (Encyclopaedia Britannica, n.d.). Religious studies and theology provide a more profound understanding of human societies by studying the origins and evolution of religious beliefs, practices, and expressions and by studying and speculating on the relations between the transcendent and the human. Furthermore, they posit questions about values, ethics, and meaning, thus shedding light on the interplay between God, faith, and reason; and how human beings thrive in a *polis* – a community of other individuals – and the institutions necessary to govern it (Encyclopaedia Britannica, n.d.).

Through the application of a rigorous research protocol (specifics on the methodology are described in the next section), we identified 58 publications in the religious studies and theology literature that investigate distinctive aspects of the relationship between religion and PA. Their analysis revealed significant findings in terms of the contents and foci of these publications, the religions that are studied in relation to their implications for PA, and methodological considerations at the crossroads between the social sciences and the humanities.

This study is important for the following reasons. First, the results complement the findings of the study by Ongaro and Tantardini (2024d) on the manifold relations between religion and PA by bringing the humanities into the picture to complement the findings from the social science literature. Second, this study bridges PA, an academic discipline regarded as an insular field (McGuigan et al., 2021), and two far-removed academic disciplines – religious studies and theology. Third, and crucial, this study is another step in the direction of remedying the neglect of the religious as a key explanatory factor employed by scholars in studying PA, an important direction of research for the reasons outlined in Ongaro and Tantardini (2023b; 2024a and 2024c).

The chapter unfolds as follows: First, we present the methodological approach employed in this review. Second, we describe the identified corpus of literature. Third, we summarise the overall findings of the review. Finally, we discuss the contribution of religious studies and theology literature to the field of PA and provide future venues for research.

METHODOLOGY

Literature Search

Following Ongaro and Tantardini (2024d), we restricted the analysis to English-language peer-reviewed journal articles, thus excluding contributions in languages other than English and the so-called "grey literature" (Rothstein & Hopewell, 2009); this is due exclusively to research resources limitations. We also confined the analysis to articles published between 1960 and 2023 (for the same reason noted above – and, also, noticing that Ongaro and Tantardini, 2024d, researched the same time span). Table 11.1 reports the Boolean string and keywords used in the title-OR-abstract-only search. The keyword "public govern*" was truncated to include derivative words such as but not limited to government(s), governance, governing; the keyword "public administrat*" was truncated to include derivative words such as but not limited to administration(s), administrator(s), administrative; the keyword "public manag*" was truncated to include derivative words such as but not limited to management, manager(s), managerial; the keyword "public leader*" was truncated to include derivative words such as but not limited to leader(s) and leadership; the keywords "public sector*" and "public institution*" were truncated to include their respective plural forms.

Table 11.1   Boolean string and keywords

Databases	Boolean string and keywords
ProQuest	"public govern*" OR "public administrat*" OR "public manag*"
Web of Science	OR "public sector*" OR "public institution*" OR "public leader*"
DOAJ	
EBSCO	
JSTOR	

Source: Author's own.

We conducted the initial searches during the month of November 2023. The first stage of the literature identification yielded a total of 333 potentially relevant articles: 176 articles identified in the ProQuest research platform, 120 articles on Web of Science, 20 articles on DOAJ, 13 articles on EBSCO, and four articles on JSTOR. Each article's author(s), title, journal name, abstract, Digital Object Identifier (DOI), and other relevant information were downloaded. After removing 62 duplicate records, there were 271 articles eligible for further screening.

Adopting the protocol also employed in Ongaro and Tantardini (2024d), both authors screened the 271 articles to assess whether they contributed or not to the field of PA (PA = YES/NO). A total of 14 disagreements were discussed and resolved by the two authors, thus increasing inter-rater reliability (Littell et al., 2008). 194 articles were deemed not to contribute to the field of PA (PA = NO) and thus excluded from full-text retrieval. A total of 74 articles were downloaded and assessed for full-text eligibility. Then 16 articles were further

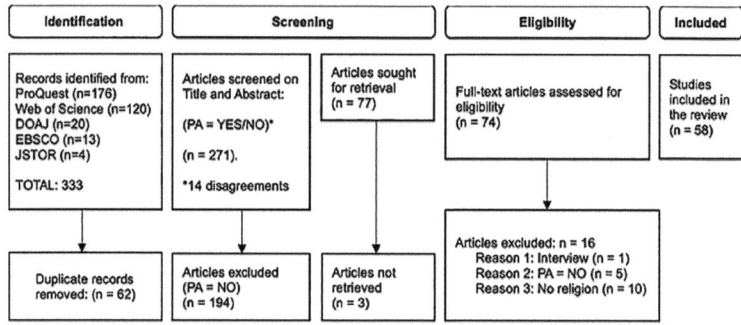

Source: Our elaboration on the PRISMA protocol flow diagram.

Figure 11.1   The literature identification, screening, eligibility, and inclusion process.

excluded: ten of them because there was no reference to (any of) religion, faith, or spirituality; five articles were excluded because after reading the full text, the authors agreed they did not contribute to the field of PA (PA = NO); and finally, one article was excluded because it was an interview. A total of 58 studies were included in the review (see Appendix A for the full list).

Review Methodology

The 58 articles were reviewed and categorised according to the categories reported in Table 11.2. Following Ongaro and Tantardini (2023a), the articles were classified on whether the level of analysis was on the individual(s) (code: Micro-level), the level of organisations, including the operations and delivery of public services (code: Meso-level), or the more macro level (code: Macro-level) of the broader configuration of public administrative systems. Furthermore, the 58 articles were attributed to one of the 18 themes identified in the book by Ongaro and Tantardini (2023a): the first ten themes were identified based on the actual detection of scientific publications in the field of social sciences that pertain to one or more of these ten thematic areas, and provide an analysis thereof, while the remaining eight themes were identified on a purely theoretical-speculative basis, as "new" themes that could be part of a broad research agenda on the manifold relations between religion and PA – an agenda widely outlined in Ongaro and Tantardini (2023a, chapter 8). Articles were also categorised based on their methodological orientation, methods of investigation, level of governance, and focus on (a) specific country(ies) and continent; Table 11.2 also reports the number of articles identified for each of the 18 themes between parentheses.

DESCRIBING THE CORPUS OF THE LITERATURE

Before presenting and discussing the themes that appeared in the religious studies and theology literature, data is first described. Figure 11.2 shows the number of publications per five-year term. While the number of publications was particularly low between 1995 and 1999, the scholarly interest for these themes increased steadily in the subsequent 15 years, with 9 articles published between 2010 and 2014, 25 between 2015 and 2019, and 18 articles published between 2020 and November 2023. It is worth noticing that although the search criteria included articles published from 1960, the final list of studies entered in the review displays only articles published from the mid-nineties.

Figure 11.3 illustrates the orientation of the studies included in the review of the literature. Interestingly, there are four times as many empirical studies (N=47) than theoretical studies (N=11). Among the empirical studies, 34 employed a qualitative approach, eight employed a quantitative approach, and

Table 11.2   Review categories and descriptions

Categories	Description
Level of Analysis	The level of analysis of the article is micro-level or the level of individual; meso-level or the level of organisations; macro-level or the level of public administrative systems
Orientation	The orientation of the article is either theoretical or empirical. If empirical it is specified whether quantitative, qualitative, or mixed methods
Methods	The specific research method employed in the study (e.g., OLS regression, semi-structured interviews, case-study, etc.)
Level of Governance	The level of governance of the articles in either local, regional, state/province, national/federal, supranational, or international
Country and Continent	The article focuses on (a) specific country(ies)
Theme	1. Person-Organisation fit perspective (5)
	2. Religion and Public Service Motivation (PSM) (2)
	3. The influence of religious beliefs on public managers' and employees' behaviour in public sector organisations (4)
	4. Religious beliefs and bureaucratic discretion (1)
	5. Religion as a moral and beliefs system affecting behaviour of citizens/users of public services (1)
	6. Religion as a factor shaping an organisation's mission and values as well as its management practices and performance (8)
	7. Faith-Based Organisations (FBOs) and implications for public service delivery (7)
	8. Government funding of external providers and religious affiliation (1)
	9. Faith organisations and leaders' participation in public governance and co-creation, and dynamics of social cohesion and interculturalism (2)
	10. Religion as ideational basis: reflection on religion as source of legitimacy and basis of accountability, exercise of power in (politics and) public administration (6)
	11. The influence of religion on public leadership and on leadership styles (5)
	12. The influence of religion and faith on wellbeing in the workplace (4)
	13. Religion as an ideational source which has a powerful social mobilisation dimension (2)
	14. The interrelationship between religion in its ideational dimension and the design (or redesign) of governance arrangements (7)
	15. Religion and institutional quality and the quality of public governance (2)
	16. Understanding how public value varies as based on and shaped by different religious teachings (0)
	17. The influence of religion on the argument of the 'intransigent context' (1)
	18. The role of religion on environmental sustainability including the effects of global warming on populations exposed to climate vulnerabilities (0)
	19. Other (please specify) (0)

Source: Author's own.

the remaining five employed a mixed-methods approach. More specifically, most qualitative studies used semi-structured interviews, case studies, and textual analysis as data collection methods, while quantitative studies used statistical techniques (OLS, logit/probit) to analyse data.

Another descriptive information about the corpus of the literature is the geographic context in which the manifold relations between religion and PA have been studied. As illustrated in Figure 11.4, North America and Europe comprise roughly 40 percent (N=23) of the geographic contexts studied in the 58 articles included in our review. Considering that most multi-country studies (N=7) include European countries and the United States of America (U.S.A.), it is plausible to state that half of the 58 studies are focused on the so-called Western Countries. Sub-Saharan Africa (N=5) and Northern Africa and the Middle East (N=4) are the second and third geographic contexts studied in the articles included in our review.

Finally, to conclude this section and to introduce the presentation of the results, we also report on the level of governance at which the studies are pitched. As shown in Figure 11.5, Micro-level studies represent a third of the articles included in this literature review (N=19). Organisational-level studies (Meso-level) accounted for about 26 per cent of studies (N=15), while Macro-level studies accounted for about 21 per cent (N=12). It is also interesting to note that 17 per cent of studies were double-coded Meso/Macro (N = 10), thus representing multi-level studies in which multiple echelons have been studied.

RESULTS

Our literature review identified a range of themes about the relations of religion and PA. With the exception of themes 16 and 18 (see Table 11.2 for the complete list of themes), for which no articles were attributed, all the other themes are here analysed. The first five themes revolve around papers that consider religion as a shaper of the personalities and behaviours of elected and tenured officials and citizens/users of public services (Micro-level themes).

1. Person-Organisation fit perspective

Two of the five articles attributed to this theme focus on PO fit strictly speaking: Craft et al. (2011) "investigate how Christian faculty members integrate their religious identity with their professional identity within public colleges and universities" (p. 92) in the US and found that the "desire of most Christian faculty is not to 'take back' the country for their faith but simply to have their faith seen as reasonable, genuine, and attractive" (p. 107). Meron (2015) with a study on Jewish engineers in Greece in the 1930s validates the hypothesis that (religious) minorities prefer to work in the private sector as opposed to the public sector to avoid discrimination. Putra et al. (2023) and Iraqi et al. (2020)

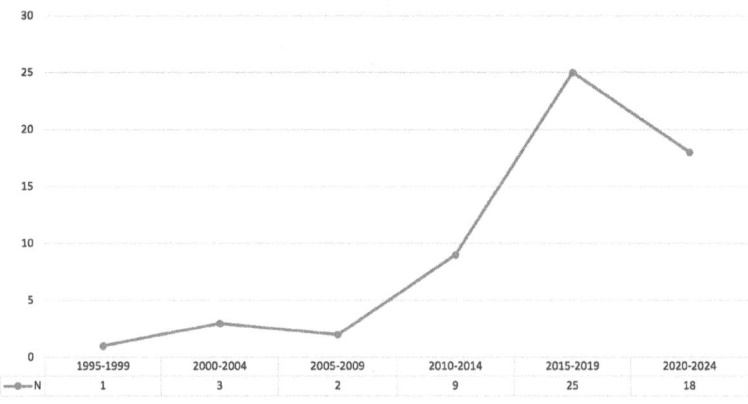

Source: Author's own.

Figure 11.2   Number of publications per five-year term

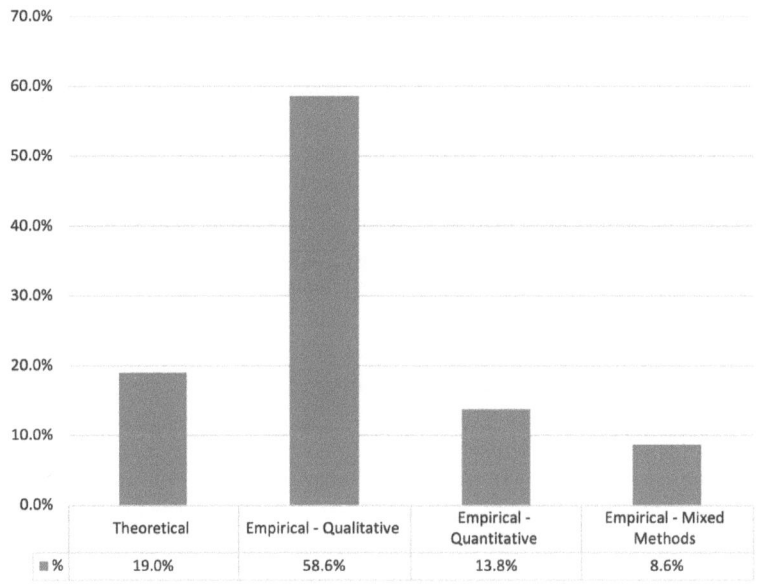

Source: Author's own.

Figure 11.3   Orientation of the studies included in the review (In percentages)

frame their respective articles in terms of P-O fit as a determinant of job satisfaction and individual performance.

2. Religion and Public Service Motivation (PSM)

Plopeanu (2022) found a positive association between religious affiliation to Christian Orthodoxy and the intentions to pursue a career in the public sector among students studying Economics and Business Administration at a major Romanian university. In a qualitative study about officers attending training at the National Institute of Public Administration (INTAN) in Kuala Lumpur, Malaysia, Yashaiya and Noh (2022) found that in evaluating the level of PSM of individuals and their intention to join the public service, ethnic heterogeneity of the organisation matters in addition to personal attributes such as education, personal values and identity, political beliefs, and socialisation.

3. The influence of religious beliefs on public managers' and employees' behaviour in public sector organisations

Collectively, the four articles attributed to this theme highlight the significance of religion in shaping attitudes and behaviours and informing the decision-making process of actors within public sector organisations. Worth mentioning is the contribution by Adler et al. (2021): in a study of local public sector officials (mayors and commissioners) in the US, the authors found that "religious factors are crucial for understanding variation in frontline officials' responses to COVID-19" (p. 418) and that religious nationalism was a strong predictor of

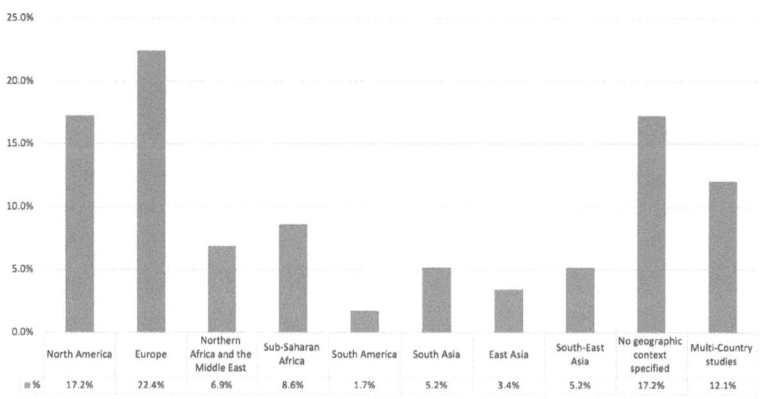

Source: Author's own.

Figure 11.4   *Percentages of the geographic contexts of the studies included in the review*

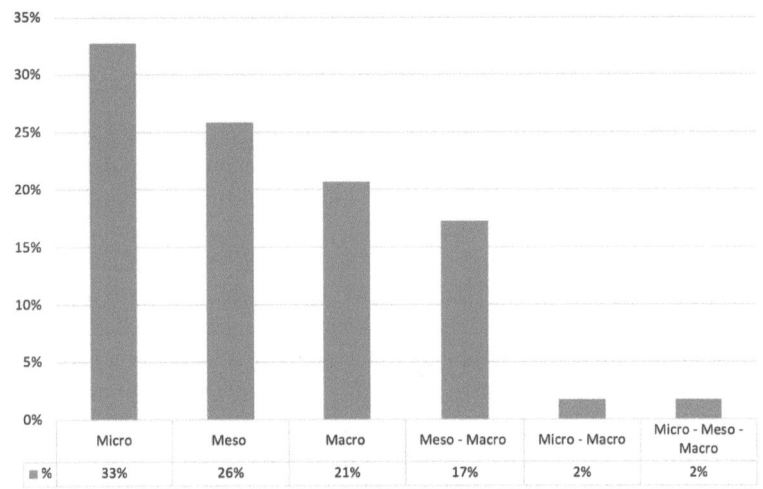

Source: Author's own.

Figure 11.5   *Level of analysis of the studies included in the review (In percentages)*

resistance of these officials to adhere to public health guidance (i.e., masking, social distancing, vaccinating, etc.). Differently, the contribution by Dudin et al. (2019) focuses on the personal cross-cultural features of managers working in multicultural education settings and their role in fostering a multicultural approach to managing these organisations.

4. Religious beliefs and bureaucratic discretion

In the only article attributed to the very closely related Theme 4, Charles et al. (2014), found that the level of spirituality could help police officers buffering toxic experiences they confront during their duty. They also found that officers with high levels of spirituality "had low levels of perceived stress, [...] fast executive processing, and high levels of brain integration" (p. 203). This is important as police officers are "expected to perform at the highest level concerning perception, planning, strategizing, motor functioning, and endurance when confronting immediate crisis or critical incident" (p. 207). The peculiarity of this study was that it employed a mixed-methods approach where police officers were first interviewed to "allow the participants to describe their police work, issues surrounding their exposure to trauma, spiritual history, and spiritual beliefs" (p. 203) and then through the use of electroencephalogram

(EEG) instrumentation, the authors studied the relation of the 11 police officers' executive functioning, brain integration and spirituality in life.

5. Religion as a moral and beliefs system affecting the behaviour of citizens/users of public services

In the only article attributed to this theme, Coons and Brennan (2002) discuss two realist strains of moral philosophy within the context of Roman Catholicism – the gnostic and the obtensionalist – that widely support school choice and parental sovereignty in the public sector. The authors conclude by articulating a Catholic position on the school choice question, stating that "parents confirm that there is a real good and that their own child is bound to honor it–with salvation as the prize" (p. 296).

6. Religion as a factor shaping an organisation's mission and values as well as its management practices and performance

The next four themes concern the link between religion and organizational behaviour, broadly intended (Meso-level themes). We assigned eight articles to Theme 6. Two of these articles (Cadge et al,2017; Gilliat-Ray, 2018) focus on methodological challenges and comparative analytical frameworks for analysing ways religion shapes public institutions in different organisational and geographical contexts. Two articles focus on the (changing) role of religion and chaplaincy in the military in the U.S. and France (Konieczny & Bertossi, 2017) and Chile (Bellolio, 2020). These articles also address the sub-theme of religious diversity within public sector organisations and institutions. One article specifically addresses the involvement of religion in public healthcare institutions in the U.S. and the U.K. (Idler & Kellehear, 2017). The authors propose a continuum for this relationship, "from completely merged identities at one end ('faith-saturated') to entirely separate ones at the other ('faith-secular partnerships')" (p. 234). Finally, the contribution by Proehl et al. (2015) presents the "challenges faced, tensions experienced, and lessons learned while transferring a Lasallian (Christian Brother) educational model into the public sector" in Illinois, U.S. (p. 125).

7. Faith-Based Organisations (FBOs) and implications for public service delivery

We attributed seven articles to Theme 7. Three articles focus on FBOs' role in providing education in Sweden (Henrekson, 2023), Ghana (Zook & Arndt, 2021), and in North Carolina, U.S. (Pearson et al., 2018). Another article focuses on the role of Hindu social service FBOs not only in providing food to those in need but also as a mode of bridging and institution building (Pandya, 2017). Gao et al. (2023) analyse the role of Christian social service FBOs in the context of China, highlighting their multiple identities as faith-based organisations – legal-person organisations, and professional organisations, – their pluralistic nature, and their ability to form relationships with non-religious professional service systems.

8. Government funding of external providers and religious affiliation

The only article assigned to Theme 8 presents a study on contracting between faith-based healthcare organisations and the public sector in four African countries (Cameroon, Chad, Tanzania, and Uganda) (Boulenger et al., 2014). According to the authors, contracting with faith-based healthcare facilities was a crucial step in developing effective and equitable healthcare delivery systems and ultimately integrating these facilities into public health systems. The study stresses the need to "dramatically improve knowledge and expertise in designing, implementing, and monitoring contractual arrangements" (p. 28) and professionally train the health management of the FBOs entering a contractual relationship with the public sector.

9. Faith organisations and leaders' participation in public governance and co-creation, and dynamics of social cohesion and interculturalism

The last Meso-level theme shows the role of faith- and community-based initiative in instances of urban governance and community development. Burgess (2015) discusses the case of the African Pentecostal Initiative in Zambia and Nigeria, which fosters "citizen mobilization through training church and community leaders, and [empowers] ordinary people to improve the quality of life in their communities" (p. 176). Dahan (2019), in a study on community-based organisations (CBOs) engaged in social activity on behalf of lower-class neighbourhoods and towns in Israel, found how the religious drives civic engagement and how this, in turn, "influences the nature of urban governance (the governance logic, strategy and the services given to community)" (p. 64).

10. Religion as ideational basis: reflection on religion as source of legitimacy and basis of accountability, exercise of power in (politics and) public administration

Religion has throughout history provided – or been used as – a source of legitimacy and basis of accountability, exercise of power in politics at large and thence, derivatively, in public administration. Our search has detected some articles which discuss issues pertaining to this category. Two consider specifically religion in Europe. The first is van Putten et al. (2019), which examines from a theoretical standpoint the meaning of the philosopher Habermas's reflections on the post-secular turn in western societies, in order to draw implications for – and outline the contours of – "the possibility of a 'post-secular public administration', which grants a more significant place to beneficial forms of religion in modern societies" (van Putten et al., 2019, p. 5).

In a post-secular society, it is not only religious citizens but also "non-religious citizens that must change on the epistemological level" (p.12), in that "Sometimes people can only speak in religious language. If that is the case, they [religious citizens] should not bear the burden of having to translate their arguments in secular terms" and "this post-secular stance requires a profound change in attitude for non-religious citizens. Habermas emphasizes that a secular tolerance towards religious convictions and practices is necessary, but not sufficient. Religious citizens are also members of an inclusive community of citizens with equal rights, in which each individual is accountable to the others for his political contributions [and] the challenge is to combine 'equal citizenship' with 'cultural difference' as complementing elements of an inclusive civil society" (p.12). In such a post-secular society and public sphere, both non-religious and religious citizens must learn how to be(come) citizens of the common, shared political community they belong to. As part of that, public administration scholars and practitioners alike must learn, and specifically "public administration students need to know about the functioning of religion in society and about its civic and public contributions to the public sphere" (p.19). Ultimately, the disciplines of public theology and public administration must be brought to talk to each other, and "such rapprochement between public theology and public administration would begin by accepting a post-secular condition that is inclusive and collaborative towards religion and its relevance for public life" (pp.19–20).

With a more empirical focus, Griera and Martínez-Ariño (2018) investigate, through a range of cases reported in the special issue for which their article constitutes the introductory paper, how state and religion encounter one another in key public institutions in western European societies, namely schools, hospitals, and prisons. The special issue takes "public institutions as privileged observatories for understanding the changing place of religion [in society] but also as laboratories in which new forms of interactions and arrangements are being experimented" (p.111).

From the perspective of Judaism and Jewish theology, Yanow (2003) criticises the approach and underpinning values adopted in the study of public administration in the US (which he claims to be grounded in Protestant-Capitalist ethic and Lockean liberalism) and considers them incompatible with Jewish values and Judaism, seen not as a religion (considering Judaism as a religion is, for Yanow, an interpretation of it derived from a Protestant conception of what a religion is), rather as practice, using the term "practice" much along the lines in which it is developed in the Pragmatism of John Dewey. For Yanow, the Protestant-Christian cultural heritage and the Jewish one differ in the way in which they conceive of "the relationship between the individual 'citizen' (using the term here to mean member of society, without reference to legal standing) and 'the public' [as well as the way in which they conceive of] the source and character of authority in 'administrative' decision-making" (Yanow, 2003, p. 143). For Yanow, the American mode and conception of public administration is not value-neutral, rather it is Protestant in character, centred as it is on the individual, while a "Jewish public administration' can only be communal in character and orientation, with the administrative apparatus 'built on a grouping, rather than on individuals" (p.144). In a Jewish administrative apparatus (which existed throughout all the 1,878 years during which Jews were without a state, and it continues – the author argues – to exist in the Jewish communities outside of the contemporary state of Israel) "a person does not have an identity as an individual. Instead, one's identity is bound up with one's location within an interlinked set of patrilineal-based relationships" (p.144) and this constitutes "one of the central distinguishing characteristics of a Jewish administrative practice: membership in 'the public' rests on one's status as a member of a family, nested within a clan, nested within a larger grouping, rather than on individual identity [therefore] Public administration is fundamentally participative in a structural sense, by virtue of membership in the public arena: the 'private' sphere almost entirely disappears from view [and] This participative element is recapitulated and reinforced in the deliberative discourse embodied in the Talmud, which is bound up in the work of communal administration" (p.145). Jewish administration is based – according to Yarow – on an inherently communal and deliberative decision-making process (rather than being hierarchical, as in the Weberian administration, and centred on majoritarian institutions where the will of the majority prevails), and "Western" public administration can become closer to Jewish public administration only insofar as it incorporates participatory democratic practices along the lines of Habermasian deliberative discourse.

11. The influence of religion on public leadership and on leadership styles

Public leadership is a burgeoning area of thriving research and inquiry. It is therefore perhaps not unexpected that in our search we have detected a number of articles examining the relevance of religious teachings for the practice of public leadership. Some of these articles explicitly distinguish between spirituality and religion, to then examine how they influence public leadership. Harris (2002), from a Christian perspective and drawing from the Old Testament, introduces the idea that the commitment to "accountability to God" may exercise a disciplining effect on public servants, driving them to restrain self-serving behaviour and give way to more altruistic courses of action, thereby shaping a "positive" form of public leadership. In a similar vein, Oke et al. (2019) trace the roots of ethical behaviour by ethical leaders in the Christian faith. In a sophisticated analysis, Nullens (2013) brings in spirituality as "mediating factor" between the Christian faith of a public leader and the societal and organisational effectiveness of its leadership for the good (the key question addressed in the paper being the normative and evaluative one of what makes leadership a "leadership for the good"), by revisiting the theology (specifically: Christology) of Dietrich Bonhoeffer. Fairholm and Gronau (2015) profile the contours of a 'whole-soul' leadership for public administration, which draws on spirituality and refuses any compartmentalisation of life that may tend to separate the person "when on-the-job" (in the domain of the professional life) from the person *tout court*. Shifting from spirituality to religion, the influence of religion, both as an ideational basis and as a personality system, on public leadership at a conceptual level is explored by Roberts and Hess-Hernandez (2012).

12. The influence of religion and faith on wellbeing in the workplace

Religious belonging and faith are deemed to have a (positive) effect on wellbeing in the workplace specifically, and wellbeing and health more broadly, in a number of the articles our literature review has identified. White et al. (2018) delve into a specific and measurable aspect, namely they investigate whether religious involvement (i.e., attendance and salience) mitigates the association between combat casualty exposure and sleep disturbance among US military veterans: they find out that religious salience both offsets and moderates (i.e., buffers) the above association, and religious attendance offsets but does not moderate the above association. Derrico et al. (2015) focus the link between an institution (in their case: Christian universities and campuses in the US) being inspired by religious belonging of both its staff and its users (i.e. Faith-Based Organisation, see also theme 7) and the thriving of the very users of its services, where thriving is conceptualized as levels of intellectual, interpersonal, and psychological vitality that result in measures of student success. Both this study and the study of Hassan et al. (2021) point to (enhanced levels of) spirituality as mediating between religion and faith, on one hand, and wellbeing of staff and users of public services, on the other (however theoretically problematic it may be to measure spirituality and gauge what "enhanced spirituality" may mean). Finally, Qaisar and Malik (2015) directly elaborate on the link between Islamic teachings and wellbeing in the workplace.

13. Religion as an ideational source which has a powerful social mobilisation dimension

Religion can be a powerful source of social mobilisation. In our literature review, we detected two papers dealing with some profiles that pertain to public administration and public services. Sikking (2014) observes that Catholic and other private schools have measurable organizational strengths that socialize students into participation in public institutions more effectively than public schools – even if the formal teaching curriculum is the same for both categories of educational organisations (the difference being attributed to the influence of the hidden curriculum being developed in the former category of schools). This points to the consideration that Faith-Based Organisations are not just alternative providers of public services, but the kind of provision they put into effect may have important implications for the users of such services, notably that they (as citizens) may end up being mobilised to engage in public institutions more and more effectively than pupils (citizens) attending public school.

In another area of public service – the healthcare policy – Altinordu (2021) observes how the government of Turkey, backed by religious parties, leveraged religion as a tool for mobilisation for managing the Covid-19 pandemic and induce citizens and residents to undertake certain courses of action and adopt certain behaviours – whether or not these were in agreement with indications from health experts and scientists. The author notices the specific (albeit not unique) conditions in Turkey, and considers three factors in particular to "have been decisive in determining the salience and political function of religion in the course of the COVID-19 pandemic in Turkey: a government party which routinely uses religion in political mobilization (the AKP), a form of secularism that relies on a centralized government bureaucracy for the management of Islam (the *Diyanet*), and the near-total control the government established over the Turkish religious field in the aftermath of the failed coup attempt of 2016" (Altinordu, 2021, p.447). The government and state apparatus may, under certain political-societal conditions, become a central force in the use of religion as a source of political mobilisation.

14. The interrelationship between religion in its ideational dimension and the design (or redesign) of governance arrangements

Religion in its ideational dimension can also provide a potent base to inspire the design of governance arrangements (or redesign thereof) fitting the mutable local circumstances. Carmichael (2017) uses a Gramscian lens to investigate how British rulers in the late 19th century attained hegemony over the coastal Muslim populations of present-day coastal Tanzania and Kenya, by co-opting religious leaders and, ultimately, taking over the existing Islamic administrative structures and officials as well as by steering the ways in which *waqf* (uniquely Islamic institutions whose specific resources are to be directed to benefit the Muslim community) were managed. In a similar vein and thrust (i.e., that of addressing the question of how a religious minority may rule over a majority of the population professing another religion), Akhund (2009) studies the governance arrangements of Ottoman rule of Macedonia, a region in which the Muslim population was a minority in an otherwise ethnically fractured, yet majority Christian, territory. Muslim officials dominated the roles of representative of the central ottoman government, yet Christian officials were co-opted to a number of administrative roles – albeit co-existence between the two groups was not without tensions, and governance was occurring in the shadow of the powerful Ottoman army present in the territory and manned mostly by Muslims. Ultimately, ethnical and religious pluralism was tolerated, but integration did not occur, nor was it pursued.

The interrelationship between religion and public governance arrangements also involves the religious policy of the state, notably encompassing the so-called denominational law – the regulation of the legal status of religious denominations in a given polity (including which denominations get officially recognised, hence regulated). This policy is investigated, with focus on the charitable activities of Churches in Poland, Hungary and the Czech Republic, in the paper by Kamiński (2021). Similarly, Zain and Zakaria (2022) consider the development of governance arrangements in Malaysia as concerns ensuring Halal principles are adopted throughout the production processes, and assess governance arrangements from the viewpoint of Islamic teachings. In this case, the perspective is in a sense reversed, and the focus is on how religious principles may guide the assessment of public governance arrangements, from the standpoint of the religion's teaching.

At times, this role in governance borders other thematic areas, like service delivery by Faith-Based Organisations (theme 7). Majority (Lutheran) Churches in the three (European) Nordic countries of Norway, Sweden and Finland are an embedded part of the large welfare system of these countries, performing both as agents of service delivery and as a source of symbolic and social capital, and in the latter role perform also as promoter of altruistic values in society, thereby contributing not just to shape public governance arrangements in their polity but also to shape individual and societal values (Pessi et al., 2009; Angell and Pessi, 2010).

The paper by Nielsen (2016) explicitly uses theoretical lenses from the field of public administration – interactive governance and discursive institutionalism – to examine the interrelationships between the majority Lutheran Church in Denmark and the Danish state, noticing how such interactions contribute to shape the level of autonomy of the Church (not just via à vis the state, but also the autonomy of congregations within the Church) as well as the ways in which the Church – while focused on its ultimate theological and pastoral mission – contributes to social cohesion in Denmark.

15. Religion and institutional quality and the quality of public governance

It is an intensely debated question the issue of whether, and if so in what direction, religion shapes the quality of public institutions and public governance: for the better or for the worse? And better or worse in what sense, according to which criteria? The paper by Rastgar (2023) aims to link the notion of transparency in the public service – an area of active research in the field of public administration – with "Islamic teachings, mainly during the short reign of Imam Ali" (Rastgar, 2023, p. 2), to then more broadly revisit the notion of "Good Governance" in the public sector in light of religious, rather than secular, notions. The main argument is that transparency as understood and conceptualised via Islamic teachings positively impacts on the quality of public governance. The paper by Wibowo (2020) works out an argument to "reveal the compatibility of Islamic teachings with the concept of Good Public Governance (GPG) represented by the Governance Index developed by the World Bank" (Wibowo, 2020, p. 53), after having observed empirically that Muslim majority countries generally score lower on the six main World Bank Good Governance indicators than the average world score, or the score of non-Muslim countries. For the author, religion as ideational basis may further the development of Good Public Governance.

16. The influence of religion on the argument of the "intransigent context"

The argument of the "intransigent context" in public administration has been put forward by Rugge (2013) in a chapter part of a book devoted to understanding the notion of context in public administration and management. The key idea of the intransigent context revolves around the hypothetical situation whereby a social group attributes to the features that characterise their political community a degree of internal cohesiveness and at the same time of diversity from any other political community up to the point that "no exogeneous pattern or institution modelled in a foreign context can ever intrude into it" (Rugge, 2013, p. 45). Whether such a context exists in reality or it is just an imagined or theoretical construct is debatable, but for the purposes of this contribution we notice that religion is a potentially apt candidate to operate as a decisive factor in shaping in the members of a political community the image of their context being unique, and hence also impossible to intrude by foreign elements: that is, of making it "intransigent".

We now turn to examine if and to what extent the literature in religious studies and theology journal addresses the issue of the intransigent context. We have only found one paper – Mullins, 2012 – which considers a somewhat related topic: the revival of religious nationalism in Japan, notably since the second half of the 1990s. The paper examines the different ideological positions related to the role of religion in public life in post WWII Japan also in relation to the preceding State Shinto period (i.e., from the Meiji Restoration till the end of WWII), and the role of the state in regulating it, thereby touching on a number of cross-cutting themes. Importantly, the paper, albeit mostly implicitly and as a given, points to the distinctive religion of Japan, Shinto, as constitutive of the public narrative and, albeit indirectly, of the distinctiveness of the "context" of Japan. While the topic of the intransigent context – and notably of whether religion can perform as a main (if not the main) factor in giving rise to an intransigent context – has not (yet) been directly tackled in religious studies, it is an area which has potential for further investigation, both speculatively and empirically.

DISCUSSION AND CONCLUSIONS

The review of the English-language peer-reviewed publications between 1960–2023 in the religious studies and theology literature reveals significant findings. *First*, the results of the review show that the manifold relations between religion and PA, which were detected in the social sciences and classified into ten themes (Ongaro & Tantardini, 2024d; 2023a), have also been explored in the broader humanities literature. The results here presented show that religious studies and theology scholars have predominantly focused their attention on studying the manifold relations between religion and PA at the level of the behaviour of individuals (Micro-level), thus considering religion as shaping the personality and behaviours of public administrators and citizens/users of public services alike (Turner, 2013). Although the articles included in the review that focused on Macro-level themes appeared to be quantitively less than Micro-level themes, the review revealed religion as an ideational basis continues to be a source for re-thinking the foundations of public administration and its core elements, including but not limited to the notions of "public", "citizen(ship)", "(administrative) authority", "(public) decision-making", and so forth.

Second, with the exceptions of Themes 16 and 18, the results of the review show that the eight themes, which were identified on a purely theoretical-speculative basis as "new" themes in Ongaro and Tantardini (2023a, chapter 8), had been already explored, albeit partially, by religious studies and theology scholars. Interestingly, this exploration seemed to have favoured both the analysis of two additional Micro-level themes (Themes 11 and 12) and of two additional Macro-level themes (Themes 14 and 15). This provides additional evidence of the influence of religion on the behaviour and motivation of public sector leaders (Themes 11) and the general well-being of public sector employees (Theme 12). It also provides additional evidence for the role of religion as an ideational source for the design of governance arrangements fitting the mutable local circumstances (Theme 14) and for the quality of public governance (Theme 15). We further note that one article has been recently published on theme 18 as part of a special issue dedicated to the topic of the relationship of religion and PA (Alibasic, 2024), and one on theme 16 (Ongaro and Tantardini, 2024b), in social sciences journals therefore not encompassed in this literature review – both represent dedicated efforts to fill the remaining gap on the themes identified in a speculative way in the research agenda that we have delineated in Ongaro and Tantardini (2023a, chapter 8).

Third, the focus of the studies included in the review has been predominantly on Roman Catholicism, Protestantism, Judaism, and Islam. With only a few exceptions – Pandya (2017) on Hindu social service FBOs and Mullins (2012) on Shintoism – Asian religions (including Hinduism, Buddhism, Confucianism, Shintoism, Jainism, Sikhism, Taoism, and Zoroastrianism) as well as other forms of religion and spiritualism (i.e., animism, druidism, shamanism) appear not to have been studied in relation to their implications for PA – at least in the English-language literature that has been reviewed here. This may be the case, but it could also mean that the exclusion of the so-called "grey literature" (Rothstein & Hopewell, 2009) may have prevented the inclusion of relevant studies, which might have provided a more complete sense of what the religious studies and theology literatures offer about the study of religion and public administration.

Fourth, regarding the research methods and data analysis techniques employed in the studies included in the literature review, three considerations can be made. First, about 60 per cent of the studies included in this review employed a qualitative approach. What we found in this literature seems to be in line with the research methods approaches described in the contribution by Griffin (2012) who listed *oral history, visual methods, discourse analysis, ethnographic research methods, interviewing,* and *textual analysis* as qualitative research methods employed in the humanities (Griffin, 2012, also discussed quantitative research methods in his contribution). Second, mixed-methods approach seem to have an appeal among religious studies scholars, including the application of neuroscience techniques to the study of religion and public administration (see Charles et al., 2014) to provide additional evidence and explanations to complement the results of other analyses. Third, as pointed out by Griffin (2012), there are "very different ideas about how to do research" (p. 94) especially across different branches of knowledge (i.e., the humanities and the social sciences). Recent calls for interdisciplinary collaborations (i.e., Ongaro & Tantardini, 2023b) require an honest and clear understanding of each other disciplines' research methods and of "what constitutes 'good' research, what counts as evidence and how to present research" (p. 94) to be successful.

To conclude this chapter, we provide two possible avenues for future research. *First,* the results of this literature review on the manifold relations between religion and PA in the religious studies and theology literature should be compared with the results of the review of the literature that Ongaro and Tantardini (2024d) carried out in the social sciences. Such a contribution may provide a more complete and well-rounded understanding of such relations. *Second,* with the caveat discussed above, we encourage interdisciplinary collaborations between scholars in the religious studies and theology disciplines and the social sciences to fill the gaps identified in this review of the literature. This would entail the exploration of uncharted themes (i.e., Themes 16 and 18, with the qualification above concerning recent and ongoing research work on these areas) or understudied themes (i.e. Themes 13, 15, and 17), and the much more systematic inclusion of the influence of Asian religions on PA. Responding to this call for future research entails both overcoming the methodological issues described above and the adoption of an ethics of responsibility in engaging with this research agenda (see Ongaro & Tantardini, 2024c) by scholars interested in understanding the role that religious factors play in administrative phenomena.

REFERENCES

Encyclopaedia Britannica (n.d.). https://www.britannica.com (accessed on 14 February 2024).

Griffin, G. (2012). Writing about research methods in the arts and humanities. In R. Buikema, G. Griffin, & N. Lykke (Eds.), *Theories and methodologies in postgraduate feminist research* (pp. 91–104). Routledge.

Littell, J. H., Corcoran, J., & Pillai, V. (2008). *Systematic reviews and meta-analysis.* Oxford University Press.

McGuigan, G. S., Morçöl, G., & Grosser, T. (2021). Using ego-network analyses to examine journal citations: a comparative study of public administration, political science, and business management. *Scientometrics, 126*, 9345–9368.

Ongaro, E., & Tantardini, M. (2023a). *Religion and public administration: An introduction.* Cheltenham, UK and Northampton, MA: Edward Elgar Publishing.

Ongaro, E & Tantardini, M. (2023b) Advancing knowledge in public administration: why religion matters. *Asia Pacific Journal of Public Administration*, 45(1), 1–6, DOI: 10.1080/23276665.2022.2155858

Ongaro, E., & Tantardini, M. (2024a). Debate: Why the religious factor has been forgotten in PA studies? (And how to remedy it). *Public Money & Management*, 44(1), 7–8. DOI: 10.1080/09540962.2023.2264054

Ongaro, E. & Tantardini, M (2024b) Bringing religion into public value theory and practice: Rationale and perspectives. *Administration and Society,* 56(8), 972–1000 DOI: 10.1177/00953997241264474

Ongaro, E. & Tantardini, M. (2024c). Contours of a research programme for the study of the relationship of religion and public administration. *Public Policy and Administration,* 39:4, 521-530.

Ongaro, E., & Tantardini, M. (2024d). Religion, spirituality, faith and public administration: A literature review and outlook. *Public Policy and Administration*, 39(4), 531–555. DOI: 09520767221146866.

Page, M. J., Moher, D., Bossuyt, P. M., Boutron, I., Hoffmann, T. C., Mulrow, C. D., ... & McKenzie, J. E. (2021). PRISMA 2020 explanation and elaboration: updated guidance and exemplars for reporting systematic reviews. *bmj, 372*.

Rothstein, H.R., & Hopewell, S. (2009). Grey literature. In: H. Cooper, L.V. Hedges, & J.C. Valentine (eds), *The handbook of research synthesis and meta-analysis* (pp. 103–127). Russell Sage.

Turner, B.S. (2013). *The religious and the political: A comparative sociology of religion*. Cambridge: Cambridge University Press.

APPENDIX: FULL LIST OF STUDIES INCLUDED IN THE REVIEW

Adler Jr, G. J., Ortiz, S. E., Plutzer, E., Mayrl, D., Coley, J. S., & Sager, R. (2021). Religion at the frontline: How religion influenced the response of local government officials to the COVID-19 pandemic. *Sociology of Religion, 82*(4), 397–425.

Akhund, N. (2009). Muslim representation in the three Ottoman Vilayets of Macedonia: Administration and military power (1878–1908). *Journal of Muslim Minority Affairs, 29*(4), 443–454.

Altınordu, A. (2021). Divine warning or prelude to secularization? Religion, politics, and the COVID-19 pandemic in Turkey. *Sociology of Religion, 82*(4), 447–470.

Angell, O. H., & Pessi, A. B. (2010). Co-operation in welfare? Inter-organizational relationships between Church-based welfare agents and the welfare state at the local level in Norway and Finland. *Diaconia, 1*(1), 62–81.

Becci, I., & Dubler, J. (2017). Religion and religions in prisons: Observations from the United States and Europe. Journal for the Scientific Study of Religion, 56(2), 241–247.

Bellolio, C. (2020). The Chilean military after Antuco: Shortcomings of a post-secular discourse. *Religions, 11*(3), 146.

Boulenger, D., Barten, F., & Criel, B. (2014). Contracting between faith-based health care organizations and the public sector in Africa. *The Review of Faith & International Affairs, 12*(1), 21–29.

Burgess, R. (2015). Pentecostals and development in Nigeria and Zambia: Community organizing as a response to poverty and violence. *Pentecostal Studies, 14*(2), 176–204.

Cadge, W., Griera, M., Lucken, K., & Michalowski, I. (2017). Religion in public institutions: Comparative perspectives from the United States, the United Kingdom, and Europe. *Journal for the Scientific Study of Religion, 56*(2), 226–233.

Cadge, W., Griera, M., Lucken, K., & Michalowski, I. (2017). Afterword: On the study of religion in public institutions. *Journal for the Scientific Study of Religion, 56*(2), 255–258.

Carmichael, T. (1997). British 'practice' towards Islam in the East Africa protectorate: Muslim officials, Waqf administration, and secular education in Mombasa and environs, 1895–1920. *Journal of Muslim Minority Affairs, 17*(2), 293–309.

Charles, G. L., Travis, F., & Smith, J. (2014). Policing and spirituality: Their impact on brain integration and consciousness. *Journal of Management, Spirituality & Religion, 11*(3), 230–244.

Coons, J. E., & Brennan, P. M. (2002). School choice among competing "Catholic" philosophies. *Journal of Catholic Education, 5*(3), 286–296.

Craft, C. M., Foubert, J. D., & Lane, J. J. (2011). Integrating religious and professional identities: Christian faculty at public institutions of higher education. *Religion & Education, 38*(2), 92–110.

Dahan, Y. (2019). Community-based organizations motivated by religious ideology as a driving force behind shaping urban governance: The Israeli case. *Politics, Religion & Ideology, 20*(1), 64–93.

Derrico, C. M., Tharp, J. L., & Schreiner, L. A. (2015). Called to make a difference: The experiences of students who thrive on faith-based campuses. *Christian Higher Education, 14*(5), 298–321.

Dudin, M. N., Pogrebinskaya, E. A., Sidorenko, V. N., Sukhova, E. I., Zubenko, N. Y., & Shishalova, J. S. (2019). Cross-cultural management in the system of harmonization of interests in the multi-confessional educational environment. *European Journal of Science and Theology, 15*(3), 191–199.

Duff, J., Battcock, M., Karam, A., & Taylor, A. R. (2016). High-level collaboration between the public sector and religious and Faith-Based Organizations: Fad or trend?. The Review of Faith & International Affairs, 14(3), 95–100.

Fairholm, M. R., & Gronau, T. W. (2015). Spiritual leadership in the work of public administrators. *Journal of Management, Spirituality & Religion, 12*(4), 354–373.

Gao, J., Shi, X., & Wu, X. (2023). The current triple-type attributes of and policy issues for Christian social service organizations in China: From a multi-disciplinary perspective. *Religions, 14*(4), 475.

Gilliat-Ray, S. (2018). Afterword: Religion in public institutions. Methodological challenges, institutional comparisons, and key variables. *Journal of Religion in Europe, 11*(2–3), 186–194.

Giorgi, A., & Accornero, G. (2018). The Catholic Church and the crisis: the case of Portugal. Journal of Contemporary Religion, 33(2), 261–276.

Griera, M., & Martínez-Ariño, J. (2018). Researching religion in public institutions: Context, object, and methods. *Journal of Religion in Europe, 11*(2–3), 110–122.

Harris, J. I. (2002). The king as public servant: Towards an ethic of public leadership based on virtues suggested in the wisdom literature of the older testament. *Journal of Theology for Southern Africa*, (113), 61.

Hassan, Z., Tnay, J. S., Sukardi Yososudarmo, S. M., & Sabil, S. (2021). The relationship between workplace spirituality and work-to-family enrichment in selected public sector organizations in Malaysia. *Journal of Religion and Health, 60*, 4132–4150.

Henrekson, E. (2023). The continuation of perceived deviance: independent confessional schools in Sweden 1795–2019. *British Journal of Religious Education, 45*(4), 313–324.

Idler, E., & Kellehear, A. (2017). Religion in public health-care institutions: US and UK perspectives. *Journal for the Scientific Study of Religion, 56*(2), 234–240.

Iraqi, K. M., Shafi, M. K., & Rafi, S. T. A. (2020). Human Resource Management practices: A case study of the Dr. Mahmud Husain Library, University of Karachi. *The Islamic Culture" As-Saqafat-ul Islamia" - Research Journal-Sheikh Zayed Islamic Centre, University of Karachi, 43.*

Kamiński, T. (2021). Religious policy and the charitable activities of Churches in Poland, the Czech Republic and Hungary after 1989. *Journal for the Study of Religions and Ideologies, 20*(58), 52–65.

Knorre, B., & Zygmont, A. (2019). "Militant Piety" in 21st-century Orthodox Christianity: Return to classical traditions or formation of a new theology of war?. Religions, 11(1), 2.

Konieczny, M. E., & Bertossi, C. (2017). Religious conflict and the chain of command in the American and French militaries. *Journal for the Scientific Study of Religion, 56*(2), 248–254.

Lindsay, D. M., & Smith, B. C. (2010). Accounting by faith: The negotiated logic of elite evangelicals' workplace decision-making. Journal of the American Academy of Religion, 78(3), 721–749.

Meron, O. C. (2015). Between private and public sectors: Jewish engineers in Greece between the wars. *Journal of Modern Jewish Studies*, *14*(3), 409–429.

Mullins, M. R. (2012). The neo-nationalist response to the aum crisis: A return of civil religion and coercion in the public sphere?. *Japanese Journal of Religious Studies*, 99–125.

Nielsen, M. V. (2016). Appealing to the state church identity in processes of change. *Journal of Church and State*, *58*(2), 213–233.

Nullens, P. (2013). Towards a spirituality of public leadership: Engaging Dietrich Bonhoeffer. *International Journal of Public Theology*, *7*(1), 91–113.

Oke, A., Brand, J., Freed, S., & Baumgartner, E. (2019). Leading with integrity under pressure: The activist leadership model. *Journal of Applied Christian Leadership*, *13*(2), 28–47.

Pandya, S. P. (2017). Food, faith, social service and institution building: The Annamrita programme of the Hare Krishna movement in India. *Religion, State & Society*, *45*(1), 4–22.

Pearson, F., Poole, K. J., Moore, W. R., Moore, L., Rife, J., & Richburg, A. R. (2018). The congregational social work education initiative: A new pathway in field education and community partnership. *Social Work & Christianity*, *45*(1).

Pessi, A. B., Angell, O. H., & Pettersson, P. (2009). Nordic majority churches as agents in the welfare state: Critical voices and/or complementary providers?. *Temenos-Nordic Journal of Comparative Religion*, *45*(2).

Plopeanu, A. P. (2022). Drawing the determinants of employment intentions in the public sector among Romanian students' religiosity, religious belonging, beliefs and attitudes. *European Journal of Science and Theology*, *18*(6), 77–96.

Proehl PhD, R. A., Starnes MA, H., & Everett MBA, S. (2015). Catalyst schools: The Catholic ethos and public charter schools. *Journal of Catholic Education*, *18*(2), 125–158.

Putra, Z., Ma'ruf, J. J., Yunus, M., Harmen, H., & Amin, H. (2023). Determinants of job satisfaction of public sector organizations' employees in six continents: A systematic review. *Nidhomul Haq: Jurnal Manajemen Pendidikan Islam*, *8*(1), 64–76.

Qaisar, M. N., & Malik, N. T. (2015). Determinants of employee health and happiness: A perceptive of well-being from Islamic and general point of view at public sector organisations in Islamic Republic of Pakistan. *Al-Idah*, 31, 84–103.

Rastgar, A. A., Davoudi, S. M. M., Surahman, H. S., & Al-Salami, A. A. A. (2023). Following Islamic teachings in the governance of Islamic society with an emphasis on transparency. *HTS Teologiese Studies/Theological Studies*, *79*(1).

Roberts, G. E., & Hess-Hernandez, D. (2012). Religious commitment and servant-leadership: The development of an exploratory conceptual model. *The International Journal of Servant-Leadership*, *8*(1), 299–329.

Rugge, Fabio (2013) 'The intransigent context: Glimpses at the history of a problem', pp. 44–54 in Christopher Pollitt (ed.) *Context in Public Policy and Management: The missing Link?* Cheltenham, UK and Northampton, MA: Edward Elgar Publishing

Sikkink, D. (2004). The hidden civic lessons of public and private schools. *Catholic Education: A Journal of Inquiry and Practice*, *7*(3), 339–365.

Țicu, D. (2013). Axiological dimensions involved in the public policies process. European Journal of Science and Theology, 9(2), 57–64.

Van Putten, R., Overeem, P., & Van Steden, R. (2019). Where public theology and public administration meet: Reflections on Jürgen Habermas' post-secular turn. *International Journal of Public Theology*, *13*(1), 5–24.

Warburg, M. (2019). By Grace: Recognition of religious minority associations in Denmark from the Reformation until 2018. Journal of Religion in Europe, 12(4), 353–383.

White, J., Xu, X., Ellison, C. G., DeAngelis, R. T., & Sunil, T. (2018). Religion, combat casualty exposure, and sleep disturbance in the US military. *Journal of Religion and Health*, *57*, 2362–2377.

Wibowo, M. G. (2020). Good public governance in Islamic perspective: An analysis on the world governance indicator in OIC member countries. *Ihtifaz: Journal of Islamic Economics, Finance, and Banking*, *3*(1), 51–66.

Yanow, D. (2003). Public administration and the Jewish ethic. *Judaism*, *52*(3/4), 140.

Yashaiya, N. H., & Noh, A. (2022). Should heterogeneity matter? Evaluating public service motivation in a non-homogenous society. *Intellectual Discourse*, *30*(1).

Zain, C. R. C. M., & Zakaria, Z. (2022). Integration of Islamic management principles and values according to the Qur'an and hadith in fostering halal governance in Malaysia. *Al-Bayan: Journal of Qur'an and Hadith Studies*, *20*(2), 157–181.

Zehavi, A. (2017). Religionization from the bottom up: Religiosity trends and institutional change mechanisms in Israeli public services. Politics and Religion, 10(3), 489–514.

Zhanat, A., Nurgul, T., Galiya, S., Kairat, Z., Kudaiberdi, B., & Maxat, M. (2023). Peculiarities of Kazakhstan and Malaysia in view of the relationship between State and religion. Journal of Islamic Thought and Civilization, 13(1), 75–88.

Zook, S., & Arndt, C. (2021). Islamic NGOs in education in Ghana: Analysis of the scope, activities, and revenue portfolios. *Journal of Education in Muslim Societies*, *2*(2), 57–81.

12. When Ideas Have Consequences: The Optical Illusion of Religion in Public Policy

Pasquale Annicchino

INTRODUCTION

The interaction between the humanities and public administration or public governance is of significant interest to scholars in the field of law and religion.[1] Law and religion scholars investigate the interaction between legal and religious frameworks across various dimensions, including theoretical, comparative, and religious law analyses, and a public administration perspective is a significant contribution to these efforts.

Over the years, some of us have also engaged in public policy activities, contributing to national and international projects with a particular focus on religion.[2] This policy work involves addressing numerous epistemological challenges, many of which pertain to the role of religion in the public square and the influence of secularization theory on policymakers' frameworks and understanding. This issue is especially pertinent in Western societies where, compared to other parts of the world, religion has historically assumed a diminished role in public governance over the past centuries. This chapter addresses some of these issues, combining a theoretical and scholarly perspective with an experiential one. While mostly adopting a Western perspective, I hope the considerations and analyses developed throughout this chapter may be of interest to a broader international readership.

---

[1] The disciplinary field is intended as the study of the interaction of law and religion. For a basic introduction, see Berman (1974).

[2] For the purpose of this contribution, I understand the term religion as defined by Ongaro and Tantardini: "Religion – broadly defined as a set of coherent answers to the core existential questions that confront any human group and pertain to the relationship of the human to the divine and their codification in creedal forms, and involving a ritual dimension and piety" (Ongaro and Tantardini, 2023b, p. 1).

This contribution is structured as follows: Section II will examine the impact of secularization theory and its implications for policymaking. Section III will address the "return" of religion in public life (in the West) and its effects on policy formulation. Section IV will highlight the dual role of religion in public policies, emphasizing the necessity of considering religion in the development of both domestic and foreign policies. Section V will provide concluding remarks. I will argue that our conceptualization of religion and its role in public policies is intricately linked to the socio-cultural developments within our societies. The presumption that secularization renders religion irrelevant in public policy design warrants a more nuanced and thorough examination.

THE OPTICAL ILLUSION OF THE SECULARIZATION THEORY

Much of the discourse concerning the role of religion in public life and governance centers on the narrative that has prevailed in the Western world since the Enlightenment and post-Enlightenment era. As Mary Ann Glendon has argued: "The image of religion as a fomenter of strife figures prominently in a grandiose historical narrative that took rise in the Enlightenment era against the background of the wars of religion that had wrecked Europe in the 16th and 17th centuries. According to this narrative, religion was expected to decline with the advance of science and education" (Glendon, 2013, p. 586). In the meta-narrative that has shaped numerous reflections in the social sciences, the advancement of secularization has been posited to lead to the marginalization of religion. Consequently, this process is expected to yield direct and significant outcomes: "The demise of religion was supposed to be accompanied by the diminution, if not disappearance, of all the ills that proponents of this story believed to be associated with religion – intolerance, violence and the stifling on individual freedom" (Glendon, 2013, p. 586). In fact, Peter Berger, who had for years sided with the authors arguing for the relevance of the secularization theory, in 1998 signaled the need for a paradigmatic shift: "The assumption that we live in a secularized world is false. The world today [...] is as furiously religious as it ever was, and in some places more so than ever" (Berger, 1999, p. 2).

These reflections have had a direct impact on legal scholars. For years, the relationships between law and religion have been built upon a fundamental principle of separation. As Harold Berman argued in 1974, the Western world entered an "era of the radical separation of subject from object, of essence from existence, of person from act, of spiritual from secular, of religion from law" (Berman, 1974, p. 111). This "separation paradigm" worked on the "assumption, common some years ago, that Western liberal democracies had solved the problem of the relationship between state and religion, with constitutional secularism as a main plank of the solution. Such assumption now seems somewhat naïve and precipitous, akin to confident declarations of the 'end of history'" (McCrudden, 2015, p. 434). Today, the "separation paradigm" and the role of constitutional secularism as a cornerstone of liberal democracy seem to be contested in many countries around the world. Religions seem to be taking a central role through a process of identitarization in many societies.

It is challenging to comprehend the rise of Hindu nationalism in India without considering the public role of religion.[3] Similarly, Christianity's significance to Donald Trump's Christian nationalism and the role of Judaism among Orthodox Jews active in Israeli politics exemplify this phenomenon. Notably, I have not included examples from the Muslim world, which are often regarded as "usual suspects" when it comes to arguing about the limits of the strict regulation of religion from the public space, nor do I discuss religion in other Asian countries in this chapter. The central issue, in my view, is that from the perspective of the humanities' contribution to the advancement of public governance and administration, we must address our understanding and framing of religion in public policy design. Should we adhere to the analyses of scholars who, for years, have argued that secularization would inevitably render religion marginal and irrelevant to public policies? Or, alternatively, should we reevaluate our assumptions and ideas to understand if and how religion has reemerged, transformed, and become pertinent to public governance and administrative actions?[4]

IS RELIGION BACK?

Our increasingly pluralistic societies are currently experiencing significant polarization, a characteristic feature of post-secular contexts. In Western

---

[3] For the case of India, Ongaro and Tantardini highlight how: "The embeddedness of the caste system into the fabric of society in India has implications also for PA studies, notably in relation to how context and contextual influences may affect such dimensions as the legitimacy of public governance, on one hand, and the delivery of public services, on the other hand" (Ongaro and Tantardini, 2023a, p. 72).

[4] The role of the epistemological factor has been underlined by Ongaro and Tantardini: "Another reason for overlooking religion is that religious factors may fit problematically into certain epistemological approaches, like forms of neopositivism, which have been ascendant in recent decades. We counter that this need not be the case, and that there is room in the field of PA – which is interdisciplinary and characterised by epistemological and methodological pluralism – for researching the influence of religion on key aspects of PA through a multitude of approaches and methods" (Ongaro and Tantardini, 2023a, p. 1).

countries, societal and religious pluralism has been managed through various legal and political arrangements, predominantly grounded in the principles of constitutional secularism. Examining the evolution of societal values on a comparative scale is crucial, as this analysis can reveal significant societal trends. In this regard, the Inglehart-Welzel Cultural Map (as of 2023; latest available when this book goes to press) serves as an invaluable resource. See Figure 12.1 where countries are grouped into cultural regions with distinct colors.

The analysis of data from the World Values Survey and European Values Survey conducted by Ronald Inglehart and Christian Welzel, focusing on cultural change and cultural traditions, has demonstrated the extent to which Western countries diverge from the rest of the world regarding the relationships between traditional versus secular values and survival versus self-expression

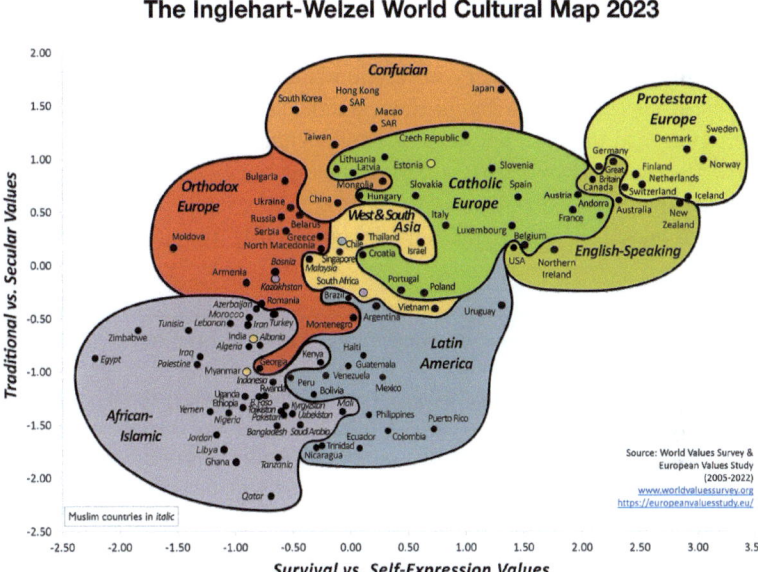

Source: World Value Survey 2023 (2023).

Figure 12.1   *The Inglehart-Welzel World Cultural Map*

values.[5] It is important to highlight some of their most pertinent findings, which may significantly impact the discourse on the role of religion in public governance.

1. "Much of the variation in human values between societies boils down to two broad dimensions: a first dimension of *'traditional vs. secular rational values'* and a second dimension of *'survival vs. self-expression values'*";[6]
2. "The value differences between societies around the world show a pronounced *culture zone pattern*. The strongest emphasis on traditional values and survival values is found in the Islamic societies of the Middle East. By contrast, the strongest emphasis on secular-rational values and self-expression values is found in the Protestant societies of Northern Europe".[7]

As Welzel has demonstrated, these data can be interpreted within the context of the human struggle for emancipation and empowerment (Welzel, 2013). While it is true that the marginalization of religion as a factor in public administration or governance can lead to optical illusions and misunderstandings, we must also recognize that the category of religion cannot be essentialized or taken for granted. There can be different elements that can contribute to the creation of a religion, and they are not necessarily the same in every case. As Olivier Roy has illustrated (Roy, 2010), a key variable is the extent to which religion separates from cultures, with secular forces breaking religion apart and creating an individualized existential experience of faith. In some contexts, this

---

[5] These are the definitions provided by the authors of the map: "*Traditional values* emphasize the importance of religion, parent-child ties, deference to authority and traditional family values. People who embrace these values also reject divorce, abortion, euthanasia and suicide. These societies have high levels of national pride and a nationalistic outlook. *Secular-rational values* have the opposite preferences to the traditional values. These societies place less emphasis on religion, traditional family values and authority. Divorce, abortion, euthanasia and suicide are seen as relatively acceptable. (Suicide is not necessarily more common.) *Survival values* place emphasis on economic and physical security. It is linked with a relatively ethnocentric outlook and low levels of trust and tolerance. *Self-expression values* give high priority to environmental protection, growing tolerance of foreigners, gays and lesbians, and gender equality, and rising demands for participation in decision-making in economic and political life" (World Value Survey, 2023, 2023).

[6] See World Value Survey 2023 (2023).

[7] See previous note.

individualized experience can become more significant than collective religious experiences. The split between religion and culture is central to Roy's "deculturation" theory, which posits that as religion individualizes and globalizes, it becomes dis-embedded from culture. Religion, therefore, can evolve and often evolves in ways that are not necessarily embedded within societal evolution and in forms that, for this reason, are not necessarily moderated by societal forces that can contain the radicalization of religions.

This cultural process can have several consequences, including a reconfiguration of the religious landscape. When examining religion in the public sphere, we must consider this "deculturation" and not necessarily look for "traditional religions". In doing so, we may, for instance, come across examples like the QAnon conspiracy theory movement, which has had a significant influence on American politics with relevant implications for national security. Annabelle Bichler has summarized the content of QAnon in the following terms:

> QAnon, as this conspiracy system has been dubbed, has ridden the line of religiosity from its inception. Emulating the Blood Libel of the Middle Ages, an antisemitic canard which falsely accused Jews of murdering Christian children in order to use their blood as part of religious rituals, as well as the 'Satanic Panic' of the 1980s, QAnon doctrine posits that a cabal of Democrats and celebrities engage in rituals of kidnapping, sexual abuse, and cannibalization of innocent children while Donald Trump acts as the sanctified savior, battling this unholy evil behind scenes. Q's posts frequently quote the Christian Bible alongside allegations of government criminality and apocalyptic predictions, citing an ongoing battle between good and evil – exemplified by the political battle between Conservatives and Liberals – as conjunctive to the Biblical battle between God and Satan (Bichler, 2020).

The example of QAnon illustrates that even in the Western context, amidst the advancement of secularization, the emergence of quasi-religious movements is possible. Western analysts have often interpreted QAnon and similar movements through the lens of fake news or conspiracy theories, deeming the category of religion outdated. However, this approach can be an epistemic flaw, as it fails to grasp the genuine commitment of the movement's participants (Smith, 2022). This can have significant implications for national security policies (Miotto and Droogan, 2024) and for our understanding of the category of religion. To comprehend how religiosity is evolving in regions affected by increasing secularization, particularly when viewed solely through the lens of "traditional" religions, we must adopt a more intellectually flexible and fluid conception of religion, which can operate transversally within PA structures both in the context of internal policies and in foreign policy.

RELIGION AND ITS IMPACT ON POLICIES: A DUALISTIC DIMENSION

The role of religion in public policies and the study of public law, particularly within public administration, has been shaped by assumptions about the role of religion in public life. Law, as a tool, has contributed to this process, serving either as an instrument to constrain the public dimension of religion or to allow it more scope for intervention and influence in the context of public policies. There seems to be an inherent tension between a conception of religion as a "problem" for public policy, and a conception of religion as a contribution to solving problems in public policy.

Intellectually, religion has often been neglected in public administration studies as "[...] scholars have often focused on secular and Western-centric models of PA, thereby overlooking the existing ones, for example Confucian PA and Islamic PA, where religion may potentially and more prominently affect key social actors and the overall configuration of the public administrative space" (Ongaro and Tantardini, 2024, pp. 7–8). In this regard, Ongaro and Tantardini have provided a comprehensive overview of the potential intersections between religion and public administration (Ongardo and Tantardini, 2023b). One analytical feature offered by Western models, which serves as further material for reflection, is the dualistic nature of the impact of religion on public policies through the distinct creation of bureaucratic structures for internal and foreign policy. This delineation is often a unique characteristic by which public administrations manage religion.

Domestic Policies

The analysis of religion in public law has frequently been conducted through the prism of national laws and their mechanisms for including or excluding religion from the process of formulation and implementation of public policies. It is not coincidental that in many countries, policies on religion are managed by the Ministry of Interior, the department in charge of the internal security of a state, reflecting the perception of religion primarily as a "problem" to be managed and contained, rather than as a potential contributor to public policies. This paradigm influences how the possible contributions of religions to public policies are conceived. For example, in Italy, religious groups that have not formalized agreements with the State under Article 8 of the Italian Constitution remain subject to a law from the fascist period (Law No. 1159/29) on "admitted religions".[8] This lower threshold of institutional recognition endangers their full participation in the administrative activities of the state, should public institutions seek to partner with various religions for the delivery of public services.

Today, this strategy of exclusion by a state vis-à-vis religion(s) is often implemented through a securitization paradigm, which tends to favor the majoritarian religion of a country while excluding or directly discriminating against minority religions. Turkey provides an example of a complex bureaucracy used to manage religion from this "internal security" perspective, also with significant foreign policy implications (Maritato, 2021). The Diyanet, or Directorate of Religious Affairs, is legally mandated to manage religious affairs, particularly Islam. The Directorate strictly regulates religion internally; for instance, the Diyanet drafts the sermons delivered in mosques, an approach that suggests a typical "religion as a problem" stance managed under national security concerns in Turkey and abroad (Yaşar, 2023). Domestically, the interaction between religion and security is a critical aspect of public administration activities in many countries. This dynamic has prompted international organizations, such as the OSCE's Office for Democratic Institutions and Human Rights (ODIHR), to engage in the debate, highlighting the need for "comprehensive security" that includes the protection of human rights (OSCE and ODIHR, 2019).

Although not a state and rather a supranational/international form of public governance, the European Union provides valuable material for reflecting on the dualistic nature of the relationship between religion and public policies (domestic and foreign levels). From the perspective of internal policies, according to Article 17 of the Lisbon Treaty:

1. The Union respects and does not prejudice the status under national law of churches and religious associations or communities in the Member States.
2. The Union equally respects the status under national law of philosophical and non-confessional organisations.

---

[8] As Francesco Alicino reminds us, the Italian government has a high degree of discretionary power in finalizing agreements, according to Article 8 of the Constitution, with different religious groups, as "there is no formal procedure of using Article 8.3, which can turn the discretionary power of the Government into unreasonable (not-constitutionally based) discriminations towards religious denominations excluded from the common legislation based on *intense*. These denominations remain in effect subject to the 1929 Law (no. 1159) on 'admitted religions' that, approved during the fascist regime, legitimize an even greater discretionary power by the Italian Government" (Alicino, 2017, p. 14).

3. Recognising their identity and their specific contribution, the Union shall maintain an open, transparent and regular dialogue with these churches and organisations.

Following this provision of the Treaty, it has been argued that the EU will not interfere with legislation on issues concerning religion, as this has been left to the individual Member States. However, from the perspective of public policies, it is challenging to precisely define what legislating on "religion" entails due to its complexity. For instance, EU regulations on education or research may also address issues relevant to religious groups. This has created a paradox where, according to a strict interpretation of this provision, the European Union should refrain from intervening in internal policies on religion but should promote policies for the protection of freedom of religion or belief abroad (Annicchino, 2014).

Foreign Policy

As we have seen, religion has consistently been framed as an issue to be addressed within the national legal orders of each state and as a matter of public order, and in certain cases, national security, rather than as a foreign policy issue. This narrative has contributed to a perception of religion as a "problem" to be managed by the government, typically through the Ministry of Interior. However, religion, and religious freedom in particular, can be highly relevant to the design of foreign policy for states with a particular interest in religion. As Thomas Farr has argued, based on his personal experience: "I spent the better part of my career as an American diplomat basically indifferent to the importance of religious freedom. Then, in 1999, I joined the Office of International Religious Freedom, which had just been created in the U.S. Department of State. I quickly lost my indifference" (Farr, 2018).

In recent years, religion and public administration have increasingly intersected, with several bureaucracies being established in different states to promote and protect freedom of religion or belief. This development, especially in Western countries, follows the example of the United States, which created a bureaucratic machinery for the promotion and protection of religious freedom with the approval of the International Religious Freedom Act in 1998. This model has inspired other countries to allocate institutional attention to this issue through their Ministries of Foreign Affairs (Annicchino, 2018). As the UN Special Rapporteur on Freedom of Religion or Belief has highlighted:

> The United States of America has the longest standing freedom of religion or belief body, which is composed of commissioners from various sectors. The European Union has a special envoy for the promotion of freedom of religion or belief outside

the European Union. These representatives and bodies largely have outward-facing, foreign policy mandates, promoting the implementation of the respective States' foreign policy on freedom of religion or belief. (UN Special Rapporteur on Freedom of Religion or Belief, 2023, par. 71)

The impact of these newly established structures on the foreign policies of various states is evident from the description provided by the UN Special Rapporteur on Freedom of Religion or Belief:

> They pursue their responsibilities in various ways, including by using social media platforms to draw attention to violations, appealing to Governments to put an end to such violations, hosting events and dialogues to address concerns, ensuring this right is included in a State's diplomatic engagements, visiting countries, funding freedom of religion or belief projects, engaging with affected communities, participating in joint letters of concern and seeking to build bridges and advance the rights of religious and belief minorities. States, civil society organizations and experts also gather through regular international ministerial level events dedicated to advancing freedom of religion or belief (UN Special Rapporteur on Freedom of Religion or Belief, 2023, par. 71).

The undertaking of actions on freedom of religion or belief within the context of EU policy has been highlighted as a contradiction to the narrative that the EU "does not do religion". As argued by Marco Ventura: "As eminently indicated by the adoption of the formula in the 2013 Guidelines, 'freedom of religion or belief' enters the space of the European Union through the door of the Union's external action" (Ventura, 2020, p. 31).[9]

In addition to the foreign policy advanced by state actors, religion can significantly influence the delivery of fundamental services through faith-based organizations (FBOs), which consistently interact with public administration in this capacity (Marshall et al., 2021). This is another crucial aspect to consider when assessing the dualistic nature of the interaction between religion and public administration in both domestic and foreign policies. Particularly in the context of foreign policies, FBOs are quintessential foreign policy actors, as they typically operate within transnational networks. As public administrations function in both domestic and foreign policies, a global approach[10] to the issue is necessary, given that religions intersect both domains of action.

---

[9] For an analysis on the role of religion in the context of the European External Action Service, see Foret, 2021, 2017.

[10] It is important to distinguish for these purposes between the global and the globalist perspective. As underlined by Ongaro and Tantardini: "In this work we take a global perspective, meaning that we aim to conceptualise and theorise the influence of religion (notably organised, institutionalised religions) on the functioning of public administrative systems in all regions of the world. However, the

CONCLUSION

Religion is not necessarily capable of explaining all phenomena, nor does everything depend on a religious variable. However, it appears that scholars and policymakers from Western countries have often suffered from a form of optical illusion. This is a direct result of flawed analyses by those who have long claimed that religion would become merely a matter of personal choice and lose its relevance as a social phenomenon. On the contrary, religion seems more relevant than ever on a global scale and continues to evolve, even in countries with high levels of secularization. As Ongaro and Tantardini have argued, "In a world where religion persists to shape individuals as well as societies, it is high time to fill this gap and – in a responsible and well-calibrated way – (re-) introduce the religious factor into PA studies" (Ongaro and Tantardini, 2024, p. 8).

This approach should likely consider the dualistic nature of the interaction between religion(s) and public administration(s): both in the sense of considering that religion in policymaking may be either (or both) perceived as a problem and as a contribution (to the solution of problems), and that religion may be treated differently in policymaking depending on whether it is domestic or foreign policies that are being considered. In the context of the interaction between the humanities and public administration or public governance, a thorough analysis of the role of religion and religious groups can contribute to improving public policies for the common good.

REFERENCES

Alicino, F. (2017). The Place of Minority Religions and the Strategy of Major Denominations: The Case of Italy, *Rivista AIC*, 2, pp. 1–20.

Annicchino, P. (2018). *Law and International Religious Freedom: The Rise and Decline of the American Model*. London, Routledge.

Annicchino, P. (2014). Coherence (and Consistency) or Organized Hypocrisy? Religious Freedom in the law of the European Union, in M.C. Foblets, K. Alidadi, J.S. Nielsen, Z. Yanasmayan (eds.), *Belief, Law and Politics. What Future for a Secular Europe?*, Ashgate, Farnham, pp. 257–263.

Berger, P. (1999). The Desecularization of the World: A Global Overview, in P. Berger (ed.), *The Desecularization of the World: Resurgent Religion and Global Politics*, Washington D.C., Eerdmans, pp. 1–18.

Berman, H.J. (1974). *The Interaction of Law and Religion*. Nashville, Abingdon Press.

---

perspective of this book is not a globalist one: we do not think there is one global ideological-theoretical perspective that may explain the relationship of religion to PA" (Ongaro and Tantardini, 2023a, p. 3).

Bichler, A. (2020, 18 December). QAnon as a Religion. *Canopy Forum on the Interactions on Law and Religion*, available at: https://canopyforum.org/2020/12/18/qanon-as-a-religion/.

Farr, T.F. (2018, 2 October). The Global Crisis of Religious Freedom: The Stakes for America and the World. Testimony before the Senate Judiciary Committee-Subcommittee on the Constitution, available at: https://www.judiciary.senate.gov/imo/media/doc/10–02–18%20Farr%20Testimony.pdf.

Foret, F. (2021). Religion and the European External Action Service, in G. Davie, L. Leustean (eds.), *The Oxford Handbook of Religion and Europe*. Oxford, Oxford University Press pp. 338–353.

Foret, F. (2017). How the European External Action Service Deals with Religion through Religious Freedom. *College of Europe-EU Diplomacy Papers*, 7, available at: http://aei.pitt.edu/87517/1/edp_7_2017_foret.pdf.

Glendon, M.A. (2013). The Quest for Peace Fifty Years after Pacem in Terris – What Role for Religion?, *The Global Quest for Tranquillitas Ordinis. Pacem in Terris, Fifty Years Later*, Pontifical Academy of Social Sciences, Acta 18, pp. 584–604.

Maritato, C. (2021). Pastors of a Dispersed Flock. Diyanet Officers and Turkey's Art of Governing Its Diaspora. *Italian Political Science Review*, 51(3), 321–338.

Marshall, K., Roy, S. Seiple, C., and Slim, H. (2021). Religious Engagement in Development: What Impact Does it Have? *The Review of Faith and International Affairs*, 19, 42–62.

McCrudden, C. (2015). Transnational Culture Wars. *International Journal of Constitutional Law*, 13(2), 434–462.

Miotto, N. and Droogan, J. (2024). "Stand Against the Wiles of the Devil": Interpreting QAnon as a Pseudo-Christian Extremist Movement. *Critical Sociology*, available at: https://journals.sagepub.com/doi/10.1177/08969205241228874.

OSCE/ODIHR. (2019). "Freedom of Religion or Belief and Security: Policy Guidance", *OSCE/ODIHR*, available at: https://www.osce.org/odihr/429389.

Ongaro, E. and Tantardini, M. (2024). Debate: Why the Religious Factor has been forgotten in PA Studies? (And How to Remedy It). *Public Money and Management*, 44, pp. 7–8.

Ongaro, E. and Tantardini, M. (2023a). Advancing Knowledge in Public Administration: Why Religion Matters. *Asia Pacific Journal of Public Administration*, 45(1), 1–6.

Ongaro, E. and Tantardini, M. (2023b). *Religion and Public Administration: An Introduction*. Cheltenham, UK and Northampton, MA: Edward Elgar.

Roy, O. (2010). *Holy Ignorance: When Religion and Culture Part Ways*. New York, Columbia University Press.

Smith, N. (2022). A Quasi-fideist Approach to QAnon. *Social Epistemology: A Journal of Knowledge, Culture and Policy*, 36, 360–377.

UN Special Rapporteur on Freedom of Religion or Belief (2023, 30 January). Landscape of Freedom of Religion or Belief, A/HRC/52/38, available at: https://www.ohchr.org/en/documents/thematic-reports/ahrc5238-landscape-freedom-religion-or-belief-report-special-rapporteur.

Ventura, M. (2020). The Formula "Freedom of Religion or Belief" in the Laboratory of the European Union. *Studia Z Prawa Wyznaniowego*, 23, 7–53.

Welzel, C. (2013). *Freedom Rising: Human Empowerment and the Quest for Emancipation*. Cambridge, Cambridge University Press.

World Value Survey 2023 (2023). Catalogue of Findings, available at: https://www.worldvaluessurvey.org/WVSContents.jsp?CMSID=Findings&title=Anna.

Yaşar, A. (2023). Diyanet Imams between Turkish Majoritarianism and German "Majority Society". *Journal of Muslims in Europe*, 12, 253–281.

13. Reconnecting government: On the existential layers of public administration

Ronald van Steden

INTRODUCTION

Charlemagne, regarded as one of the greatest rulers in history, confronted numerous challenges, including social unrest, raging wars, crop failures, and famine during the Middle Ages. In his efforts to establish peace and security, the emperor implemented various measures. He commanded bishops, cardinals, churches, and monasteries to organise prayers and mandated knights to distribute alms and engage in charitable deeds, while urging ordinary believers to kneel and pray for divine intervention. Later, Charlemagne adopted more practical solutions such as constructing grain silos and restructuring notoriously unstable governance systems (De Graaf, 2014). Both religious and profane measures were indispensable to ensure public order and prosperity in the long term.

Times have significantly changed since Charlemagne's passing in 814. A cornerstone of modern Western democracy is the separation of church and state. Although interpreted variably across different countries (Ferrari, 1988) and not uniformly legislated and implemented (Audi, 1989), this principle broadly safeguards the liberty of individual conscience and disentangles religion from politics and public administration. It ensures that matters concerning religion and the nation-state remain distinct, protecting each from undue influence (Witte, 2006). The outcome is a 'secular' – disenchanted and value-neutral – government nurturing a social environment where pluralistic worldviews, religions, and belief systems can coexist harmoniously.

The study of public administration has a secular character too. Still, scholars have studied the relevance of religion within this field. Ongaro and Tantardini offer a thorough study of how religion, which they define as 'the relationship of the human to the divine' (2023a, p. 2), may enhance our understanding of public administration around the world. Current empirical inquiries encompass the funding of faith-based organisations, the involvement of religious groups in public service delivery, and the influence of individual religious beliefs on the conduct of civil servants (Ongaro & Tantardini, 2023a, 2023b). Yet, despite the significance of these studies, compared to other areas within public administration scholarship, research on the intersection of religion, government, and governance remains relatively limited and dispersed. Religion as a subject has mostly been overlooked or confined to the periphery of the scientific discipline.

Against this background, I explore how public administration can benefit from the humanities, most prominently theology and philosophy. The relevance of this endeavour lies in the observation that, not unlike the era of Charlemagne, our contemporary world is riddled with uncertainty, discontent, and distrust in public institutions. Public administration, both as a practice and as a scientific discipline, struggles to find a convincing response to the challenge of how governments develop worthwhile relations with the citizens they ought to serve. Government systems are bureaucratic and impersonal and, at times, even pathological and inhumane. My central argument is that religious wisdom may help find promising routes to reconnect government to society. In particular, the question of how positive forms of 'resonance' (Rosa, 2019) shape personal contacts between civil servants and citizens requires attention. Street-level bureaucrats (SLBs) have a key role to play (Golan-Nadir, 2024). Public service provision, after all, takes place at the micro level of human interaction.

SOCIETAL DISCONTENT

Despite high levels of individual well-being in many developed countries, there seems to be a growing collective sense of doom and gloom around the Western world. We may speak of a lingering zeitgeist – i.e., a shared 'evaluation of the state (and future) of society' – of societal discontent. For example, in the Netherlands, citizens judge negatively the quality of collective life, while Americans express even greater concerns about their perception of society in decline (Van der Bles et al., 2015). Another study confirms that 'societal pessimism', as a public mood, has been apprehensive in the Netherlands, the United States, and Japan over the past quarter-century. Although the three countries have different historical trajectories, citizens converge around a common anxiety about the future (Van Houwelingen, 2016). Across the West, rising pessimism and discontent can be pictured as an 'ink stain' (Tiemeijer & Keizer, 2023), which flows into feelings of increasing personal vulnerability and decreasing control over one's own life. To a certain degree, societal discontent is a productive force in signaling and fighting social evils such as discrimination and exclusion, but it becomes problematic when people start to refrain from participating in society and blame the government for their precarious situation. Multiple interconnected factors explaining the rise of undermining forms of societal discontent are at stake.

A first set of factors relates to what Bauman (2000) has vividly described as 'liquid' modernity. According to his view, previously stable social relationships, moral standards, and national boundaries have evaporated into 'thin air' due to the twin dynamics of individualisation and globalisation. Although individualisation has brought about a lot of personal autonomy and sparked processes of emancipation, critics point to the collapse of social networks and civic engagement (Bellah et al., 2008 [1985]; Putnam, 2000). Developments such as declining voluntary participation in communities, churches, and sports clubs contribute to the erosion of social and moral ties essential for trust and cooperation in society. Moreover, international economic, political, and cultural integration, coupled with technological innovation, offer unprecedented opportunities but also raise grave concerns about, for example, the loss of local traditions, job displacement, and economic inequality. These developments shake all segments of society, but particularly exacerbate the gap between the affluent and the middle and lower classes, with the latter bearing the brunt of a boundless world. Back in the 1980s, Beck (1990 [1986]) was already warning of the dawn of a 'risk society' full of insecurity and unpredictability. His observations remain as, if not more, pertinent in today's nervous social climate.

A second set of factors refers to a diminishing social welfare ideal. In his analysis of our late modernity, Rosa (2013 [2005]) highlights a phenomenon he calls 'frenetic stillstand': individuals grapple with perpetual transformations while battling paralysing inertia. This paradoxical experience of stagnation arises from the ongoing necessity to toil harder, deplete more natural resources, and expend greater psychological energy merely to maintain the status quo. Consequently, apart from ecological catastrophe and personal burnout, citizens are nervous about the financial sustainability of social welfare systems that guarantee old age pensions, quality healthcare, accessible education, and social protection against unforeseen adversities. A related point is the 'fear of falling' (Ehrenreich, 1989): an anxiety about social descent that permeates the middle classes, causing many reasonably affluent and privileged groups of citizens to feel uncertain about their future. More specifically, the belief that people's own offspring will be better off in terms of social status and financial position than themselves is no longer a given (Putnam, 2015). This trend has resulted in a decline in solidarity and empathy with more vulnerable members of society and a retreat from liberal values. Widespread populism and searches for scapegoats such as migrants are troubling signals.

A final set of factors pertains to the waning trust and confidence in public institutions. Within liquid modernity, 'reflexive' citizens exhibit a critical stance toward government policies and performances (Giddens, 1990). While their reflexivity is largely beneficial for the quality of democratic processes, it can become detrimental, if not toxic, when significant portions of society start questioning the legitimacy of government institutions. For example, only about 20 percent of Americans express trust in the federal state, with a majority expressing dissatisfaction with how the state addresses their individual needs and allocates taxpayers' money (PEW Research Centre, 2022). Furthermore, according to the United Nations (2021), while levels of trust in public services and institutions vary greatly worldwide, experts signal an overarching negative trend compelled by economic insecurity and negative perceptions of state agencies. These issues have been exacerbated by the COVID-19 pandemic (Eurofound, 2022). Likewise, and despite divergence between countries, the OECD (2022) reports that 'just four in ten people indicate high or moderate high trust in their national government'. Administrations are generally seen as sufficiently reliable but could do better in acting on citizens' concerns and in being responsive to public feedback. Disadvantaged groups and younger people have the lowest levels of trust in government.

PATHOLOGIES OF PUBLIC ADMINISTRATION

Societal discontent is not a recent phenomenon. Insecurities and uncertainties arising from deteriorating social connections, economic instability, and wavering trust in government have been pervasive over the last three decades (OECD, 2021). At the same time, through scientific movements of New Social Governance, New Welfare, and New Public Management, governments have invested considerable effort in what can be described as 'social engineering' and 'manufacturability' – endeavours aimed at mastering tragedy and fate. These endeavours have fostered a 'worldview of the machine, with a mechanistic-rational and instrumental view of society and governance' (Van Putten, 2020, p. 279). The net result is what Trommel (2009) terms 'greedy governance' – a culture of control that inadvertently leads to unforeseen consequences, persistent pathologies, and the emergence of new issues that undermine government authority and legitimacy. It is fair to say that high hopes about manufacturability and managerialism have had detrimental effects on the normative aspects of compassion, connection, and resonance in public service work. Following Trommel's analysis, I will provide a discussion of each movement and examine their associated pitfalls below.

In liquid times, where informal networks of mutual solidarity have come under pressure, the New Social Governance movement aspires to strengthen local communities. As spontaneous forms of social cohesion become less common, governments desperately try 'to restore the social fibre of society' (Vonk, 2014, p. 195). Policies manifest in various forms, including the stimulation of active citizenship and community care. The overall objective is to encourage individual activism and collective action to revitalise (deteriorated) neighbourhoods (Foster-Fishman et al., 2007). Similarly, collaborative partnerships between municipal departments, law enforcement, social services, housing associations, and other agencies formulate normative notions of 'safe, orderly and clean' areas. These partnerships implement interventions ranging from financial incentives to strict sanctions. For example, the city of New York heavily invested in aggressive public order maintenance, the removal of homeless individuals from the streets, and a zero-tolerance policy for minor infractions (Chronopoulos, 2020). However, the downside of these aspirations is a 'hypochondriac fixation' on deviations from the norm, often at the expense of marginalised populations, such as migrants and the poor (Schinkel & Van Houdt, 2010).

While the sustainability and affordability of national welfare systems were increasingly questioned, the emergence of New Welfare demonstrated a shift towards policies designed to discipline individual life trajectories: 'the self-regulation of risky behaviour is regarded as being integral to personal well-being and integration within society' (Ellison & Fenger, 2013, p. 549). The fundamental premise underlying these policies is the expectation for citizens to lead sensible and productive lives contributing to collective prosperity. Therefore, policymakers have introduced an array of precautionary measures to invigorate this kind of behaviour (no smoking, healthy eating, adequate exercise, smooth careers) and counteract deliberate abuse of welfare state facilities. Yet, a negative consequence has been the development of a 'preventive gaze' that penetrates people's whereabouts since everybody is a potential perpetrator (Peeters, 2013). The Daycare Benefit Scandal in the Netherlands epitomises what can happen. In 2021, the Dutch cabinet resigned following revelations that the Tax Administration wrongfully accused thousands of families of fraud, causing loss of jobs, financial ruin, and other severe distress (Peeters & Widlak, 2023). It appeared that algorithms indirectly discriminated based on ethnicity and race.

Finally, inspired by market-oriented ideologies, governments have embraced New Public Management (NPM) as a philosophy and set of practices that elevate efficiency, effectiveness, flexibility, customer service, and performance measurement. Osborne and Gaebler (1992) famously advised that the welfare state should 'steer' not 'row': instead of being directly involved in the delivery of public services (rowing), the government's role, in their view, is to set standards for facilitating (steering) other agencies, including private businesses and non-profit organisations, to do the actual work. NPM, albeit in various forms, has had a tremendous impact on public sector restructurings, but also received criticism (Pollitt & Bouckaert, 2017). Opponents have argued that an overemphasis on efficiency and effectiveness might lead to a neglect of other public values (such as social justice) and the quality of government services. The decoupling between the facilitation and execution of services may also lead to fragmentation, a focus on short-term planning, less motivated employees, and accountability gaps in monitoring outsourced service providers (Diefenbach, 2009). For citizens, the 'hollowing out of the state' (Rhodes, 1994) has literally distanced public services. Libraries, schools, police stations, and public transport have disappeared from their neighbourhoods, villages, and towns.

THE BÖCKENFÖRDE PARADOX

The NPM movement can be further criticised for how it extends a market logic to government and society. Governments have incorporated business-like practices, and citizens are increasingly perceived as 'responsibilised' entities adopting an economic language of commodities and self-help (Shamir, 2008). For example, in both Britain and the Netherlands, collective welfare state arrangements have been outsourced to private companies and social enterprises, which are expected to provide citizens with public services, while (weak) informal networks of families, friends, neighbours, and informal caregivers are empowered to take on support roles for vulnerable individuals (Verhoeven & Tonkens, 2013). Yet, when placing public officials at too much distance from individual citizens, responsibilisation is not without implications, as it tends to overlook the symbolic power of government agents and agencies. Following Loader, the police, but we may consider social services too, are 'principally *affective* in character, something which people evince a deep emotional commitment to and which is closely integrated with their sense of self' (1997, p. 3; emphasis in the original). In other words, civil servants should convey that citizens are well looked after, thereby strengthening communities of attachment. Public services ideally embody a narrative through which people comprehend society and experience 'ontological' or 'existential' security (Giddens, 1990, p. 92) – a sensation of reliability and stability that involves basic trust in the social system and activates a conception of good citizenship. Responsibilisation tends to cut this string between government and its inhabitants.

Taken together, market-embedded morality and responsibilisation strategies are at odds with the ideal of public officials who serve the common good and uphold public trust. Nothing less than the legitimacy of democratic government is facing severe challenges. This disturbing conclusion reminds us of the so-called 'Böckenförde paradox' that '*[t]he liberal, secularised state is sustained by conditions it cannot itself guarantee*' (Böckenförde, 2020 [1967], p. 167; emphasis in the original). With his dictum, Böckenförde, a well-known German legal scholar, points to the emergence of nation-states as the outcome of historical secularisation processes that gradually released political and legal systems from metaphysical oversight. Policies and laws became valid because they accorded with sovereign, not religious, consent, affirming that modern governments solely derive their authority and legitimacy from citizen support. The 'great gamble' now is how individualised and responsibilised citizens find a form of unity and integration in the modern state. Böckenförde dismisses the answer of coercive authority because this puts the axe at the roots of liberal democracy. The stability of democratic government, it seems, requires symbolic expression in the form of a shared set of beliefs, norms, and values. Put differently, on an existential level, the legitimacy of public institutions rests on moral association and social attunement that precludes laws, bureaucratic procedures, and government actions.

From his travels around North America, Alexis de Tocqueville, the nineteenth-century philosopher and sociologist, asserted that the foundation of a democratic government lies not solely within legal and constitutional frameworks, but also within 'the mores of society' (Fradkin, 2000, p. 90). These mores are cultivated and upheld in an intermediate space between government, market, and private life that comprises non-profit organisations, churches, schools, universities, corporations, and voluntary associations. Within such institutions, citizens embrace values other than self-interest and learn to develop social skills and invest in the common good (Alexander, 2006). A pluralistic civil sphere is key to experiencing recognition, belonging, and purpose, all of which contribute to feelings of basic trust and security. The primary function of government agencies and civil servants is to serve rather than to steer this civil sphere, articulate the preferences of citizens, and engage them in the promotion of general welfare. '[I]n a democratic society', Denhardt and Denhardt (2000, p. 557) argue, 'a concern for democratic values should be paramount in the way we think about systems of governance. Values such as efficiency and productivity should not be lost but should be placed in the larger context of democracy, community, and the public interest'. Indeed, alongside the *'efficient* parts' of a constitution and government (those by which it 'works and rules'), attention must also be given to the *'dignified* parts', which are essential for winning 'the loyalty and confidence of mankind' (Bagehot, 1867 [2001], p. 5; emphasis in the original). Religious traditions and wisdom may help maintain this spirit and wield 'symbolic' and 'normative' power (Tsai, 2016) to endorse citizens' trust in government and democracy.

A POST-SECULAR TURN

A renewed receptiveness to religion is not self-evident. Back in 1984, Neuhaus cautioned against popular political discourse evolving into a 'naked public square,' devoid of religious voices that serve as essential carriers of values and responsibilities. This may end, he suggests, in the death of democracy over the long run (Neuhaus, 1984). According to Taylor (2007), the situation is less dramatic as the secular age still leaves room for a plurality of voices, including religious ones. Religious beliefs and practices have undeniably changed and indeed retracted from the public sphere in Western societies, but, since the turn of the new millennium, we also witness a renewed global presence of religion, both in its constructive and destructive forms (Berger, 1999). While acknowledging that religious traditions possess negative aspects such as sectarianism, terrorism, and church scandals, they continue to carry a vital 'apologetic dimension' (Graham, 2014) spilling over into the ideational and motivational characteristics of governments, societies, and individuals.

Habermas (2001; 2006; 2008; 2019), one of the spearheads of Enlightenment, rationality, and deliberation, is currently at the forefront of advocating a fresh intellectual receptivity for religion and religious wisdom within the Western hemisphere. Through his hypothesis of a post-secular turn, Habermas calls attention to the renewed importance of religious discourses in politics and society. However, his analysis has been largely ignored by most scholars (and practitioners) in the field of public administration (Van Putten et al., 2019). Their neglect can be attributed, in part, to the inherently secular nature of public administration as an international academic discipline. Its historical roots are firmly embedded in Enlightenment principles, which fuelled the rejection of a higher moral authority beyond human reason (Raadschelders, 2008; Rutgers, 1997). This foundational stance has significantly contributed to the secularisation of Western thought and practice. Notably, early manifestations of public administration science, such as *Kameralistiek* in Germany, as well as *Science administrative* in France, were directly influenced by Enlightenment thinkers and lacked substantial connections with religious traditions. Max Weber, one of the greatest intellectual fathers of European administrative science and practice, was even virulently opposed to Christianity.

More fundamentally, the science of public administration has predominantly embraced logical positivism, heavily relying on stringent liberal distinctions between 'public' and 'private', 'politics' and 'administration' (Rutgers, 2001), and 'state' and 'church'. Herbert Simon, an influential proponent of this view, asserts that administrative science and practice should focus on facts, with limited or no attention to values and metaphysical positions in decision-making, as they are deemed sub-rational and outside the realm of scientific argumentation. While religious expressions might be (reluctantly) tolerated in the legislature and the presidency, other branches of government, especially the judiciary and the bureaucracy, are expected to be neutral (Lynch et al., 1997). Indeed, there exists a prevalent apprehension that religion could potentially have detrimental effects on society. Habermas opposes this apprehension by adopting a more lenient attitude towards religion. He indicates 'a change in consciousness' (Habermas, 2008, p. 20) – that is, an awareness of the remainder of religion that challenges the taken-for-granted recognition of the West as completely secularised. The idea that religion, often employed by social scientists in abstract and unspecified ways, would simply vanish due to modernisation processes has been proven incorrect.

Habermas stresses that contemporary secularism is characterised by moral detachment, exacerbated by social engineering, bureaucratisation, and marketisation, which have eroded shared values and solidarity among people. Religion, implicitly defined by Habermas as the substance of belief systems and worldviews influencing individuals' engagement in public life, can be a positive force in society. It serves as a crucial source of morality and social cohesion, fostering civic commitment to democracy (Habermas, 2001; 2019). Furthermore, Habermas warns against conflating the neutrality of a secular state with hostility towards religion. State neutrality, he contends, involves maintaining impartiality regarding a plurality of worldviews, rather than excluding religion from public life. Nevertheless, he underscores the importance of respecting the separation of church (or mosque and synagogue) and state, as well as upholding 'public reason'. There should always be a 'filter' between formal and informal discourses: 'in a constitutional state, all norms that can be legally implemented must be formulated and *publicly justified* in a language that all citizens understand' (Habermas, 2008, p. 28; emphasis in the original). While people have the right to express their own convictions, they must embrace the secular state and disavow possible harmful elements within their religion.

CONTRACT AND COVENANT

The roots of the modern secular state trace back to philosophers such as Thomas Hobbes, who theoretically established the legitimacy of public institutions through a legal concept: the social contract. Hobbes' concept emerges from a hypothetical (not a historical) 'state of nature' where people are engaged in a civil war of 'all against all'. Fearing violence, brutality, and pain, they collectively decide to relinquish their freedoms to a robust state. The gist of the social contract thought experiment, Ongaro (2020, p. 172) writes, is that modern public institutions ultimately rest on 'our will in a deliberate [...] choice to surrender to the authority of the state in order to preserve certain conditions for our individual lives – primarily safety and security'. Regulatory and disciplinary measures are prevalent in this respect. From social contract theories, we may cautiously infer that prevailing public administration movements – New Social Governance, New Welfare, and New Public Management – trace their roots to rationalistic and legalistic concepts of the state. Such movements have, at least, displayed a strong appetite for bureaucratic and managerial ways of doing. Recall the earlier described modes of 'greedy governance' aspiring to manufacture society by means of public interventions. Trust in public institutions globally has not seen an upward trajectory as a result.

In daily life, the legitimacy of public administration, which is closely related to citizens' trust in public institutions, can hardly be distinguished from its embeddedness in and subordination to politics and political systems. Changes in one domain will ultimately affect the other. It can nevertheless be useful to make an analytical distinction between public administrations and political systems for the purpose of studying how public sector reforms and routines, like NPM, may have an impact on issues of legitimacy and trust (Ongaro, 2020). Although trust levels differ among countries (Bouckaert, 2012) and proving causality between government performance and public trust levels is challenging (Van der Walle & Bouckaert, 2003), scholars point out that citizens may not fully appreciate government actions aimed at achieving greater efficiency, effectiveness, and accountability. Instead, empirical evidence from the Netherlands, the United States, and South Korea converges around what citizens do want from civil servants, namely responsiveness, service, and dedication (Neo et al., 2023). Public values rather than managerial skills have their merits here.

Specifically, at the micro-level of street-level bureaucrats' behaviour, principles and practices of mutual trust and recognition between civil servants and citizens are vital for governments to function at their full democratic capacity. A cross-national overview of studies concludes that citizens judge the government and civil servants on 'good governance', proper performance, professional competence, procedural fairness, and ethical conduct (Houston et al., 2016). From their perspective, civil servants tend to hold a neutral – neither trusting nor distrusting – view of citizens (Yang, 2005). An efficient and effective use of public resources remains, of course, integral to good governance (Paanakker et al., 2020), and public values are inevitably rife with conflict (Van der Wal et al., 2011). However, this does not negate the fact that civil servants must cultivate a 'listening heart' (Rosa, 2024) towards the struggles, worries, expectations, and demands of citizens. A secular age marked by discontent and cynicism about public administration urgently calls for a richer comprehension of what good governance entails.

Beyond the pragmatic reasons of a well-functioning public administration to ensure trust, satisfaction, and legitimacy on the citizens' side, good governance, with all its internal ambiguities, is desirable in itself. It supports and sustains conditions for citizens to pursue the good life – an exertion of the heart and the soul to promote *eudaimonia* (Van Steden, 2020). Philosophy and theology contribute to this insight by emphasising not only the managerial and legal but also the existential and moral dimensions of good governance. Indeed, as Ongaro (2020, p. 178) says, 'NPM-inspired recipes can hardly address the issue of how to improve lives in terms of fulfilment (living a full life, the *eudaimonia*)'. His observation is vital considering frictions between groups of citizens and what they perceive as distant and occasionally dysfunctional or even hostile government agencies (think of the discriminatory fraud hunts). Public administration scholars and practitioners have a duty to respond in thoughtful and benevolent ways. Delving into the connection between religion, morality, and public administration holds significant potential for exploration.

Building on the discussion about a post-secular turn sparked by Habermas (2001; 2006; 2008; 2019), it follows that religious traditions, wisdom, and language do matter for public administration practices and scholarship. Religion can be a wellspring of wisdom for good governance, as moral foundations and the doctrine of vocation encourage civil servants and other public officials to develop 'a genuine care for their fellow citizens' (Dwivedi, 1987, p. 705). Contrary to modern contract theories, which prioritise rational will and individual (self-)interest, a pre-modern discernment of institutional legitimacy revolves around the conception of the social covenant. While Hobbes' contract theory reflects a negative anarchical worldview, the social covenant offers a more positive framework, expecting (heavenly) citizenship rooted in notions of loyalty, responsibility, and reciprocity. Ongaro and Tantardini (2023a) locate the covenant idea in the Book of Genesis where God, through the old prophets, builds a pact with the people of Israel. In Christian theology, the social covenant was brought to completion in the person of Jesus Christ and His message of universal love for humankind.

The Western heritage of Christianity also influences the ancient Greek interpretation of *eudaimonia*. While Aristotle posited that *eudaimonia* arises from a collective pursuit of the common good within the confines of a *polis*, a city-state, Saint Augustine wrote that 'being in communion with God is the end of human flourishing' (Vos, 2023, p. 203). His theology implies that caring for one's neighbour extends to forms of justice that embrace the entire world – every human being – rather than being confined to a limited group of wealthy males, as was the case in Aristotle's *polis* (and still is today). Augustine's religious teachings serve as a poignant reminder that universalistic inclusion is essential for a well-functioning democratic government and a compassionate society. His heritage echoes through the notion that society is an intricate network of interpersonal relationships moulded by normative beliefs in respect, loyalty, and solidarity, converging within what Sztompka (2019) terms a 'moral space'. The dedication of civil servants to normative principles, professional values, and good governance is crucial for the establishment and maintenance of this space.

THE QUESTION OF RESONANCE

The moral aspects of SLBs' work are a recurring theme in public administration literature. Max Weber once contrasted 'instrumental rationality' with 'value rationality'. Instrumental rationality involves a calculated assessment of the costs and benefits, as well as the advantages and disadvantages, of policies and interventions. In contrast, personal worldviews and religion are rooted in value rationality, which pertains to ideals, moral standards, and normative orientations (Ongaro & Tantardini, 2023, 2024). Maynard-Moody and Musheno (2003), for their part, introduce a 'state-agent' narrative in which SLBs are charged with carrying out government plans and policies, and a 'citizen-agent' narrative that takes seriously who citizens are, what they do, and what they need. The challenge lies in striking a balance between the legal and moral obligations of SLBs in their interactions with ordinary people.

To be sure, value rationality can influence the behaviour of public officials both positively and negatively. Normative convictions might contribute to unequal treatment within the civil service and towards the citizenry. However, in exploring the question of how to reconnect government and the public, attention goes to positive forms of 'resonance' (Rosa, 2019) in SLB-citizen contact. Theological and philosophic answers are a case in point. Resonance, which literally means 'giving back sound' (Gregersen, 2020, p. 101), signifies a feeling of being touched by encounters with people, music, art, nature, and more. It is like a pendulum swinging between two poles whose frequencies attune in harmony. These 'good vibrations' (Vandenberghe, 2023) serve as an antidote to alienation, which represents the problematic separation between the self and the other, or the self and the wider environment. Societal discontent and public distrust in government can be interpreted as a lack of resonance in human relationships.

Theissen (2019), an eminent New Testament scholar, juxtaposes resonance with what he labels the 'absurd' – the drama of being thrown into a cold, heartless, and silent universe. This may lead to the spiritual and existential disillusionment of not feeling 'at home' (Christoffersen & Gregersen, 2019). Conversely, resonance denotes an atmosphere of connection, reciprocity, and appreciation: '*something clicked*' (Peters & Majid, 2022, p. 3; emphasis in the original). In seeking meaning, religious-minded individuals long for God, who is, for Theissen, not just an anthropomorphic projection. Believers are 'carried into the world' (Gregersen, 2020, p. 95), which represents an emotional experience of resonance that takes place prior to self-productive human intentionality and purpose. They are touched by a pre-existing reality, an all-encompassing love, that 'demands' a personal pledge. Distinct from purely aesthetic experiences (pleasures like beautiful movies or thrilling soccer matches), religious experiences come with a moral obligation.

Conceiving human beings as *homo resonans* offers a promising route forward to uncovering the frequently neglected existential – religious and spiritual – layers in human interactions. Through resonance, so to speak, civil servants feel addressed and motivated to reach out to others. They turn from a 'buffered self' to a 'porous self' (Taylor, 2007), exhibiting greater sensitivity for what is requested from them. A sense of resonance, akin to the ancient pursuit of *eudaimonia* or human flourishing and happiness (Rosa, 2019), may shield civil servants against unjust treatments of citizens and support an ethos of empathy, proportionality, and compassion. As such, the acoustic metaphor of resonance helps to grasp what 'happens when practitioners make sense of momentary gestures, signs and sentences that occur in their practices, which includes how they attune to these practices' (Olsman, 2022, p. 315). Public administration has something to learn from the humanities here.

It can be argued that the concept of resonance provides a sort of bridge between the irreducibility of existential (religious, spiritual) experiences, on the one hand, and the necessity to empirically study what takes place in the everyday routines of public administration, on the other hand. How can we understand this in a secular context of SLB-citizen contact? In opposition to Theissen, Rosa deploys 'the same notion of resonance to both inner-worldly and divine-human relations' (Christoffersen & Gregersen, 2019, p. 22). Meaningful encounters with the world and with fellow human beings also signify an existential moment of resonance. Rosa's horizontal view of religion is open to the criticism of becoming overly secular (Quintana & Combalia, 2023), but we should not forget that the etymology of religion is derived from *'re-ligare*, the Latin term for being "rebound" into the basic relations' (Christoffersen & Gregersen, 2019, p. 20; emphasis in the original). Religion promises that somebody (or Somebody) is responsive to the needs of others, that people are seen and heard. The quest for this responsiveness lies at the core of debates within public administration about SLB-citizen contacts, interactions, and their outcomes.

IN SEARCH OF RESONANCE

This concluding section outlines a research agenda examining how resonance in SLB-citizen interactions is fostered by unspoken existential layers of religious and broader humanistic worldviews. Since their interactions are imbued with intersubjective meaning, rational and positivist currents in public administration science, which are limited to empirical observation and 'brute' objective data, fall short. Alternatively, scholars should embrace hermeneutical and interpretative branches of the social sciences to gain a profound understanding of resonating contacts (Taylor, 1971). Qualitative methods and techniques, such as in-depth interviewing, participant observation, and narrative analyses, have the power to provide an authentic presentation of SLBs' and citizens' communications, experiences, beliefs, and perceptions. Rosa (2024) identifies four elements of resonance – affection, self-efficacy, transformation, and uncontrollability – that will guide my research agenda.

The element of affection denotes moments when the self is 'called upon', stirring one's emotions and triggering a personal reaction (Rosa, 2019). This inner voice, as described in the public administration literature, evokes terms like 'calling' or 'vocation', whether rooted in a personal relationship with God or in a secular faith in the constitutional state (Houston et al., 2008). Work can be viewed simply as a means of earning a living or advancing one's career, but, particularly in e realm of public service, it holds richer significance too. In Bellah et al.'s words, a '"calling" […] constitutes a practical ideal of activity and character that makes a person's work morally inseparable from his or her life' (2008 [1985], p. 66). Civil servants, in their commitment to their (local) communities, may thus embrace their work not merely as a means to an end but also as an intrinsic value. This attitude leads us to ponder the following questions: Do civil servants indeed view their work as a calling? If so, how do (religious) worldviews affect their calling? How do SLBs' worldviews and beliefs (value rationality) relate to bureaucratic procedures and cost/benefit calculations (instrumental rationality)?

Sympathy or, on a deeper level, affection among individuals extends into 'self-efficacy', Rosa's second element: '[t]he subject responds to this affection in a self-efficacious mode of reaching out and touching or influencing the object or entity encountered' (2020, p. 398). For civil servants, their religion, faith, and worldview may serve as a moral compass that guides their intuitions of what is just and fair, translating into concrete behaviour characterised by a genuine 'desire to serve' others (Bisesi & Lidman, 2009). Indeed, SLBs, in their direct contacts with citizens, strongly feel the urgency of suitable interventions to address situations effectively: 'to a degree, the society seeks not only impartiality from its public agencies but also compassion for special circumstances and flexibility in dealing with them' (Lipsky, 2010 [1980], p. 15). Attention to this 'moral agency' (Zacka, 2017) of SLBs can be advanced by exploring questions like: How do SLBs reach out to citizens? Do their contacts result in tailor-made responses necessary to 'fit' people's individual situations and needs? In what ways are these contacts affected by SLBs' (religious) worldviews and beliefs?

Such questions directly speak to the third element of transformation in Rosa's framework: 'the experiencing self has to change during the relationship, because [of] the ways she is involved in the two-directionality of affection and emotion' (Peters & Majid, 2022, p. 18). Transformation occurs both within individuals and between them. NPM and other public administration movements exhibit a preference for strict guidelines, performance targets, precautionary measures, and so on, which create tension with the SLBs' room to manoeuvre. This may frustrate their personal and professional calling to serve others. Citizens also struggle with bureaucratic government agencies but may find concrete assistance from SLBs. In their interactions, citizens can be emotionally and morally moved by the efforts of SLBs, potentially leading to a change in their view of public administration. Related research questions include: Do the efforts of SLBs positively impact the situations and requirements of citizens? How do the outcomes of SLBs' efforts influence public perceptions of government? Do SLB-citizen contacts give SLBs a sense of purpose in their work?

Finally, despite public administration's inclination towards 'social engineering' and 'manufacturability', resonance in citizen-SLB interactions is uncontrollable and unpredictable – the fourth element of resonance. As Rosa asserts, 'it is constitutionally impossible to predict its occurrence, and [...] if it happens, it is absolutely impossible to predict or control the outcome or result of the ensuing transformation' (2020, p. 398). Grasping the interactions between SLBs and citizens and what occurs there necessitates detailed research about the last set of questions: Had SLBs and citizens anticipated the outcomes of their contacts? What are the similarities and differences between the intentions and outcomes of SLB-citizen contact? How can the experiences of both SLBs and citizens be explained? Answering these questions should provide greater insight into the social routines and practices at the frontline of government institutions. It is there where bureaucracy gets a human face, and where vicious cycles of discontent and distrust might be turned into virtuous cycles of resonance and reconnection.

ACKNOWLEDGEMENTS

The section on 'a post-secular turn' is drawn from a previous paper authored by Robert van Putten, Patrick Overeem, and me (van Putten et al., 2019). I would like to express my gratitude to Edoardo Ongaro for inviting me to the seminar on Public Administration and the Humanities in Rome, which served as the foundation for this chapter, and for his insightful comments on an earlier draft.

REFERENCES

Alexander, J.C. (2006). *The Civil Sphere.* Oxford: Oxford University Press.
Audi, R. (1989). The Separation of Church and State and the Obligations of Citizenship. *Philosophy & Public Affairs, 18*(3), 259–296.
Bagehot, W. (1867 [2001]). *The English Constitution.* Cambridge: Cambridge University Press.
Bauman, Z. (2000). *Liquid Modernity.* Cambridge: Polity Press.
Beck, U. (1990 [1986]). *Risk Society: Towards a New Modernity.* London: Sage.
Bellah, R.N., Madsen, R., Sullivan, W.M., Shidler, A., & Tipton, S.M. (2008 [1985]). *Habits of the Heart: Individualism and Commitment in American Life.* Berkeley, CA: University of California Press.

Berger, P.L. (ed.) (1999). *The Desecularization of the World: Resurgent Religion and World Politics*. Washington D.C./Grand Rapids, MI: Ethics and Public Policy Centre/Eerdmans.

Bisesi, M. & Lidman, R. (2009). Compassion and Power: Religion, Spirituality, and Public Administration. *International Journal of Public Administration*, 32(1), 4–23.

Böckenförde, E.W. (2020 [1967]). The Rise of the State as a Process of Secularization. In: M. Künkler & T. Stein (eds.) *Religion, Law, and Democracy: Selected Writings*: Oxford: Oxford University Press, pp. 152–167.

Bouckaert, G. (2012). Trust and Public Administration. *Administration, 60*(1), 91–115.

Christoffersen, M.G. & Gregersen, N.H. (2019). Resonance, Risk, and Religion: Gerd Theissen and Hartmut Rosa on Religious Resonance. *Philosophy, Theology and the Sciences*, 6(1), 6–32.

Chronopoulos, T. (2020). The Making of the Orderly City: New York since the 1980s. *Journal of Urban History*, 46(5), 1085–1116.

De Graaf, B. (2014). *Waar zijn we bang voor?: Een religieus-theologische benadering van veiligheid [What Are We Afraid of?: A Religious-Theological Approach towards Security]*. Amsterdam/Groningen: PThU.

Denhardt, R.B. & Denhardt, J.V. (2000). The New Public Service: Serving Rather than Steering. *Public Administration Review*, 60(6), 549–559.

Diefenbach, T. (2009). New Public Management in Public Sector Organisations: The Dark Sides of Managerialistic 'Enlightenment'. *Public Administration, 87*(4), 892–909.

Dwivedi, O.P. (1987). Moral Dimensions of Statecraft: A Plea for an Administrative Theology. *Canadian Journal of Political Science/Revue Canadienne de Science Politique, 20*(4), 699–709.

Ehrenreich, B. (1989). *Fear of Falling: The Inner Life of the Middle Class*. New York: Twelve/Hachette Book Group.

Ellison, M. & Fenger, M. (2013). Introduction – 'New' Welfare in Practice: Trends, Challenges and Dilemmas. *Social Policy and* Society, *12*(4), 547–552.

Eurofound (2022). *Fifth Round of the Living, Working and COVID-19 e-Survey: Living in a New Era of Uncertainty*. Publication Office of the European Union, retrieved from: www.eurofound.europa.eu/en/publications.

Ferrari, S. (1988). Separation of Church and State in Contemporary European Society. *Journal of Church and State*, 30(3), 533–547.

Foster-Fishman P.G., Cantillon D., Pierce S.J., & Van Egeren, L.A. (2007). Building an Active Citizenry: The Role of Neighbourhood Problems, Readiness, and Capacity for Change. *American Journal of Community Psychology*, 39(1–2), 91–106.

Fradkin, H. (2000). Does Democracy Need Religion?. *Journal of Democracy, 11*(1), 87–94.

Giddens, A. (1990). *The Consequences of Modernity*. Cambridge: Polity Press.

Golan-Nadir, N. (2024). Religion and Public Administration at the Micro Level: The Lens of Street-Level Bureaucracy Theory in Democracies. *Australian Journal of Public Administration*, 83(4), 736–748.

Graham, E. (2014). Between a Rock and a Hard Place: Public Theology in a Post-Secular Age. *Practical Theology* 7(4), 235–251.

Gregersen, N.H. (2020). Resilient Selves: A Theology of Resonance and Secularity. *Dialog, 59*(2), 93–102.

Habermas, J. (2001). *Glaube und Wissen: Rede zum Friedenspreis des Deutschen Buchhandels [Faith and Knowledge: Speech for the Peace Price of the German Bookstores]*. Berlin: Suhrkamp Verlag.

Habermas, J. (2006). Religion in the Public Sphere. *European Journal of Philosophy*, *14*(1), 1–25.

Habermas, J. (2008). Notes on Post-Secular Society. *New Perspectives Quarterly*, *25*(4), 17–29.

Habermas, J. (2019). *Auch eine Geschichte der Philosophie – Band 2: Vernünftige Freiheit: Spuren des Diskurses über Glauben und Wissen [An Alternative History of Philosophy – Volume 2: Rational Freedom: Traces of Discourses on Faith and Knowledge]*. Berlin: Suhrkamp.

Houston, D.J., Aitalieva, N.R., Morelock, A.L. & Shults, C.A. (2016). Citizen Trust in Civil Servants: A Cross-National Examination. *International Journal of Public Administration*, *39*(14), 1203–1214.

Houston, D.J., Freeman, P.K. & Feldman, D.L. (2008). How Naked Is the Public Square?: Religion, Public Service, and Implications for Public Administration. *Public Administration Review*, *68*(3), 428–444.

Lipsky, M. (2010 [1980]). *Streel-Level Bureaucracy: Dilemmas of the Individual in Public Services* (30th anniversary expanded edition). New York: Russell Sage Foundation.

Loader, I. (1997). Policing and the Social: Questions of Symbolic Power. *The British Journal of Sociology*, *48*(1), 1–18.

Lynch, T.D., Omdal, R., & Cruise, P.L. (1997). Secularization of Public Administration. *Journal of Public Administration Research and Theory*, *7*(3), 473–487.

Maynard-Moody, S. & Musheno, M. (2003). *Cops, Teachers, Counselors: Stories from the Front Lines of Public Service*. Ann Arbor, MA: The University of Michigan Press.

Neo, S., Grimmelikhuijsen, S., & Tummers, L. (2023). Core Values for Ideal Civil Servants: Service-Oriented, Responsive and Dedicated. *Public Administration Review*, *83*(4), 838–862.

Neuhaus, R.J. (1984). *The Naked Public Square: Religion and Democracy in America*. Grand Rapids, MI: Eerdmans.

OECD (2021). *Perspectives on Global Development 2021: From Protest to Progress?*. Paris: OECD Publishing.

OECD (2022). *Building Trust to Reinforce Democracy: Main Findings from the OECD Trust Survey*. Presentation retrieved from: http://oe.cd/trust.

Olsman, E. (2022). Resonance in a Theopoetics of Practice in Practical Theology. *International Journal of Practical Theology*, *26*(2), 311–328.

Ongaro, E. (2020). *Philosophy and Public Administration: An Introduction* (second edition). Cheltenham, UK and Northampton, MA: Edward Elgar.

Ongaro, E. & Tantardini, M. (2023). *Religion and Public Administration: An Introduction*. Cheltenham, UK and Northampton, MA: Edward Elgar.

Ongaro, E. & Tantardini, M. (2024). Religion, Spirituality, Faith and Public Administration: A Literature Review and Outlook. *Public Policy and Administration*, *39*(4), 531-555.

Osborne, D. & Gaebler, T. (1992) *Reinventing Government: How the Entrepreneurial Spirit is Transforming the Public Sector*. Reading: Addison-Wesley.

Paanakker, H.L., Masters, A.B., & Huberts, L.W.J.C. (eds.) (2020). *Quality of Governance: Values and Violations*. Basingstoke: Palgrave Macmillan.

Peeters, R. (2013). *The Preventive Gaze: How Prevention Transforms our Understanding of the State*. The Hague: Eleven International Publishing.

Peeters, R. & Widlak, A. (2023). Administrative Exclusion in the Infrastructure-Level Bureaucracy: The Case of the Dutch Daycare Benefit Scandal. *Public Administration Review, 83*(4), 863–877.

Peters, M. & Majid, B. (2022). *Exploring Hartmut Rosa's Concept of Resonance.* Basingstoke: Palgrave Macmillan.

PEW Research Centre (2022). *America's Views of Government: Decades of Distrust, Enduring Support for its Role.* Report retrieved from: www.pewresearch.org.

Pollitt, C. & Bouckaert, G. (2017). *Public Management Reform: A Comparative Analysis – Into the Age of Austerity* (fourth edition). Oxford: Oxford University Press.

Putnam, R.D. (2000). *Bowling Alone: The Collapse and Revival of American Community.* New York: Simon & Schuster.

Putnam, R.D. (2015). *Our Kids: The American Dream in Crisis.* New York: Simon & Schuster.

Quintana, O. & Combalia X.C. (2023). Resonance: The Final Dissolution of Religions or the Last Stage of Secularization. *Religions, 14*(6), 689.

Raadschelders, J.C.N. (2008). Understanding Government: Four Intellectual Traditions in the Study of Public Administration. *Public Administration, 86*(4), 925–949.

Rhodes, R.A.W. (1994). The Hollowing Out of the State: The Changing Nature of the Public Service in Britain. *Political Quarterly, 65*(2), 138–151.

Rosa, H. (2013 [2005]). *Social Acceleration: A New Theory of Modernity.* New York: Columbia University Press.

Rosa, H. (2019). *Resonance: A Sociology of Our Relationship to the World.* Cambridge: Polity Press.

Rosa, H. (2020). Beethoven, the Sailor, the Boy and the Nazi: A Reply to My Critics. *Journal of Political Power, 13*(3), 397–414.

Rosa, H. (2024). *Democracy needs Religion.* Cambridge: Polity Press.

Rutgers, M. R. (1997). Beyond Woodrow Wilson: The Identity of the Study of Public Administration in Historical Perspective. *Administration & Society, 29*(3), 276–300.

Rutgers, M. R. (2001). Splitting the Universe: On the Relevance of Dichotomies for the Study of Public Administration. *Administration & Society, 33*(1), 3–20.

Schinkel, W. & Van Houdt, F. (2010). The Double Helix of Cultural Assimilationism and Neo-Liberalism: Citizenship in Contemporary Governmentality. *British Journal of Sociology, 61*(4), 696–715.

Shamir, R. (2008). The Age of Responsibilization: On Market-Embedded Morality. *Economy and Society, 37*(1), 1–19.

Sztompka, P. (2019). Trust in the Moral Space. In: M. Sasaki (ed.). *Trust in Contemporary Society.* Leiden: Brill, pp. 31–40.

Taylor, C. (1971). Interpretation and the Sciences of Man. *The Review of Metaphysics, 25*(1), 3–51.

Taylor, C. (2007). *A Secular Age.* Cambridge, MA: Harvard University Press.

Theissen, G. (2019). Religious Experience: Experience of Transparency and Resonance. *Open Philosophy, 2*(1), 679–699.

Tiemeijer, W. & Keizer, A.G. (2023). *Onzekerheid, maatschappelijk onbehagen en persoonlijke controle: een conceptuele en empirische analyse* [*Uncertainty, Societal Discontent and Personal Control: A Conceptual and Empirical Analysis*]. Den Haag: WRR.

Trommel, W.A. (2009). *Gulzig bestuur* [*Greedy Governance*]. Den Haag: Boom-Lemma.

Tsai, G. (2016). The Morality of State Symbolic Power. *Social Theory and Practice*, *42*(2), 318–342.

United Nations (2021). *Trust in Public Institutions: Trends and Implications for Economic Security*. Policy brief retrieved from: www.un.org/development/desa/dspd/.

Vandenberghe, F. (2023). Tuning into Harmut Rosa's Systematic Romanticism. *The Journal of Chinese Sociology*, *10*, 12.

Van der Bles, A.M., Postmes, T., & Meijer, R. (2015). Understanding Collective Discontents: A Psychological Approach to Measuring Zeitgeist. *PLos One*, *10*(6), 1–26.

Van der Wal, Z., De Graaf, G. & Lawton, A. (2011). Competing Values in Public Management. *Public Management Review*, *13*(3), 331–341.

Van der Walle, S. & Bouckaert, G. (2003). Public Service Performance and Trust in Government: The Problem of Causality. *International Journal of Public Administration*, *26*(8–9), 891–913.

Van Houwelingen, P. (2016). Societal Pessimism in Japan, the United States, and the Netherlands. *Japanese Journal of Political Science*, *17*(3), 427–450.

Van Putten, R.J. (2020). *De ban van beheersing: naar een reflexieve bestuurskunst [The Spell of Control: Governance as Reflexive Art]*. The Hague: Boom Bestuurskunde.

Van Putten, R.J., Overeem, P. & Van Steden, R. (2019). Where Public Theology and Public Administration Meet: Reflections on Jürgen Habermas' Post-Secular Turn. *International Journal of Public Theology*, *13*(1), 5–24.

Van Steden, R. (2020). Blind Spots in Public Ethics and Integrity Research: What Scholars can Learn from Aristotle. *Public Integrity*, *22*(3), 236–244.

Verhoeven, I. & Tonkens, E. (2013). Talking Active Citizenship: Framing Welfare State Reform in England and the Netherlands. *Social Policy and Society*, *12*(3), 415–426.

Vonk, G. (2014). Repressive Welfare States: The Spiral of Obligations and Sanctions in Social Security. *European Journal of Social Security*, *16*(3), 188–203.

Vos, P.H. (2023). Aristotelian Eudaimonism as Common Ground for Dialogue on the Good Life. In: L. Huppes-Cluysenaer & N.M.M.S. Coelho (eds.). *Aristotle on Truth, Dialogue, Justice and Decision*. Cham: Springer, pp. 193–210.

Witte, J. (2006). Facts and Fictions About the History of Separation of Church and State. *Journal of Church and State*, *48*(1), 15–45.

Yang, K. (2005). Public Administrators' Trust in Citizens: A Missing Link in Citizen Involvement Efforts. *Public Administration Review*, *65*(3), 273–285.

Zacka, B. (2017). *When the State meets the Street: Public Service and Moral Agency*. Cambridge, MA: The Belknap Press of Harvard University Press.

14. The Arts and Public Administration: How the Consideration of the Nature of Art can Provide Novel Ways to Understand Public Administration

Edoardo Ongaro

INTRODUCTION AND RATIONALE

This chapter argues that the arts (more on definitions in the next section) can contribute to the study and practice of public administration in manifold ways. Adding the arts to the other branches of the humanities can provide a deeper and broader array of perspectives and approaches from which to understand public governance, government, public administration and public management (hereafter collectively referred to as PA). Indeed, given the overall thesis put forth in this book, that the humanities and the social sciences represent two complementary perspectives to the study and practice of PA (located at different ontological-logical as well as epistemological levels, and yet, or perhaps exactly because of this, complementary to each other), adding the arts brings the entirety of the 'arts, humanities and social sciences' to the fore as a source of knowledge for the advancement of PA studies (the 'arts, humanities and social sciences' are one of the three main areas in which academic disciplines are commonly clustered, with the other two being the life sciences and STEM – science, technology, engineering, and mathematics).

It may be useful at this point to clarify that this chapter focuses on the arts as such – in their essence, so to speak – and is not confined to the (very significant) case in which an artistic work chooses PA as its subject, as with the most famous masterpiece *Allegory of Good Government* (*Il Buon Governo*) by Ambrogio Lorenzetti. There is already important literature in the field of PA on Lorenzetti's piece specifically, and more broadly on the significance of artistic works that are specifically about PA (government, public governance, public service and public servants) – for example, see de Graaf and van Asperen (2018) and Drechsler (2001), authors who also revisit this artwork and their analysis of it for this book (see Chapters 15 and 16 in this volume). The goal of this chapter is to complement these 'mainstays' in the field with a reflection on the multifaceted nature of the arts, and especially artistic work, by outlining (sketching) possible lines of inquiry about how consideration of the nature of artistic work may provide guidance for both the study and the practice of PA.

The chapter unfolds as follows: first, a (necessarily very brief) analysis and consideration of the nature of the arts and artistic work is wrought out, for purposes of application to PA. Then five key traits of artistic work are considered, to delineate possible lines of inquiry and ways of understanding and 'making sense' of the contribution a reflection on the nature of artistic work can bring to PA. These connecting points are: (1) art as craftsmanship and PA; (2) art as creation and PA; (3) art as a means of expression and PA; (4) art as knowledge and PA; (5) art as beauty and PA. The chapter then concludes by bundling the threads together on the manifold ways in which art and artistic work may support our understanding of PA.

WHAT IS ART/WHAT ARE THE ARTS?

If we confine our focus to the fine arts (not encompassing, e.g., the applied arts) and we take a very canonical definition, the arts in the plural refer to the seven arts. These are generally grouped into:

- The *visual arts*, namely *painting*, *sculpture* and *architecture*. These arts have been deemed to be based on drawing and design. Drawing is pivotal to the visual arts, and it is (at least conceptually) what makes them possible and characterises the visual arts — as most famously argued by Renaissance artist Michelangelo Buonarroti, though the notion is debated. Design – which, it should be noted, is an English language word which may not have an exact equivalent in other languages (and it is, in fact, almost universally used in English) – is also key to the visual arts. Drawing is the (mental-physical) activity that makes the visual arts possible, while design is the process whereby the imagined (in the mind of the artist-designer) becomes real.
- The *performing arts*, namely *music*, *drama/theatre* and (albeit problematically; the philosopher Roger Scruton famously denied it being an art) *cinema*. Such arts are characterised by their being executed – performed – as a constitutive trait of theirs.
- *Writing/literature*, in poetry or prose.

The term 'art', used in the singular, refers to the essence of what is artistic: a major topic in philosophy (the branch of philosophy called aesthetics). It concerns 'doing/making' by human beings, the capacity and the actual act of 'creation' of something. The term derives from the Latin word '*ars*', refer-ring to 'skill' or 'craft', the capacity to make something, to create something starting from 'raw materials', from 'matter', to infuse something into matter, or at least to process and give shape to matter. Etymologically, it is apposite to notice that the ancient Greek term '*poiesis*' (noun), or '*poiein*' (verb), from which the term 'poetry' in the English language derives, means 'to make'. Therefore inherent in the notion of 'art' is the activity of 'making', 'creating', 'transforming/giving form' to an initially indistinct, inchoate something. Both craftsmanship (the capacity to craft something) and the creation of something previously non-existent (the result of such capacity and activity) are constitu-tive of the artistic process.

The art also provides means of expression that are alternative or comple-mentary – but nonetheless distinct and different – to verbal (often verbal-numerical) 'scientific' communication. Additionally, literature, while relying on the verbal form of communication, does so in ways that are distinct and different (often afar) to the language of scientific communication: i.e., it is 'artistic,' not 'scientific' verbal communication.

Importantly, especially since Romanticism, artistic activity has been con-ceived of as (also) a way of knowing and understanding reality, as a distinctive (and privileged, according to exponents of Romanticism like the philosopher Friedrich Schlegel) form of knowledge and understanding of reality. Though this quasi-divine nature of the arts is contested and amply debated, the men-tioning of Romanticism and Schlegel also provides us with the opportunity to alert the reader to a major limitation of this chapter: it refers almost entirely to a Western conception of art and artistic tradition, due to both knowledge limitations of the author and the requirement to keep the argument within the constraints of a single chapter.

Finally, yet crucially, in the most classic 'last but not least' fashion, the art and the arts concern the experience of beauty by human beings.

Importantly, the art – any art – is always about the relationship between the work of art and the spectator: the beholder/listener/reader re-enacts the work of art every time they contemplate the work of art, which is, in this sense always present. Indeed, 'all is presence in art – art is only "there" during "the act" – interpretation, in the sense of engagement, is what makes the work of art' (Drechsler, 2001, pp.7–8, also citing Gadamer, 1997).

The remainder of the chapter examines the implications for PA – the study and the practice of public governance, public administration and public management – in relation to the nature of art as, respectively, an activity of craftsmanship; an act of creation; a means of expression; a form of knowledge and understanding; and a way to attain, as well as an expression of, beauty.

ART AS CRAFTSMANSHIP AND PA

This notion may appear controversial: with a sweeping simplification, we may say that, at least since Romanticism, artistic work is considered to be a matter of inspiration, a privileged activity, and a source of high status for the artist, also entwined with her/his (alleged) capacity to connect with the ultimate nature of things and the divine (at least until the mid-20th century, as later on a critical reflection on artistic work, expressed in the visual arts in such movements as minimalism or *arte povera*, has revisited the work and scope, and ultimate ambitions, of the artist and artistic work). However, the capacity of making things by employing non-codifiable knowledge has always been distinctive of the arts – a process which has inherently a craftsmanship nature. Indeed, over western history and at least until the Renaissance, the artist was likened to an artisan, and the artist's capacity to make things, the distinctive set of non-codifiable (yet which can be learnt via processes of apprenticeship), non-verbally expressible (or not entirely at least) skills, is what has characterised artistic work.

Administering, as a form of human action and human work, contains key elements of craftsmanship (for example, Lynn, 2006, pp. 27–29, who proposes a tri-dimensional view of public management, of which craft is one of these foundational dimensions; also Goodsell, 1992). Building on this line of reasoning, the appreciation of administering as an activity that contains key elements of craftsmanship may be interpreted to mean that administering constitutively possesses something of the artistic way of doing things, the 'making things happen' that is constitutive of the artistic process, and which relies also on non-codifiable skills (especially in terms of 'how-to' and behavioural skills), skills that inherently have an artistic component embedded in them, or at least can also be understood through the lens of artistic-like skills. We should further add that it is not only public administration and public management that are interested in learning about craftsmanship, craft work and what it entails; the field of business administration and management is also interested in craftsmanship (see Bell et al., 2021).

One more consideration on this point: it is not just the 'pure' artistic process that may be used as a term of reference or as a source of inspiration for making sense of the activity of administering the public sector and public services. In fact, even art-related activities that are considered as less 'pure and noble', at least after Romanticism, because they are deemed to lack the creative component and are more 'technical' – like the reproduction (copying) of an already existing work of art, or the work of restoring a masterpiece – may entail forms of craftsmanship and creativity (not least when minimal yet highly meaningful adaptations for the different context of an audience from a different place and time are performed in reproducing a masterpiece of the past), which may provide a valuable metaphor for how decisions occur in PA.[1]

The artistic way of doing things through craftsmanship is therefore inherently a property of what PA is about: of how administering and managing public services and public organisations occurs and unfolds.

ART AS CREATION AND PA

Each administrative system is unique, and the outcome of creative processes (often centuries- or millennia-long) to which we refer as statecraft: in a sense, each administrative system (present and past, tied to a nation-state or other forms of supra- or sub-national polity) is a work of art (though not all are equally beautiful), and each is uniquely adapted to the circumstances into which it was established and by which it has been shaped (and which, in turn, it has shaped after it has been established), to which we refer as 'context' (Pollitt, 2013).

If context matters in public governance and administration, then art as creation is a way of understanding state-building and the development of administrative systems (their features and their 'performance') in their own context. Like all artistic work, it does not happen in a vacuum; rather, each work of art has the potential to inspire others: inspiration from previous works of art shapes the next ones. Similarly, previous administrative systems, their configuration, processes, structures, institutions and culture, have the potential to inspire others (when not outright influencing them, as the policy transfer literature explains). Hence, we would argue that the analogy with artistic work may provide insights into both our understanding of the uniqueness of each administrative system, which has been creatively adapted for its own distinctive context, and how processes of learning from other instances of administrative systems may occur, thereby providing another conceptual tool – or at least another metaphor – for enhancing our comprehension of comparative public administration.

There is another sense in which art as creation may enable the development of PA. Art is, well, poetic – a term which derives from *poietic*, a word whose semantics evoke the making of things, and thereby the word also evokes the idea of knowing things because we (humans) are the makers of such things, because they have been made by us. This is a notion that is central to one very important strand of philosophical thinking in the Aristotelian-Thomistic

---

[1] I'm indebted to Bert George for pointing this aspect out to me.

philosophy as well as found in the work of philosophers like Francis Bacon and Thomas Hobbes and, crucially, Giambattista Vico, who coined the expression *verum factum est*; that is, what is true in the social world is such because it has been made, we know it because we are its makers; we have made it and thereby we are the cause of it. A maker's conception of philosophy is an approach recently revitalised by Luciano Floridi who has developed a constructionist (not constructivist) notion of philosophy as conceptual design (Floridi, 2019); a philosophical perspective which may provide a pathway for an (uncommitted) ontology grounding a philosophy of PA for the 21st century, the century of the information age. This approach is centred on the notion of *design* – think of the visual arts, architecture (design par excellence), painting, sculpture – and the social world being designed by information agents; in other words, a maker's conception of philosophy which may provide an important underpinning for the development of a philosophy of public administration.

ART AS MEANS OF EXPRESSION: THE ROLE OF THE SPECTATOR AND PA

The arts provide means of expression, which are alternative or complementary to verbal (often verbal-numerical) 'scientific' communication. The clearest example is Ambrogio Lorenzetti's most famous work, *The Good Government*), the frescoes painted in the Hall of the Nine Governors (the 'City Hall') of the Italian city of Siena between 1338 and 1339 CE. Drechsler and de Graaf have widely elaborated on the benefit of employing visual forms of communication to the study of PA problems, and a dedicated part of this book (Chapters 15 and 16) elaborates on the perennial inspiration and source of knowledge and understanding that Lorenzetti's work can provide to PA.

Indeed, in the professional community of art experts, there are specific groups of experts focusing on forms of artistic representation of people in government – public officials – and how they are represented in paintings and the visual arts.[2]

Also, for the arts that (also) use verbal forms of communication – like writing/poetry, drama/theatre, cinema – these forms of communication are radically different from the verbal-scientific communication, which is the standard means of expression in the administrative sciences. That verbal communication in the arts, like within poetry, is radically different from scientific communication has been forcefully argued by Heidegger in his most famous treatment of the works of Friedrich Hölderlin and reflections on the essence of poetry.

---

[2]   I am indebted to Wolfgang Drechsler for pointing me to this.

It is not only the means of expression and form of communication that change when shifting from verbal, or verbal-numerical, scientific communication to an 'artistic expression' – it is also the role and function of the receiver of the 'message'; in fact 'the art is engagement by the spectator with the masterpiece, the fruition of the art is an act which makes the "contents" of the artistic expression present [...] [A]ll is presence in the art, it becomes present (Gadamer, 1997, p. 25). This is so because art is only "there" during "the act" – interpretation, in the sense of engagement, is what makes the work of art [...] if we look seriously at, and engage with, Lorenzetti's fresco ... It becomes alive at that moment, and on a level that is neither merely aesthetic nor purely intellectual or historical' (Drechsler, 2001, pp. 7–8). The receiver/spectator performs an active role in artistic 'fruition'. Therefore, the arts not only provide a different – be it alternative or complementary – means of expression to study and understand PA, they also cast a different role for the students of public administration; by student, we do not refer only to university graduates, rather we mean whoever is learning about what PA is and how it works, including public administration scholars and practitioners alike.

ART AS KNOWLEDGE AND PA

Art can be the source of a different form of knowledge and understanding – a different level[3] of reasoning than the logic and reasoning that inform the sciences in general, and notably, for our purposes, the social sciences specifically. In this sense, the arts share with the humanities the property of bringing human reasoning to a different level than scientific reasoning; an alternative or complementary form of approaching the understanding and comprehension of reality.

Notably, the arts can help us navigate the maze and learn about ourselves as human beings living and operating in society at multiple levels ('from the person to the group to the world', as aptly subtitled in the book by Raadschelders, 2020), which may provide crucial underpinnings for theorising and practising public administration.

---

[3] We are here assuming that 'levelism' – i.e., the approach of studying reality at different levels – can still be used in contemporary philosophising, at least from an epistemological perspective, as Floridi argues (Floridi, 2013, chapter 3).

ART AS BEAUTY AND PA

It may be appropriate to start this section with a quote:

> Beauty is truth, truth beauty – that is all.
>
> Ye know on earth, and all ye need to know.
>
> *John Keats, 'Ode on a Grecian Urn' (concluding two verses), 1819, published*
> *in Annals of the Fine Arts for 1819.*

Why, then, has PA, in this akin to large swathes of the contemporary social sciences, forgotten beauty? If PA as a field of study is about attaining truth – however narrow and specific the domain of reality about which truth in PA specifically is being sought may be – why does the pursuit of beauty seem to have disappeared from PA studies? There has long been a debate, notably in the natural sciences, about whether a theory should also be 'elegant', whether considerations about its beauty should inform the appraisal of a theory. Shouldn't this debate be discovered and taken onboard by PA studies too? Shouldn't PA theories also be appraised and appreciated on the basis of their elegance – the beauty of theories? And analogously, isn't the discovery of opportunities for creating public value, or for promoting public values, something that may well be called 'beautiful'? If so, shouldn't PA scholars and practitioners alike rediscover beauty in what they do? To this purpose, the arts may be an invaluable source of inspiration.

CONCLUSION

Hegel placed art as the first moment of the supreme dialectical triadic moment of the Absolute Spirit (i.e., God and Reality in its fullness), next to religion and (the ultimate synthesis of reality for Hegel) philosophy. If such is the status of art according to a giant of philosophy like Hegel, why, then, has PA developed in ways that are oblivious to it?

If the mention of Hegel raises eyebrows, and we adopt a less lofty and more 'down-to-earth' view than Hegel's ambitious (pretentious?) dialectical synthesis of reality, we can still ask the question: Why are art and the arts – alongside philosophy and religious studies – not (or at least in a very limited way) mobilised in contemporary PA studies? Why are artistic studies – alongside religious studies and philosophical studies (on which, see recently Ongaro, 2020, on philosophy and PA; and Ongaro and Tantardini, 2023, on religion and PA) – not part and parcel of the intellectual sources on which PA relies and which PA deploys to generate knowledge and understanding in its field?

Taking these questions not rhetorically but as an entry point to issues of academic organisation of knowledge and sociology of knowledge may lead us to important considerations about how the field of PA has developed over the past decades, probably since at least WWII. Taking instead the questions rhetorically, that is, as a call to fill a gap, may prompt scholars (and practitioners) to make steps in an important direction – the one taken by this and all the chapters thematically related to the topic of art and PA in the present book. These chapters have, in fact, from different angles, set for themselves the very ambitious and very important goal of obviating such oblivion. More analytically, patterned on the structure specifically of this chapter, we argue that drawing parallels between the arts and PA can lead to developing, or at least critically revisiting, the field of PA in manifold ways.

First, by enhancing our understanding of the nature of PA as craft. Drawing parallels between the arts and PA and reflecting on the nature of the arts can generate and foster an understanding of the nature of craft work and craftsmanship – and hence lead to a reflection on the nature of the very activity of administering and managing public services as craft work and craftsmanship.

Second, the creative nature of art may provide inspiration for generating a better understanding of the interplay of PA and the context in which it operates (both the factual context within which administrative systems work and the intellectual context of the scholars investigating it; see Virtanen, 2013). Drawing parallels between the arts and PA can enable a better understanding of how administrative systems develop in ways to dynamically 'fit' their own distinctive contexts, and at the same time, can lead to a better appreciation of how each administrative system may be a source of inspiration for other administrative systems by way of analogy and analogical reasoning – a thrust and an endeavour which is at the origin of the very field of comparative public administration.

Third, by considering the nature of the arts as a different means of expression, we can be inspired to expand the means of expression that are being used in PA studies and practice. This process can lead to enable studying PA in ways that also systematically include non-verbal forms of communication. This in turn can lead to novel ways in which PA is being understood and comprehended, to novel viewpoints and perspectives from which to look at PA problems and practices (the most obvious example being what PA can learn from a visual artistic work like Ambrogio Lorenzetti's *Allegory of Good Government* – see De Graaf and Van Asperen, 2018 and Chapter 15 in this volume; Drechsler, 2001 and Chapter 16 in this volume).

Fourth – and related to the preceding point centred on the consideration of the arts as alternative means of expression – by redefining and critically rethinking the role of the public administrationist (the scholar of PA) and the public administrator (the practitioner of PA) as having an active role in engaging with PA as the 'object of study', the arts may provide a way of redefining the very role of both the PA scholar and the practitioner as co-producers of PA – in the same way the receiver of an artistic work is never passive and always an active agent in co-constructing the artistic 'object'. Both scholars and practitioners of PA may be inspired by the re-thinking of themselves in relation to PA as object of study and practice in the way in which the spectator performs an active role in the process of artistic 'fruition'.

Fifth, the appreciation of art and the arts as the source of a different form of knowledge and understanding – a different level of reasoning – which may enable a different form of comprehending reality (Floridi, 2013, chapter 3), enables the development of different forms of reasoning in the field of PA, which may lead to generating novel forms of knowledge and understanding about PA, seen as part and parcel of (social) reality.

Sixth, the art enables the appreciation of beauty – art *is* beauty. Engaging the arts for PA may therefore enable the development of the field of PA in ways that may help rediscover beauty in and for PA.

In conclusion, this endeavour – that is, to mobilise the kind of appreciation of knowledge, of understanding, of reasoning, of inspiration that is being brought about by art and the arts – can be central to the re-foundation of both PA studies and the practice of PA, indeed leading to 'the art of PA' for the 21st century.

REFERENCES

Bell, E., Dacin, M. T. and Toraldo, M. L. (2021) 'Craft Imaginaries – Past, Present and Future', *Organization Theory,* 2(1). https://doi.org/10.1177/2631787721991141.

de Graaf, G. and van Asperen, H. (2018 – online first 2016) 'The Art of Good Governance: How Images from the Past Provide Inspiration for Modern Practice', *International Review of Administrative Sciences,* 84(2), 405–420.

Drechsler, W. (2001) 'Good and Bad Government. Ambrogio Lorenzetti's Frescoes in the Sienna Town Hall as Mission Statement for Public Administration Today'. Local Government and Public Service Reform Initiative, Discussion Papers, No. 20, pp. 1–29.

Floridi, L. (2013) *The Philosophy of Information.* Oxford: Oxford University Press.

Floridi, L. (2019) *The Logic of Information: A Theory of Philosophy as Conceptual Design.* Oxford: Oxford University Press.

Gadamer, Hans Georg (1997) 'The Philosophy of Hans-Georg Gadamer', *Library of Living Philosophers, Volume 24,* edited by Lewis Edwin Hahn, Open Court (ISBN 0812693426, 9780812693423)

Goodsell, C. T. (1992) 'The Public Administrator as Artisan', *Public Administration Review,* 52(3), 246–253.

Lynn, L. E., Jr. (2006) *Public Management: Old and New.* New York and London: Routledge.

Ongaro, E. (2020) *Philosophy and Public Administration: An Introduction.* 2nd edition. Cheltenham, UK and Northampton, MA: Edward Elgar.

Ongaro, E and Tantardini, M. (2023) *Religion and Public Administration: An Introduction.* Cheltenham, UK and Northampton, MA: Edward Elgar.

Pollitt, C. (2013) *Context in Public Policy and Management: The Missing Link?* Cheltenham, UK and Northampton, MA: Edward Elgar.

Raadschelders, J. (2020) *The Three Ages of Government: From the Person, to the Group, to the World.* Ann Arbor: University of Michigan Press.

Virtanen, T. (2013) 'Context in the Context: Missing the Missing Links in Public Administration', in C. Pollitt (ed.) *Context in Public Policy and Management: The Missing Link?* Cheltenham, UK and Northampton, MA: Edward Elgar, pp. 3–34.

15. The Arts and Public Administration: How Artworks Can Be a Source of Knowledge, Inspiration, Motivation, and Understanding in Public Administration

Gjalt de Graaf and Hanneke van Asperen

THE ARTICLE *THE ART OF GOOD GOVERNANCE*

In this chapter we argue that *art can be a source of knowledge, inspiration, motivation, and understanding in PA* and thus enrich the field of PA. We made the same argument in the 2016 article *The Art of Good Governance: How Images from the Past Provide Inspiration for Modern Practice* (De Graaf & Van Asperen, 2016). In it we answer the research question: How can Lorenzetti's frescoes of Good Governance (Fig. 15.1) inspire our modern-day conception of Good Governance? In order to answer it we used a well-known image from the past, not as an illustration, but the as the core of our argument (Drechsler, 2001). In the search for insight into the concept of good governance, our goal was to see whether the frescoes can inspire us to develop a fresh perspective on what makes governance *good* governance. In other words, we used the hermeneutics of art.

This research method raises interesting questions. Can we use a work that is from a distant past, depicting a society that is so clearly not ours? Can we possibly know what Lorenzetti wanted to say to his audience, and is this even relevant if we want to use his frescos for inspiration today? These questions behind all history of thought and/or political philosophy, are supposedly relevant for the present. The popular scholarly answer, more often than not, is: No, we cannot use such works today (Drechsler, 2001, p. 7).

Yet, like Drechsler, we argue that we could, because: "interpretation, in the sense of engagement, is what makes the work of art. This is a-temporal; if we look seriously at, and engage with Lorenzetti's fresco –[…] it becomes alive at that moment, and on a level that is neither merely aesthetic nor purely intellectual." (Drechsler, 2001, p. 7/8). One might even say that a visual art work only exists in the eyes of its beholders. A work of art is never just a static unchanging product made by an artist. A public engages with it, takes things away from it, adding new layers of meaning to it, making it relevant or irrelevant to present-day problems, fashions and fascinations. To use a popular phrase from the modern artist and writer Marchel Duchamp in 1961 "the creative act is not performed by the artist alone; the spectator brings the work into contact with the external worlds by deciphering and interpreting its inner qualification and thus adds his (or her or their) contribution to the creative act." (Duchamps, 1978, p. 140). Taking it one step further, one could state that the creative act is not finished until the last person has looked at the artwork.

In a postmodern sense, one could also argue that an audience, including a scholarly one of (art) historians, can never look at an artwork without bias. A person's background, interests, affinities, and concerns, also those of a scholar, always consciously and unconsciously color and affect their perspective. So why not accept the idea that a vision of an artwork is never without bias and instead embrace the idea that art from any time and any place can help us gain a clearer perspective of our own time and place? Following this line of thought, we argue that, under the right circumstances, the analysis of a work of art can also lead to inspired insights about the present.

Works of art offer unfamiliar views, and that is exactly why they can be inspiring. Furthermore, in art history, images – paintings, statues, prints, or miniatures – do not serve as illustrations of "how it used to be." Most historians nowadays agree that there is no straightforward answer to that question anyway. They realize that "the audience" is not one static entity, but a polymorphic group of people. Art historians always take into consideration that the "message" of the artist – if there is such a thing – might differ from the message that contemporary audiences take away from it. In other words, the artist, the image, its context, and its (intended and actual) audience(s) are just the first points of departure for (art) historians – in combination with other archival, literary, and visual sources – to expose various concepts and practices which differ per context and per audience.

Even in a short timeframe after an artwork was created it could take on different meanings depending on changing contexts, circumstances, and events. So, at what time after an artwork's creation do we stop investigating its effect on its audiences or stop studying the ways that an audience from a certain time used it to shape their reality? The answer is: never. Many art and culture historians study the effects of (old and new) artworks in the present. If we realize that artworks, especially those in the public eye, such as Lorenzetti's frescoes, still inspire people today, why not make this the point of departure in a scholarly debate on how artworks can inspire the scholarly debate? Art can inspire anyone at any moment. When the discussion involves a thought-through art historical interpretation of iconographic detail, as we offered in our previous study, this can lead to a new, fresh, and inspired vision of good governance. Moreover, with an art historical analysis does the argument become a serious discussion about the inspirational power of imagery? Only when an argument integrates a thought-through interpretation of iconographic detail and a vision which goes beyond the purely historical, does it become a serious discussion about the inspirational potential of imagery.

Artworks can be inspiring by themselves, but we may take inspiration to a new level by including art history in the discussion, because art historical analyses can lead to new and freshly inspired visions of familiar art works. After all, art historical methods can help to see a well-known image in a new light, for example by focusing on details that may otherwise be overlooked, or by pointing out connections that would otherwise go unnoticed. In a way, a thought-through interpretation of iconographic detail can have as much inspirational potential as a work of art, because of the new insights it can lead to.

Seen this way, our study was not on fourteenth-century Sienese values, or on the governance of fourteenth century city states. Although interesting in itself, it is not what has informed us on modern-day (good) governance and public values. Instead, using a research method from art history, we looked for inspiration for our modern-day conception of good governance by focusing on some of the values of good governance that were visualised by Lorenzetti in this piece of art.

Current ideas on governance have influenced (and will always color) the ways we look at Lorenzetti's frescoes. We decided that it was time to reverse things and have the work of art and art historical analysis of the artwork inspire and color our current ideas on governance. To a certain extent, the inability to look objectively at images from a distant past justifies – in our minds – our use of the frescoes in a debate on modern practice.

MANAGERIALISM VERSUS THE HERMENEUTICS OF ART

From the first draft of the manuscript onwards, PA scholars either seem to love or hate it (with the latter group in the great majority). Before the journal *International Review of Administrative Sciences* accepted the manuscript, it was submitted to the journal *Public Administration*. The editor remarked: "Two of the reviewers liked your paper, three others found the connection with PA issues underdeveloped." Examples of both sides: "This is an excellent, methodologically au-courant essay that very well balances the 'normal science' papers more commonly found in top-tier PA journals." Yet another reviewer replied: "I am sorry to conclude that I do not think this manuscript has the quality needed for publication in *Public Administration*. Compared to the (many) articles about Lorenzetti it lacks to provide substantial new insights relevant for a PA audience."

We had the same experience before we submitted the manuscript to journals. A draft paper was presented during a lunch seminar organized by the department of Political Science and Public Administration at the Vrije Universiteit Amsterdam. The political scientists in the department, in particular, were not satisfied with the answers to the question of what we can learn for modern-day governance from fourteenth-century Italian frescoes. Yet we got the opposite reaction when presenting the same draft paper to the permanent *Study Group on Quality and Ethics of Governance*, European Group of Public Administration (EGPA), in September 2014 in Speyer. The presentation received a very enthusiastic reaction; the paper was judged to be inspiring.

Around 10 years later, we can conclude that the idea of using the hermeneutics of art in PA did not attract followers. According to Google Scholar[1] the English-language article has been cited 21 times. Almost none of these publications engage with the hermeneutics of art as a way of inspiring modern-day conceptions of (good) governance. The article is mostly cited when the Good Governance concept is being introduced. The only exceptions to this are publications where Ongaro is the author or co-author (Ongaro, 2019, 2020; Ongaro & Tantardini, 2023a, 2023b). These publications discuss the article and its hermeneutics sympathetically (especially, Ongaro, 2020).

Arguably, the reactions to *The Art of Good Governance* article say something about the managerial state of the discipline and practice of PA. Although public governance is value laden, normativity of governance has seldom taken center stage in the study of PA (De Graaf, 1996). Despite their omnipresence, values are under-acknowledged in its study, "they are 'leached out' of positive policy analysis in favor of interest-based and institutionalist approaches." (Stewart, 2009, p. 15). The origins of PA lie in a practical imperative: the search for solutions to (public) problems where the dominant value is efficiency (Ringeling, 2017, pp. 44–45). Traditionally, much of the discipline has had the self-image of an instrumental discipline, apolitically and neutrally advising the powers that be. Instrumental, not normative. The discipline of Public Administration is mostly focused on professionalizing public governance (Braun et al., 2015), with the values of effectiveness and efficiency central.

The practice of current Western public governance is often described as a matter of the "politics of expertise," as technocratic (Fischer, 1990). Public governance has become a marketplace of interests and services delivered by public organizations or private organizations backed by government. MacIntyre

---

[1]   On 26 January 2024.

speaks of managerialism pervading modern society, with a strong narrow-minded focus on the value of effectiveness (MacIntyre, 1991; Overeem, 2011). We see this dominant management logic nowadays echoed in the practice and the discourse of Western governance. Politics has become problem management. Trommel (2019) speaks of the "managerial state." In policy making of the past decennia, the management perspective has been dominant (Putters, 2021). A characteristic of this managerialism "is its reliance on technical expertise (Fischer, 1990) and the science-for-policy model as a source of authoritativeness (Hajer, 2009)" (Prettner et al., 2023, p. 141).

The positive reactions to *The Art of Good Governance* article seem to come mostly from scholars who study the normative side of public governance, as in the EGPA permanent *Study Group on Quality and Ethics of Governance*. Among those studying the technical issues of governance and management, the inspirational and informative values of a fresco from the fourteenth century have a smaller chance of touching a chord, than among those looking at the moral aspects of governance. Carol Lewis (2013, p. 2): "We need imagery and feelings to tap into our moral intuition and so to affect behavior. Art is an effective heuristic for ethics because, as the moral psychologist Jonathan Haidt (2001, p. 818), notes, 'Moral intuition is ... akin to aesthetic judgment.'" The hermeneutics of art can be especially helpful in PA when studying the moral dimension of the value-laden practice; for example when answering the question of when governance is *good* governance.

As said, in *The Art of Good Governance* article the hermeneutics of art was used to inspire modern-day conceptions of good governance in PA. We maintain, therefore, that art can be a source of knowledge and understanding in PA and thus enrich the field. Art can be studied in PA to enrich our understanding of previous conceptions of (good) governance and can thus lead to new inspiration and motivation in today's governance. After all, "Artists and writers often use widely shared symbols and romanticized experiences to communicate the ideal. They intentionally display powerful icons that convey an attitude and a viewpoint. As such, they are meant to push buttons and stir up responses that are strengthened by the power of emotions and engagement" (Lewis, 2013, p. 2). To illustrate this point, just compare the difference in inspiration and motivation on good governance suggested by Lorenzetti's murals (Fig. 15.1) and the visual presentation of the eight principles of Good Governance by the United Nations (Fig. 15.2).

Of course, within the field of PA there are useful historical analyses of public governance which can inform and inspire us, yet these analyses are often based on written documents. In art history, the analysis is centered – just as in the article *The Art of Good Governance* – on art. Images have a different function from written documents. Their audiences sometimes partially overlap, but they can also differ substantially. Studying objects of art that visualize

Figure 15.1   *Ambrogio Lorenzetti, Allegory of Justice and Good*
Government, fresco, 1337–39. Siena, Palazzo Pubblico, Sala
dei Nove. © Comune di Siena; Fondazione Musei Senesi.

ideas and ideals of (good) government has thus an added value. An image
more directly engages with its audience than a written text. With an image,

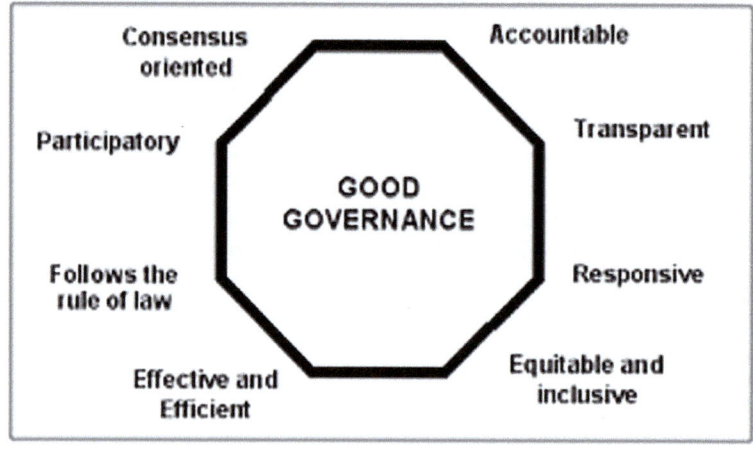

Source: Author's own.

Figure 15.2   *8 Principles of Good Governance by the United Nations*

observers focus on the details that appeal to them; a picture is worth a thousand words. A text takes longer to process. Furthermore a text usually has a smaller readership than a visual work of art, although admittedly the latter depends on the context in which an image is on display. Lewis (2013, p. 5): "Public works of art invariably are statements about political power and often about the link between power and ethical behavior. The British political theorist David Miller (2003, pp. 2–3) writes: 'There is no better way to understand what political philosophy is and why we need it than by looking at Lorenzetti's magnificent mural.'"

BRIDGES BETWEEN THE ARTS AND PA

The idea that the arts in general – including literature and film – can contribute in several ways to PA is far from new. Dobel (1996, p. 154) wrote almost three decades ago:

> In a field haunted by the hubris of social science, the question periodically arises as to what kind of knowledge the humanities might provide for public administration. In earlier centuries, it was taken for granted the humanities and arts helped improve the character and judgement of public officials. The legacy of scientific management, positivism, and behaviorism, however, displaced humanistic knowledge as hopelessly incapable of providing verifiable knowledge about social phenomenon. … Today amid the flux of methodological pluralism and the discovery of the moral dimension of public administration, a wide ranging group of public administration scholars are attempting to integrate the humanities into scholarship and teaching.

The arts can contribute PA in more ways than just inspiring and motivating values and virtues. Around the times of Dobel's words, Goodsell and Murray (1995b) published a wonderful edited book entitled *Public Administration Illuminated and Inspired by the Arts.* "To us, public administration, as a field of academic study and realm of management and policy practice, has since its origins been cut off, for the most part, from a rich source of cultural nourishment. This source is the humane, provocative, imagination-firing qualities of the arts, both fine and applied" (Goodsell & Murray, 1995a, p. 4).

Just like argued in *The Art of Good Governance* article, Goodsell and Murray (1995a) conclude in the prologue that the arts can contribute to PA by identifying and animating moral values. This is what they call the Values Bridge. Yet, the focus of Goodsell and Murray is on other art forms than paintings, mainly on literature. Novels and other forms of fiction can inform us of insights otherwise not attained; it can animate specific values in PA. E.g., Kroll (1995, p. 93) maintains that films can help public administrators to "become more aware of the subtleties inherent in the interplay between complex situations and individual personalities. The essence of public management involves this interplay". Another example is by Adams and Marini (1995), who study what Kesey's *One Flew Over the Cuckoo's Nest* can contribute to the theory of bureaucracy, and especially to what values it can inspire in public governance.

In addition to identifying and animating values – the Values Bridge – Goodsell and Murray (1995a, pp. 6–7) see four other "bridges" to be built across the divide separating the arts and PA. The first bridge is the Theory Bridge. The philosophy of aesthetics can enhance theoretical development of PA. Especially by analogy, the comprehension of beauty can inform PA theory. As Rhodes and Hodgett maintain: "Geertz argues 'theory, scientific or otherwise, moves mainly by analogy' and increasingly these analogies are drawn from theatre, painting, and literature … With this shift to the analogies of game, drama, and text, the Social Sciences are no longer burdened by naturalism. They can escape the idea that 'the human sciences should strive to develop predictive and causal explanations akin to those found in the natural sciences' (Bevir & Kedar, 2008, p. 503)." (Rhodes & Hodgett, 2022, p. 1/2). Goodsell (1995), for example, sketches an explicit theory of "artisan" public administration drawing on analogies with aesthetic philosophy, with the goal of public actors gaining a sense of self-worth and achievement. He highlights the craft and creativity of public administrators. Borrowing from the theory of art, Goodsell (1992) lays the foundations of a normative theory for the micro level of governance, which supplements the focus in PA – also evident back in 1992 – on effectiveness and efficiency. This type of PA approach fits well with viewing PA "as an art and a craft as much as it is a science, and public servants are generalists—that is, a profession based on craft knowledge" (Rhodes, 2016, p. 639). Murray (1995a) provides another example of the Theory Bridge in addressing two principles of artistic form, harmony, and balance. "The Pythagorean values of proportion and regularity have influenced the structures of our administrative systems. Cost-benefit analysis is widely acclaimed as providing a balanced approach to important macro-level policy questions of equity and efficiency" (Murray, 1995a, p. 46).

Related to the Values Bridge is the Leadership Bridge that focuses on the leaders in PA, in order to lead both well and "good" (De Graaf & Paanakker, 2015). The Leadership Bridge "enables us to bring alive the pathos and humanity of individual leaders depicted in the arts, particularly literature but also film and video" (Goodsell & Murray, 1995a, p. 6). Leaders of all times have looked for all kinds of inspiration and motivation on the art of leadership. Many writers – both in fiction and nonfiction – have provided such motivation and inspiration. As an example, Gira (1995) draws lessons for leadership from the work of Shakespeare. "Shakespeare chose through his plays to hold a mirror up to life, wherein we may observe why some leaders succeed, despite the burdens of office, and why others fail" (Gira, 1995, p. 110). Also, the frescoes by Lorenzetti can be seen as an example of the Leadership Bridge; after all, the frescoes reflected the essential governing virtues of those in power, but at the same time were to inspire "the nine" who represented and governed the commune of Siena.

Then there is the Policy Bridge that is related to the outcome of public governance. Maybe this seems farfetched at first, since the outcomes of public governance are dependent on so many contingencies that the arts seem far removed from them. Yet art can influence the climate of opinion around policies. Goodsell and Murray (1995a, p. 7):

> Yet all of these efforts to make policy take place in a democracy, in the arena of broader public discourse. Here, influences build not merely from attempts to control but also from the subtle and unpredictable flow of ideas. At times the trends of popular culture or even works of fine art may set the stage for emergence of "an idea whose time has come." Key novels decisively shaped public opinion on the abolition of slavery and the regulation of meatpackers, for example. Dramatic paintings of the American West stimulated settlements beyond the plains and the creation of national parks. In more recent times, the popularity of science fiction set the stage for space exploration.

We don't have to go so far as looking for some landmark policies influenced by art. McCurdy (1995) states that what all public administrators do is to a considerable extend shaped by art. "The policies they administer often germinate in the popular culture that art helps us to sustain ... Literature, paintings, movies, and television all work to create a receptive audience for new ideas" (McCurdy, 1995, p. 177). Another example would be Goodsell (2022) who coined the term "architectural power" to mean that features of public buildings such as parliaments or state houses, can have significant influence on the legitimacy of the regimes that occupy them. In this respect we are again reminded of the frescoes in Siena city hall as well as the city hall itself with its imposing tower, because these were also intended to legitimize those in power.

The fifth and final bridge is the Teaching Bridge. For a long time, and across disciplines, popular (fine) arts have been used in teaching; art can animate and deepen teaching in the classroom (Rhodes & Hodgett, 2022, p. 24; Waldo, 1968). An example in PA would be Adams, Marini, and Pugh (1995), who use Shakespeare's *The Merchant of Venice* to enhance the understanding and teaching of the concept of social equity. A more recent example in PA comes from Zavatarro (2022, p. 703/704): "This research builds on the growing literature – and long history in public management recognizing the power of novels, television shows, and films to teach various administrative concepts ... Other authors (Brainard, 2021; Herbel, 2015; Love & Fox, 2021) have turned to literature to supplement public administration education." Linking the Teaching and the Values Bridge, Dubnick (2000) shows how film can be used in the administrative classroom, and maintains that films are particularly effective in stimulating and energizing the moral imagination of students.

Note that up to now, in this section, the focus on bridges between PA and art has been mainly on public administrators, yet of course there are many more actors in public governance. Fischer (2005) speaks of participatory governance; the increasing role of citizens – often called public/citizen participation – in public governance has been widely acknowledged (Nabatchi & Leighninger, 2015). Ansell and Gash (2007) speak of collaborative governance to describe how public and private stakeholders together in collective agencies engage in consensus-oriented decision making. The arts can also play a role here. E.g., Denhardt and Denhardt (2015, p. 667) mentioned that the arts can be used to get more inclusive citizen engagement: "citizen engagement approaches based on the arts are being employed to attract people who might not typically be involved in civic activities express ideas that they find difficult to communicate. A wide variety of tools can be used to create these kinds of opportunities, including art, dance, theater, and storytelling (Goldbard, 2010)".

Despite the best hopes three decades ago of authors such as Dobel, Goodsell, and Murray, the usage of art in the discipline of PA has not really taken off. The "rebirth in the field" (Murray, 1995b, p. 211) they proposed – in which the theoretical base of PA is built upon scientific as well as aesthetic assumptions – has not materialized. Of the five bridges, the Teaching Bridge seems to have the most followers and applications nowadays.

THE VIRTUES BRIDGE

We began this chapter by giving arguments that there was value for PA in art historical analysis. We would like to end by actually carrying out that analysis, elaborating on our previous study with some other inspirational artworks visualizing virtues of past government. We could call it the Virtues Bridge, a subcategory of the Values Bridge (values and virtues are obviously closely connected). Lorenzetti's frescoes are often studied in splendid isolation, because they give so much food for thought in themselves, but values and virtues are actually omnipresent in the context of public administration in Italy and elsewhere. Nevertheless, we have to be aware of their presence in order to see them and look closely in order be inspired by them.

Inspired by new forms of government Lorenzetti and others depicted their (ideal) government in new ways. The pre-humanist ideas expressed by Lorenzetti's fresco found fertile soil in other countries. For example, many city halls in the Low Countries were decorated with statues of the political and divine virtues. Again, Charity and Justice are always present and often given pride of place. A beautiful example is the fourteenth-century city hall of the Dutch Hanseatic city of Kampen that was thriving during the Middle Ages

Figure 15.3   *Justice and Charity dispensing coins, Kampen city hall. Rijksdienst voor het Cultureel Erfgoed (Netherlands), photo collection, document no. D-06161. Photographer: A.J. van der Wal, 1984.*

because of its location on the busy waterway between the Zuiderzee (South Sea, now IJsselmeer) and the river Rhine. Statues of blindfolded Justice, and of Mercy, Temperance, and Loyalty decorate the facade.[2] They are accompanied by the Emperor Charlemagne and Alexander the Great as two well-known exemplary figures for governors to admire and emulate. The virtues are placed alongside each other, without a clear hierarchy. They are virtues that Charlemagne and Alexander the Great possessed (according to contemporary belief) and Kampen's governors should strive for. Charity is not one of the virtues depicted, but Mercy (an important element of Charity) is. She is depicted as a woman giving a coin to a pauper at her feet, reminiscent of the depiction of Magnanimity in Lorenzetti's fresco, on the bench right beside the good ruler. Magnanimity in Siena is depicted with a bowl of coins in her lap, Mercy in Kampen dispenses a coin. She reminds the governors that they should pay attention to the poor members of their community. Summarizing, the four virtues on the facade on Kampen are virtues of good governors. With Mercy among them, the decorative program focuses on virtues that make up the active life rooted in daily practice of governing.

The virtues are different in the alderman's room in Kampen city hall that also functioned as a court room (not unlike the room of the nine in Siena). Sculptor Colijn de Nole made a large sandstone mantlepiece (Fig. 15.4) in 1543–44 after a fire had destroyed a big part of the city hall's interior. In line with the primary function of the room, the sculptor combined scenes of justice and wise rule from the Bible (i.e. Judgment of Solomon) with scenes from Roman history. Several virtues flank the scenes; Charity is in their midst as the pivot of human virtues. Both the narrative scenes and the allegorical virtues are surmounted by a personification of Justice. The text below reads: "The sword of Justice ends the violence of Mars" (Bedaux et al., 1992). Mars, the Roman god of war, is lying at her feet and her sword is at his throat. Here, Justice is linked with the outcome of good government which is Peace, visualized by Lorenzetti as a separate figure in his fresco of good government. Notably, Peace in Lorenzetti's fresco is reclining against a body of armour. Lorenzetti thus visualizes peace as the result of good government. Telling the same story in a somewhat different vocabulary, Colijn de Nole combined Justice and Peace in one and the same figure.

As in Siena, these depictions are directed towards the individual governors; they represent stories and allegories that the individual governors knew,

---

[2] The statues on the facade have been replaced with replicas by J. Nolet in 1933–1938. The original statues are currently in the Koornmarktspoort, a part of the city museum of Kampen. Stenvert, R., Kolman, C., Olde Meierink, B., ten Hove, J., Knuijt, M., & Kooij, B. (1998). *Monumenten in Nederland. Overijssel.* Rijksdienst voor de Monumentenzorg.

Sources: Rijksdienst voor het Cultureel Erfgoed (Netherlands), photo collection, docu-
ment no. 402.692. Photographer: G.J. (Gerard) Dukker, 1997. Source: Rijksdienst voor het
Cultureel Erfgoed, https://beeldbank.cultureelerfgoed.nl/rce-mediabank.
Rijksdienst voor het Cultureel Erfgoed(Netherlands), photo collection, document no. 163.277.
Photographer: A.J. van der Wal, 1974. Source: Rijksdienst voor het Cultureel Erfgoed,
https://beeldbank.cultureelerfgoed.nl/rce-mediabank.

Figure 15.4   Colijn de Nole, mantlepiece, 1543–44 (Fig # detail: Justice).
Kampen, city hall, room of the aldermen.

understood, and identified with. Importantly, their focus is always on (a selection of) important virtues. Because the images show the virtues the governors strive for, the depictions at the same time have a legitimizing role. In other words, governors' virtues legitimize their position of power.

In the nineteenth century, growing centralization and nation building gave rise to new depictions of national government that supplemented images of local government. Charity again plays an important part. In France, as in other countries around Europe, administrative reforms and bureaucratic efficiency had led to a centralization of power. Over the years, the responsibilities and the involvement of federal government in local affairs increased. In 1848, painter Honoré Daumier contributed an oil sketch to a national contest in search of the "painted face of the republic" after its proclamation on 24 February, 1848. The goal of the competition was to create an official portrait of the young State. Daumier produced an oil sketch with an impressive imposing personification of the new Republic of France recognizable by the large flag at her side (Fig. 15.5). He chose to depict the Republic as a woman nursing her children. At her feet is a child, reading.

Daumier never worked up his sketch, but the personification of the Republic is obviously inspired by images of Charity who had often been depicted from the fourteenth century onwards as a woman nursing a child. Daumier's figure of the Republic was even mistaken for Charity by contemporaries of the artist.

Source: Public Domain, Wikimedia Commons. Also found in Musée d'Orsay, https://www.musee-orsay.fr/fr/oeuvres/la-republique-10865.

Figure 15.5   *Honoré Daumier, La République nourrit ses enfants en les instruit, oil on canvas, 1848. Paris, Musée d'Orsay, donation Etienne Moreau-Nélaton, 1906, inv. RF1644. © RMN-Grand Palais (Musée d'Orsay) / Hervé Lewandowski.*

It was not clear to everyone that Daumier primarily intended to depict the Republic of France. However, it is interesting that the painter modeled her on a personification of Charity and not, for example, on Justice which was also considered an important virtue of governors, as we have seen. Charity's children symbolized both the needy depending on others for sustenance and clothes as well as spiritual salvation.

But Daumier's State-Charity is not just feeding her children: A child at her feet is reading a book. Here, Charity is combined with an element visualizing education. In the seventeenth century, artists had started to add a reading child to the figure of Charity in line with the growing belief that it was a duty of the local governments to educate orphans and children of the poor (Van Asperen, 2013). The reading child perfectly fitted the image of Charity as a mother, because since the Middle Ages it was considered to be a mother's task to take care of childhood education. For those children who did not have parents, or whose parents could not provide a proper education, city government took up this responsibility. Therefore, images combining the personification of charity with a reading child were considered a suitable decoration for orphanages, for example. During the nineteenth century however, charity education was no longer dependent on the benevolence of local governors: the State assumed (part of) the responsibility of caring for its needy citizens. Because of these developments, the personification of the State, as painted by Daumier, merged with the well-known allegorical depiction of Charity as a mother and as educator.

As in Lorenzetti's fresco, Charity plays an important part in the depiction of government, but Charity is no longer depicted as a contemplative virtue. Lorenzetti presented Charity as an etherical figure, depicted with wings and hovering above the head of the just ruler. With Daumier, the accent shifts to charitable acts, which is more in line with the way we define charity today. For many of us in a secularized society, charity is no longer primarily the love of God for humans and vice versa, but rather the love of one's neighbor. Clearly, Daumier's image was produced in a different era and intended for a different audience than Lorenzetti's frescoes. Lorenzetti depicted his frescoes in the *sala dei nove* where the nine would gather to administer justice. Lorenzetti was painting an image to uplift the governors of Siena. The nine were its primary audience. However, Daumier was producing a public image for an audience of citizens. He did not primarily depict someone the governors could identify with, but an image of government that most citizens could appreciate and feel secure with. Merging the good ruler with the personification of Charity, the artist chose to depict government in a female role. Still, she is an imposing figure, a woman who can both cherish and protect her children. Moreover, Charity is no longer just one of the personified virtues flanking a (often male) personification of the good ruler (Siena) or historical figures as Charlemagne and Alexander the Great (Kampen). Charity has become the most important virtue. Government itself is depicted as a mother and the love of government for the citizens of the state is compared to a mother's caring and protective love for her children.

In this short section, we took giant leaps from the fourteenth to the nineteenth century, from Italy to the Low Countries and France, cherry picking just a few images that centralize good government. We looked at frescoes, sculpture, and oil painting, produced in different contexts and for different occasions and with different intentions. From each of these works of art we can learn different things. However, in all of these we see that *virtues are fundamental to ideas about government and that virtues provide the foundation of good rule.* Second, we can see how different artists, in consultation with the governors who commissioned the works of art, picked their models, ranging from personifications to biblical stories, scenes from Roman history, and exemplary historical figures. Each work of art places different accents. Finally, the virtue of charity always plays a prominent role in ideas about good government. Clearly, people in the past have had different interpretations of charity and charity nowadays does not mean what it did in the nineteenth century or before. Still, works of art from the past can inspire us to look at the virtue of charity (or benevolence) as a guiding principle of good government and think of ways to give new meaning to the virtue of charity in government today.

REFERENCES

Adams, E., & Marini, F. (1995). Regimentation and Rebellion in One Flew Over the Cuckoo's Nest. In C. T. Goodsell & N. Murray (Eds.), *Public Administration Illuminated and Inspired by the Arts* (pp. 59–74). Praeger.

Adams, E., Marini, F., & Pugh, D. (1995). Teaching Social Equity in a Diverse Society: The Merchant of Venice. In C. T. Goodsell & N. Murray (Eds.), *Public Administration Illuminated and Inspired by the Arts* (pp. 189–202). Praeger.

Ansell, C., & Gash, A. (2007). Collaborative Governance in Theory and Practice. *Journal of Public Administration Research and Theory, 18*, 543–571.

Bedaux, J. B., Groot, A., & Hagen, A. (1992). Allegorieën van goed bestuur. Het decoratieprogramma van het stadhuis van Enkhuizen (1687–1710). In *Jaarboek Monumentenzorg* (pp. 142–118). Rijksdienst voor de Monumentenzorg.

Bevir, M., & Kedar, A. (2008). Concept Formation in Political Science: An Anti-Naturalist Critique of Qualitative Methodology. *Perspectives on Politics, 6*, 503–517.

Brainard, L. A. (2021). Putting "Perspectives" in Perspective: Literary Fiction, Empathy & Diversity in the Public Affairs Classroom. *Public Integrity, 23*(3), 310–327.

Braun, C., Fenger, M., 't Hart, P., Van der Veer, J., & Verheij, T. (2015). Qua vadis, Nederlandse Bestuurskunde? *Bestuurskunde, 24*(4), 82–92.

De Graaf, G. (1996). *Bestuurskunde is waarde-loos* Erasmus University Rotterdam.

De Graaf, G., & Paanakker, H. (2015). Good Governance: Performance Values and Procedural Values in Conflict. *American Review of Public Administration, 45*(6), 635–652. https://doi.org/10.1177/0275074014529361

De Graaf, G., & Van Asperen, H. (2016). The art of good governance: how images from the past provide inspiration for modern practice. *International Review of the Administrative Sciences*, *84*(4). https://doi.org/10.1177/0020852316630392

Denhardt, J. V., & Denhardt, R. B. (2015). The New Public Service Revisited. *Public Administration Review*, *75*(5), 664–672.

Dobel, J. P. (1996). Public Administration Illuminated and Inspired by the Arts by Charles T. Goodsell, Nancy Murray. *Administrative Theory & Praxis*, *18*(1), 154–157.

Drechsler, W. (2001). Good and Bad Government. Amrogio Lorenzetti's Frescoes in the Sienna Town Hall as Mission Statement for Public Administration Today. *Local Government and Public Service Reform Initiative, Discussion Papers, No 20*, 1–29.

Dubnick, M. (2000). Movies and Morals: Energizing Ethical Thinking among Professionals. *Journal of Public Affairs Education*, *6*(3), 147–159.

Duchamps, M. (1978). *The Essential Writings of Marcel Duchamps ('The Creative Act', lecture at the Museum of Modern Art, New York, October 19, 1961)*. Thames and Hudson.

Fischer, F. (1990). *Technocracy and the Politics of Expertise*. Sage.

Fischer, F. (2005). Participatory Governance as Deliberative Empowerment. The Cultural Politics of Discursive Space. *American Review of Public Administration*, *36*(1), 19–40.

Gira, C. (1995). Lessons in Leadership from Shakespeare. In C. T. Goodsell & N. Murray (Eds.), *Public Administration Illuminated and Inspired by The Arts* (pp. 109–119). Praeger.

Goldbard, A. (2010). The Art of Engagement: Creativity in the Service of Citizenship. In J. Svara & J. Denhardt (Eds.), *Connected Communities: Local Governance as a Partner in Citizen Engagement and Community Building*. Alliance for Innovation.

Goodsell, C. T. (1992). The Public Administrator as Artisan. *Public Administration Review*, *52*(3), 246–253.

Goodsell, C. T. (1995). The Public Administrator as Artisan. In C. T. Goodsell & N. Murray (Eds.), *Public Administration Illuminated and Inspired by the Arts* (pp. 27–41). Praeger.

Goodsell, C. T. (2022). Architectual Power. In R. A. W. Rhodes & S. Hodgett (Eds.), *What Political Science Can Learn from the Humanities* (pp. 181–231). Palgrave Macmillan.

Goodsell, C. T., & Murray, N. (1995a). Prologue: Building New Bridges. In C. T. Goodsell & N. Murray (Eds.), *Public Administration Illuminated and Inspired by the Arts* (pp. 3–23). Prager Publishers.

Goodsell, C. T., & Murray, N. (Eds.). (1995b). *Public Administration Illuminated and Inspired by the Arts*. Praeger Publishers

Haidt, J. (2001). The emotiponal dog and its rational tail: A social intuitionist approach to moral judgement. *Psychological Review*(108), 814–834.

Hajer, M. (2009). *Authoritative Governance: Policy Making in the Age of Mediatization* Oxford University Press.

Herbel, J. E. J. (2015). Shakespeare's Machiavellian moment: Discovering Ethics and Forming a Leadership Narrative in Henry V. *Public Integrity*, *17*(3), 265–278.

Kroll, M. (1995). The Administrator-Viewer Reviewed, Through Film. In C. T. Goodsell & N. Murray (Eds.), *Public Administration Illuminated and Inspired by the Arts* (pp. 91–106). Praeger.

Lewis, C. W. (2013). Visions of Good Governance: Through Artists' eyes. *Public Voices*, *13*(1), 1–16.

Love, J. M., & Fox, C. (2021). Social Dreaming for Social Justice: Power and Resistance in Chaos Walking. *Public Integrity*, *23*(3), 296–309.

MacIntyre, A. (1991). *After Virtue*. University of Notre Dame Press.

McCurdy, H. (1995). Public Policy and Public Imagination. In C. T. Goodsell & N. Murray (Eds.), *Public Administration Illuminated and Inspired by the Arts* (pp. 177–188). Praeger.

Miller, D. (2003). *Political Philosophy: A Very Short Introduction*. Oxford University Press.

Murray, N. (1995a). The Eastern Aesthetic in Administration. In C. T. Goodsell & N. Murray (Eds.), *Public Administration Illuminated and Inspired by the Arts* (pp. 43–55). Praeger.

Murray, N. (1995b). Epilogue: Toward Enriched Administration. In R. E. Goodin & N. Murray (Eds.), *Public Administration Illuminated and Inspired by the Arts* (pp. 205–214). Praegr.

Nabatchi, T., & Leighninger, M. (2015). *Public Participation for the 21st Century*. Jossey-Bass.

Ongaro, E. (2019). The teaching of philosophy in public administration programmes. *Teaching Public Administration*, *37*(2), 135–146.

Ongaro, E. (2020). *Philosophy and Public Administration: An Introduction (Second Edition)*. Cheltenham, UK and Northampton, MA: Edward Elgar.

Ongaro, E., & Tantardini, M. (2023a). *Religion and public administration: An introduction*. Cheltenham, UK and Northampton, MA: Edward Elgar.

Ongaro, E., & Tantardini, M. (2023b). Religion, spirituality, faith and public administration: A literature review and outlook. *Public Policy and Administration*, *39*(4), 531–555.

Overeem, P. (2011). After Managerialism: MacIntyre's Lessons for the Study of Public Administration. *Administration & Society*, *43*(7), 722–748.

Prettner, R., te Molder, H., Hajer, M., & Vliegenthart, R. (2023). Light at the End of the Tunnel? The Staging of Expertise during the COVID-19 Vaccination Campaign. *Journal of Digital Social Research*, *5*(3), 140–170.

Putters, K. (2021). *Nieuwe bestuurscultuur begint bij herijking van het sociaal contract. Van Slingelandtlezing*. Sociaal Cultureel Planbureau.

Rhodes, R. A. W. (2016). Recovering the Craft of Public Administration. *Public Administration Review*, *76*(4), 638–647.

Rhodes, R. A. W., & Hodgett, S. (2022). Blurring Genres: An Agenda for Political Studies. In R. A. W. Rhodes & S. Hodgett (Eds.), *What Political Science Can Learn from the Humanities. Blurring Genres* (pp. 1–29). Palgrave Macmillan.

Ringeling, A. (2017). *Public Administration as a Study of the Public Sphere. A Normative View*. Eleven International Publishing.

Stenvert, R., Kolman, C., Olde Meierink, B., ten Hove, J., Knuijt, M., & Kooij, B. (1998). *Monumenten in Nederland. Overijssel*. Rijksdienst voor de Monumentenzorg.

Stewart, J. (2009). *Public Policy Values*. Palgrave Macmillan.

Trommel, W. (2019). Niet meer dan een speldenprik. *Bestuurskunde*, *28*(3), 41–57.

Van Asperen, H. (2013). Charity Instructing the Poor: Concepts and Practices of Education Reflected in Images of Charity. *Zeitschrift für Kunstgeschichte*, *76*(4), 541–556.

Waldo, D. (1968). *The Novelist on Organization & Administration: An Inquiry into the Relationship between Two Worlds.* Institute of Governmental Studies, University of California.

Zavattaro, S. (2022). "We'll See Who's Powerless Now!" Using WALL-E to Teach Administrative Ethics. *Public Integrity, 24*(7), 702–716.

16. Ambrogio Lorenzetti's Siena Frescoes and Public Administration Today

Wolfgang Drechsler

LORENZETTI REVISITED: ART AS HUMANITY FOR PUBLIC ADMINISTRATION

When asked to participate in a Lorenzetti, the Arts, and Public Administration (PA) panel for the conference on which this book and its essays are based, I assumed that the frescoes in the Siena town hall, iconic as they are in every sense, were to be the focus of the arts-PA connection, as they are in Edoardo Ongaro's modern-classic introduction to *Philosophy and Public Administration* (2020). The panel and conference, however, dealt less with concrete manifestations of PA and humanities – cases, if you will – and more with theorizing about this topic, in this instance as well as generally.

Ongaro's discussion of these frescoes for PA (2020, pp. 213–230) builds on earlier work by Gjalt de Graaf and Hanneke van Asperen (2018) and even earlier work by myself (Drechsler, 2001), and these three items seem to form the core of PA-related Lorenzetti scholarship during the last quarter-century. The current volume unites all four authors once again, with the former three (Ongaro, 2025; de Graaf and van Asperen, 2025) reflecting on their previous discussions. Notwithstanding the success of Ongaro's introduction, de Graaf and van Asperen are right to point out that the take-up of their essay, as measured by Google Scholar citations, has been low, with 21 hits (my own for Drechsler, 2001 is also just 39, a bit less than a short piece on Max Weber I wrote and edited within three hours; Drechsler, 2020).

But they also refer to the great success of presenting the paper during (some) conferences, and I have taught and lectured about Lorenzetti with mostly the same feedback. I have also used the Lorenzetti frescoes in other papers about Siena, with a focus on the Palio and the *contrade*, including a virtually uncited keynote for IASIA in a largely stillborn IIAS journal (Drechsler, 2016; but see the somewhat more successful Drechsler, 2006). So, I decided not to meta-reflect on the topic – except in the present introduction – but rather to update (not fully revise), after said quarter-century, the original Lorenzetti text (Drechsler, 2001), with some additions from the later essays, and some cuts of parts that were suggested externally. Seeing that this booklet was, apparently, the first 21st-century Lorenzetti-for-PA text and a somewhat grey publication,[1] I hope that this is neither an exercise in *vanagloria* nor *superbia*, but rather a contribution *in itself* to the discussion of PA and the humanities generally, and the visual arts specifically. Via Gadamer's discussion of art, parts of the text already served that purpose, if *en passant*, in the original.

SIENA, THE *CAMPO*, AND THE *PALAZZO PUBBLICO*

The Italian city republics, especially the Tuscan cities of Florence, Siena, and Lucca, as well as Venice, particularly during their peak between about 1200 and 1400 AD, have been called 'a singular experience, without parallel since antiquity, without sequel until the modern age' (Jones, 1997, p. 1). At least since the 19th century, intellectuals and scholars have had a fascination for these city-states because they seemed fairly democratic, fairly non-religious, and fairly civilized. Their aesthetics are very close to ours today, and their climate, cuisine, and atmosphere make the region the 'Chiantishire' of an ultimate arcadia. Venice's romantic allure, only enhanced by its atmosphere of decay and decline since the 1800s, needs hardly to be mentioned.

In this chapter, we will deal with Siena, the most Gothic and still the most medieval of the four. This is because Siena had already ceased to be a centre of power and wealth from around 1400, remaining prominent in several fields, but declining completely after 1555. For centuries, it formed a veritable backwater until its rediscovery by Romantic tourists (see Bowsky, 1981).

---

[1] This independent booklet, with a then unusually high print run of 1,250, was published by the Open Society Foundation's Local Government and Public Service Reform Initiative in Budapest, which was dissolved a decade later. The text is based on the first NISPAcee Alena Brunovská Award Lecture, delivered on 10 May 2001 in Riga. The lecture style was retained. To cite the 2001 acknowledgments:

"I am particularly indebted to Erik S. Reinert, the convenor of *The Other Canon* and the first to conceive of the relevance of Lorenzetti in the present context (see Reinert, 1999); to my revered teacher Hans-Georg Gadamer, with whom I discussed the validity of the argument on 16 November 2000 in Heidelberg-Ziegelhausen; and to Rainer Kattel for his, as always, crucial feedback and critical comments, especially during a research excursion to Siena in June 2000. For comments, criticism, and improvement, I should like to thank György Jenei, Sanjaya Lall, Tiina Laats, and Violetta Zentai."

For the current version, I thank Mehmet Orpak for support with the illustrations and their accompanying texts.

When coming from the right direction, one approaches Siena, a city set on top of a hill, with the first impression that she hardly seems to have changed over a very long period of time. Siena is a small city, surrounded by country-side – and indeed, it has been said that it is possible, from any spot in Siena, to reach the fields within less than ten minutes. There is a harmony of colours and shapes, while two towers dominate – one of them, the Cathedral's *campanile*. The Cathedral is built on top of the main hill; it bears the characteristic verti-cal black and white stripes of Sienese architecture so often imitated. But there is another spire that actually exceeds, or at least seems to exceed, the *campa-nile* in height, and this is the tower of the Town Hall, the Palazzo Pubblico, called Torre del Mangia. In this Mariolatrous city, it shows very clearly where the centre of the *polis* lies.

Making one's way to this centre, one arrives at the *campo*, the famous scal-lop-shaped, amphitheater-like market square – which is neither a marketplace nor a square at all. During the summer, it is here that the most famous public event in Tuscany is held, the Palio di Siena, a horse race between the different quarters of the city, the *contrade* (see Drechsler, 2006). Right now, however, our attention must fully focus on the very impressive Town Hall itself.

THE *SALA DEI NOVE* AND LORENZETTI'S FRESCOES

Between 1287 and 1355, Siena was governed by a college of patricians called 'the Nine', *I Nove*. The nine members of this college rotated extremely fre-quently to ensure maximum protection against tyranny and takeover by one person or family, a constant worry of the city republics, and a central worry already for the Greek city-states and in Plato's political philosophy (Koyré, 1945).

If one looks at the Town Hall, on the right side on the first floor – second floor in American counting – there is a room at the back where the last two windows on the right are, and this is the council chamber of the Nine, thus called the Sala dei Nove. It was here that the Nine met both in public and in closed session to administer and govern the City of Siena.

Towards the end of their power, the Nine had the room decorated by one of Siena's greatest painters, Magister Ambrogio Lorenzetti, famous also for his Madonnas (see Rowley, 1958). Lorenzetti's fresco-cycle spans over three of the four walls (the window wall is not used) of the room. It forms one general idea or makes one overall point, but it has various titles; scholars, of course, debate which one is appropriate (see Riklin, 1996). Often, the room has been and is referred to as the 'Hall of Peace' or 'Hall of Good Government', but this is taking *pars pro toto*. What we have here are the Allegories of Good and Bad Government and their respective Effects on the City and on the Country.

Of these six sets, if we stand with our backs to the windows, we see in front of us, and thus dominating the room, the *Allegory of Good Government*. To its right, on the long wall, there are the Effects of this Good Government, first on the City, then – the picture flows along but is separated by the city walls – on the Country. On the left long wall, we are shown, from the right, the *Allegory of Bad Government*, its *Effects on the City*, and its *Effects on the Country* in one long picture.[2]

Most of us will have seen, in reproduction, at least parts of the *Allegory of Good Government* – such as the seated centre figure and the Peace figure – and of the *Effects on the City*. But if one stands in front of the frescoes for the first time, one is simply overwhelmed by their immense scale, their wealth of scenes, forms, figures, and landscapes, and by the astounding colours, which cannot satisfactorily be reproduced.

This is a work of art that speaks to us directly and immediately, that has something to say to us if we 'listen' – but in any case, it is something that most of us will call beautiful, although or because this is early art, it is not quite the stylish, finished work we associate with the term Renaissance. Indeed, this is the first large-scale secular fresco, even the first large-scale piece of secular art in the West at all since the decline of Ancient Rome. For program and imagery, there are precedents, but not really on this scale, nor really in

Figure 16.1   *Lorenzetti, Allegory of Good Government, Siena Town Hall (public domain)*

---

[2] My one issue with the otherwise excellent 'second' discussion of Lorenzetti for PA (de Graaf and van Asperen 2018), is that it does not address the Bad Government part, which for me is an integral part of the 'text' of the frescoe(s).

substance – although naturally, scholarship, as scholarship must, tries to trace them.

THE *EFFECTS OF GOOD GOVERNMENT ON THE CITY*

The *Effects of Good Government on the City* (see Figure 16.2), from the corner of the room towards the city walls, seems to me to have the most unambiguous meaning today; indeed, it has a clear lesson to teach even 700 years after its creation.

And what do we see? (Castelnuovo, 1995; and Starn, 1994 provide good reproductions.) What strikes us immediately is that this is a *happy* scene. Happy is not a scholarly concept in the global West (see Drechsler, 2019), often not even an intellectual one, which is why it is so important that it is visualized here. We see a beautiful city, prosperous, in which well-fed, well-clad people are living happily. As we see in the upper left corner, from the Cathedral *campanile*, this is – albeit in idealized form – Siena. The houses are pleasantly ordered and, their individuality notwithstanding, nicely fitting – the result of regulation, of course, as in all beautiful cities. There is dancing in the street; a bride is riding to her wedding; farmers are bringing supplies to the city; there are goods aplenty in the shops, and people have money enough to purchase what they wish; there is leisure enough, and people are sitting in café-like bars. Someone is watering her window-ledge flowers, and a bird is singing in a cage in an open window – lovely for us, if not for the bird itself.

Particularly noteworthy is the building scene in the upper center-right, reproduced in Figure 16.3.

Figure 16.2   *Ambrogio Lorenzetti, Effects of Good Government on the City, Siena Town Hall (public domain)*

Figure 16.3   Lorenzetti, Effects of Good Government on the City (detail; sharpened), Siena Town Hall (public domain)

Not only is it shown here how these towers or townhouses were built (walled up from the outside) and why there are holes in these brick buildings (for the scaffolding); we are also able to recognize a construction site, a work scene, as something good and indeed vital. A city in which houses are built is, or so it is argued here, a good city. What makes Lorenzetti special is that most political utopias then and now – and to a good extent, this is one – are anti-business, but this one is not.

We also notice, quite at the centre of the bigger picture, a school scene – this is a learning society at work. It has been quipped that this scene proves that we have a utopia here: most students actually seem to be listening, which is quite a feat even before the rise of the smartphone.

In sum, people are living a good life in what – if this is the effect of good government – must be a good state.

THE GOOD LIFE IN THE GOOD STATE

As Aristotle says in the *Politika*, 'a state comes into existence for the purpose of ensuring life, and it continues to exist for the purpose of the good life' (I 1252b). And as Marsilius of Padua – arguably the most important political philosopher of Lorenzetti's time – comments upon this passage, the good life 'is the perfect final cause of the state' (*Defensor pacis* I. iv.1.). I would argue, programmatically, that this is clearly what this specific part of the fresco (but also the cycle as a whole) visualizes, thus presenting it to us with full immediacy. State is, as opposed to any legal(istic) or other more narrow definition, widely understood here as *polis*, or better even as structured human living-together, usually in a designated space. And so, the fresco can directly address us because the Good Life in the Good State, which are mutually dependent on each other, is still, or so I would claim (and that is all that can be done in matters such as these), the only way to guarantee happiness for the *polis* and – and thus! – for the individual, which means: for all of us.

THE IMMEDIACY OF ART

But can we really use a work that is so old, so distant, and from such a hidden past, depicting a life that is so clearly not ours? Can we even know what Lorenzetti wants to tell us? This is the question posed to all history of thought and/or political philosophy deliberations that are supposedly relevant, let alone serve as a form of instruction, for the present. And one popular scholarly answer is: No, we cannot use such works today.

This position would argue that all thought relates to its own time and its own time only, that there are no perennial problems, let alone answers, and that we should deal with the great thinkers of the past in an, if you will, antiquarian manner, reconstructing their world of thought as well as we can (see Skinner, 2002). This seems in line with the received hermeneutical wisdom that, in order to find out what the author of a text intended, we need to reconstruct the author's horizon.

But this is not true anyway – hermeneutics, and today this largely means Gadamerian hermeneutics, is based precisely on the insight that we can*not* fully reconstruct any historical horizon, that an author always says more as well as less than intended, and that communication happens at the moment of reading, or perceiving, the formulated message (Gadamer, 1990). But in our case, in the case of Lorenzetti, this is especially untrue.

The reason is that what we have here is a work of art, specifically a visual work of art, and in this case, the normal questions of text, context, and time do not apply. As Gadamer himself says, "art is the overcoming of the past. All is presence in art. It becomes presence." (Gadamer, 1997, p. 25) This is so because art is *only* 'there' during 'the act' – interpretation, in the sense of engagement, is what makes the work of art. This is a-temporal; if we look seriously at, and engage with, Lorenzetti's fresco – I called it 'listening' earlier on – it becomes alive right then, and on a level that is neither merely aesthetic nor purely intellectual or historical.

The 'magic' effect here is that through art-specific access, we overcome the problems of hermeneutics and of historicism. We can, may, and indeed should look at this fresco, 'listen' to it, and 'get' all the messages we can get and that we want to get. Context, as well as Lorenzetti's – or his sponsors' – intentions, may be interesting and helpful to access the fresco, but they are not decisive. As Gadamer says for poetry, although what he says is even more valid for visual art, 'What does the reader need to know? … He must know as much as he needs and as much as he can cope with. He must know as much as he really can and has to bring it into his reading … into his listening' (Gadamer, 1986, p. 155). Thus, through the artistic medium, something perennial or general makes itself apparent, although the painter's intentions may have been quite different.

Why do we – or most of us – still find an Aristophanes' comedy so funny that we laugh? And why does a Goya painting still shock us? I am thinking specifically of the famous *Third of May 1808 in Madrid* (*El Tres de Mayo 1808 en Madrid*) in Figure 16.4.

Figure 16.4   *Francisco de Goya, El Tres de Mayo 1808 en Madrid (1814), Madrid, Museo del Prado (public domain: https://commons .wikimedia.org/wiki/File:El_Tres_de_Mayo,_by_Francisco _de_Goya,_from_Prado_thin_black_margin.jpg)*

This famous painting is highly context-specific, referring to a particular event in history: the Napoleonic invasion of Spain between 1808 and 1814. On the 'journalistic' level, Goya is condemning the invasion, more specifically the executions depicted here and named in the title just by date, emphasizing the specificity. On a broader level, this is a condemnation of war, or such executions, generally (and to understand this we would no longer need to know the date of the title). On a third, aesthetic, level, this is a grand painting with artistic and aesthetic values completely separate from any statement.

The French occupation of Spain can be quite differently interpreted as well – Edgar Allan Poe's *The Pit and the Pendulum* (1842), one of his most famous short stories, clearly makes the opposite point; here, the French victory is one of Enlightenment over the horrors of the Inquisition and indeed torture. But by means of Goya's aesthetic immediacy, the 'third level', a non-context-specific yet socially relevant and not at all aesthetic message, the 'second level', is transmitted as well. In the case of this painting, it says that war is generally bad, evil, and senseless, no matter what. In Lorenzetti's case, it is to convey the idea of the Good Life in the Good City.

And this is an accomplishment that visual art – not only, but particularly – can achieve without becoming too contextual, vague, or abstract; hence the great value of visual artistic sources in such complex fields as PA. To verbalize this message, we would need dozens of pages, if we could verbalize it at all. This is not to argue, of course, for any reduction of PA to images, but for consideration of the use of visual communication where feasible.

MYTH OR REALITY? THE VENETIAN ANSWER

But how seriously can such a message as Lorenzetti's be taken? Against the above-mentioned Tuscany-as-Arcadia, 20th century historians have asserted that the world of 14th-century Tuscany was not half as nice. Indeed, it was an oligarchy; there existed discrimination, war, and insecurity of the highest order, and the rationalization, propaganda, and utopianism of either artistic or literary-philosophical treatises on Good Government can thus be taken as not so interesting. However, this approach reveals a naive view of utopias (as well as of history and of philosophy). Suffice it here to say that, normatively, utopias are both crucial in human development and necessary for the formulation of any kind of policy at all (see Drechsler, 2003).

In Lorenzetti, we certainly find a mixture of instruction, utopia, and description. Also, the government of the *Nove* was relatively short-lived, and indeed the problem of the city republics was that they were quite unstable. And true enough, Siena perished as a form of human consociation as depicted by Lorenzetti. Yet, one city republic proved, or so I would argue, that it was not the principle but extraneous circumstances that were the problem. This republic turned out to be the most stable and most successful structured form of human consociation in the history of humankind, or at least in the West: Venice (see Chambers, 1970). In view of this, we shall take a brief look at Venice now to dispel the myth of the impossibility, or lack of viability, of a *polis* organized along Lorenzettian lines.

Venice has been a highly successful promoter of her own myth – she was usually very good at sales – and studies of the 'Myth of Venice' actually formed the historiography of Venice for at least a century. However, what must be admitted is that much of it *was* real – of which the myth itself surely is a part, within as well as without Venice herself (see Drechsler, 2002 for further arguments).

Of course, Venice's situation was and is highly specific, not least because of her physical location. The lagoon made successful defence, thanks to the fleet, quite easily possible. And yet, one would think that in a host of other respects, Venice was more comparable than not to her Tuscan sisters.

In Venice, we see a *polis* that was not conquered for 1,000 years. This must be an absolute record, and for those who do not realize what this means for the life of all citizens, indeed of all people living in Venice, some pause for thought is suggested. Inner strife was also minimal – there were attempts at takeovers, there were revolts and revolutions, but amazingly few, and with very minor side effects. In the end, it is arguable that there was no real revolution, but just adaptation and reform – compare that with any other city over that period of time!

One should also not forget that the political franchise in Venice was probably larger than anywhere else at the time. There is also a functional reason for the oligarchic or aristocratic limitation of the electorate. In Venice (and Siena), one thus had a large pool of qualified people who could take over political, administrative, or judicial functions at a moment's notice – because they were up-to-date on the state's business, the rules and regulations, and the policies, as they were voting on them every week. Only such a large, viable recruitment pool makes rapid turnover in appointments possible.

This Venice excursus was about demonstrating that the model of a city run along the lines of Siena, as depicted in the frescoes, was indeed possible; that it was not a utopia at all – only that it was realized in Venice, rather than Tuscany, where certain extraneous circumstances were better. It is not to argue that such a system would be transferable, let alone applicable today. If anything, its value for us is heuristic. However, in all of Venice, this treasure-house of art, perhaps the most astounding place of political iconography, we do not find a work of art that demonstrates directly and immediately why Venice as a state worked as well as Lorenzetti's fresco cycle in Siena.

THE STATE OF LAW

But, as the late Sanjaya Lall remarked during a conference in Venice where an earlier form of this argument was presented, no state is visible in the *Effects of Good Governance* picture – it could almost be called a neoliberal fantasy. This criticism, too, can be quite easily met within Lorenzetti's frescoes – we just need to swing our eyes 90 degrees to the left. Then we face the perhaps even more famous part of the fresco, the *Allegory of Good Government*, which shows us the strong but limited state (not an oxymoron, but a necessity) that creates what are literally its *effects* (see Figure 16.5).

(Sienese) (Good) Government is enthroned at the centre, encircled by the six key virtues, of which the one immediately to the right (from our perspective left) is the most important. This is Aristotle's *phronesis*, appropriateness, the main insight into any public policy and order. The Government's sceptre hand is tied by a rope that runs from Justice's scales (Justice under Wisdom, who has the highest position; not the 'simple' Justice to the very right of our perspective). *Concordia*, unity, links the two ropes together, and it is *the citizens*, or at least their representatives, who pass the rope on to Government. Never is such Good Government absolute; not only is it subject to negotiation and discourse, rather, it is tied to Justice under Wisdom; and without unity and participation of the citizens, it all comes to nothing. In other words, it needs to be a *Rechtsstaat*, a state of law – but it remains a strong state that, if you will,

Note: Blue follows the rope from wisdom via the two forms of justice and the citizens, to tying the hand of Sienese Good Government that holds the scept.

Figure 16.5   *Lorenzetti, Allegory of Good Government, Siena Town Hall (public domain); systematic graph by the author. re.*

shapes and creates the market(s) that we see in its, the Good Government's, effects.

Now, the concept of the state of law might have evolved in juxtaposition to the welfare state, i.e., it might have stood for a state that does not become involved in any affairs of the citizens, assuming – with whatever justification – that all individuals are not only of equal worth but also, under all circumstances, capable of the same. Yet, in historical development, it is the combination of both the welfare state and the state of law that has been successful, at least in the 'West' – and as Jeane J. Kirkpatrick had pointed out, 'Every modern democracy is a welfare state in the sense that it seeks to provide basic minimum standards of well-being to its citizens' (1988, p. 2).

But, as I have argued here, it is not the minimum that matters; it is the maximum of citizen well-being that the *polis* can provide. The problems inherent in this approach, such as the tendency to tell people how they should be happy, can – and must – be kept in check precisely by the institutions and process, and by retaining the individualist-collectivist balance, or better: necessary tensions, which define any structured human living-together. And both aspects are precisely what the *Allegory of Good Government* depicts so beautifully, and thus how the Good Life in the Good State is created.

THE *EFFECTS OF BAD GOVERNMENT*

And finally, for those still not convinced, by moving our eyes a further 90 degrees to the left, we see in a single sweeping and – appropriately enough – heavily damaged fresco, the *Allegory* and *Effects* of Bad Government on City and Country (see Figure 16.6).

Here, it is made clear what we do not want: ruined houses, no commerce except the arms industry, a deserted landscape, and of course the ever-apparent violence, with the marauding foreign or even local, *soldateska*, plundering,

Figure 16.6   *Lorenzetti, Allegory of Bad Government and its Effects on City and Country, Siena Town Hall (public domain)*

dressing fancily, and molesting, raping, and killing on the street. These rape scenes, indirectly but very hauntingly depicted, are among the strongest and most innovative figures of Lorenzetti.

Being subjected to such violence, often fatal, was and is precisely the lot of so many civilians – men, women, and children – in medieval, earlier, and later Italy, Europe, and the world. The original purpose of the state, according to Aristotle, as already mentioned, is survival; it is peace within and without; no crime and no war. The denial of such peace is something that is almost always made from a secure home, but something that does not consider the citizens' most basic rights, unless they – as in Myanmar today – actively decide otherwise. It once again brings to mind the amazing success of Venice, which might have been in some sense a police state (although with very few police), but one in which violence was, and incidentally is, less likely than in almost any other city of that size – foreshadowing the Singapore today, with similar results.

But have a careful look at the space, just between the ruined houses of the bad city and the *Allegory of Bad Government*, where the houses are actually still fine (see Figure 16.7).

Somebody is living quite well between the slums and bad government, but who is that? They stepped outside, but we don't see their faces anymore as they have been worn away. This is very enigmatic, but there are two people, just standing above the corpse, who are not dressed fancily but fairly well, like the bourgeois aristocrats in the first painting, looking at all this mayhem. And that may be a reminder that even bad government does not go without profit for a few at least. And that is why some people are actually in favour of bad government, and they will defend it and its ideology – today's junta in Myanmar and its domestic and neighbourly profiteers may come to mind again.

Finally, for theory's sake, one might glance briefly at the hauntingly beautiful *Allegory of Bad Government* (see Figure 16.8).

The monster in the middle, Tyranny, encircled by vainglory, pride, and avarice or greed (which are the same in traditional virtue ethics), and betwixt angel-faced but bat-clawed and -winged fraud, and stone-throwing, dagger-slinging blind fury, is a perfect allegory of bad PA. So, arrogance, inflated pride, cocksureness, trying to save and keep money at all costs all of the time, these are the worst things. Saving money is not the point of the city, of the country. The country is no little kid saving for a bike – or today, for an iPhone – because that is not the point of human living-together. If one thinks about it, this description of the vices of bad government catches exactly the essence of NPM and of what is wrong with it, from arrogance to miserliness and even plain fraud (see Drechsler, 2005). To ask whether these days it may be the ideology easily endorsable by the profiteers from the urban-effects scene right next to it, however, will probably go too far …

*Figure 16.7   Lorenzetti, Bad Government's Effects on the City (detail),
Siena Town Hall (public domain)*

Figure 16.8   Lorenzetti, Allegory of Bad Government (detail), Siena Town Hall (public domain)

This train of thought allows me to finish with one of my favorite Aristotelian sentences, which also expresses very well one of the key insights of Lorenzetti. This is a fragment that serves to emphasize what is wrong with reductionist PA, as well as with reductionism anywhere in the social sciences, because we have a yardstick that is much more important than any self-referential numbers and amounts: *viz.*, that 'the good is the most accurate measure of everything' (*Politikos*, fragm. 79 Rose[1870]).

CODA: PUBLIC ADMINISTRATION AND THE ARTS

Good PA has a *telos*, a goal: The Good Life and/in the Good State. Only the discourse of the stakeholders brings out what these constitute at a given point and place in time. As Lorenz von Stein makes the point in his *Verwaltungslehre* (2010 [1870]), good PA is only good as long as one remembers this insight, in practice as a civil servant, as well as in theory and teaching. But precisely for that purpose, an obsolete legalistic state focus is not enough; indeed, it obscures the importance and resilience of the state. Economic sustainability, security, and other public goods, as well as general happiness and high-quality PA need to be seen together, in the 21st century more than ever. The state, the economy, the third sector: their interaction is what needs to be discussed in order to get anywhere.

It is not very profound to say that good PA is in the end about human happiness. But a reminder is often necessary, particularly for all of us who deal with PA every day. One of the best, most direct, and most apt reminders of this goal are Ambrogio Lorenzetti's frescoes in the Siena Town Hall – and, not coincidentally, arguably also the most beautiful.

If this is so, then the importance of visual art, because of its power to transcend hermeneutical problems and confront the viewer directly and immediately, becomes apparent – and with it, the importance of the humanities approach generally. In the Lorenzetti case, the artwork presents a normative philosophical discourse, utopia, and reality in this direct way – not unambiguously, and not challenge-free, but then, that is the case for anything that is not trivial. Again, this visual-artistic approach, distinctly as part of a humanistic endeavour, cannot be the only avenue to good PA today, but good PA will lose, and lose severely, if that path is blocked – and this, in turn, would reduce the possibility to think, and to realize, the Good Life in the Good State.

REFERENCES

Bowsky, William M. (1981). *A Medieval Italian Commune. Siena under the Nine, 1287–1355.* Berkeley – Los Angeles: University of California Press.

Castelnuovo, Enrico (ed.) (1995). *Ambrogio Lorenzetti – Il Buon Governo.* Milano: Electa.

Chambers, D.S. (1970). *The Imperial Age of Venice, 1380–1580.* London: Thames and Hudson.

de Graaf, Gjalt and Hanneke van Asperen (2025). 'How Artworks Can Be a Source of Knowledge, Inspiration, Motivation, and Understanding in Public Administration.' Chapter 15 in E. Ongaro, G. Orsina and L. Castellani 'The Humanities and Public Administration: An Introduction', Cheltenham, UK and Northampton, MA: Edward Elgar Publishing -this volume.

de Graaf, Gjalt and Hanneke van Asperen (2018). 'The Art of Good Governance: How Images from the Past Provide Inspiration for Modern Practice.' *International Review of Administrative Sciences*, vol. 84, no. 2, pp. 405–420.

Drechsler, Wolfgang (2020, July). 'Good Bureaucracy: Max Weber and Public Administration Today.' *Max Weber Studies*, vol. 20, no. 2, pp. 219–224.

Drechsler, Wolfgang (2019). 'The Reality and Diversity of Buddhist Economics.' *American Journal of Economics and Sociology*, vol. 78, no. 2, pp. 523–560.

Drechsler, Wolfgang (2016, Summer). "Il Buon Governo Senese: Classic Aspects of (Alternative) Public Service Delivery." *Developments in Administration / Développements de l'administration*, vol. 1, no. 1, pp. 5–23.

Drechsler, Wolfgang (2006, Summer). 'The Contrade, the Palio and the Ben Comune: Lessons from Siena.' *Trames*, vol. 10, no. 2, pp. 99–125.

Drechsler, Wolfgang (2005, 14 September). 'The Rise and Demise of the New Public Management.' *Post-autistic Economics Review*, issue 33.

Drechsler, Wolfgang (2003). '*Les Lois de Platon*, fondement de l'Économie du droit.' *Revue Française d'Histoire des Idées Politiques*, no. 16 (2/2002): *Les Lois de Platon*, pp. 399–410.

Drechsler, Wolfgang (2002). 'Venice Misappropriated. A Review of John Martin / Dennis Romano, eds. *Venice Reconsidered.*' *Trames*, vol. 6 (56/51), no. 2, pp. 192–201.

Drechsler, Wolfgang (2001). *Good and Bad Government: Ambrogio Lorenzetti's Frescoes in the Siena Town Hall as Mission Statement for Public Administration Today*. LGI Discussion Paper, no. 20. Budapest: Open Society Institute and Local Government Initiative.

Gadamer, Hans-Georg (1997). Remarks in 'Galeriegespräch.' In '*Zukunft ist Herkunft.' Hans-Georg Gadamer und Emil Schumacher – Ehrenbürger der Universität Jena*. Klaus Manger, ed., Jenaer Universitätsreden, vol. 7, pp. 9–34.

Gadamer, Hans-Georg (1990). *Wahrheit und Methode. Grundzüge einer philosophischen Hermeneutik = Hermeneutik, vol. 1, Gesammelte Werke*, 6th edn. Tübingen: Mohr Siebeck.

Gadamer, Hans-Georg (1986). *Wer bin ich und wer bist Du? Ein Kommentar zu Paul Celans Gedichtfolge 'Atemkristall'*, 2nd edn. Frankfurt/Main: Suhrkamp.

Jones, Philip (1997). *The Italian City-State. From Commune to Signoria*. Oxford: Clarendon Press of Oxford University Press.

Kirkpatrick, Jeane J. (1988, Spring). 'Welfare State Conservatism' [interview]. *Policy Review*, no. 44, pp. 2–6.

Koyré, Alexandre (1945). *Introduction à la lecture de Platon*. New York: Brentano.

Ongaro, Edoardo (2025). 'How the Consideration of the Nature of Art Can Provide Novel Ways to Understand Public Administration.' this volume – pp. 207–2016 in E. Ongaro, G. Orsina and L. Castellani 'The Humanities and Public Administration: An Introduction', Cheltenham, UK and Northampton, MA: Edward Elgar Publishing - this volume

Ongaro, Edoardo (2020). *Philosophy and Public Administration. An Introduction*, 2nd edn. Cheltenham, UK and Northampton, MA: Edward Elgar: Edward Elgar.

Poe, Edgar Allan (1842). *The Pit and the Pendulum*. Retrieved from: https://poestories .com/read/pit (last accessed 23 June 2024).

Reinert, Erik S. (1999). 'The Role of the State in Economic Growth.' *Journal of Economic Studies*, vol. 26, nos. 4/5, pp. 268–326.

Riklin, Alois (1996). *Ambrogio Lorenzettis politische Summe*. Bern/Wien: Stämpfli/ Manzsche Verlags- und Universitätsbuchhandlung.

Rowley, George (1958). *Ambrogio Lorenzetti*, 2 vols. Princeton: Princeton University Press.

Skinner, Quentin (2002). *Visions of Politics, vol. 1: Regarding Method*. Cambridge: Cambridge University Press.

Starn, Randolph (1994). *Ambrogio Lorenzetti – The Palazzo Pubblico, Siena*. New York: George Braziller.

Stein, Lorenz v. (2010 [1870]). *Handbuch der Verwaltungslehre und des Verwaltungsrechts*. Utz Schliesky, ed. Tübingen: Mohr Siebeck.

17. Mind the Gap: A Strategy to connect Humanities (Arts) with Social Sciences (Public Administration)

Geert Bouckaert

In the past, 'Science and Art' (S&A) always enjoyed a level of connection, whether it was in an individual person like Leonardo da Vinci, or in an interactive process in *ad hoc* projects. In the course of history, science and art diverged, and this divergence resulted in specialization within distinct science and art 'silos'. In addition to ongoing specialization, however, recent experiences show a new convergence within both science and the arts, and ultimately between science and art. This convergence is not an automatic process. Rather, it requires an openness between the 'cultures' of scientific research and artistic research.

In 1959, C.P. Snow delivered his influential Rede Lecture at the Senate House of Cambridge University about the 'two cultures' (Snow, 1959). He talked about education's need for greater equilibrium between the arts and humanities (which were too dominant), and the 'hard' sciences (such as engineering, physics, etc.) for the benefit of society. The current debate to move from STEM (Science, Technology, Engineering, Mathematics) to STEAM (Science, Technology, Engineering, Art, Mathematics) is related to this recognized need to encourage cross-fertilization in teaching and research.

It goes without saying that any such interaction between science and art should be two-way traffic: from art to science and from science to art.

Umberto Eco wrote in his seminal book *The Open Work* (1962/1989: 83): "Here is a culture that allows for different methods of research not because they might come up with identical results but because they contradict and complement each other in a dialectic opposition that will generate new perspectives".

In his introduction to the 2019 Venice Biennale, curator Ralph Rugoff referred to the artists selected by quoting this passage from Eco and by commenting that "Umberto Eco drew attention to the art's capacity to inspire novel ways of seeing and behaving [...] Taking nothing for granted, these artists have fashioned ways of making art that are essentially inquisitive, speculative, and exploratory" (Rugoff, 2019: 38).

Wagemans is optimistic when he states that it helps to look for commonalities, even when there are differences. He argues that both science and art ask questions and look for answers. Both, likewise, have an intrinsic motivation: for scientists to explain ('*erklären*'), for artists to understand ('*verstehen*', in Dilthey's words). His conclusion is that additional space and time to meet at the bridge would benefit us more than just staying in our own labs, workspaces, studios, or libraries (Wagemans, 2013: 191).

This chapter will focus on linking humanities as an academic cluster in general, with a focus on contemporary art, to social sciences in general, with a focus on contemporary public administration.

But what is 'contemporary'? There are different views about the meaning of 'contemporary,' what it is, and why it is important. There are different 'contemporaries' because there are different temporalities.

'The qualifier "contemporary" has different meanings and different affordances according to the specific discursive practice to which it refers. In the sciences, to give a counter example, it would be redundant (if not absurd) to talk about *contemporary science*' (de Assis, 2019: 17). According to Paulo de Assis, 'the notion of *contemporary music* does not apply to all music that is composed "today," which in fact in the vast majority of cases is not *contemporary* at all. Music of today is certainly *contemporaneous*, it is coeval to us, but nobody would say that, for example, a composer today composing a Classical symphony in the style of Haydn is making 'contemporary music''' (de Assis, 2019: 19).

According to Aira, given that we have past, present, and future, which all have 'contemporary' moments, 'contemporary' thus becomes ahistorical, or even 'anachronistic': 'Contemporary Art is its own documentation – it is writing its own history simultaneously with its appearance and doesn't need time to pass' (Aira, 2018: 33).

However, according to de Assis, '(T)o live in a given time is to be contemporaneous with it, which is a piece of factual evidence and does not carry any critical stance over one's own presence in that particular time [...] Thus, contemporary music, like contemporary art, implies a critical dimension, a distance from the everyday world, a detachment from habitus, conventions, and stratifications of forms and media' (de Assis, 2019: 9, 19).

What is the objective or the purpose of being 'contemporary'? Why do we need contemporary art?

> [...] I decidedly point towards *futures of the contemporary*, and those futures' manifold possibilities of constitution, formation, and reinvention. More so than other modes of research, artistic research has the power to reverse the arrow of research [...] artistic researchers can look into the abysses of the present in order to grasp its futures, exploring the diagnostic function of art, contributing to a symptomatology of one's own epoch [...] artistic research's most interesting perspectives are those

that more explicitly relate to the future. Such quests do not try to find out *how things really were in the past*, nor are they aiming at understanding *how we became what we are today* [...] Rather, the really challenging discoveries today are to find out *how we can become* today *what today we aim to be*. Or, *how we can depart from today, even without a clear destination in mind or safe ports to reach*. (de Assis, 2019: 28–29)

There is 'immense courage required in order to be contemporary, to engage in the difficult negotiation between the past and the future' (Obrist, 2010: 67).

Even if most of these quotations are about art and contemporary art, they also apply, *mutatis mutandis*, to science. If 'contemporary' is not just about what is produced today in art and science, but about what is produced today and what is relevant for tomorrow in terms of relevant futures, then we can only be interested in contemporary art and in contemporary science. Combining these two contemporalities has the potential to lead us to possible and conceivable futures.

What is the objective or the purpose of being 'contemporary'? Why do we need 'contemporary public administration'?

Even when 'history' and 'the past' are crucial to understanding public administration as a current reality, as defined and dependent by its own paths, it is crucial to anticipate the next public administrations, and therefore the next way of organizing our academic field of public administration. In this sense, 'contemporary' does not only mean 'today', but implies 'today with relevance for the future'. Contemporary public administration then means today's public administration as relevant for its future. This is based on a proposal made within the EPPA (European Perspectives for Public Administration) (Bouckaert and Jann, 2020: 30), which states that current:

1. "Public Administration research and teaching run too much behind facts and developments; however they should also be in front of the facts, they should not just be pushed by realities but also pull realities;
2. Public Administration is too much dominated by disciplinary boundaries and epistemological concerns; however, it should be much more taking several disciplines and approaches into account and result in an equilibrated approach;
3. Public Administration is thinking too much in causal terms; however, it s hould also, as a social science, think in teleological terms;
4. Public Administration is often pretending to be disconnected from time and space; however, it should actively and positively take context and culture into account;

5.   Public Administration research aims to be relevant for practice; however, it should critically anticipate its future relevance for public administration and governance."

One way to anticipate and prepare for this future of public administration is to consolidate futures (as in utopias), to include new disciplines and cultures (such as art and culture) and to connect to practice.

SCIENCE AND ART: FIRST TO DISTINGUISH, NOT TO SEPARATE, THEN TO COMBINE

It is clear that art and science, as expressions of creativity in our society, have been heavily marketized, globalized, and institutionalized. A central question is thus how we prepare for the future by developing research-based knowledge while trying to capture the unforeseeable. To this end, a combination of trained research capacities is needed, with sufficient curiosity and imagination to be innovative and to be able to handle uncertainties.

Helga Nowotny, Emeritus Professor at the ETH Zürich and former president of the European Research Council, states:

> To put research (back) into the arts, to (again) make visible and explicit the functions of research in the arts and in the act of 'creating knowledge' is a truly ambitious undertaking, because it takes up a vision and a project that originated in the Renaissance [...] If a world-leading university like Harvard sets up a commission to deal with the role and function of the arts within its own research-intensive premises, this sends a powerful signal to the rest of the academic world that cross-fertilization between domains of the arts and the sciences is not only possible, but a most welcome and much desired way of enhancing creativity across presumed disciplinary borderlines. (Nowotny, 2011: xix, xx–xxi)

Borgdorff (2011), Professor of Research in the Arts at the University of the Arts in the Hague, states that scientific research and development stand side by side with artistic research and development. This inspires him to distinguish between "research *on* the arts" (as historical and theoretical research about the arts), "research *in* the arts" (as research within the artistic practices of creating and designing), and "research *for* the arts" (a supporting instrumental function of methods and techniques) (Borgdorff, 2011: 46). Borgdorff's basic assumption is that, alongside its differences, artistic research has a multiplicity of links and connotations with research in the humanities, aesthetics, and social sciences in addition to science and technology.

Nowotny confirms this statement:

> Human creativity in its manifold expressions has found a privileged home in the structure of universities and research institutions, although it is by no means confined to them [...] If innovation is contemporary society's way of coping with the

vacuum that inhabits its present concept of the future, artistic research – and not just the production of art – may lead to forms of innovation that shape the elusive phenomena and events that only the individual and collective imagination can conjure [...] But the techno-sciences, important as they are, are not alone in leading these explorations and pursuits. Artists have quickly realized the artistic challenges offered by hybrid forms and the vast domain of crossing the natural with the artificial. Most significantly, they extend their creativity beyond the range covered by the techno-sciences. (Nowotny, 2011: xxv, xxvi)

Peter Weibel, President of the Zentrum für Kunst und Medientechnologie (ZKM) in Karlsruhe (Goethe Institut), also confirms this position from the point of view of the centrality of (big) data and media:

Following representation and simulation, the new working terrain of art is, therefore, reality, substitution and construction. Art will become part of technical systems that will remove human helplessness and enrich both itself and its environment in an apparatus-related manner in the form of augmented reality [...] The modern may have terminated Da Vinci's programme, but, with media art, it has begun to restore the severed link to classical art in a new form. The Renaissance, as the scientification of art is called, will return as the Renaissance 2.0 in the data and media age. (Weibel, 2014: 20)

According to Eric R. Kandel, winner of the 2000 Nobel Prize for medicine, it is necessary to bridge the two cultures of art and science. In his book *Reductionism in Art and Brain Science* (2016) he claims that "(B)oth brain science and abstract art address, in direct and compelling fashion, questions and goals that are central to humanistic thought. In this pursuit they share, to a surprising degree, common methodologies" (Kandel, 2016: 3). He continues: "(M)y central premise is that although the reductionist approaches of scientists and artists are not identical in their aims – scientists use reductionism to solve a complex problem and artists use it to elicit a new perceptual and emotional response in the beholder – they are analogous" (Kandel, 2016: 6). In his conclusion "The Emerging Dialogue between Abstract Art and Science", he appeals for "A Return to the Two Cultures": "Wilson argues that knowledge is gained and science progresses through a process of conflict and resolution. For every parent discipline, there is a more fundamental field, and antidiscipline that challenges its methods and claims [...] Art and art history are the parent disciplines, and brain science is their antidiscipline" (Kandel, 2016: 187–188).

In conclusion, it seems that every branch of scientific research (biomedical, science and technology, and social sciences and humanities) agrees on the need to connect science and art. As a consequence, artistic research, as research within the arts, and scientific research in general – and specific scientific research about, for, and with the arts – have become equivalent, and it is essential to combine them.

Science and Art are Converging

In the second half of the twentieth century, specialization in various fields of science significantly extended our levels of knowledge. This had an impact on how universities and scientific communities organized themselves. At the same time, however, it resulted in a process of pillarization, confining particular sciences to isolated silos. While this was a familiar mechanism in the organizational sciences, the lack of possibilities, opportunities, and incentives to coordinate and collaborate tended to have negative effects. It is obvious today that every effort is being made to make multidisciplinary, interdisciplinary, and trans-disciplinary research happen. This, however, is easier said than done. Nevertheless, increasingly mixed or hybrid labs and research units have been established (medicine/engineering, medicine/psychology, law/economics, engineering/sociology, etc.). Horizon 2020 invites us to share our concern and awareness that expanding knowledge is not only about specialization, but perhaps more about collaboration. To create new knowledge, synergies between silos are required. This has resulted in a converging scientific research strategy.

In the community of the arts, research and teaching likewise evolved into silos and specialization. After this period of specialization, however, a similar movement towards convergence has been evolving within the arts, a movement away from the isolated silos of the past. It goes without saying that specialization continues within the various branches of the arts, but borders are blurring. Mixed media, hybrid methods, the use of performance, etc., have resulted in a wave of artists and art that combines image, music, words, pictures, and video. To expand new art, new artistic research and expressions have developed, creating synergies between different media. This has resulted in a converging artistic research strategy.

The potential influence of arts on science is likewise evident, given a shared vision on innovation, creativity, the need to define new concepts and spaces, and experimentation. Winner of the Nobel Prize in Physics, Frank Wilczek refers in his book *Quantum Beauty* (2015) to mathematical models of Mandelbrot and to symmetry theories.

It is from these blurred borderlines within the sciences, within the arts, and between science and art, and a converging momentum for synergies, that a focus on how to combine contemporary science and contemporary art is needed.

How should we organize science and arts/culture to generate (better) synergies?

FROM SCIENTIFIC INSTITUTIONS ENGAGED IN SCIENTIFIC RESEARCH, TO SCIENTIFIC INSTITUTIONS ENGAGED IN SCIENTIFIC AND ARTISTIC RESEARCH

Most high-ranking universities have put the synergy between scientific and artistic research high on the agenda. Table 17.1 provides an overview of the top 50 (2015 Times Higher Education, THE) universities with, or without, a museum/art school. The top 25 consist mostly of American universities with their characteristic culture and (fiscal) tradition of having campus museums. The challenge remains, however, in the genuineness of their integration, and not just in a "nice-to-have" attitude.

Martel states that "within the 4,200 higher education colleges and universities in the US, there are 700 museums, 300 radio stations, 350 rock/jazz facilities, 120 publishers, 3,500 libraries and 2,300 performing arts centres. So, if you look at the US system [...] art life and academic life are closely linked" (Martel, 2014: 7).

Why do major universities invest in art and culture, and in artistic research?

Stanford University has concluded that art and creativity are vital when it comes to tackling major problems and challenges. One of the university's associate deans has been quoted as saying that researchers who explore problems from many different angles are likely to be better equipped to grasp and track solutions.

When reference is made to "museums", however, universities would be better advised to avoid focusing on classical museums. Their focus, rather, should be on a "gallery", a science gallery, or a science/art gallery, in which all university functions can be developed in this emerging spirit of interaction between scientific and artistic research (and teaching) (see also Bouckaert et al., 2023).

Table 17.1   *Times Higher Education Top 50 (2015): Universities with/ without an art school/museum/"gallery" (Bouckaert, 2016:4).*

Times Higher Education (THE) 2015 Ranking	Universities **without an** Art School / Museum / Gallery	Universities **with an** Art School / Museum / Gallery
1–25	2	23
26–50	10	15

Source: Bouckaert, 2016: 4

FROM MUSEUMS TO MUSEUMS WITH SCIENTISTS IN RESIDENCE

Museums are changing their identity (Brenton and Bouckaert, 2020). The fact that a number of artists and curators are clearly keeping an eye on scientists and scientific research should be evident from the following four examples.
1. In his 2015 exhibition 'Heartlands and Headwaters' at the National Gallery of Victoria in Melbourne (Australia), John Wolseley exhibited work on landscapes and eco-art. For this artist, "The media and activities used by environmental artists are incredibly diverse, including [...] scientific inventions. Scientific information frequently inspires or is incorporated into such works."2. At the "Biennale di Venezia, 56th International Art Exhibition, All the World's Futures" (2015), the German artist Hans Haacke exhibited the results of his "surveys" and presented "real-time systems": "The results were compiled and later displayed in a series of graphs, charts, and maps" (Young, 2015: 108).3. In certain cases, science becomes a part of an artistic strategy for exhibitions and dance performances. Anne-Teresa De Keersmaeker (Rosas) presented this in her "exhibition" in Wiels (Work/Travail/Arbeid): "In general a logic is followed that, as it were, is 'choreographing' itself according to a mathematical logic and strict geometrics that underscore the whole choreography" (De Keersmaeker, 2015). This exhibition/performance was organized in March 2016 at the Centre Pompidou in Paris and also at MoMA in New York.4. The main theme of the 14th Biennale of Istanbul (2015) was "Saltwater: A Theory of Thought Forms". The curator, Carolyn Christov-Bakargiev (who also curated Dokumenta at Kassel in 2012), explains her approach: "It looks for where to draw the line, to withdraw, to draw upon, and to draw out through organic and non-linear forms that reconnect research in art and its processes with other knowledges, including bio-sciences, physics, mathematics, as well as story-telling, philosophy, psychoanalysis and its counterpoint in the brain studies of today's neuroscience" (Christov-Bakargiev, 2015: XLIII). It is no coincidence, therefore, that this biennale had a lot of "scientific" art, or science as art, including works by scientists – e.g., a painting with "waves" made in 1870 by Santiago Ramón y Cajal (1906 Nobel Prize winner for the discovery of the neuron) (Christov-Bakargiev, 2015: 54) – and plant designs by Darwin and Blossfeldt (p. 586). The biennale included clear references to representations of what is "invisible", such as the "aurora borealis", with calculations by the scientist Carl Størmer (1874–1957) (Christov-Bakargiev, 2015: 22); to the "intentions to know", with work from Annie Besant (Christov-Bakargiev, 2015: 54, 65); scientific videos of deep-sea rivers by Jeffrey Peak (Christov-Bakargiev, 2015: 60); and a reference to "Knots Theory", with representations of "nods" by the Scottish physicist Peter Tait (Christov-Bakargiev, 2015: 87).

Artist Liam Gillick also painted the Bernoulli formula on the riverfront wall of the Istanbul Museum of Modern Art as a metaphor for societal, administrative, and political pressure in Turkey. The bridge between science and art is also obvious in art institutions. I provide six examples.

1. One of the first examples is Black Mountain College, a sui generis American College (1933–1957) near Asheville, North Carolina. It was founded to teach art and science in a spirit of interdisciplinarity and experimentation to promote collaboration. Didactically, a "forward-thinking educational system" (John Dewey) was adopted. "What set the college apart was Rice's belief that the curriculum should not just include natural sciences and the humanities, but that the students should also receive teaching in the various disciplines of art" (Hamburger Bahnhof, 2015). Teaching personnel included Gropius, Albers, Einstein, Cage, and Rauschenberg. The Freie Universität Berlin's "Dahlem Humanities Center" organized an exhibition about this experiment (Black Mountain: An Interdisciplinary Experiment, 1933–1957) at the Hamburger Bahnhof Museum in Berlin: "The exhibition aims not only to offer a historical retrospective but also to spotlight current debates on aspects of the education and training of artists today" (www.black-mountain-research.com).

2. On the occasion of its opening exhibition, the Fondazione Prada in Milan (2015) stated clear objectives: "What is a cultural institution for? This is the central question of today. We embrace the idea that culture is deeply useful and necessary as well as attractive and engaging. Culture should help us with our everyday lives, and understand how we, and the world are changing. This assumption will be key for the Fondazione's future activities. Our main interest is ideas, and the ways in which mankind has transformed ideas into specific disciplines and cultural products; literature, cinema, music, philosophy, art and science [...] We will find new ways for sharing ideas" (Fondazione Prada, May-August 2015). Its "south" gallery is the result of a dialogue "alluding to a path between institutional and personal, leading to methods of research and collecting" (ibid.).

3. One of the primary goals of KIASMA in Helsinki, the most important Finnish museum for contemporary art, is to encourage more interaction between science and art, and it is considering hiring a scientist in residence.

4. One of the most important and impressive initiatives in Europe is the Humboldt Forum in Berlin. Since 2020, in the spirit of Wilhelm and Alexander von Humboldt, a forum has been established to connect art, culture, science, and education. The Forum consists of the Stiftung Preussischer Kulturbesitz, the Staatliche Museen zu Berlin

(Ethnologisches Museum, and Museum für Asiatische Kunst), the Zentral-
und Landesbibliothek, and Humboldt-Universität.

5.   At the Pirelli HangarBicocca Foundation in Milan, at least two examples
of combining art and science stand out as remarkable. The first is entitled
Terre Vulnerabili. From October 2010 to July 2011, Chiara Bertola and
Andrea Lissoni organized four major exhibitions and research sessions
on the major topic of "vulnerability". "The project is all about acknowledging the concept of vulnerability from the physical and moral points
of view, embracing it as a positive and vital element in life. Vulnerability
is that singular capacity for empathy that allows us, as human beings, to
recognise and accept our own ethical responsibilities towards others, the
wider community and the environment. This is an evolving, germinat-
ing, organic project, which will be developed over the course of its lifes-
pan, enabling the public to play their part in it and allowing the artists to
continue to cultivate and nourish it. In this way, all those involved will
become in some sense responsible for the exhibition and for its continued
existence [...] The project aims, then, to indicate a direction and propose
a new language at a time in which our planet and the systems that govern
it are showing serious signs of breakdown" (https://pirellihangarbicocca
.org/).

The second example is entitled *On Space Time Foam* (2013). An
encounter was organized between Tomás Saraceno (the artist), Bruno
Latour (sociologist), Molly Nesbit (art historian), and Joseph Grima
(architect). The debate produced distinct layers of thought and knowledge
that affected and related to each other in real time. Saraceno's *On Space
Time Foam*, is a floating structure, that can be accessed by the public,
consisting of three levels of transparent film. It draws its inspiration from
the cubic shape of the exhibition space. The work required months of
preparation and experimentation with a multidisciplinary team of archi-
tects and engineers, and it will have its natural continuation in an important project the artist will work on during a residency period at MIT (the
Massachusetts Institute of Technology in Cambridge). The question of an
abstract arrangement and location, and the meaning of creative space, also
informed Bruno Latour's discourse. The sociologist applied some of his
central concepts to the analysis of Saraceno's work in a simplified way,
namely the actor-network theory – an overview of how people, ideas, and
technologies interact to form coherent elements – by defining a habitat as
a shapeless entity that possesses a potential inhabitable space in which
nature and society are indistinguishable, and by offering an overall reevaluation of man's relation with the past, in particular with modernism
(https://www.domusweb.it/en/art/2013/02/07/a-stream-of-aesthetic-philo-
sophical-and-pure-ideas.html).

6. Singapore: ArtScience Museum: Where Art Meets Science

    "ArtScience Museum is devoted to the exploration of art, science and the connections between them. In the permanent exhibition, *Future World*, the creative threads by which art and science, technology and culture are inextricably bound are expressed in the immersive, interactive artworks by teamLab. teamLab is a group of ultra-technologists known for their innovative use of digital technology as a medium for art. They are made up of hundreds of artists, engineers, animators, mathematicians and architects. Working as one, they consistently break new ground in artistic expressions, creating worlds of magic and metaphor" (Folder of the ArtScience Museum at Marina Bay Sands, Singapore) (https://www.marinabaysands.com/museum/exhibitions-and-events.html).

HUMANITIES AND PUBLIC ADMINISTRATION: CLOSING THE GAP

As a central and general framework for interaction within the university (Biomedical, Science and Technology, and Humanities), the following scheme might apply (see Figure 17.1). The "initial" situation shows an interaction between "Society and Science," and between "Society and Art". By connecting "Science and Art", we shift to an interaction between "Society with Science & Art", which affects the relationships between Society on the one hand, and Science and art on the other.

Currently, there are interactions between society and the scientific world (Figure 17.1: 1 and 2), and between society and the artistic world (Figure 17.1: 3 and 4). A simple interaction suggests that a society has questions, which then invite answers, or where science and art try to provide answers, responses, and discussions.

This interaction has become difficult, however, and in some cases even resulted in a mismatch of expectations, perceptions, and strategies leading to misunderstandings and even distrust. This chapter will not develop this mismatch. It has become increasingly clear, nevertheless, that major societal problems need to be solved with scientific support, e.g., climate change, important economic and financial crises, (political) leadership in a state context with responsive citizens, or governance and control of big data clouds and new technologies. All these risk becoming unmanageable. At the highest political level within the UN, 17 Sustainable Development Goals (SDGs) have been agreed upon, with 2030 as the goal for their realization. In their own way, these 17 SDGs are perhaps utopian in their ambitions and conviction that societies are capable of solving major problems (see also, Achten et al., 2016). Science is and should be focused on developing strategies to help realize these ambitious objectives.

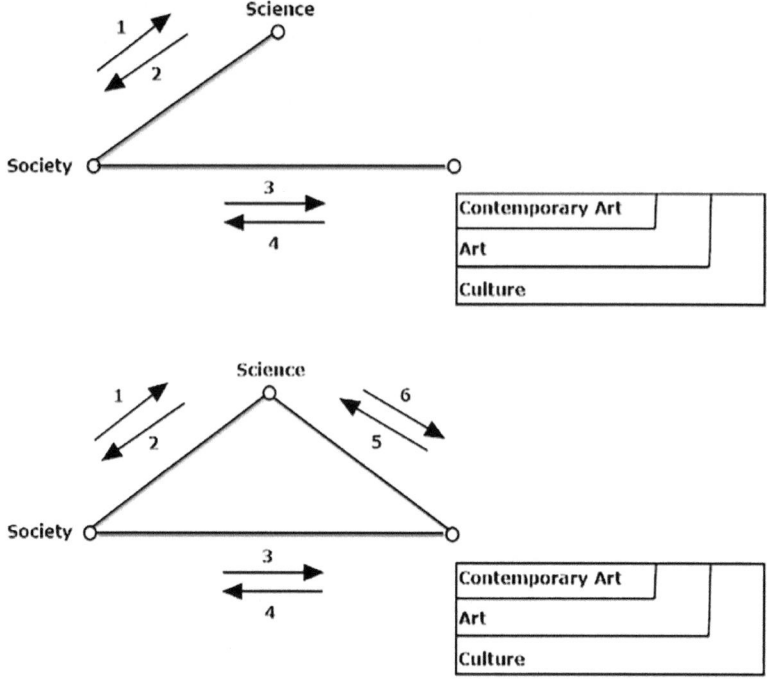

Source: Bouckaert, 2019.

*Figure 17.1   Redefining interactions between Society, Science, and Art:
                  Closing the Triangle*

On the other hand, there is a clear counter-movement of distrust of and among experts, and even the promotion of "alternative truths", or a conviction that ideologies should dominate and overrule evidence-based policies.

    When science and art become too disconnected from reality, these intellectual infrastructures become disconnected from emerging problems. They become too technocratic and are increasingly perceived as the "ivory towers" of self-serving and self-protecting elites, which are irrelevant and not accountable for the resources they receive. During the COVID-19 pandemic, it was also clear that biomedical sciences needed to be complemented with humanities to communicate to different segments in society, to convince society of measures taken, and to explain sometimes conflicting positions of academic disciplines in evidence-based measures (Bouckaert et al., 2020).

    It goes without saying that the scientific and artistic communities will develop their own strategies to counter these pressures. To further support this, however, science and art should connect in an effort to create a new agenda with a shared ambition of re-inventing realities and developing possible futures. In the face of societal fatalism, indifference, distrust, and desperate disbelief, this positive strategy for new capacity to trigger new possible futures needs to bring back societal hope, belief, and trust in these futures. This will also demonstrate that science in general, and humanities in particular, along with culture and art, together, have a shared and mutually reinforcing voluntarist approach to tackle societal problems and create added value.

This needs to – or potentially can – happen via the creation of new shared spaces for experiments, which can result in creativity, discovery, and innovation, not only for the immediate resolution of specific problems but, more importantly, to generate new visions, paradigms, and trajectories. By organizing a cross-fertilizing context between science and art, and by establishing platforms for serendipity, science and art will not only re-invent their interactions with society, but they are also likely to become even more socially responsible, accountable, and relevant. This is the purpose of closing the triangle of society, science, and art.

In the art market, frontline art galleries are called '*galerie de combat*'. In the same way, frontline universities, organizing cross-overs between science in general, and humanities with 'public administration' included in particular, with culture and art, should turn themselves into a '*université de combat*'.

HOW TO CONCEPTUALIZE AND CONNECT HUMANITIES (ART) WITH SOCIAL SCIENCES (PUBLIC ADMINISTRATION)?

When we are convinced or have an intuition of the potential benefits of the need to combine scientific and artistic research, we are immediately faced with practical questions, namely, how do we go about it and how should we best organize ourselves to make it happen? Before answering this question, we need first to reflect on how we can conceptualize science and art together. This is an *intellectual* strategy. Derived from the intellectual strategy, there is also a need to have the *infrastructure* to do so and a solid *system of governance* that includes the allocation of resources, the organization of activities, steering and guiding, allocation of responsibilities, and parallel accountability mechanisms. Three I's need to be developed: Intellectual, Infrastructural, and Institutional.

The development of the 'Intellectual Pillar' to connect science in general with humanities, and art can be conceived in three stages, which can be developed in both a sequential and a simultaneous way. These three intellectual models could be labeled as 3Cs: Co-operations, Constellations, and Co-productions.

By facilitating a transition to the 3Cs, we actually transition from scientific research as a circle to scientific and artistic research as an ellipse with two focal points, one scientific and one artistic (see Figure 17.2).

C1: Co-operations

The first model, "co-operations", places art and science in a functional relationship of "utility" and "use". In C1.1, art and artistic research uses scientific research, and in C1.2 science uses artistic research (see Figure 17.3).

What we have here is a relationship between art and science that leads to open dialogue and an exchange of ideas, expertise, and experiences. These exchanges may lead to a position of one serving the other.

The interaction of supplying and absorbing practices and expertise can run in both directions: artistic research serving science, but also scientific research serving art and artistic research. In the context of science serving art (C1.1), artistic research and expressions use, for example, technologies (e.g., 3D), virtual realities for simulations, databases, or digital tools. In the context of art serving science (C1.2), one might think, for example, of artistic design supporting aerodynamic or ergonomic models. One might also think of art as part of physical or psychological therapies.

In the proposed model, there is a juxtaposition of artistic and scientific research. This requires a proximity of expertise to cross-fertilise, and to bridge supply and demand. It needs sufficient overlap and difference based on shared concepts and complementary approaches. It requires an openness to other "cultures" of research and a willingness to be exposed to the other "culture".

The risk involved in bringing the two traditions together is a potential absence of communication, because neither is willing to leave its comfort

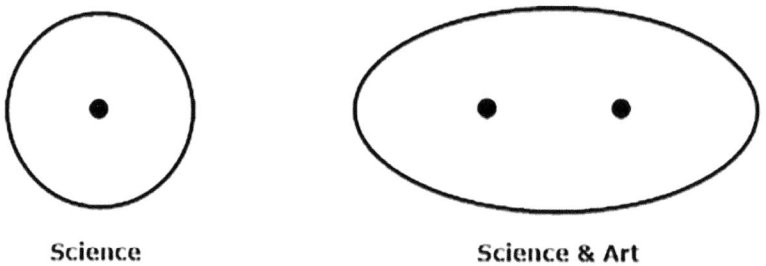

Science   Science & Art

Source: Bouckaert, 2019,

Figure 17.2   *From scientific to scientific and artistic research: From circle to ellipse*

Co-operation (C1)

C1.1   C1.2

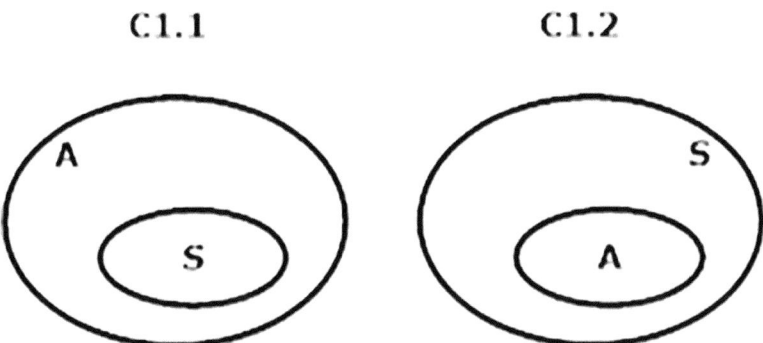

Figure 17.3   C1: Co-operation between science and art

zone. A lack of research empathy, in both directions, can obstruct communication and hence the exchange, and thereby the matching of supply and demand. It is also clear that too much emphasis on direct and immediate results can become dysfunctional, even if the potential for acquiring direct results is most tangible in the C1 model, which is about "using" "art for science", or "using" "science for art".

It is important to create a situation in which bringing potential supply and demand together in a context of shared inputs can lead to an active exchange of ideas. Co-operation as a model is the first layer of bridging scientific and artistic research.

The implications of connecting and bridging humanities and public administration are obvious.

Art could be integrated as a policy instrument. There is considerable literature and practice to "use" art as and in therapy. Also, the communication of policy issues and measures is increasingly common practice. Film and theatre are functional in mobilising and convincing audiences and target groups. On the wicked policy topic of climate change, Bruno Latour pushed theatre to show the need for network theories and enhance awareness of climate change. The Pirelli HangarBicocca in Milan organised exhibitions and scientific seminars on *Terre Vulnerabili*, curated by Chiara Bertola and Andrea Lissoni.

C2: Constellations

A constellation is a network of visions and insights that creates a field of knowledge. Different disciplines provide input to these visions and insights, as fields of knowledge on different realities – the constellations – allow for synergies. There are constellations based on scientific research, and there are constellations based on artistic research. The assumption here is that combining scientific and artistic research can lead to new constellations, new networks of visions and insights, thereby creating new knowledge.

Constellations can be seen as a second layer of interaction between science and art, where both contribute to a new constellation or mind-map. In C2.1, art drives the constellation with science; in C2.2, science drives the new constellation with art (see Figure 17.4). Drivers can be critical questions, contradictory debates, or the exposure of cognitive dissonances between scientific and artistic research.

According to Benjamin, "(I)deas are to objects as constellations are to stars" (Benjamin, 2003, as translated by Osborne, p. 34). This means that ideas are not more present in reality than constellations in the skies. This also means that artistic research may lead to empirical models of these constellations.

In this second layer of interaction between scientific and artistic research, there is a mutual understanding of how to look at reality by sharing, developing, and reinforcing a constellation of ideas about realities. This can happen in two directions. Science can drive the constellation (C2.1), or art can drive the constellation (C2.2).

C2.1: In the field of "vision sciences", there is a shared constellation with inputs from the "vision sciences" about how we perceive things. The constellation raises questions such as: What is the steering perception: color or shape? Why is there a general preference for curves, and much less for straight lines? Eye-tracking methodologies are used by both artistic and scientific research based on a shared modeling of a constellation.

Constellations (C2)

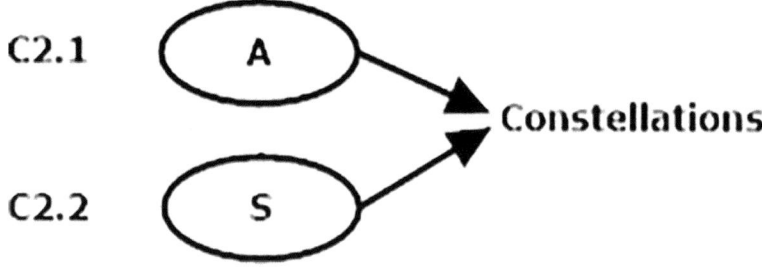

Figure 17.4   C2: Constellations between science and art

Another example of science-driven constellations driving artistic research is based on the beauty of mathematical models (e.g., Mandelbrot).

C2.2: An arts-driven constellation, including scientists, is obvious in problem-driven thematic exhibitions that result in a kaleidoscopic approach to a societal issue.

> A work of art establishes a state of potentiality, challenging us to change or readjust the way we understand the world. Faced with an object or image we don't understand, we seek an explanation within our existing epistemological map. When none emerges, we then turn to the map itself – our own consciousness – and begin to examine our own assumptions and to question the preconceived notions upon which they are built (Huberman as quoted by Garabedian, 2015: 183).

Garabedian further observes that art, and by extension artistic research, "unsettle the codes that we frequently tend to use to compose explanations [...] art can disturb the habits of a world in which people wish to explain everything and put everything in order, in categories and definitions" (Garabedian, 2015: 183). As a result, artistic and scientific research have a combined potential to create new "constellations" of realities.

There is a risk that artistic research is considered inferior since its metaphors for reality may be viewed as less strong. There is a clear asymmetry in mutual interest and knowledge of the "other side". Artists and artistic researchers are much more interested in, and knowledgeable about, science than scientists and scientific researchers are knowledgeable about, and interested in, art and artistic research.

However, by having a range of complementary outputs from artistic and scientific research, a shared constellation can become a second layer of interaction.

In developing strategic management for the public sector, a VUCA context of volatility (V), uncertainty (U), complexity (C), and ambiguity (A) becomes even more complicated when wickedness is multiplied with system quakes (Bouckaert & Galego, 2024) in a TODO context where environments are not just volatile but become *turbulent and disruptive* (T); where knowledge quality is not just uncertain but *oscillates* and becomes unpredictable and unknown (O); interdependence is not just complex but triggers policy *dominoes falling in an unknown sequence* (D); and where sustainable 'solutions' are not just ambiguous but sets of solutions are *opposing, wicked, and disputed* (O). How do we map the "known unknown" and even the "unknown unknown" in public administration? This requires combining facts and fantasy, which is about imagining the unthinkable. Artistic research could trigger "thinking outside of our public administration boxes".

Another indispensable field for public administration is that of utopias/dystopias (Achten et al, 2016; Bouckaert and Crompvoets, 2016). Utopias drive changes of societal models and create possible futures which we try to envision. Utopias are constellations based on facts and imagination. The counter-thinking is dystopias to prevent certain models and possible unwanted futures. To combine utopian literature with public administration, we need to transcend and complement causality by embracing "teleology", defining omegas as utopias, and then recognizing the values and methods of reverse mapping.

Also, imagining cultures of administration (Hofstede) by imaging these different cultures, becomes another vehicle to rethink cultures of public administration. The imaging of "Bureaucrats", by Jan Banning shows and represents "an army of millions of government officials, they show how civil servants mirror the character of their nation" (Banning, 2016) in countries such as Bolivia, France, Yemen, Russia, India, Liberia, the US, or China. This clearly underscores the importance of cultural contexts for public administration.

C3: CO-PRODUCTIONS

A third layer is the effective co-production of "knowledge" about realities. In this layer, one observes a push for synergies and a pull for shared results. Pushing and pulling together toward a shared outcome to solve a shared problem results in developing a shared supply and demand of research. This leads to a science and art think-and-do-tank. In a way, it is adding art as a fully-fledged discipline into an interdisciplinary research approach.

In the C3 model, science and art are both and jointly pushing and pulling for a new shared outcome (see Figure 17.5).

The effort to provide images of "black holes" in astronomy has been pushed and pulled by both artistic and scientific research. Historically, during the Second World War, the development of "operational research" was pushed and pulled by "Blackett's Circus," where Lord Blackett gathered and forced a flamboyant team of researchers to work together to solve problems. This is ultimately about the required diversity of research teams to acquire kaleidoscopic approaches toward realities.

The approach requires that shared outputs and outcomes be defined. It requires interactive research, with a team spirit similar to "Blackett's Circus". Diversity in teams allows us to have a broader picture, to ask more questions, to be kaleidoscopic. Scientific and artistic researchers try to explain to one another their own way of looking at realities.

Distrust between research strategies is a major risk. This can also be generated by a lack of knowledge between the two cultures. Ultimately, co-production will only work when partners are considered to be equal in their capacity to contribute to a shared agenda for a shared outcome.

The implications of connecting and bridging humanities and public administration are obvious.

Co-production (C3)

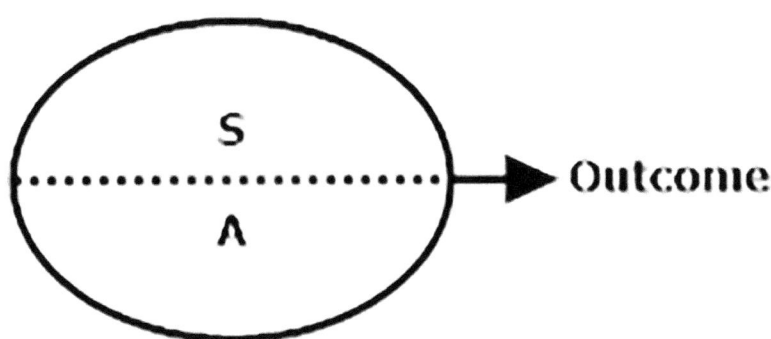

Figure 17.5   C3: Co-production between science and art

In 1956, the American artist Joseph Kosuth showed his *One and Three Plants* (1965): a physical cactus, a photographed picture of the same cactus, and a printed dictionary definition of a plant. These were three ways to define and look at a reality and to image and imagine this reality. In 1957, Herbert Simon wrote his *Models of Man* in which he emphasized that our models of man are confined and limited by knowledge, cognitive capacity, and time, resulting in bounded rationality which affects our decision-making. Both researchers, Kosuth as an artistic researcher, and Simon, as a scientific researcher, challenged our "ontology" by recognizing new types of reality, which are emerging even more in the future (virtual, artificial, experimental, etc.). The ontological contribution of art to PA is about creating and recognizing new realities. Kosuth and Simon also shared a vision on epistemology by accepting new ways to get to know new types and existing types of reality. The epistemological contribution of art to PA is that the reality of "performance" is about putting something on stage, about making the invisible visible. Finally, Kosuth and Simon impacted methodologies which are required when we take these new ontologies and epistemologies seriously. Next to "empirical positivism" (surveys and statistics) and "critical realism" (including 'case' studies), there is a need to add "radical constructivism" (language theory, semiotics, etc.). These three methodological schools need to be triangulated to have a more refined image of realities. The methodological contribution of Art to PA is to add and to triangulate with "radical constructivism".

Art supports public administration by stretching typologies of reality and handles "noise", "bias", "error", "variance", and "deviation". It implies blending concepts of "time", handling the tension between order versus chaos (on reducing complexity, self-organizing systems, or dissipative structures [Prigogine]). It helps to think in terms of reversibility versus irreversibility, linearity versus non-linearity, or hazard versus necessity.

SOME CONCLUDING REMARKS

From all these testimonies and experiences, it is clear that all types of interaction take time and trust. Box 17.1 provides some recommendations for collaborating scientists and artists. C1 has a greater chance of having a more direct focus on a concrete result built around a concrete project. Within C1, artistic research is more knowledgeable of and interested in using scientific research than vice versa. Currently, there is more artistic research using scientific research than the other way around.

C2 requires a fundamental exchange of concepts and visions with a kaleidoscopic approach, which allows adjustments to models for looking at realities and creating mind-maps. This affects the way we image and imagine reality. C3 is ambitious in its design to have a shared, equilibrated synergy of two research strategies. C2, and certainly C3, require much more time, trust, and a belief in added value, which can be more indirect. As the degree of serendipity increases from C1 to C3, the degree of immediate results decreases accordingly.

One potential strategy to develop an intellectual plan might be to move and allow C1 first, and then move to C2 and C3. This expansion is realistic and feasible, especially since there are fragments of evidence of all three practices. However, it may also be realistic to aim for C1, C2, and C3 simultaneously, when a sufficiently broad platform is created.

By integrating C1, C2, and C3 in our universities, we expand a scientific research circle to a broader elliptic space with two foci, one scientific and the other artistic.

BOX 17.1   RECOMMENDATIONS FOR COLLABORATING SCIENTISTS AND ARTISTS

Some recommendations for collaborating scientists and artists:

- Start a cross-over with a positive attitude of wonder and interest in the other;
- Embrace diversity and reflect upon your own frames and opinions;
- Invest the time needed to get to know one another and to trust each other;

- Keep a certain rhythm in the meeting frequency, while making sure there are sufficient breaks in between. A too rigidly controlled process may be suffocating. On the other hand, one should not postpone meetings for too long;
- Allow a change of direction of processes from the original plan. Unexpected turns are sometimes unavoidable and may lead to interesting results;
- Give written expression from time to time about what you have learned or experienced;
- Do not think too rigidly in terms of results, certainly not in financial terms;
- Take time to reflect on what the indirect effects are of the crossover.

Source: Depuydt, 2017: 67, own translation

REFERENCES

Achten Veerle, Bouckaert, Geert, and Schokkaert, Eric (eds.) (2016) *A Truly Golden Handbook, The Scholarly Quest for Utopia*. Leuven University Press.

Aira, César (2018) *On Contemporary Art*. David Zwirner Books.

Banning, Jan (2016) *Bureaucratics*. Nazraeli.

Benjamin, Walter (2003, originally in 1928) The Origin of German Tragic Drama (translated by Osborne, John). Verso.

Borgdorff, Henk (2011) The Production of Knowledge in Artistic Research. In Biggs, Michael and Karlsson, Henrik (eds.) *The Routledge Companion to Research in the Arts*. Routledge, pp. 44–63.

Bouckaert, Geert (2016) LUCA@KU Leuven. KU Leuven Instituut voor de Overheid, Leuven.

Bouckaert, Geert (2019) KU Leuven 'Science & Art': 'Mind the Gap', A Strategy to Connect Contemporary Science and Contemporary Art. KU Leuven, Leuven..

Bouckaert Geert and Crompvoets, Joep (2016) Utopian Public Governance: Cloudy, Cloudier, Cloudiest. In Achten Veerle, Bouckaert, Geert, and Schokkaert, Eric (eds.) *The Scholarly Quest for Utopia*. Leuven University Press, pp. 158–171.

Bouckaert, Geert, and Jann, Werner (2016) *European Perspectives for Public Administration*. The Way Forward. Leuven, Leuven University Press.

Bouckaert Geert and Galego, Diego (2024) System-quake proof "Systemic Resilience Governance": Six Measures for Readiness. *Global Policy*, 15(6): 1–9. doi.org/10.1111/1758-5899.13433.

Bouckaert, Geert, Dekoninck, Ralph, Hambersin, Michel, Martens, Maximiliaan, Monard, Elisabeth, Périer-D'Ieteren, Catheline, Samyn, Philippe, Steels, Luc, Van Kerckhoven, Anne-Mie, and Wagemans, Johan (2023) Arts with Science and Technology (AST): How to Walk the Talk ? In Académie Royale de Belgique (ed.) *Serving Society: Academies and the Challenges of a Complex World*. ARB, pp. 81–103.

Bouckaert, Geert, Galli, Davide, Kuhlmann, Sabine, Reiter, Renate, and Van Hecke, Steven (2020) European Coronationalism? A Hot Spot Governing a Pandemic

Crisis. *Public Administration Review*, 80(5): 765–773. https://doi.org/10.1111/puar
.13242.

Brenton, Scott and Bouckaert, Geert (2020) The Distinctiveness and Diversity of
Leading Public Museums: Assessing Logics of Consequences and Appropriateness.
Public Administration Review, 81(4): 715–727. https://doi.org/10.1111/puar.13323.

Christov-Bakargiev, Carolyn (ed.) (2015) *Saltwater, A Theory of Thougth Forms. The
14th Istanbul Bien-nial Catalogue.* Istanbul Foundation for Culture and Arts, Yapi
Kredi Publications, Vehbi Koç Foundation, Istanbul.

de Assis, Paulo (2019) The Contemporary: In the Midst of Multiple Hurricanes of
Time. In de Assis, Paulo and Schwab, Michael (eds.) Futures of the Contemporary:
Contemporaneity, Untimeliness, and Artistic Research. Orpheus Institute, Leuven
University Press.

De Keersmaeker, Anne-Teresa (2015) *Work/Travail/Arbeid.* Wiels.

Depuydt, Christine (2017) *Cross-Overs, (Meer)Waarde van Cross-Overs tussen Kunst
en Wetenschap en Bedrijven.* VIVES.

Eco, Umberto (1962/1989) *The Open Work.* Harvard University Press.

Fondazione Prada (2015) *Programma.* May–August 2015.

Garabedian, Mekhitar (2015) *To a Stranger from a Stranger.* AraMer.

Hamburger Bahnhof (2015) *Ausstellungen Frühling/Sommer 2015.*

Humboldt Forum (2015) Humboldt Forum, Berlin (https://www.humboldtforum.org/
en).

Hofstede, G. (2001) *Culture's consequences: comparing values, behaviors, institutions
and organizations across countries.* Thousand Oaks, CA, Sage.

Kandel, Eric R. (2016) *Reductionism in Art and Brain Science, Bridging the Two
Cultures.* Columbia University Press.

Martel, Frédéric (2014) Arts and Education in a Time of Digital Mutation. In Corcoran
Kieran, Del-fos, Carla, and Maxwell, Jessica (eds.) *Artfutures: Working with
Contradictions in Higher Arts Education.* ELIA, pp. 7–13.

Nowotny, Helga (2011) Foreword. In Biggs, Michael, and Karlsson, Henrik (eds.) *The
Routledge Companion to Research in the Arts.* Oxon, pp. xvii–xxvi.

Obrist, Hans Ulrich (2010) Manifestos for the Future. In Aranda, Julieta, Wood, Brian
Kuan, Vidokle, An-ton (eds.) *What is Contemporary Art? E-Flux journal.* Sternberg
Press, pp. 58–69.

Prigogine Ilya and Stengers, Isabelle (1984) *Order out of Chaos.* Bantam Publishers,
Penguin Random House.

Rugoff, Ralph (2019) May You Live in Interesting Times. In La Biennale di Venezia
(ed.) *May you Live in Interesting Times*, pp. 36–43.

Snow, C.P. (1959) *The Rede Lecture: The Two Cultures.* Cambridge University Press.

Wagemans, Johan (2013) Wetenschap en Kunst, een raar paar? In Boenders, Frans
(ed.) *Mee met morgen, Vijftig kortessays over de toekomst van wetenschap en
kunst samengebracht door de Koninklijke Vlaamse Academie van België voor
Wetenschappen en Kunsten.* Academia Press, pp. 189–191.

Weibel, Peter (2014) When Science and Art Meet. In Corcoran, Kieran, Delfos, Carla,
and Maxwell, Jessica (eds.) *Artfutures: Working with Contradictions in Higher Arts
Education.* ELIA, pp. 14–20.

Wilczek, Frank (2015) *A Beautiful Question: Finding Nature's Deep Design.* NY,
Allen Lane.

Young, Allison (2015) Hans Haacke. In La Biennale di Venezia (ed.), *All the World's
Futures, Biennale Arte 2015, Short Guide.* Biennale, pp. 108–109.

18. Humanism and Public Administration: Profiling the contours of Public Administration as Practical Humanism

Stefano Biancu and Edoardo Ongaro

INTRODUCTION[1]

This chapter shifts the focus from the humanities as academic disciplines and perspectives to the very notion of *humanism*, and it tackles the issue of the relationship of humanism and public administration (hereafter: PA, the term being here used to encompass the notions of public governance, government and public administration, and public management). We ask the question: can we speak of humanism of and for PA, and if so, what is its meaning and how ought humanism to infuse PA? In order to address this gargantuan question – for which we can only propose here some tentative elements – we first revisit defining issues about the very notion of 'humanism', to then reflect on how humanism intended as a mythical and axiological reference can – indeed should – provide a horizon of sense within which PA can be both studied (investigated and understood) and practised.

HUMANISM: DEFINITIONS AND PERSPECTIVES

We at first provide some conceptual elements about how humanism can be defined, which hopefully can pave the way to deal with our ultimate, and quite arduous, question: 'can we speak of humanism of and for PA, and if so, what is its meaning and how ought humanism to infuse PA?'.

Let us start by saying that the notion of humanism is highly polysemic. We deem it necessary to distinguish at least three ways in which the term may

---

[1] The chapter is the joint work of the authors; however, in the final writing Stefano Biancu has written the sections "Introduction" and "Humanism: Definitions and Perspectives", while Edoardo Ongaro has written the other section of the chapter.

serve: the historiographic use, the cultural one and the axiological (Biancu, 2019a; Biancu, 2019b; Biancu, 2019c).

Humanism is above all a historical and historiographic term with a descriptive and interpretative function applied to certain points in European (and Western) intellectual history: Italian Humanism of the 15th Century, German New Humanism of the 18th (the *Goethezeit*), and the various humanisms of the 20th Century: the pedagogical humanism (Jaeger, 1934–1947); the Christian one (Maritain, 1936); the Marxist (Fromm, 1965; Merleau-Ponty, 1947); the existential(ist) (Sartre, 1946; Jaspers, 1949); and the many humanisms of the Anglo-American humanist movements. Then there are the reactions to such humanisms: the anti-humanisms of the 20th Century (Althusser, 2018; Foucault, 2001; Lévi-Strauss, 1956, Lacan, 1978), and the various post- and trans-humanisms of the 21st century.

Still, humanism is also a broad term in culture, or rather a synthesising category that perhaps better than any other expresses the self-consciousness of European civilisation as a whole. As such, humanism is not only a term representative of a given historical period, rather it is a term that serves as catalyst for a *Weltanschauung* (a worldview) and an *ethos* that implies social and political institutions of a certain form. Humanism is at this point nothing less than an eponym for European civilisation (Tognon, 2019). Humanism is here understood as that generative category which – for better or worse – gave rise to a particular civilisation, *i.e.* to a culture and its social and political institutions.

Other than being a historical and cultural term, humanism also carries an axiological meaning; as such, it has performed the role of a regulative ideal. It is no coincidence that at each and every crisis that European civilisation has undergone, the term "humanism" has been evoked as a synthesising term standing for "civilisation" in a time of barbarism. This has been the case with the Italian Humanism in the aftermath of the crisis of medieval Europe, and afterwards with the various humanisms of the 20th Century, in the wake of the two World Wars.

Now, these three applications of the term "humanism" – the historical, cultural and axiological – are not located at the same conceptual-ideational level. In its historical and historiographical meaning, the term "humanism" has a clear and definite referent, *i.e.* precise moments in the intellectual history of Europe and the West. This is no longer the case, however, when the term is applied in the broad cultural sense and in its axiological meaning. In these cases, the term "humanism" functions more as a mythical than a logical concept. "Humanism" is not intended here as a descriptive or informative term, but rather as a regulative ideal that aims to establish a space of reciprocal recognition and a just order of relationships (relationships with ourselves, between subjects of thinking and acting, with the world, and even with what is perhaps beyond the world or at its foundation).

This is a point well appreciated by Michel Foucault: humanism is, to all effects and purposes, a myth. According to Foucault, however, humankind is today discovering that it can operate without myths: *'l'humanité commence à découvrir qu'elle peut fonctionner sans mythes'* (['humankind is starting to discover it can operate without myths' – our translation], Foucault, 2001). We wonder whether this claim is not itself a myth, *i.e.* the myth of a humanity devoid of myths. Can we do without myths and a symbolic order within which to think and live? Is it not instead the case that in the absence of a preceding, pre-established, space of meaning, reason itself cannot operate?

We have just said that humanism has been evoked as a synthesising term standing for 'civilisation in times of barbarism'. As Tzvetan Todorov has pointed out, the term 'civilisation' stands for the recognition of the common humanity of all human beings, including those belonging to a civilisation other than one's own (Todorov, 2008). Civilisation is an acknowledgement of a plurality of modes within which humanity itself might be accomplished. Barbarism, on the contrary, is disinclined to make this acknowledgment. Each time the acknowledgment of a form of humanity other than my own becomes less obvious, a form of humanism rises to its defence. When it rises, it does so in an axiological and mythical way, inclined to reconcile a given civilisation with the regulative ideal of 'civilisation'. Are the ideas of 'humanity' and of 'civilisation' that constitute the regulative ideal of humanism mythical constructs themselves? Indeed, they are. The question is whether we should – or indeed whether we can at all – do without a symbolical and mythical space of this kind. The term 'mythical' does not mean false, *i.e.* the opposite of 'true': terms like 'humanism' and 'humanity' are to all effects mythical categories that aim to establish a symbolic space where recognition and a just order of relationships are made possible, and reason can operate.

Humanism understood as an axiological category has over time performed at least two fundamental historical functions. The first has been to legitimise anthropocentric claims. The second has been the defence of the weakest and the most vulnerable among human beings. The first function traditionally performed by humanism – that of vindicating anthropocentric ambitions – has meanwhile become unfeasible. Some of the moral claims traditionally put forward by humanity, for instance the claim to dominance over nature and that of moral superiority in dignity over other animals, are being contested from many standpoints, and often with good reason. In this perspective, as Maritain pointed out, the misfortune of classical humanism is to have been anthropocentric, and not to have been humanism: *'Le malheur de l'humanisme classique est d'avoir été anthropocentrique, et non pas d'avoir été humanisme'* (Maritain, 1984, p. 322).

The second function, on the other hand, has been that of securing a boundary from below. Humanism has traditionally operated as a synthesising and generative category at the core of a constellation of notions such as, amongst others, 'human dignity' and 'human rights'. In principle, these are terms universally shared, but their material and substantial content is not self-evident (at least not any longer), and they need to be continuously renegotiated. Once again: can we do without such a mythical and symbolic space? The category of 'natural law' (*i.e.* the idea according to which all human beings share an inherited common moral law) serves, to our mind, as a good example: it is a quintessentially mythical category, impossible to implement as a descriptive, clear and articulate idea. But then again: can we do without this kind of regulatory ideal when it comes to assert the safekeeping of the weakest, namely those who do not perfectly fit with the canonical image of human being as an adult, healthy, civilised, preferably male individual? (Bonhoeffer, 1998).

In particular, there are two distinct but inseparable claims related to humanism in the axiological sense: first, the recognition of the shared humanity of all human beings; and, second, the nature of task of this shared humanity. These claims – *i.e.* the recognition of the shared humanity, the realisation of which is a task falling to every human being – cannot develop in opposition to particular cultures. Without culture there is no humanity. Yet every culture is itself a means to humanisation only under the condition that a universal – axiological and mythical – point of reference delivers it from the temptation of narcissistic leaning. This humanist claim should not be mistaken for a dissolving of cultures into conforming universalism. Humanism is therefore to be understood not as a universal claim of reason in which particular cultures are superseded, rather as a recognition of the shared humanity of all human beings, the realisation of which is a task to be taken up by every human being.

To conclude this 'defining' section: is 'humanism' an ambiguous term? Likely so, but – as we hope to have shown – what we are dealing with is a term conveying a mythical and axiological reference that we simply cannot do without. This in order not to make our self-esteem great again (as the populist rhetoric of our time would like us to), but as the claim of championing those who are unable to fend for themselves, particularly in dark times (Arendt, 1968). Which is certainly one of the main tasks of PA. In this sense we are certainly at liberty to discard the term 'humanism', but we will then be required to find another one, one not yet available. To conclude this part of our reflection, we may ask whether we ought to dare humanism, as Julia Kristeva suggests (Kristeva, 2011). To this question, we need to answer that we certainly ought to dare, to the extent that among PA's duties there is the protection of the most vulnerable, those without power and therefore subjected to the power of others. We elaborate on this 'mission' and sense of purpose for PA in the next and final section of this chapter.

PROFILING THE CONTOURS OF PUBLIC ADMINISTRATION AS PRACTICAL HUMANISM

Public Administration is indeed about the practical exercise of power, specifically public power, as well as – indeed exactly because of it – about the protection of the most vulnerable, of those without power. Or so it ought to be – as this is essentially a normative stance.

The manifold practical ways in which PA is about the protection of the most vulnerable can be seen across all key domains of living together in a society. In fact, PA is about the administration of justice to redress the torts; it is about the police and policing to protect the victims (better: pre-empting them to become victim in the first instance); it is about the actual delivery of forms of welfare to support each and every resident throughout adverse circumstances; it is about tackling unemployment and creating the conditions for life-long learning and self-realisation through work, as well as social security and a safe retirement; it is about the protection of the political community from external threats (via the national defence and other forms of security governance), and so forth. We also notice that 'vulnerable' is a category which may vary over time and place, also dramatically with the changing circumstances of life: for example, a wealthy, healthy, accomplished and civilised citizen may all of a sudden become vulnerable when attacked defenceless while walking on a street. All of these functions that characterise what PA stands for and what it does – better: what PA ought to stand for and do – are predicated on a fundamentally normative (as opposed to factual-descriptive) stance, that is, they embody a conception of PA infused with humanism as regulative ideal. In fact, of course, PA, far from protecting the vulnerable, in many factual instances can and does become itself the main source of threat for the vulnerable and the powerless, when it is used by and for the powerful to further their own power to the detriment of the others – meaning everyone else who does not submit to the powerful and complies with their whims.

It is in this perspective that - to go back to Julia Kristeva's question about the need to dare humanism – in this contribution and, indeed, throughout this book we authors dare to dare humanism, and specifically we dare to dare to assert that humanism could and ought to infuse PA. We claim that PA needs humanism – indeed, yes, as a mythical and axiological reference within which it can be both studied (investigated and understood) and practised. The design of public administrative systems, public governance arrangements, public management systems, and the practice of them, that is, making them function 'well' for the good or at least the betterment of things, could and should be driven by an ultimate ethos, an evolving system of values, an axiology that is premised on the recognition of our shared humanity as its regulatory foundational ideal.

Such regulative stance enables to make sense of the exercise of (public) reason in conducting public affairs, within any specific political community as well as among them (that is, both in government and in inter-governmental relations – both in the public governance of a(ny) political community, and in international and global governance). This approach we are suggesting is centred on conceiving of PA as a form of practical humanism, a way of defining PA, of considering what PA is, that has been put forward by one of the authors of this chapter in another book (Ongaro, 2020, pp.16–17 in particular, explicitly referring also to Waldo, 1948/84 – and see also Overeem, this volume – and to Raadschelders's conception of PA as practical wisdom as one intellectual tradition in the field, see Raadschelders, 2008 and 2011), to make sense of and embed the study and the practice of PA into a symbolic space where recognition and a just order of relationships are made possible, and reason can operate.

The humanism we are delineating here as mythical an axiological reference is one which recognises the plurality of human cultures and the uniqueness of each human culture as a key component of the distinctive context within which a political community and its public governance and administration system unfold and evolve over time. Culture is a defining system of the distinctive context into which each and every PA system across space and time operates (Bouckaert, 2007; Ongaro and van Thiel, 2018; Schedler and Proeller, 2007; Pollitt and Bouckaert, 2017), thus enabling and substantiating the varieties of human societies. And at the same time, each culture can become a vehicle of humanisation for each and every society only under the condition that humanism as a universal – axiological and mythical – point of reference delivers it from the risk of sliding into a straitjacket constricting the fulfilment and well-being of the people that are socialised and live their lives into it (this has been aptly referred to as 'the intransigent context' by Rugge, 2013). A humanism-infused PA can be(come) part and agent of a(ny) culture that may aspire to be vehicle of humanisation.

Humanism in this perspective operates as a synthesising and generative category at the core of a constellation of notions – like human dignity and human rights – which are in need of being continuously renegotiated while remaining universally shared by humankind and always needing to be continually upheld, lest the vulnerable and the weakest get trumpled by the very administrative systems and governance regimes that ought to support and protect them. The humanism that substantiates the very notion of PA as practical humanism is a humanism, whose contours we evoke here, which is respectful towards and cares for nature and all other living beings, and which by providing a grounding for human dignity can provide a regulatory ideal normatively driving the redesign of public governance and public administration and management for addressing the evolving challenges of humankind and of nature in the 21st century.

Ultimately, humanism provides a civilisational horizon – the horizon of human civilisation, the horizon of the humanity in all human beings as end and not just means for the benefit of the few (Kant, 1781), the horizon of thinking teleologically and not just in terms of efficient causation (Kant, 1790; and see Bouckaert, 2020) – within which to pursue the effort of improving societies and living well together, living dignified human lives, by leveraging for the improvement of PA both the kind of understanding provided for by the humanities and the kind of knowledge furnished by the social sciences (alongside the natural and medical sciences and technological disciplines) within a horizon of sense. We dare to dare to conceive of PA as practical humanism!

REFERENCES

Althusser, L. (2018) *Pour Marx* (original 1965). Paris: La Découverte.

Arendt, H. (1968) *On Humanity in Dark Times. Thoughts about Lessing* (orig. 1960), New York: Harcourt Brace.

Biancu, S. (2019a) 'The Human Measure and the (Impossible?) Legacy of Humanism', *ETICA & POLITICA / ETHICS & POLITICS*, 21, pp. 9–23.

Biancu, S. (2019b) 'L'humanisme: (im)pertinence d'une notion pour l'éthique', *Revue d'éthique et de théologie morale*, 303, pp. 11–26.

Biancu, S. (2019c) 'Competing Paradigms. A Century of Humanism and homo symbolicus', *Munera. Rivista europea di cultura»*, special issue, pp. 111–127.

Bonhoeffer, D. (1998) *Ethik*, I.Tödt, H.E. Tödt, E. Feil, C. Green (eds.). 2nd Edition. München Kaiser Verlag, pp. 163–217.

Bouckaert, G. (2007) 'Cultural Characteristics from Public Management Reforms Worldwide', pp. 29–64 in K. Schedler and I. Pröller (eds) *Cultural Aspects of Public Management Reform*. Amsterdam: Elsevier.

Bouckaert, G. (2020) 'From Public Administration in Utopia to Utopia in Public Administration', pp. 71–83 in Bouckaert, G. and W. Jann (2020) *European Perspectives on Public Administration*. Leuven, Belgium: KU Leuven University Press.

Foucault, M. (2001) 'Qui êtes-vous, professeur Foucault?', in: M. Foucault, *Dits et écrits (1954–1988)*, tome I (1954–1975), pp. 601–620, Paris: Gallimard.

Fromm, E. (1965) (ed.) *Socialist humanism. An international symposium*. Garden City: Doubleday.

Jaeger, W. (1934–1947) *Paideia. Die Formung des griechischen Menschen*. 3 voll. Berlin: Walter de Gruyter & Co.

Jaspers, K. (1949) 'Conditions et possibilités d'un nouvel humanisme', pp. 181–210 in: Pour un nouvel humanisme. Rencontres internationals de Genève (tome IV), Neuchatel: Éditions de la Baconnière.

Kant, I. (1781) *Kritik der reinen Vernunft*. Riga: Hartknoch.

Kant, I. (1790) *Kritik der Urteilskraft*. Berlin-Libau: Verlag Lagarde und Friedrich.

Kristeva, J. (2011) 'Oser l'humanisme'. *Revue des deux mondes*. Septembre. pp. 79–102.

Lacan, J. (1978) *Le Séminaire. II*. Paris : Éd du Seuil.

Lévi-Strauss, C. (1996) 'Les trois humanismes' (1956), in Id., *Anthropologie structurale II* (1973), pp. 319–322. Paris: Plon.

Maritain, J. (1984) 'Humanisme intégral. Problèmes temporels et spirituels d'une nouvelle chrétienté' (1936). In: Maritain J. and R., *Œuvres complètes*, vol VI (1935–1938), Fribourg-Paris: Éditions Universitaires Fribourg Suisse - Éditions Saint Paul.

Merleau-Ponty, M. (1947) *Humanisme et terreur: essai sur le problème communiste.* Paris: Gallimard.

Ongaro, Edoardo (2020) *Philosophy and Public Administration: An Introduction.* Cheltenham, UK and Northampton, MA: Elgar.

Ongaro, Edoardo and Sandra van Thiel (2018) 'Introduction', pp. 3-10 in Edoardo Ongaro and Sandra van Thiel (eds.) *The Palgrave Handbook of Public Administration and Management in Europe.* London: Palgrave

Pollitt, C. and Bouckaert, G. (2017) *Public Management Reform. A Comparative Analysis: Into the Age of Austerity.* 4th edition. Oxford: Oxford University Press.

Raadschelders, J. (2008) Understanding Government: Four Intellectual Traditions in the Study of Public Administration. *Public Administration*, 86(4), pp. 925–949.

Raadschelders, J. (2011) *Public Administration: The Interdisciplinary Study of Government.* Oxford: Oxford University Press.

Rugge, Fabio (2013) 'The Intransigent Context: Glimpses at the History of a Problem', pp. 44–54 in C. Pollitt (ed.) *Context in Public Policy and Management: The Missing Link?* Cheltenham, UK and Northampton, MA: Elgar.

Sartre, J.-P. (1946) *L'Existentialisme est un humanisme.* Paris: Nagel.

Schedler, K. and Pröller, I (eds) (2007) *Cultural Aspects of Public Management Reform.* Oxford, Amsterdam: Elsevier.

Todorov, T. (2008) *La peur des barbares. Au-delà du choc des civilisations.* Paris: Éditions Robert Laffont.

Tognon, G. (2019) 'Humanism. Reflections on an Eponymous' Idea, in: Contemporary Humanism – Questioning an Idea: A Time of Fragility, a Time of Opportunity?. *Munera. Rivista europea di cultura*, special issue.

Waldo, D. (1948/1984) *The Administrative State: A Study of the Political Theory of Public Administration.* New York, NY: Ronald Press.

Index

14th Biennale of Istanbul (2015) 261
17 Sustainable Development Goals
    (SDGs) 264
1948 Universal Declaration of Human
    Rights 71
2019 Venice Biennale 254

academic philosophy 38
Academy of Social Sciences (UK) 96,
    104
Adams, E. 224–6
Adams, G. B. 146
Addams, J. 57–8, 63
Adler Jr, G. J. 159
Administration & Society 64
Administrative Behavior 61
administrative discretion 45, 45–6
administrative history 120, 133, 148
    to administrative histories 134–5
    defined 134, 135
    interpretations 135–6
    and methodology 136–8
    public administration (PA) 135
        applied history 138–40
        usefulness of applied
            administrative history 140–2
    relationship with other disciplines
        146–8
        evolution 146
        public administration 147
    story of disciplines 119
        Alabama 120–21
        Baden-Baden, Germany 125–7
        Brussels, Belgium 124–5
        Cambridge, UK 121–2
        Milan, Italy 122–4
    toolkit of historian 142
        analogy 144
        contextualization 143–4
        evidences, integration of 145–6
        periodization 142–3

administrative law 110
*Administrative Reforms of Frederick
    William I of Prussia, The* 121
Administrative State, The 24, 27–8, 32,
    120
Aira, C. 255
Akhund, N. 166
Albers 262
Alexander the Great 228, 232
Allegory of Bad Government 249, 251
Allegory of Good Government 207, 240,
    247
Allison, G. 138
Altinordu, A. 166
ambiguity 85
*American Political Science Review, The
    (1959–1963)* 120
American Public Administration 28
analytic eclecticism 54
Anglo-American humanist movements
    276
Anglo-Saxon research 113
Annals (Annali) 123
*Annals of the Association of American
    Geographers* 98
Annals of the Fine Arts 214
Annicchino, P. 14
Ansell, C. 9, 63, 226
anti-pluralist reform agenda 37
anti-statism 37
applied history 138–40
    instruments of historiographic
        investigation 142
    for public administration 138–40
Aquinas, T. 70
architecture 5, 208
Arellano-Gault, D. 42
Arendt, H. 40, 43–4, 46, 147
Aristotelian republicanism 43
Aristotle 26, 103, 199, 242, 247–8
Armbrüster, T. 43

art 208–10
  Art of Good Governance, The
    (article) 217–19
  creative nature of 216
  described 210
  immediacy of 243–5
  institutions 262
  managerialism vs. hermeneutics
    221–4
  and PA 224
  PA and 251–2
    art as humanity for 236–7
    beauty, art as 214, 216
    craft, nature of PA as 215
    craftsmanship, art as 210–11
    creation, art as 212–13
    knowledge, art as 213, 216
    Leadership Bridge 224
    means of expression, art as 213,
      215
    moral values: Values Bridge 224
    Policy Bridge 225
    Teaching Bridge 225
    Theory Bridge 224
    art as humanity for 236–7
    beauty, art as 214, 216
    craft, nature of PA as 216
    craftsmanship, art as 210–11
    creation, art as 212–13
    knowledge, art as 213, 216
    Leadership Bridge 224
    means of expression, art as 213,
      215
    moral values: Values Bridge 224
    Policy Bridge 225
    Teaching Bridge 225
    Theory Bridge 224
  performing 208
  Venice 245–6
  Virtues Bridge 226
  visual 208
  writing/literature 208
artificial intelligence (AI) 91
artistic expression 213
artistic 'fruition' 213, 216
Art of Good Governance, The (article)
  217–19, 221
  art history 219
  hermeneutics of art 222

modern-day (good) governance and
    public values 219
  positive reactions 222
  principles by United Nations 222
arts 208
ArtScience Museum (Sinapore) 264
Ashmore, P. 98
Augustine, S. 199
axiology 279

Bacon, F. 212
Baleste, M. 95
Banning, J. 271
barbarism 277
Barczewski, B. M. 44–5
Baruch, B. 137
Barzelay, M. 4
Bauer, M. W. 37
Bauman, Z. 191
Beard, C. A. 120
beauty, art as 214
Beaver, S. H. 97
Becker, S. 37
Beck, U. 191
behaviour of public manager 79
    field and research questions 81–2
    micro-foundations 82
    see also micro-foundationsBeiner,
      R. S. 38
Bellah, R. N. 39, 202
Beneduce, A. 137
benevolence 74–5
Benjamin, W. 269
Benvenuti, F. 123
Berger, P. 178
Berk, G. 41
Berman, H. 178
Bertelli, A. M. 30
Bertola, C. 263, 268
Besant, A. 261
Beveridge Report 96, 104
Beveridge, W. 95
Biancu, S. 10, 16
Bichler, A. 182
"Biennale di Venezia, 56th International
    Art Exhibition, All the World's
    Futures" (2015) 261
Black Mountain College (North
    Carolina) 262
Blacksburg movement 31

Blair, T. 97
Blokker, P. 44
Blossfeldt, K. 261
Böckenförde, E. W. 72, 195
Böckenförde paradox 194–5
Boda, Z. 90
Boin, A. 64
Borgdorff, H. 257
Bouckaert, G. 5, 16
Brendel, D. H. 51
Brennan, P. M. 161
Bringing the State Back In 112–13, 116
Brister, E. 40
British Academy (BA) 95
Brussels, Belgium: story of discipline
    124
Buonarroti, M. 208
Burdeau, F. 126
bureaucracy 44
bureaucratic anonymity 40
bureaucrats 90
bureau men 40
Burgess, R. 162

Cage 262
Cahiers 125
Caldwell, L. K. 134–5, 140
Carmichael, T. 166
Carnap, R. 61
Carr, E. H. 122
Castellani, L. 12
Centre for Urban and Regional
    Development Studies (CURDS)
    (UK) 99
*Chapters in the Administrative History
    of Mediaeval England* 121
Charlemagne 189–90, 228, 231
Charles, G. L. 160
chat-bots 91
Christov-Bakargiev, C. 261
cinema 208
civilisation 277
classical liberalism 42
    modern vs. 43
Clegg 115
collaborative governance (CG) 75
Common Sense Policy Group 105
community-based organisations (CBOs)
    162
community of inquiry 55, 63

concept of State 108
    administrative State 115
    autonomy of political actor 117
    bureaucratic power and decision-
        making processes 116
    crisis of Nation-State 110
    cultural influence for studies 111
    defined 134
    European historiography *see*
        European historiography
    governance and legitimacy 110
    historical and sociological inquiries
        115
    interdisciplinarity 112
    Italy 111
    legitimacy 116
    Nation-State 116
    normative frameworks and real-world
        implementation 116
    political power 115–16
    public administration 147
    research group 112
    research tracks 113
    revolutions 112
    sovereignty 109
contemporary art 16, 255
    objective or purpose 255
contemporary music 255
contemporary public administration
    61–4, 256
Coons, J. E. 161
Costa, P. 110, 114
Courpasson 115
COVID-19 pandemic 100
Craft, C. M. 157
craftsmanship, art as 210–11
creation, art as 211–12
Creel, H. G. 137
critical studies 33
cultural bias against the State 108

Dahan, Y. 162
Darwin 261
Das Deutsche Kaiserreich (1871–1918)
    112
Daumier, H. 230–31
    State-Charity 231
da Vinci, L. 254
Daycare Benefit Scandal 193
Dearing Report 95

de Assis, P. 255
Debré, M. 137
deculturation theory 181
de Graaf, G. 5, 15, 73, 208, 213, 236
De Keersmaeker, A.-T. 261
Demangeon, A. 97
democracy 45
    administrative discretion defended
        45–6
democratic backsliding 37
Denhardt, J. V. 195, 226
Denhardt, R. B. 195, 226
Dennard, L. 46
de Nole, C. 228
Derrico, C. M. 165
de Tocqueville, A. 137, 195
Deutsch, K. 85
Dewey, J. 40, 50, 53, 55–9, 61–4, 129,
    163
Dimock, M. E. 58
*Discourses of Voluntary Action at two
    'Transformational Moments' of the
    Welfare State, the 1940s and 2010s
    project* 100
Diyanet, or Directorate of Religious
    Affairs 184
Dobel, J. P. 224, 226
domestic policies 183
Dorwart, R. A. 121
Downing, B. 113
drama/theatre 208
Drechsler, W. 5, 15, 73, 208, 213, 218
Dubnick, M. 225
Duchamp, M. 218
Dudin, M. N. 160
du Gay, P. 42
Dunlop, C. A. 86
duty 71
    anthropological level 71
    ethical level 71
    legal level 71
    supererogation and 71

Eco, U. 254
Effects of Bad Government 248–9
Eichmann, A. 40
Eichmann in Jerusalem 40
Einstein 262
Ellul, J. 123
Elton, G. R. 121–3

Emerson, B. 40
emotions 80
equality 72
eudaimonia 198–9, 201
European historiography *see* European
    historiography
    France 111
    Germany 110, 112
    Italy 110
European Perspectives for Public
    Administration (EPPA) 256
Evans, K. G. 63, 112
evolution 146
extrinsic motivation 74

face-to-face interaction 62
Fairholm, M. R. 165
faith-based organisations (FBOs) 161,
    186
Farr, T. F. 185
Federal Trade Commission (FTC) 41
Ferguson, N. 138
FISA: Fondazione Italiana per la storia
    amministrativa 122, 124
Fischer, F. 226
Floridi, L. 3, 213
Fondazione Prada in Milan 262
Foucault, M. 276
*Foundations of Modern Political
    Thought, The* 43
fraternity 72
Frederickson, G. 73
French historiography 111
Fries, H. S. 58
frontline art galleries 266
frontline universities 266

Gadamer, H.-G. 15, 238, 243–4
Gadamerian hermeneutics 243
Gaebler, T. 193
Galli, C. 113
Galton, F. 60
Gao, J. 161
Garabedian, M. 270
garbage can-like process 86
Gash, A. 226
Gaus, J. M. 58
genres de vie 97
German historiography 110, 125

Baden-Baden: story of discipline 126–7
State for Estates 114
Geschichte der Staatsgewalt 116
Geyer, R. 64
Giddens, A 113
Gillick, L. 262
Gira, C. 224
Glendon, M. N. 178
Good and Bad Government and their Effects on City and Country 15
Good Governance 168, 217, 221
good governance 15, 222
    see also Art of Good Governance, The (article) principles by United Nations 221
Good Government, The 213
Good Life in the Good State, the 243
Good Public Governance (GPG) 168
Goodsell, C. T. 224–7
government-citizen relations 190
    contract and covenant 197–9
        good governance' 198
        legitimacy of public administration 198
        religion 180–2
    post-secular turn 196–7
    public administration pathologies 192
        greedy governance 192
        New Social Governance 192
        New Welfare 193
        NPM 193
    resonance 199
        affection 202
        human beings as homo resonans 201
        instrumental rationality 199
        meaning 38, 200
        self-efficacy 202
        SLB-citizen contact 201
        transformation 202
        uncontrollability 203
        value rationality 200
    societal discontent *see* societal discontent
Goya, F. 245
Goya painting 244
greedy governance 192
grey literature 153, 171
Griera, M. 163

Griffin, G. 171
Grima, J. 263
Gronau, T. W. 165
Gropius 262
Gulick, L. 57

Haacke, H. 261
Habermas, J. 162, 196–7, 199
Haidt, J. 221
Halal principles 167
Handbook of Administrative History 128
Handbook of Public Administration 128
Hanson, S. 99
Hardill, I. 11
Harris, J. I. 164
Hassan, Z. 165
Heath, J. 42
Heclo, H. 80, 85–6
Hegel 214
Heller, H. 109
Hempel, C. 61
hermeneutics vs. managerialism of art 221–4
Hess-Hernandez, D. 165
Heyen, E. V. 126–7
Heyworth Report 95
Hintze, O. 108, 111, 113, 123
historiography 12, 27, 111, 113, 119
    public administration 147
    and public administration 264–6
    story of disciplines *see* administrative history
Hobbes, T. 42, 197, 199, 212
Hodgett, S. 225
Hoffmann, S. 110
homo discentis (HD) 85–7, 88
    policy making, ontology of 87
    public decision-maker 86
    stability and equilibrium 86
homo economicus approach 61
homo faber 89, 90–1
homo oeconomicus (HE) 80
    administrative science and public policy analysis 84
    full/perfect rationality 83
    public finance theories 83
    rational choice models 83
    representative agents 82
homo politicus 90
Hood, C. 17

Huberts, L. 73
human dignity 6, 16, 278, 280
human geography 11, 94
    knowledge production 103–4
    private archives 103
    and public policy nexus 101
    regional 94
    systematic 94
    UK and study of governance and
        society 97–101
humanism 5, 16, 147, 275
    claims 278
    contours of public administration as
        practical humanism, profiling
        279–81
    definitions and perspectives 275–78
    historical functions 276–7
humanities 6, 18, 46, 147, 255
    society, science, and art, interaction
        betweenpublic administration
        and 264
    public servants 147
human rights 6, 16, 278, 280
Humboldt Forum in Berlin 263

Il Buon Governo 15
Industrial Training Act (1962) 99
Inglehart, R. 180
Inglehart-Welzel World Cultural Map
    180
Institute for the Science of Public
    Administration (ISAP) 123
institutionalist historical research 110–11
institutionalist historiography 111
International Institute of Administrative
    Sciences (IIAS) 124
*International Review of Administrative
    Sciences (journal)* 219
intrinsic motivation 74
Iraqi, K. M. 157
Italian historiography 114, 122

Jahrbuch 126
James, D. 100
James, W. 52–4, 57, 61, 64
Johnson 101
Judaism 163

Kamiński, T. 167
Kamkhaji, J. C. 11

Kandel, E. R. 258
Kant, I. 7
Katzenstein, P. J. 54
Keats, J. 214
Kelsen, H. 109
Kesey, K. 224
KIASMA in Helsinki 262
Kirkpatrick, J. J. 248
"Knots Theory" 261
knowledge, art as 213
Koch, I. 100
Kosuth, J. 272
Kristeva, J. 279
Kroll, M. 223
Kuhnian paradigm 53–4
Kuhn, T. 55

La France: les 22 regions 95
Latour, B. 263, 268
Laudan, L. 53, 60
Lawler, P. A. 31
learning 85
    HD *see* homo discentis (HD)
    micro-foundations 82
    see also micro-foundationsontology
        of policy making 86
Le Carte e la Storia 127
Legendre, P. 123
Les Isles Britanniques 97
Lessons of the past 144
levelism 3
Leverhulme Trust 99, 105
Lewis, C. W. 223
liberal interventionism 43
liberty 72
limited State 111
Lippmann, W. 40
Lisbon Treaty 184
Lissoni, A. 263, 268
Logic: The theory of inquiry 54
Long, N. E. 31, 58
'L'ordinamento giuridico' essay 109
Lorenzetti, A. 15, 208, 213, 217–18, 222,
    224, 226, 231, 252
    art as humanity for public
        administration 236–7
    Siena *see* Siena
Lorenzetti's frescoes 217–18, 226, 228,
    231, 246
    Charity 231

Sala dei Nove and 239, 239–40
Louis D. Brandeis and the Making of Regulated Competition, 1900–1932 41
Luton, L. S. 140
Lynn, L. E. 30

Maastricht Treaty 117
Macaulay, M. 73
Machiavellian Moment, The 43
MacIntyre, A. 222
Mackinder, H. J. 97
Madonnas 239
Malik, N. T. 165
Mann, M. 113
Mansfield, H. C. 120
Marcus, G. E. 89
Marini, F. 224–25
Maritain, J. 277
Marshall Plan 144
Marsilius of Padua 242
Martínez-Ariño, J. 163
Marx, K. 31
Massey, D. 99
Mass Observation Archive 100
Mass Observation Project (MOP) 105
May, E. R. 141, 144
Maynard-Moody, S. 200
McCurdy, H. 225
McDowell, L. 99
means of expression, art as 216
Melis, G. 108, 127
Menand, L. 57
Merchant of Venice, The 225
Meriggi, M. 117
Meron, O. C. 157
"The Metaphysical Club" 57
micro-foundations 82
    characteristic of homo in bureaucracy 90
    hierarchical order 90
    homo discentis (HD) 85–7
    homo emotionalis (HEM) 87–9
    homo faber 90–1
    homo oeconomicus 83–5
Miewald, R. D. 141
Miglio, G. 122–4
Miller, D. 224
Mills, S. 102
Milward, A. S. 116

Mitchell, D. 98
Mobilising Voluntary Action in the four UK jurisdictions: Learning from today, prepared for tomorrow project 101
Models of Man 272
modern liberalism 42
    classical vs. 43
Molitor, A. 124–6
Monk, J. J. 99
Moore, M. 10, 73
Mullins, M. R. 171
Muno, W. 37
Murray, N. 224–7
museums 261
    museums with scientists in residence, to 261
    art/arts 208–9
    scientists and scientific research 261
    vulnerability 263
Musheno, M. 200
music 208
mutatis mutandis 256
'Myth of Venice' 246

National Archive (UK) 100
National Institute of Public Administration (INTAN) (Malaysia) 159
Nation-State 116
Nesbit, M. 263
Neuhaus, R. J. 195
Neustadt, R. E. 141
New Public Management (NPM) 75, 193, 197
Nielsen, M. V. 167
Noh, A. 159
Nowotny, H. 257
Nullens, P. 165
Nussbaum, M. C. 37

Oestreich, G. 123
Oke, A. 165
old public administration (OPA) 75
One and Three Plants (1965) 271
One Flew Over the Cuckoo's Nest 224
Ongaro, E. 10, 13, 15–16, 103, 152–5, 170–1, 183, 186, 189, 197–9, 221, 236

Open Work, The 254
Orlando, V. E. 109
Osborne, D. 193
Ostrom, V. 53
Overeem, P. 8, 12

painting 208
Pandya, S. P. 170
participation, defined 54
'Peace through Law' essay 109
Peak, J. 261
Pearl, J. 60
Pearson, K. 60
Pedersen, K. Z. 64
Peirce, C. S. 52, 55–7
Pendleton Civil Service Reform Act
    (1883) 57
performing arts 208
personal autonomy 41
Perspectives on Administration 120
Petit, P. 43
Pfeiffer, C. 37
Philipps 115
philosophical anthropology 68, 73–4, 76
philosophy 28, 59
    pragmatism *see* pragmatism
Philosophy and Public Administration
    103, 236
phronesis 247
Pirelli HangarBicocca Foundation in
    Milan 263
Pit and the Pendulum, The 245
Plato 25, 103, 239
Plopeanu, A. P. 159
Plumb, J. H. 140
pluralism 53
    pragmatism 53
pluralistic universe, A 53
Pocock 43
Poe, E. A. 245
policy-making 14
polis 199
political power 115
    defined 134
'Political Theology' essay 109
political theory 27
    Public Administration as 27
Politika 242
Popper, K. 129
populism 41, 41–2, 44, 46–7

Portinaro, P. P. 109
postmodernism 30
post-modern State 111
power State 112
Practice of History, The 122
"practices of the self" approach 41
pragmatic maxim 52
pragmatism 9, 30, 51, 163
    participatory 54–6
    pluralism 53
    practical 52–3
    principles 51–6
    provisional 56
    and public administration 264–6
        contemporary 61–4
        history 57–9
        logical positivism, pragmatism by
            59–61
Prince and Discourses on Livy, The 104
Proehl, R. A. 161
pro-social motivation 74
Protestant-Christian cultural heritage
    163
public administration 147
    art *see* art
    pathologies 192
    pragmatism and *see* pragmatism
    religious studies and theology
        literature 152–3
see also religious studies and theology
        literature*Public Administration
        Illuminated and Inspired by the
        Arts* 224
Public Administration (journal) 219
public administration (PA) 3, 133, 135
    administrative history 148
        see also administrative history art as
            humanity for 236–7
    as profession 4–5
    defined 134
*Public Administration Review (1958–
    1966)* 120
public and its problems, The 40, 58, 61,
    64
public decision-maker 86
public ethics 73
public governance 13, 221, 279–81
public management 4, 279
    definition 4
public philosophy 36, 46–7

administrative discretion defended in
    democracy 45–6
civic republicanism 43–4
faces 9
features 9
humanities 39
    as creative 40
    as illuminating 40
    moral, ethical choice and 41
    revealing, as 39
    values-in-action and 41
interpretations 135–6
liberalism 42
meaning 38
neutrality of state 44
    civic republicanism 43–4
    populism 41–2
non-arbitrary 38
populism 41–2
practical reasoning 38
public life 38
synoptic meaning 38
public policy 177
    religion role in *see* religion
public service 73–4
public service motivation (PSM) 74, 159
    nature of 74
    supererogation 76–7
Public Service Motivation theory 10
public services 76
*Public's Law: Origins and Architecture
    of Progressive Democracy, The* 40
public value (PV) 68, 74
Public Value theory 10
Pugh, D. 225
Putnam, H. 60
Putra, Z. 157
PV theory 73–4

Qaisar, M. N. 165
QAnon 181
Quantum Beauty 259

Raadschelders, J. C. N. 17, 29–30, 54,
    125, 128, 134–6, 140
Radaelli, C. M. 11, 86
Ranke, L. 122
Rastgar, A. A. 167
rationality 88
    bounded 85–8

emotions 89
and inferential learning 89
Rauschenberg 262
Rawls, J. 39
Rayner, D. 137
Reductionism in Art and Brain Science
    258
*'The Regional Implications of
    Restructuring in the Wool Textile
    Industry' thesis* 99
Reichenbach, H. 61
Reinhard, W. 116
religion 14, 180–2
    defined 134
    epistemological factor, role of 0
    ideational basis, as 162
    marginalization 181
    moral and beliefs system affecting
        behaviour of citizens/users of
        public services 161
    and organizational behaviour 161
    in public governance 181
    public policies, in 187
        domestic 183–4
        foreign 185–6
    secularization theory 178–9
    social mobilisation, as source of 166
    studies and theology literature *see*
        religious studies and theology
        literature
Religious Freedom Act (1998) 185
religious studies and theology literature
    152–3
    corpus of literature 155–60
    future research 171
    literature search 153–5
        Boolean string and keywords
            153–4
        identification, screening, eligibility,
            and inclusion process 154
    research methods and data analysis
        techniques 171
    results: themes analysis 170
        faith- and community-based
            initiative 162
        FBOs and public service delivery
            161
        government funding of external
            providers and religious
            affiliation 162

ideational basis, religion as 162–5
ideational dimension and design
    (or redesign) of governance,
    religion in 166–7
influence of religion and faith on
    wellbeing in workplace 165
intransigent context, religion on
    168
person-organisation (PO) fit
    perspective 157
public institutions and public
    governance, religion in
    quality of 167
religion and organizational
    behaviour 161
religion and PSM 159
religion as moral and beliefs
    system affecting behaviour
    of citizens/users of public
    services 161
religion influence on public
    leadership and leadership
    styles 164
religious beliefs and bureaucratic
    discretion 160
religious beliefs influence on public
    managers' and employees'
    behaviour in public sector
    organisatons 160
social mobilisation, religion as
    source of 165
review methodology 155
    articles 155
    categories and descriptions 156
Roman Catholicism, Protestantism,
    Judaism, and Islam, review on
    171
Report on the Banality of Evil, A 40
representative agents 82
republican experimentalism 41
republicanism 47
Research Excellence Framework (UK)
    96
Rhodes, R. A. W. 224
Roberts, G. E. 165
Rocco, A. 109
Rockefeller, N. 120
Roger Il (King) 138
Romanelli, R. 114
Romano, S. 109

Roman republicanism 43
Roosevelt, F. 58
Roosevelt, T. 58
Rorty, R. 60
Rosa, H. 191, 201–3
Rotelli, E. 111, 127
Rowse, A. L. 133
Roy, O. 181
Rueschemeyer 112
Ruffilli, R. 111, 114
Rugge, F. 11, 168
Rugoff, R. 254
Rutgers, M. 73
'Saints and Heroes' (essay) 70

Sala dei Nove and Lorenzetti's Frescoes
    239–40
Sandel, M. J. 38, 43–4
Santiago Ramón y Cajal 262
Saraceno, T. 263
Schiera, P. 111
Schmitt, C. 109, 122
science and art 257, 259
    data and media 258
    human creativity 258
        and public administration 264–6
    interaction between 254
    knowledge 259
    museums to museums with scientists
        in residence, from 261
    reductionism 258
    research and development 257
    scientific institutions 260
    social sciences and humanities (art)
        272
        constellations: C2 269–71
        co-operations: C1 267–8
        co-productions: C3 271–3
        constellations: C2 269–71
        co-operations: C1 267–8
        co-productions: C3 271–3
scientific management 32
scientific populism 31
Scruton, R. 208
sculpture 208
secularization theory 178–9
Seidenfeld, M. 43, 45
separation paradigms 14
settlement women 40
Shakespeare, W. 225

Shields, P. M. 10, 51, 54–5, 61–4
Siena 238
  campo, the and Palazzo Pubblico, the
    238–9
  Effects of Good Government on the
    City 241–2
  state of law 247–8
Sikking, D. 165
Sil, R. 54
Simon, H. A. 24, 28–9, 61, 80, 84, 120,
    196, 272
Skinner, Q. 43, 122
Skocpol, T. 112–13
SLB-citizen contact 200
Smith, A. 83
Snider, K. F. 58
Snow, C. P. 254
social contract 197
Social Science of Public Philosophy
    (SSPP) approach 39
Social Science Research Council (SSRC)
    104
societal discontent 190
  frenetic stillstand 191
  liquid modernity 191
  public institutions 191
  societal pessimism 190
societal pessimism 190
Socrates 8, 25–6
Socrates of Public Administration 25–6
Socratic Public Administration *see*
    Waldo, D.
On Space Time Foam (2013) 264
Staeheli, L. A. 98
Stamp, D. 97
Star Chamber Stories 122
state of law concept 247–8
State of the apparatus 111
State paradigm 111, 113
Stato immaginario 114
Stearns, P. 139
Stever, J. A. 62
Stivers, C. 39, 44, 46
Storia Amministrazione Costituzione
    (SAC) 127
Storing, H. J. 31
Størmer, C. 262
Strayer, J. 134
street-level bureaucrats (SLBs) 190, 200

Structure of Scientific Revolutions, The
    55
Study of Public Administration, The 120
supererogation 76–7
  actions 68–70
  PSM 74
  public ethics 73
synoptic, meaning 38
Sztompka, P. 199

Tait, P. 261
Tantardini, M. 13, 152–5, 170–1, 183,
    186, 189, 199
Taylor, C. 195
Tedoldi, L. 11
Theissen, G. 200–1
theology literature *see* religious studies
    and theology literature
Theory of Justice, A 39
theory-pluralism 53
Thinking in time: The uses of history for
    decision makers 141
Third of May 1808 in Madrid 244
Thrasymachus 25
Thuillier, G. 125
Todorov, T. 277
Tosh, J. 138
tout court philosophy 17
Tout, T. F. 120
Trommel, W. A. 192, 222
Trump, D. 179, 182
Tsien, J. 123
Tsien, T.-H. 123
Tudor Revolution in Government:
    Administrative Changes in the
    Reign of Henry VIII, The 121

UKRI COVID-19 programme 101
uneven development 99
United Kingdom (UK) 94
  Cambridge: story of discipline 121–2
  higher education: policy context 95
    audit culture 96
    careers of individuals 95
    decisions of universities 96
    financial support 95
    social problems, study of 95
  human geography and study of
      governance and society 97
    archives 98

government-funded projects
98–101
regional approach 97
terroire concept 97
UN Special Rapporteur on Freedom of
Religion or Belief 185
Urbinati, N. 41
Urmson, J. 70

value rationality 32
Values Bridge 224
van Asperen, H. 5, 15, 207, 236
Van Putten , R. 162
van Steden, R. 14
Venice 245–6
Ventura, M. 186
Verwaltungslehre 251
Vico, G. 212
Vidal de la Blache, P. 97
virtue ethics 41
Virtues Bridge 226
vision sciences 269
visual arts 208
voluntary sector archives 100
von Stein, L. 25, 127, 251

Wagemans, J. 255
Waldo, D. 8, 12, 23, 25, 43, 58, 120–21,
127, 134
and beyond 31–3
and practical wisdom 29–31
Public Administration as political
theory 28–9
re-reading Waldo today 26–7

Ward, K. 98
Watts, G. 39
Webber, J. 42
Weberian principles 112
Weber, M. 25, 47, 80, 90, 111, 113, 120,
123, 128, 196, 199
Wehler, H. -U. 112
Weibel, P. 258
Welzel, C. 180–1
*When the State Meets the Street: Public
Service and Moral Agency* 41
Whetsell, T. A. 9, 61, 64
White, J. 165
White, L. 25
Wibowo, M. G. 168
Wilczek, F. 259
Wilson, W. 25, 47, 133
Winckelmann, J. 123, 128
Wolseley, J. 261
Wool Textile Scheme, The 99
World Bank Good Governance 168
Wright, V. 125–6
writing/literature 208

Yanow, D. 163
Yashaiya, N. H. 159
*Yearbook of European Administrative
History (JEV)* 126

Zacka, B. 41, 45
Zain, C. R. C. M. 167
Zakaria, Z. 167
Zavatarro, S. 225